MODELS OF INCOME DETERMINATION

NATIONAL BUREAU OF ECONOMIC RESEARCH
CONFERENCE ON RESEARCH IN INCOME AND WEALTH

Models
of Income
Determination

STUDIES IN INCOME AND WEALTH

VOLUME TWENTY-EIGHT

BY THE CONFERENCE ON RESEARCH

IN INCOME AND WEALTH

A REPORT OF THE

NATIONAL BUREAU OF ECONOMIC RESEARCH

PUBLISHED BY

PRINCETON UNIVERSITY PRESS, PRINCETON

1964

Printed in the United States of America

by The Colonial Press Inc., Clinton, Massachusetts

Prefatory Note

This volume of Studies in Income and Wealth contains the papers presented at the Conference on Models of Income Determination held in February 1962 at Chapel Hill, North Carolina. We are indebted to the University of North Carolina for making its facilities available to us; to Irwin Friend (chairman), Edward F. Denison, Raymond W. Goldsmith, Lawrence R. Klein, and James Tobin, who served on the Program Committee; to Irwin Friend, who prepared the Introduction; and to Edward F. Denison and Lawrence R. Klein, who served as conference editors. Ester Moskowitz prepared the manuscript for press, and H. Irving Forman drew the charts.

Contents

CONTENTS

CONTENTS

MODELS OF INCOME DETERMINATION

Introduction

IRWIN FRIEND

UNIVERSITY OF PENNSYLVANIA

THE Conference on Models of Income Determination reflected an attempt to bring together economists and statisticians interested in national income theory and measurement with those interested in using national income and related data for constructing either "complete" models of income determination or individual "structural" relations which can be used in such models. The papers in this volume, prepared for that conference, will well repay the reader's effort. They are of high quality, present substantive new results as well as methodological insights, and deal with some of the more basic problems of economic analysis in general and of income models in particular. Even a hasty perusal of the volume will indicate the progress made in the state of these arts in recent years. However, it will also indicate how much more remains to be done before we have reasonably satisfactory models for forecasting, policy-making, or better understanding of economic behavior. As a result, prior to consideration of the individual papers it may be useful to comment briefly on a fundamental difficulty of model construction.

In constructing a model of income determination, there are an impressive number of possible ways of combining different forms of each of a number of structural equations if the number of equations and the number of forms fitted or tested for each equation are at all large. Thus, for a system of thirty equations and ten forms tested per equation, the theoretical number of combinations is 10^{30}. The number of time series observations available for distinguishing among these combinations is painfully limited. Consequently, it is extremely difficult if not impossible to choose among a glittering array of estimates of even the most basic parameters of the system, such as the (short-term or long-term) marginal propensity to consume out of income, to say nothing of the more esoteric parameters.

An obvious approach to the solution of this problem, which has been experimented with to a very limited extent, is to make use of cross-section data for households and business firms (whether they are obtained by special surveys or other means) to derive as many as possible of the parameters in the model. However, this approach has probably led to less reliable parameters in general than even the time series data, for reasons which should by now be well known,

1

including in particular the difficulty of inferring intertemporal behavior from interpersonal data and of separating long-run from short-run income and other effects.

A more satisfactory solution to the problem would seem to require the collection and use of continuous cross-section data, where the response of economic behavior to changes in relevant variables can be traced either as these variables change normally over time or in response to special stimuli. Thus, continuous cross-section or panel data for households should be able to provide reasonably reliable estimates of the marginal propensity to consume out of different types of income or out of wealth. Such data for business firms—which already exist—might provide more reliable estimates of the key parameters in the relationships for inventory and perhaps also for plant and equipment demand. To give one other type of example, specially designed surveys could measure the relation of hours of work or length of the workday or workweek to productivity (the importance of which for growth models is indicated in Edward F. Denison's *The Sources of Economic Growth in the United States*).[1] It would probably not be a very fruitful exercise to try to determine this effect in the usual framework of a production function embedded in a complete economic model all of whose parameters were derived from time series data.

One further comment on model construction may be in order. Virtually everyone will agree that the model used should depend on the subject of the analysis and that it is highly unlikely (at least in our time) that the same model will explain the national income in a period, the price of wheat, the quantity of steel produced and consumed, interest rates, stock prices, and the level of assets of various financial intermediaries. However, as some of the subsequent papers and comments will indicate, there does not seem to be the same agreement on the likelihood that different models of income determination may be useful for different objectives, e.g., for forecasting versus more ambitious purposes, or for short-run versus longer-run forecasting. These papers and comments show a substantial divergence of opinion about the relative superiority of the large-scale models for short-run forecasting of the national income—a method increasingly being used by econometricians—versus smaller models which concentrate on variables and relationships of primary cyclical importance. It may be useful therefore to point out that, regardless of

[1] Committee for Economic Development, 1962.

2

the merits of these different views, if secondary variables are introduced into the analysis, the models may have to be made considerably more complicated than even the large-scale models now customarily used.

Thus, if an attempt is made to integrate financial variables into a model of income determination in order to analyze the interrelation of the financial and real variables, I suspect that the usual introduction of an interest rate (or sometimes short-term and long-term rates separately) would be inadequate without expanding the model by introducing also the cost of equity financing, since these two costs may frequently move in opposite directions. Short-run forecasting can conceivably be done best on the basis of a simple model consisting of a few key relationships which may or may not require financial variables, but once an attempt is made to assess the effect of financial variables of a somewhat lower order of importance it is essential that all interrelated "secondary" variables also be included.

I shall now touch briefly on each of the papers to give some indication of their coverage, with a minimum of reference to the illuminating and often spirited comments made by the discussants of these papers or to the answers by the authors.

Lawrence R. Klein's paper is of particular interest since it describes, for the first time probably, the most comprehensive short-run model of the United States economy available and has already been used for forecasting. The paper presents and analyzes the utility of a large-scale quarterly model which consists of twenty-nine structural relations plus some accounting identities and tax and transfer payment relations, makes use of some *ex ante* as well as *ex post* variables, some financial as well as real variables, and is fitted to the period from 1948 through 1958, with all the parameters determined from time series data. The results seem promising, though it is too early to appraise this model adequately. However, a number of questions are raised by various discussants—including Edward F. Denison, Franco Modigliani, and Irwin Friend and Robert Jones— ranging from data problems to the rationale of signs and magnitudes of several regression coefficients, the degree of aggregation, the justification of some of the variables and equation forms employed, and the predictive accuracy obtained. The numerous issues and the different viewpoints are spelled out in the comments by these discussants and in the replies by Klein.

T. M. Brown's article represents a detailed description of the annual moderate-size Canadian model (nine structural equations plus a large number of tax and transfer equations and accounting identities) on which he and his associates have been working for a number of years. The model is fitted to the periods 1926–41 and 1946–56. Again, the magnitudes of some of the regression coefficients seem suspect. Thus, the extremely high (0.94) long-run marginal propensity to consume services and perishables out of wage and salary disposable income does not seem plausible. Other questions are raised by Carl Christ, who compares the Brown and Klein models, and by William C. Hood, who points out that only half of the gross national product is covered by structural equations, the other half being exogenous. The information on goodness of fit and forecasts is not sufficient to appraise the results satisfactorily. However, many of the tentative results and the discussion of their possible policy implications are interesting, and a number of useful recommendations are made to improve the model. Thus, Brown suggests that comprehensive monthly economic data be collected from a stratified sample of households and firms to test for changes in structure from the past to the current period. This suggestion should probably be expanded, as noted earlier, to cover the determination of the historical "time series" structural coefficients themselves wherever possible.

While the first two papers are devoted to the presentation and discussion of specific complete economic models (in the United States and Canada), the four papers that follow are concerned with recent developments relating to individual major structural relationships. The paper by Jean Crockett starts with the thesis that we have been unable so far to measure accurately the effects of income or assets on consumption primarily as a result of three factors: inability, using either time series or cross-section data, to separate satisfactorily various "permanent" and "transitory" components of income which may have different effects on consumption; inability to differentiate among consumption (or saving) propensities of various groups in the population which, particularly in cross-section data, may greatly distort measurable asset effects; and failure to take account of the interaction between income and asset effects. Crockett next offers a careful examination of the biases involved in estimating income and asset effects, in which she notes the promise of continuous cross-section data for avoiding such biases. She then sets up a model containing six groups of families, classified on the basis of the relative magnitude of their saving propensities and the sign of their transitory income, for each of which she derives a theoretical consumption function which is tested qualitatively against the 1950 BLS-Wharton data and the 1955 *Life* data. She concludes that the results indicate the desirability of grouping families in cross-section studies on the basis of both saving propensities and the relation of actual to normal income. Using time series data as an interim device, she estimates transitory income as the deviation from a time trend of actual income and relates consumption to actual income and transitory income; to actual income and a variable whose value depends jointly on liquid assets and transitory income; and to actual income, transitory income, and the deviation of actual from "normal" liquid assets. A tentative conclusion of this analysis is that the marginal propensity to consume with respect to normal income is a little higher than with respect to actual income, while the marginal propensity with respect to transitory income is distinctly lower, though well above zero. The discussant of Crockett's paper, Daniel B. Suits, discusses a different method, which he has utilized to achieve the same objectives.

Robert Eisner's paper is another in a series of interesting studies by the author of the relative utility of a distributive lag accelerator versus past or current profits in explaining investment in plant and equipment. Eisner, using cross-section data, for each of the years 1955–58, to which he applies a wide variety of tests, concludes that the acceleration principle is highly useful in explaining plant and equipment expenditures, whereas any influence of past or current profits is "in large part, if not entirely, . . . a 'proxy' [effect]." The evidence he presents on this important proposition is impressive, though the discussant of his paper, Bert G. Hickman, presents a number of reasons for questioning the conclusiveness of Eisner's findings, which attribute an insignificant role to realized profits and internal funds in investment decisions. Eisner's finding is rather surprising, since there is no theoretical presumption that the large fraction of plant and equipment expenditures for cost-cutting and new products is affected by the acceleration principle, whereas they are presumed to be greatly influenced by the past and current profits environment and perhaps to a lesser extent by the availability of internal funds. The empirical evidence he adduces relies largely on a profits variable which is the ratio of profits before taxes to gross fixed assets, rather than the ratio of profits after taxes to net worth; and in the one set of regressions where the latter variable is employed, profits become relatively more important. It would be interesting to test what would happen to the relative importance of change-in-sales (accelerator) and profits variables if, in addition to change-in-sales variables for a number of different years and the ratio of a single year's profits to net worth, profits to net worth for other years were introduced, to put the two types of variables on a more equal footing. It might also be useful to test change in (rather than the level of) profits versus change-in-sales variables.

Michael Lovell's paper on "Determinants of Inventory Investment" provides a highly thoughtful review of prior work, including that relating to the determination of equilibrium inventories, adjustment lags, and the usefulness of anticipated sales data versus suitable proxies based on *ex post* data. On this last point, he argues that the anticipations data give only marginal improvement over suitable proxies. In common with authors of several of the other papers, he notes the importance of continuous cross-section data (for individual firms) to answer the relevant questions for setting up a satisfactory structural equation in this area. The relative stress on unfilled orders and changes in unfilled orders as determinants of inventory investment in equations which Lovell presents is questioned by Ruth P. Mack, who states that ". . . unfilled orders and their rates of change explain too much and sales too little of inventory investment." In this connection, Mack points out that orders held by the machinery and transportation equipment industries alone "constitute on the average over 70 per cent of total outstanding orders and also dominate rates of change." It is interesting to note that a subsequent paper in this volume finds plant and equipment anticipations to be a more useful variable than unfilled orders in explaining inventory investment, suggesting that the former is a more powerful expectational variable.

The paper by Wilfred Lewis, Jr., on "The Federal Sector in National Income Models" covers a sector of the economy for which structural relationships obviously cannot be derived in the same manner as for the private sectors. However, Lewis does attempt to determine some of the interrelations between the federal sector (receipts and expenditures) and the rest of the economy "in the hope of increasing, if only slightly, the precision with which the government sector can be handled in long-term and short-term economic models." A wealth of useful results and hypotheses are presented on such matters as the long-range income elasticities of different types of federal revenues (and of total revenues), long-range projections of federal spending, and the short-run behavior of the built-in stabilizers. One discussant, Bert G. Hickman, is dubious about the success of Lewis's interesting "shortfall method" of measuring the response of consumption to changes in income during economic contractions, which Lewis uses in arriving at his conclusion that the importance of the "direct" stabilizers has increased over the postwar period. The other discussant, Joseph A. Pechman, also questions the conclusion that the direct stabilizers have been materially strengthened.

The last three papers in this volume are concerned with different kinds of problems than those associated with the derivation of the usual type of "complete" economic models or individual structural relationships. In their paper on "Short-Run Forecasting Models Incorporating Anticipatory Data," Irwin Friend and Robert Jones tentatively conclude, both on a priori and empirical grounds, that *for short-run forecasting* a simple small-scale model is likely to do at least as well as the more complex large-scale models. They find that the specific quarterly, semiannual, and annual models utilized, containing four structural equations and one identity, seem to give both good fits for 1951–60 and relatively good "forecasts" for 1961–62, and that none of the coefficients seems unreasonable. The semiannual and apparently also the annual models give somewhat better results than the quarterly models, even though they entail forecasts for substantially longer periods ahead. This improvement in results may reflect the averaging out of erratic short-term changes in the data (including errors of observation). Of the business and consumer anticipations series tested in these time series models, only plant and equipment anticipations clearly and consistently add to predictive ability. Both discussants of this paper, F. Thomas Juster and Lawrence R. Klein, express reservations about the promise of small-scale models for short-run forecasting, with the former also questioning the form in which the anticipations data are introduced into the models.

Albert Ando's paper is an imaginative attempt to spell out the implications and statistically to derive the parameters of several growth models. Some of the assumptions include a linear consumption function homogeneous in labor income and consumer net worth, a Cobb-Douglas production function for each type of good, a constant rate of neutral technological change characterizing each production function, perfect competition in all markets, and labor which

7

is homogeneous and increasing at a constant rate over time. The last model, which receives most empirical attention, distinguishes two types of goods, consumption and investment, and introduces a government which purchases goods and imposes taxes on income of individuals, and a banking system which issues money in exchange for individuals' indebtedness to it. Ando notes that his models explain constancies in the relative shares of income, the rate of return on capital, the saving-income ratio, etc., without making these assumptions explicitly, and that they lead to empirical estimates of several key parameters which are not too unreasonable. However, Ando also points out the unsatisfactory nature of some of his results, including the substantial understatement of the required rate of return on capital (which he tentatively attributes, at least in part, to the absence of uncertainty from his models) and the evidence of an appreciable historical decline in the coefficient of capital in the production function for investment goods (which if taken at face value would invalidate the assumption of a Cobb-Douglas production function with neutral technological change). These models, as Ando points out, are not intended to reflect factors which cause the economy to deviate significantly from the smooth path of equilibrium growth defined by them, i.e., the models essentially are set up to explain full-employment periods. In his discussion, Ralph W. Pfouts observes that two of the three variables used to explain output—technological change and employment (capital is the third)—are determined as functions of time and that this seems unsatisfactory, at least for employment. He also questions the "passive" role assigned to investment in the models, which, he states, contain no "realistic" explanation of the determinants of investment, since the demand for investment is determined by marginal productivity, saving is determined by the consumption function, and the model adjusts so that saving equals investment.

The final paper, by Zvi Griliches, is largely a critical analysis of price data from the viewpoints of general reliability and economic relevance to the basic problems to which they are applied. Griliches discusses a suggestion he had made earlier on how to measure quality changes through cross-section price specification regressions; e.g., prices of automobiles (in logarithmic form) are related annually, for 1950–61, to such specifications as brake horsepower, shipping weight, and over-all length, showing the impact on price of a unit change in a particular specification, holding other specifications constant.

Griliches then uses this information to obtain "quality-adjusted" price indexes. The first discussant, George Jaszi, states that the conventional approach would give the same results in principle as Griliches' method and concludes ". . . it is a mistaken idea that we can get at a better measure of quality by a study of consumer evaluations of the various features inherent in a good than by a comparison of costs." The second discussant, Edward F. Denison, emphasizes that the real disagreement between Griliches and the national income statisticians (including Denison) relates to the determination of the commodity or service to be priced and points out that "switching the criterion for the 'commodity' to be priced from what the consumer actually buys (hospital care, surgeon's time, drugs, etc.) to what he 'really' wants is a dangerous and inconclusive game for the statistician to play." In reply, Griliches states that he considers this regression approach as more clean-cut operationally than the conventional method but more generally "as only a first step toward the construction of constant utility or productivity level price indexes." He disagrees with the "Denison-Gilbert-Jaszi position" in that he does not consider it feasible or of economic interest to construct "a value-free set of price and output indexes, independent of a welfare framework or of production or utility function considerations." The basic differences of opinion involved may or may not revive one of the older arguments in the national income literature.

A Postwar Quarterly Model: Description and Applications

LAWRENCE R. KLEIN

UNIVERSITY OF PENNSYLVANIA

Introduction

THE National Bureau of Economic Research has often made the point that annual data are inadequate in business cycle analysis. This is not to claim that they are worthless but merely to recognize that we ought to try to do better. Without going to the extreme that the NBER reaches in doing most of its analysis with monthly data, we in econometric model-building research ought to go at least as far as the construction of quarterly systems. Eventually, we shall build monthly models, but the first step is naturally a quarterly model. There is serious doubt whether suitable data could be found for our methods on a monthly basis. The quarterly national income accounts are now plentiful, though not necessarily ultimately refined, and we have had a good span of time since the end of World War II in which to build up a sample of respectable size.

Some prewar quarterly data stretch back as far as World War I. These have already been exploited in econometric model building by Harold Barger and myself, but our investigation dealt only with a small model to be used for methodological purposes.[1] It might be possible to prepare an approximate set of quarterly series covering the period before as well as after World War II on the scale needed for the present model, but the expenditure of time would be enormous. We made a pragmatic decision to confine the analysis to postwar quarterly data. That alone posed substantial problems of data processing. A possible advantage of this decision was that we obtained

NOTE: The research on this model was supported by the Rockefeller Foundation. Participating at various times over the course of the development of the model were Motoo Abe, R. J. Ball, Hidekazu Eguchi, K. Krishnamurty, Kanta Marwah, Mitsugu Nakamura, Joel Popkin, and Yoichi Shinkai. Harry Eisenpress of the IBM Corporation rendered invaluable computing assistance. Machine time was generously made available to us by IBM.

[1] "A Quarterly Model for the United States Economy," *Journal of the American Statistical Association*, September 1954, pp. 413–437.

a more homogeneous sample, but we lost in terms of richness of experience.

We made another basic decision at the outset, namely, to use seasonally adjusted data. The alternative would have been to introduce explicit seasonal variables, as was done in the recent British model.[2] Consumers of economic data and of the results of economic analysis appear to be more receptive to seasonally adjusted than to unadjusted data; therefore, we decided to make our findings available immediately in adjusted form. This freed us from a certain amount of routine work by making the number of variables smaller in each equation. Theoretically, there is much to be said in favor of using seasonal variables with unadjusted data, but an adequate treatment may, in several cases, take us beyond the simple additive process used in the British model.

It may be useful, at the outset, to distinguish the present model from its annual predecessors, using the Klein-Goldberger model as a reference point.[3]

1. The present model is less aggregative. There are more equations in the present model. Some represent obvious decomposition of national product elements; others stem from more subtle theorizing about patterns of behavior.

2. Anticipatory data are used in the present model. In applications of the Klein-Goldberger model to problems of forecasting, frequent use was made of expectations about consumer purchases and investment outlays, but these subjective variables were not built into the models directly. Now we have introduced realization functions which express actual behavior as a function of expectations. In *short-run* forecasting these equations can be used; but since we do not provide an endogenous explanation of expectations, only limited use can be made of such relations. Nevertheless, we feel that this is an important first step in macroeconomic model building.

3. Explicit relations among inventories, sales, backlogs, and order flow appear in the new model. The Klein-Goldberger model slurred over the whole question of inventory investment. Later work has extended that model annually, using more explicit inventory behavior; but the essence of inventory-order patterns probably cannot

[2] Lawrence R. Klein *et al.*, *An Econometric Model of the United Kingdom*, Oxford, Eng., 1961.
[3] Lawrence R. Klein and A. S. Goldberger, *An Econometric Model of the United States, 1929–1952*, Amsterdam, 1955.

be discerned with annual data. Our quarterly model is more promising in this respect.

4. The concept of capacity, together with the rate of utilization, is introduced in the new model. It is difficult to define capacity and to measure it. Nonetheless, this concept figures importantly in much economic analysis. We attempt, at the Wharton School, to measure capacity utilization; and, imperfect though our series may be, it appears to be of significance in the structure of our model.

5. The accounting identities are properly expressed in current prices, while the behavioral and technical equations are, save for appropriate exceptions, in real terms, relative prices, or deflated incomes. There was a distortion in the older annual models, caused by requiring the national income identities to hold in real or deflated variables. When prices change by large amounts, these distortions grow in significance.

There are other points of difference between the new and the older models, but those above are the differences that motivated the present research. Others will be brought out in the discussion of the equations of the model.

The Model

The sample data include the quarters from I-1948 to IV-1958. For lagged values we used some earlier quarters. Time has elapsed since the model was estimated, and quarterly data for 1959, 1960, and 1961 are now available. Eventually, the whole system will be re-estimated. The estimates are limited-information maximum-likelihood estimates. In some cases two-stage least-squares estimates have been used because of problems of multicollinearity. It has been found that limited information estimates are more sensitive than two-stage estimates to the presence of multicollinearity. In cases where the limited-information method gave obviously nonsensical results, we used two-stage estimates instead. Multicollinearity problems among the set of predetermined variables also proved troublesome, and we estimated the system in two major groups of equations with a somewhat different set of predetermined variables in each group.

LIST OF VARIABLES

$*C_d$ Expenditures on consumer durables, billions of 1954 dollars
$*C_n$ Expenditures on consumer nondurables, billions of 1954 dollars

13

$*C_s$	Expenditures on consumer services, billions of 1954 dollars
$*Y - T$	Disposable personal income, billions of current dollars
$*W$	Wages, salaries, and other labor income, billions of current dollars
$*P$	Nonlabor personal income, billions of current dollars
C_d^e	Index of consumer buying plans for durable goods
$*L$	End-of-quarter cash balances, billions of current dollars
$*p_d$	Implicit deflator, consumer durables, 1954 = 1.00
$*p_n$	Implicit deflator, consumer nondurables, 1954 = 1.00
$*p_s$	Implicit deflator, consumer services, 1954 = 1.00
N	Population, millions of persons
$*I_p$	Expenditures on private producers' plant and equipment, billions of 1954 dollars
$*I_h$	Expenditures on nonfarm residential construction, billions of 1954 dollars
$*I_i$	Inventory investment, billions of 1954 dollars
$*X$	Private gross national product, billions of 1954 dollars
$*X_c$	Private gross national product at full capacity, billions of 1954 dollars
I_p^e	Intended investment outlays, billions of 1954 dollars
$*q_h$	Implicit deflator, nonfarm residential construction, 1954 = 1.00
$*i_L$	Average yield, corporate bonds, per cent
F_s	Number of marriages, thousands
I_h^s	Number of housing starts
$*h$	Hours worked per week, index
$*i_s$	Average yield, ninety-day commercial paper
$*O$	Manufacturers' new orders, billions of 1954 dollars
$*U$	Manufacturers' unfilled orders, billions of 1954 dollars
$*S_c$	Corporate retained earnings, billions of current dollars
$*P_c$	Corporate profits, billions of current dollars
T_c	Corporate income taxes, billions of current dollars
$*q_p$	Implicit deflator, plant and equipment expenditures, 1954 = 1.00
$*D_r$	Capital consumption allowances, replacement cost, billions of 1954 dollars
$*N_w$	Number of employees, millions of persons
N_g	Number of government employees, millions of persons

N_e Number of self-employed, millions of persons

W_g Government wages, salaries, and other labor income, billions of current dollars

*p Implicit deflator, gross national product, 1954 = 1.00

*w Average annual wage, current dollars

*N_L Labor force, millions of persons

*F_e Exports of goods and services, billions of 1954 dollars

X_w Index of world production, 1954 = 1.00

*F_{im} Imports of crude food and materials, billions of 1954 dollars

p_i Implicit deflator, imports of goods and services, 1954 = 1.00

*F_{if} Other imports, billions of 1954 dollars

R End-of-quarter percentage of total bank reserves held in excess of required reserves

i_r Federal Reserve average discount rate

U_d Manufacturers' unfilled orders of durable goods, billions of 1954 dollars

U_n Manufacturers' unfilled orders of nondurable goods, billions of 1954 dollars

*C Total consumer expenditures, billions of 1954 dollars

p_w Index of prices of competing exports, 1954 = 1.00

*p_e Implicit deflator, exports of goods and services, 1954 = 1.00

G Government expenditures on goods and services, billions of current dollars

D_a Capital consumption allowances, accounting prices, billions of current dollars

T_i Reconciling item between net national product and national income, billions of current dollars

* Denotes endogenous variable.

Variables taken from the national income accounts in dollar totals are seasonally adjusted at annual rates. Most other variables are also seasonally adjusted.

In the equations written below, the numbers in parentheses under each coefficient are estimated standard errors. The correlation measures, $\overline{R}$, are computed from the formula

$$R = \sqrt{1 - \left(\frac{\Sigma\, r^2}{T - m}\right)\left(\frac{T - 1}{\Sigma\, x^2}\right)}$$

15

where r is the residual, x is the dependent variable, and m is the number of parameters in the equation. The equations that have been estimated by the two-stage, least-squares method are marked TSLS below the number.

ESTIMATED EQUATIONS

(1)
$$C_d = -67.1 + .363 \frac{Y - T}{p_d} + 58.4 \frac{P}{W}$$
$$(51.0) \quad (.15) \qquad\qquad (79.0)$$

$$- 1.14 \frac{1}{8} \sum_{i=1}^{8} (C_d)_{-i} + .174 C_d^e \qquad \bar{R} = 0.40$$
$$(.86) \qquad\qquad\qquad (.093)$$

(2)
$$C_n = 27.7 + .259 \frac{Y - T}{p_n} + 8.88 \frac{P}{W}$$
$$(8.1) \quad (.044) \qquad\qquad (15.0)$$

$$+ .191 \frac{1}{8} \sum_{i=1}^{8} (C_n)_{-i} + .0056 \left(\frac{L}{p_n}\right)_{-1} \qquad \bar{R} = 0.99$$
$$(.095) \qquad\qquad\qquad (.055)$$

(3)
$$C_s = -152.0 + .103 \frac{Y - T}{p_s} + 41.1 \frac{P}{W}$$
$$(19.0) \quad (.017) \qquad\qquad (6.9)$$

$$+ .0188 \frac{1}{8} \sum_{i=1}^{8} (C_s)_{-i} + .0596 \left(\frac{L}{p_s}\right)_{-1} + 1.13N$$
$$(.13) \qquad\qquad\qquad (.024) \qquad\qquad (.16)$$
$$\bar{R} = 0.99$$

(4)
$$I_p = -8.18 + 32.5(X/X_c) + .557 I_p^e \qquad \bar{R} = 0.91$$
$$(4.16) \quad (4.76) \qquad\qquad (.0486)$$

(5)
$$I_h = -11.3 + .0764 \frac{Y - T}{q_h} - .776 i_L + .0011F$$
$$(1.2) \quad (.0091) \qquad\qquad (.47) \qquad (.0015)$$

$$+ .00812 (I_h^s)_{-1} \qquad \bar{R} = 0.96$$
$$(.0007)$$

(6)
$$I_i = -48.42 + .2675(X - I_i) - .2997 \sum_{j=1}^{\infty} (I_i)_{-j}$$
$$(13.5) \quad (.0707) \qquad\qquad (.06)$$

$$+ 269.3(p - p_{-1}) + .2031 U_{-1}$$
$$(75) \qquad\qquad (.047)$$
$$\bar{R} = 0.99 \text{ (stockform)}$$

16

(7) $$S_c/q_p = -.448 + .938 \frac{P_c - T_c}{q_p}$$
$$ (2.5) \quad (.061)$$

$$ - .853 \frac{1}{8} \sum_{i=1}^{8} \left(\frac{P_c - T_c - S_c}{q_p} \right)_{-i} \qquad \bar{R} = 0.96$$
$$ (.17)$$

(8) $$P_c = 5.49 + .627 \left(P - \frac{1}{3}^{P-1} \right) \qquad \bar{R} = 0.59$$
$$ (5.1) \quad (.10)$$

(9) $$D_r = 10.8 + .0664X + .00599 \sum_{i=1}^{\infty} (I_p + I_h - D_r)_{-i}$$
$$ (3.10) \quad (.017) \qquad (.0034)$$
$$ \bar{R} = 0.94$$

(10)
TSLS $$X = 90.9 + 1.758[h(N_w - N_g) + N_e]$$
$$ (60.83) \quad (1.485)$$

$$ + .196(X/X_c) \sum_{i=0}^{\infty} (I_p + I_h - D_r)_{-i} + .135t$$
$$ (.062) \qquad\qquad\qquad\qquad (.640)$$
$$ \bar{R} = 0.99$$

(11)
TSLS $$X_c = 90.9 + 1.758N_L + .196 \sum_{i=0}^{\infty} (I_p + I_h - D_r)_{-i}$$
$$ (60.83) \quad (1.485) \quad (.062)$$

$$ + .135t \qquad\qquad\qquad \bar{R} = 0.93$$
$$ (.640) \qquad \text{(residual variance about mean)}$$

(12) $$\frac{W - W_g}{p} = 7.19 + .254X + .254X_{-1} + .221t \qquad \bar{R} = 0.99$$
$$\phantom{\frac{W - W_g}{p} =} (7.4) \quad (.015) \quad (.015) \quad (.083)$$

(13) $$w - w_{-4} = 169.0 - 38.2 \frac{1}{4} \sum_{i=0}^{3} (N_L - N_w - N_e)_{-i}$$
$$\phantom{w - w_{-4} =} (46.0) \quad (15.0)$$

$$\phantom{w - w_{-4} =} + 2110 \frac{1}{4} \sum_{i=0}^{3} (p - p_{-4})_{-i} + 1.56t \qquad \bar{R} = 0.56$$
$$\phantom{w - w_{-4} =} (540.0) \qquad\qquad\qquad (.80)$$

(14) $$h = .721 + .320(X/X_c) + .00217(X - X_{-1})$$
$$ (.047) \quad (.052) \qquad (.0006)$$

$$ - .00026t \qquad \bar{R} = 0.51$$
$$ (.00017)$$

(15) $$N_L = 61.2 - .308(N_L - N_w - N_e) + .226t$$
$$ (.21) \quad (.075) \qquad\qquad (.0053)$$

$$ \bar{R} = 0.99$$

(16)
$$U = -101 + 2.12O + 111(X/X_c) \qquad \bar{R} = 0.62$$
TSLS
$$(44) \quad (.84) \quad (55)$$

(17)
$$O = 2.56 + .0589(X - I_i)_{-1} + 387(p - p_{-1})$$
$$(3.2) \quad (.0098) \qquad\qquad (72.0)$$
$$\bar{R} = 0.60$$

(18)
$$F_e = 2.98 + .160(X_w)_{-1} \qquad\qquad \bar{R} = 0.90$$
$$(1.112) \; (.0115)$$

(19)
$$F_{im} = 3.82 + .0065X_{-1} - 1.04(p_i/p)_{-1} \qquad \bar{R} = 0.53$$
$$(.867) \; (.0015) \qquad\qquad (.804)$$

(20)
$$F_{if} = 8.11 + .039\,\frac{Y - T}{p_i} - 24.1\,\frac{P}{W}$$
$$(2.62) \quad (.0082) \qquad\qquad (5.3)$$
$$+ .286\,\frac{1}{8}\sum_{i=1}^{8} (F_{if})_{-i} \qquad \bar{R} = 0.97$$
$$(.15)$$

(21)
$$\frac{L}{pX + W_g} = .815 - .0743i_L - 1.38(p - p_{-1}) \qquad \bar{R} = 0.64$$
TSLS
$$(.058) \quad (.0131) \qquad (.92)$$

(22)
$$i_L = .0541 + .0497i_s + .959(i_L)_{-1} \qquad \bar{R} = 0.97$$
$$(.15) \qquad (.034) \qquad (.060)$$

(23)
$$i_s = .502 - .146R_{-1} + 1.18i_r \qquad \bar{R} = 0.96$$
$$(.399) \quad (.060) \qquad\quad (.096)$$

(24)
$$p_d = .548 + .422p + .00067(U_d)_{-1} \qquad \bar{R} = 0.94$$
$$(.034) \quad (.039) \quad (.00017)$$

(25)
$$p_n = .346 + .618p + .00946(U_n)_{-1} \qquad \bar{R} = 0.97$$
$$(.027) \quad (.024) \quad (.0021)$$

(26)
$$p_s = .716 + .000179w - 1.08(C_s/C) \qquad \bar{R} = 0.99$$
$$(.090) \quad (.000005) \qquad (.29)$$

(27)
$$q_p = -.508 + 1.52p \qquad\qquad \bar{R} = 0.99$$
$$(.028) \quad (.029)$$

(28)
$$q_h = .492 + .000144w \qquad\qquad \bar{R} = 0.96$$
$$(.021) \quad (.000006)$$

(29)
$$p_e = .374 + .0688p_w + .572p \qquad \bar{R} = 0.83$$
$$(.063) \quad (.088) \qquad (.12)$$

(30)
$$p_dC_d + p_nC_n + p_sC_s + q_pI_p + q_hI_h + pI_i + p_eF_e$$
$$- p_i(F_{im} + F_{if}) + G = pX + W_g$$

(31) $W + P + S_c - pX = W_g - D_a - T_i$

(32) $hwN_w = W\,10^8$

(33) $W + P = Y$

(34) $C = C_d + C_n + C_s$

Discussion of the Equations

To make the system more comprehensible before we discuss applications of the model and its actual performance, we shall comment briefly on each equation or group of equations, comparing it with related work in econometrics.

THE CONSUMPTION EQUATIONS

Consumer expenditures have been split into three obvious components—durables, nondurables, and services. Starting from the time-honored proposition that consumption (or consumption type) is dependent on aggregate income, we introduce the following qualifications:

1. Income should be adjusted for taxes and transfers. We use disposable income.
2. Relative prices might be relevant when dealing with subgroups of consumption. We deflate disposable income by the price index of the consumption type considered.
3. Income distribution as well as aggregate income may affect consumption. We use a separate variable to measure the ratio of wage to other personal income.
4. There may be lags in consumer behavior. We introduce average consumption (by type) of the past eight quarters to show the effect of the past.[4]
5. Consumer wealth as well as income may influence behavior. We used total stock of cash as a particular wealth variable of strategic importance in consumer spending.
6. Population growth may affect consumption. We introduced an explicit population variable, although we could have measured

---

[4] In the Barger-Klein quarterly model, last quarter's consumption was used, in direct analogy to the successful use of last year's consumption in the annual models. There is so much pure autocorrelation that this kind of quarterly relation was not satisfactory. If past consumption is to represent a standard or norm from which adjustments to current conditions take place, it seems better to use average consumption of the recent past. All these schemes using past consumption are transformations of distributed lag processes.

consumption, income, and cash balances on a per capita basis as an alternative.

We made these adjustments uniformly to all three consumption functions, but in the end settled for selective use of certain variables in certain equations. This was an empirical selection that has been used throughout the model. Many experimental calculations were made for each equation. We finally settled upon a set of parameter estimates for each equation that looked reasonable. Reasonableness was based on a priori notions about sign and order of magnitude of coefficients. The degree of experimentation was limited because we committed ourselves to a set of predetermined variables for the whole group of calculations by the method of limited information. We introduced one special variable in the equation for consumer durables. This variable is an index of consumer buying plans for new cars and other household items. We do not explain this variable within the system.

THE INVESTMENT EQUATIONS

Capital formation is divided into producers' plant and equipment, residential construction, and inventory investment. In the plant and equipment equation, investment intentions are introduced explicitly. These are the data of the Office of Business Economics—Securities and Exchange Commission on first intentions deflated by the price index of capital goods as of the (future) date to which the intentions refer. One may justifiably argue that we should deflate them as of the date at which the intentions are expressed. A similar anticipatory variable appears in the residential construction equation. It is the lagged value of starts.

The system is open with respect to these two anticipatory variables; i.e., we offer no endogenous explanation of investment intentions or housing starts; therefore, the extrapolation period for the model is limited. Our treatment here is parallel to that in the equation for consumer durables, where we introduce the index of consumer buying plans. In the inventory investment equation, we have proceeded somewhat differently. We have the backlog of orders as a kind of anticipatory variable there, but we attempt to give, at a later stage in the model, an endogenous explanation of unfilled orders, bringing new orders into the system as well.

The positive correlation between inventory investment and unfilled orders may seem to be strange, for businessmen ought not to be accumulating stocks while they still have backlogs of unfilled orders on hand. Our disaggregation was not carried far enough in this system to distinguish among inventories of raw materials, goods in process, and finished goods. The first two ought to be positively associated with unfilled orders, while the third ought to be negatively associated. A similar result is found by Duesenberry, Eckstein, and Fromm in their quarterly model.[5]

In the housing demand equation we use a long-term interest rate variable to show the effect of credit terms, and a marriage variable to show the effect of demographic pressures on facilities.

The capacity variable, which we have estimated with considerable expenditure of research effort, appears to be highly significant in the equation for plant and equipment.

The inventory equation, apart from the usual transactions and stock adjustment terms, contains an indication of price speculation. We did not separate farm from nonfarm inventories. This is another direction in which future disaggregation ought to go.

THE ELEMENTS OF NONWAGE INCOME

There are three equations for nonwage income components. One covers corporate saving; one relates noncorporate (excluding wages) to corporate income; and one deals with depreciation. The fundamental national accounting identity equating national income to national product, with appropriate reconciling items, requires the separate explanation of corporate saving. In the explanation of corporate saving a variable measuring corporate income, as distinct from other nonwage income, must be used. This necessitates an equation. Finally, depreciation in the system must be explained; for the capital formation variables are measured gross, and they must be cumulated for measurement of capital stock.

Corporate savings are made to depend on corporate income (after taxes) and lagged dividend payments of the past eight quarters. The explanation of the particular lag scheme here is the same as in the consumption equations.

When we use depreciation variables in the model for the purposes of measuring capital stock, we reckon depreciation at replacement costs. In other instances, we reckon in accounting prices. Here, we

[5] James S. Duesenberry, Otto Eckstein, and Gary Fromm, "A Simulation of the United States Economy in Recession," *Econometrica*, October 1960, pp. 749–809.

are interested in relating depreciation to the accumulated stock of fixed capital and the rate of economic activity.

The relation between corporate and total nonwage income is purely empirical. It may be wiser to separate dividend and interest income from the nonwage noncorporate amounts, explaining this slow-moving component by a simple trend or autoregression, and to relate corporate income to income from noncorporate self-employment. The particular combination of variables used in the estimation of this empirical relation has been chosen so as to avoid some complications of multicollinearity.

PRODUCTION FUNCTIONS

The ordinary version of the production function is estimated by equation 10. There we have a relationship between real private output [GNP less government wages and salaries, deflated by the GNP deflator (see equation 30)], the input of labor, the input of capital, and a technological time trend. Labor input is measured as private employment $(N_w - N_g)$ adjusted by an index of hours worked (h) plus the number of self-employed (N_e). Since h is an index value on a unit base, we express adjusted employees and self-employed in conformable units: $h(N_w - N_g) + N_e$. Capital input is measured as the accumulated stock of capital, based on statistics of net investment in fixed capital, times the rate of utilization of capacity. Strictly speaking, we would want to have the rate of utilization of capital as the multiplying factor, but lacking a direct estimate of capital utilization we use an over-all measure of capacity utilization.

Capacity as expressed in equation 11 must be explained.[6] It is an important, but elusive, concept in its own right, and it plays an important role in this model. By capacity output, in the aggregate, we mean a *point* on the macro-economic production function corresponding to full utilization of inputs—labor and capital in this case. We might write

$$X_c = \alpha_0 + \alpha_1 N_L + \alpha_2 K + \alpha_3 t + v$$

where X_c = capacity output

N_L = labor force

K = stock of capital [shorthand for $\sum_{i=0}^{\infty} (I_p + I_h - D_r)_{-i}$]

v = random error.

[6] The discussion of capacity and the production function bears heavily on ideas put forward by Professor Morishima of Osaka University.

Perhaps we should write $0.97(N_L - N_g)$, or some other high fraction of the private labor force, for full-utilization labor input in order to allow for frictional unemployment and public employment. In this paper, $1.0N_L$ is used, since the applied work to be described was based on this value.

This is not an independent relationship. Its parameters should be the same as those of the ordinary production function, expressed in terms of actual output, employment, and utilized capital. Two separate linear functions might be used to approximate a single nonlinear production surface—one linear function approximating actual operations and the other approximating full-capacity operations. In the actual process of equation estimation we found difficulties in estimating the full-capacity version of the production function, because N_L, K, and t are obviously strongly intercorrelated. They are all smooth trends. The problem in estimating the ordinary production function directly is that direct estimates of capital utilization cannot be obtained. We have direct estimates for labor in the form of employment and hours statistics. We approximated the solution of this problem by estimating

$$X = \alpha_0 + \alpha_1[h(N_w - N_g) + N_e] + \alpha_2(X/X_c)K + \alpha_3 t + u.$$

We were able to do this because we had independent estimates of X/X_c.

These independent estimates have come to be known as the Wharton School index of capacity utilization. The index is constructed in the following way: Each of thirty major components of the Federal Reserve index of industrial production is plotted on time charts. Seasonally adjusted monthly series, averaged to quarters, are plotted. Trend lines through peaks are established. These are linear segments connecting pairs of successive peaks. Peaks are established by inspection, with minor or temporary peaks eliminated. Some simple rules are established for recognizing peaks. From the last peak in a series, the trend lines are continued linearly with the same slope as the last completed segment. When actual production is rising and goes above the extrapolated trend, we increase the slope of the extrapolated line until a definite peak is established. When the trend lines are revised, we revise capacity calculations back to the last previous peak. The ratios of actual production to trends drawn through peaks give us figures on the percentage of capacity utilized by industry. The industry figures are averaged with weights into a national figure. The weights are those used to combine the Federal Reserve output series in its national index of production.

It would require an extensive argument and documented research study to give full justification to this method of estimating capacity utilization rates. In this paper, we merely want to describe our procedures and definitions of variables in the model. Many criticisms could obviously be raised about our method of measuring capacity. In our use of this measure we have implicitly assumed that industrial capacity, as we measure it from the FRB index components, is indicative (in an index sense) of capacity to produce private national product.

Using our estimates of the production function in (10), we find that the same coefficients inserted into (11) produce calculated values of X_c that are also close to those independently derived by our method of trends through peaks.

The relation between (10) and (11) may be further clarified by multiplying the production function, on both sides, by X_c/X. We then transform

$$X = \alpha_0 + \alpha_1[h(N_w - N_g) + N_e] + \alpha_2(X/X_c)K + \alpha_3 t + u$$

into

$$X_c = \alpha_0(X_c/X) + \alpha_1(X_c/X)[h(N_w - N_g) + N_e] + \alpha_2 K \\ + \alpha_3(X_c/X)t + (X_c/X)u.$$

The employment variable, in brackets, is marked up by the factor X_c/X. This should bring it close to N_L or $0.97(N_L - N_g)$. The coefficients of α_0, α_3, and u make this form differ slightly from the full-capacity version

$$X_c = \alpha_0 + \alpha_1 N_L + \alpha_2 K + \alpha_3 t + v$$

with which we started this discussion.

WAGES, HOURS, AND LABOR FORCE

Associated with the technical conditions of production are the demand for labor and hours of work. Labor demand is converted into wage payments through valuation of employment by the wage rate.

The private wage bill, deflated by the general price index, is made a linear function of current and lagged output, with an upward time trend. This is a straightforward generalization of the constancy of labor's share. To avoid problems of collinearity between X and X_{-1}, we make their coefficients equal before estimating the equation.

The wage rate (quarterly earnings at an annual rate) is made to depend on the state of the labor market, the general price level, and a trend. This is a familiar interpretation of the "law of supply and demand" used in the annual models that preceded the present work. Wage changes (over a four-quarter span) are made to depend on unemployment (averaged over the past four quarters), price changes (over a four-quarter span, averaged over the past four quarters), and a trend.

Unemployment is the residual difference between labor force and employment; therefore, we need an equation for labor force. We considered the standard hypothesis that makes labor supply depend upon the real wage rate, but found no satisfactory relationship. Labor force follows a smooth trend that we represent by a purely chronological variable. There is, however, an elastic cyclical element in the labor supply. This is largely accounted for by housewives, students, and semiretired people. They appear to swell the ranks of the labor force when jobs are plentiful and to withdraw when jobs are scarce. In our equation we represent this by a negative association between labor supply and unemployment.

ORDERS AND BACKLOGS

The inventory equation discussed above contained a variable representing unfilled orders. In the endogenous explanation of unfilled orders we use the rate of capacity operation and the flow of new orders. This requires an additional equation to explain new orders, which we do in terms of recent sales and price changes. Our orders series are limited to the manufacturing sector, and eventually we would want to extend this part of the model on a disaggregated basis to nonmanufacturing sectors.

FOREIGN TRADE

In a formal sense, both imports and exports are endogenous in this model. The explanation of exports is carried no further than to relate it directly to world production. Relative prices, as we have been able to measure such a magnitude, have not been found to be of significance in this equation. Overseas reserves, trade liberalization, and other variables may eventually prove to be important in a more detailed study of exports. In the applications we have made with the model, exports have been set at predetermined levels, and the export equation used here has been purely formal.

Import demand, however, has been more closely geared to the domestic economy. We divide imports into two classes, imports of unfinished and imports of finished goods. The former are determined directly from statistics of crude food and material imports. Imports recorded in the GNP accounts less these crude food and material imports are called "finished" imports. They are a residual, consisting of goods and services. We treat them like consumer goods. Equation 20, therefore, is simply an import analogue of the consumption equations.

MONEY AND INTEREST

Demand for cash balances, which appears as a variable in the consumption equations, is made to depend on the long-run interest rate as a standard formulation of the doctrine of liquidity preference. One version of that theory is to assume that velocity, instead of being a constant, is a function of the interest rate. We have made the reciprocal of velocity our dependent variable. We have extended the dependence of cash holdings to price movements as well as the level of the interest rate.

In most versions of the modern theory of employment, the monetary authorities are assumed to control the stock of cash directly. Our assumption here is that they influence or control bank reserves and the discount rate. These influence the short-term rate, which then has a bearing on the long-term rate. These lines of reasoning are brought out in equations 22 and 23. The long-term rate is assumed to be a Koyck-type distributed lag function of past short-term rates. After transformation, this becomes a linear relation with the current short rate and the lagged long rate as explanatory variables.

PRICES

In various individual equations of the system, specific price levels occur. For example in equations 1, 2, and 3, there are three separate consumer prices. We follow a general rule on all the specific price variables. Each specific price is related to the general price or wage level and possibly to some particular factor affecting that price.

Our system is interrelated; nevertheless, we can pick out certain main lines of causation. For a given output level, including a rate of capital formation as a component, the production function (10) shows labor requirements. Equation 13 is responsible for wage rate determination, and equation 12 can be transformed into a markup of price over unit labor costs. Thus, both the general price level and the wage rate are determined in the system. In equations 24 through 29, specific prices are related to one of these two general variables. The backlog variables used in (24) and (25) are subclasses of total unfilled orders. While the total is explained within the system, the components are not. The coefficient of C_s/C, the fraction of total consumption accounted for by services, is statistically significant but negative. This does not appear to be a reasonable result.

IDENTITIES

The remaining equations in the systems are identities. Components of national product, valued in current prices, add to the total. This is expressed as private GNP (pX) plus government wages and salaries (W_g). In the next identity, the components of net national income ($W + P + S_c$) are equated with GNP ($pX + W_g$) less depreciation (D_a) and a reconciling item (T_i), which consists of indirect taxes less subsidies, the statistical discrepancy, and other small items. In this relation, depreciation is valued at accounting prices. We do not give an explicit relation between accounting price and replacement cost depreciation in the model, but we do use some simple proportions between these two for short-period applications.

Equation 32 expresses the wage bill as the product of employment, hours, and the wage rate. The final two equations are self-evident.

APPLICATIONS—1961 FORECASTS

In the first trial calculations using this model, we extrapolated beyond the terminal sample date, IV-1958, for predictions of the first three quarters of 1961. These calculations were started in March 1961, and were completed in April. Results for the first quarter were not known but could be guessed in broad outline.

To keep the algebra of solution simple we fixed values over the forecast period for some variables in order to make the system linear. This required the assignment of prices. We were not generally satisfied with equations 24 through 29, in any case, and thought that prices could be predicted a priori for the three quarters of 1961 as well as they could be predicted by these equations. We also set the general price level at predetermined values. Interest rates and exports were similarly fixed at predetermined levels.

27

In order to solve the remaining equations linearly, we needed to fix values for P/W in (1)–(3) and (20). This required the suppression of equation 13. Capacity output was estimated from (11), using last period's labor force and capital stock with the constant item adjusted so as to make the computed value agree with the first quarter's observation, I-1961; and the denominator of X/X_c could thus be computed in advance of the other variables for each forecast solution. This, too, was done to preserve linearity. We added three equations, determined from recent observations, on tax-transfer variables.

$$T = -45.16 + 0.198\,Y$$
$$T_c = -4.59 + 0.599P_c$$
$$T_i = -39.86 + 0.213pX$$

Using the values of predetermined variables in Table 1, we solved the system for endogenous variables in I-1961. First, however, we made estimates of variables in this model from a starting point in the fourth quarter of 1960.

We reduced the system algebraically to two equations in I_i and X. One was directly obtained from the inventory equation (6) with predetermined values substituted for the other variables. The other was obtained by substitution and algebraic reduction of the other variables in (30). This gave a residual equation in I_i and X. We adjusted the constant terms of each equation so that they gave us the correct values, simultaneously, for I_i and X corresponding to our best estimates of these in the observation period, IV-1960. Keeping these adjustments in the constant terms of the two equations in I_i and X, we solved the system sequentially in I-, II-, III-1961. We used computed values from one quarter as lagged inputs for successive quarters. *We did not adjust individual equations, apart from the two relations between I_i and X, which kept a constant adjustment throughout the time sequence of solutions.* Some component series of national product may therefore be biased, but the quarter-to-quarter variation should not be seriously distorted. *Some of our computed components do not add to national totals.* Selected results are given in Table 2.[7] Actual values are in Table 3.

On the surface, this appears to have been a good forecast. The prediction of an upturn in the economy after the low point in the first quarter of 1961 was not surprising. Opinion was much divided,

---

[7] This table was circulated privately to more than 100 technicians in April 1961. It was a genuine forecast.

TABLE 1
Predetermined Variables Used in 1961 Forecasts

Variables	Value Assumed			Actual Value*		
	I	II	III	I	II	III
P/W	0.36	0.36	0.36	0.36	0.35	0.35
$\frac{1}{8}\Sigma(C_d)_{-i}$	41.0	computed		41.3		
C_d^e	110.0	110.0	110.0	117.0	110.0	113.0
$\frac{1}{8}\Sigma(C_n)_{-i}$	140.6	computed		140.3		
$(L/p_n)_{-1}$	227.7	228.5	229.0	227.7	231.1	238.9
$\frac{1}{8}\Sigma(C_s)_{-i}$	111.5	computed		112.1		
$(L/p_s)_{-1}$	210.8	211.5	212.0	212.4	214.8	219.9
N	182.5	183.3	184.1	182.5	183.2	(183.95)p
I_p^e	28.5	28.0	28.0	28.9	27.9	(28.6)p
i_L	4.64	4.60	4.50	4.59	4.59	4.72
F	296.0	450.0	461.0	291.0	430.0	(430.0)p
$(I_i^s)_{-1}$	1,003.0	1,050.0	1,100.0	1,003.0	1,016.0	1,100.0
X_{-1}	394.0	computed		395.0		
t	61.0	62.0	63.0	61.0	62.0	63.0
q_p	1.22	1.22	1.22	1.23	1.23	(1.23)p
$\frac{1}{8}\Sigma\frac{1}{q_p}(P_c - T_c - S_c)$	11.2	computed		11.3		
P_{-1}	102.9	computed		101.7		
W_g	51.0	52.0	53.0	50.4	51.3	52.1
$p\dagger$	1.153	1.153	1.153	1.156	1.158	1.164
$\Sigma(I_i)_{-j}$	239.3	computed		246.4		
$(X - I_i)_{-1}$	396.4	computed		396.2		
$(p_i/p)_{-1}$	0.841	0.840	0.840	0.841	0.835	0.830
$\frac{1}{8}\Sigma(F_{if})_{-i}$	19.72	computed		19.0		
G	103.0	104.0	105.0	105.0	107.3	108.5
p_e	1.085	1.085	1.085	1.105	1.204	(111.0)p
F_e	25.0	25.0	25.0	25.0	21.9	(24.0)p
D_a	44.5	45.0	45.5	44.2	45.0	45.5
p_d	1.045	1.045	1.045	1.048	1.055	1.055
p_n	1.085	1.085	1.085	1.085	1.081	1.081
p_s	1.175	1.180	1.185	1.167	1.174	1.174
q_h	1.170	1.170	1.170	1.170	1.170	(1.175)p
p_i	0.97	0.97	0.97	0.97	0.96	(0.96)p
N_e	9,200.0	9,200.0	9,200.0	9,410.0	9,100.0	8,820.0
N_g	8,600.0	8,700.0	8,800.0	8,670.0	8,700.0	8,450.0
$\Sigma(I_p)_{-i}$	2,224.86	computed		2,224.86		
$\Sigma(I_h)_{-i}$	1,006.27	computed		1,006.27		
U_{-1}	44.6	computed		44.3		

p = preliminary.
* Available at later date—after the forecast.
† The value for IV-1960 was estimated to be 1.152.

however, on the magnitude of the recovery. There is no doubt that many persons were surprised (in government and business) by the magnitude of our increments from first to second quarter and from second to third quarter. This is not to say that we were alone in pre-

29

TABLE 2

SELECTED FORECAST VALUES, 1960–61
(billions of 1954 dollars unless otherwise stated)

Variable	Starting Value 1960 (IV)	Estimate 1961 (I)	Forecast 1961 (II)	Forecast 1961 (III)
C_d—durable consumption	43.5	41.4	43.4	47.9
C_n—nondurable consumption	144.7	143.9	145.4	148.2
C_s—services consumption	115.0	115.5	116.9	118.7
I_p—plant and equipment	36.4	35.4	35.4	36.3
I_h—residential construction	18.2	17.7	18.2	19.9
I_i—inventory investment	−2.4	−4.4	−2.7	0.7
X—private GNP	394.0	388.4	396.2	412.1
GNP (current prices)	503.8	498.8	508.8	528.2
X/X_c (capacity rate)	0.89	0.87	0.88	0.90

TABLE 3

ACTUAL VALUES OF SELECTED FORECAST VARIABLES, 1960–61
(billions of 1954 dollars)

Variable	1960 (IV)	1961 (I)	1961 (II)	1961 (III)
C_d—durable consumption	41.6	37.6	39.8	40.3
C_n—nondurable consumption	141.3	141.6	142.6	145.2
C_s—services consumption	116.6	117.8	119.2	121.4
I_p—plant and equipment	38.5	36.3	36.9	36.6
I_h—residential construction	17.5	16.5	17.6	19.9
I_i—inventory investment	−1.1	−3.2	2.9	3.9
X—private GNP	395.1	389.6	401.4	407.0
GNP (current prices)	504.5	500.8	516.1	525.8
X/X_c (capacity rate)	0.88	0.86	0.90	0.92

dicting a substantial improvement in real output, but the model came out in the correct neighborhood when there were great doubts in the minds of many persons that the recovery would be this strong. It is also important to note that the prediction was for a surprisingly large increase in output associated with quite modest increments in our estimate of capacity utilization.

While our estimate of GNP for the third quarter is close to the outcome, the model underestimated the growth from the first to the second quarter and overestimated it from the second to the third. We had too little inventory investment and too much durable consumption. Our other errors were less remarkable.

These are only surface observations. A more detailed appraisal requires two considerations: (1) data revision and (2) accuracy of assumptions. We made our forecast for the second and third quarters on the basis of preliminary estimates of the fourth quarter of 1960 and informed guesses about the first quarter of 1961, which had just passed. Data were not fully collected for the first quarter of 1961, and many of the fourth quarter estimates for 1960 were highly tentative. Our base period (IV-1960) estimates of output were too high by approximately $1 billion, and our inventory estimates were too low by the same magnitude. These two variables were forced by our adjustment process to give the "correct" values as we estimated them at the time for the base period. *We did not adjust the other component equations of the model;* therefore, in the "back" solution, which gives the distribution of values of individual variables, all the identities do not necessarily hold; and we may start off from biased values in the base period. This bias is not serious, though, since we can see its magnitude in IV-1960. C_d is, for example, overestimated by about $2.0 billion in the base period. This bias value in C_d is not adequate to account for the large value of durable consumption in the third quarter. We definitely overestimated the rise in C_d. Apart from the underestimate of inventory change, no other GNP component is seriously enough distorted in the forecast to merit special consideration. Our index of capacity utilization was revised in the summer of 1961.[8] Although it is not apparent in the comparison of the values for IV-1960, the new index tends to run about one or two points above the old one that was used in the forecast.

One of the drawbacks of the model is that it contains so many predetermined variables that a large amount of nonmodel forecasting is necessary before the model can be used in forecasting. A month's work at data processing and extrapolation of exogenous variables is required in preparation for a forecast. The large number of predetermined variables in Table 1 indicates the magnitude of initial input. There are many variables, covering many aspects of the economy here. It is easy to be right on some values, too high on some, and too low on others. We underestimated the growth in money supply. Government spending was set too low in the initial period and grew slightly less than was actually the case. The interest rate should have risen slightly instead of declining by a small amount.

---

[8] The index was computed from the FRB indexes on a 1957 base in the revision. The older indexes on a base of 1947–49 had been previously used.

Housing starts were actually fixed in advance. Price increases were too low. Population growth was closely estimated, and so on.

Major sources of error in the forecast are not to be sought in the assumptions made for predetermined variables or in data revisions. The model is only a statistical estimate of reality and is subject to error. Imperfect knowledge of the true relationships in the economy and some large disturbances probably account for the great part of the forecast error. Strikes and hurricane damage in the third quarter probably had substantial effects on changes in variables between the second and third quarters.

APPLICATIONS—THE RECESSIONS OF 1953–54 AND 1957–58

Models can be tested by *ex post* as well as by *ex ante* forecasts. In the previous section, we described *ex ante* forecasting. In this section we shall summarize the results of a simulation study prepared for the Joint Economic Committee of the Congress of the United States.[9] This is an example of *ex post* forecasting and has the advantage of controlling error in the assumptions for predetermined variables. Since it is an application after the event, good estimates of the predetermined variables are available.

Ex post extrapolations of a model outside the sample data to which the model is fitted provide better tests than do *ex post* calculations using internal sample data. The present example uses internal data and is, therefore, not as stringent a test as we hope, eventually, to apply. At the moment this example is cited as an interesting application.

The problem posed in this application was how to determine, from the model, whether and how much specific dampening of inventory fluctuation in past recessions would have contributed to total output stabilization. This is a hypothetical problem, exemplifying how models can be used in policy formulation, and is not a test of the model. However, the first step in attacking the inventory stabilization issue was to let the model run through the course of each of the two recessions considered to see whether it duplicated actual output fluctuations. Predetermined variables were inserted into the equations for the first quarter of 1953 (and the first quarter of 1957). The

[9] Lawrence R. Klein and Joel Popkin, "An Econometric Analysis of the Post-War Relationship Between Inventory Fluctuations and Changes in Aggregate Economic Activity," *Inventory Fluctuations and Economic Stabilization*, 87th Cong., 1st sess., December, 1961, III, 69–89.

system was then successively solved as a dynamic model through the fourth quarter of 1954 (and the fourth quarter of 1958). Exogenous variables were assigned their actual values for each quarter's solution, but lagged endogenous variables were generated within the model after starting from given initial conditions. As in the case of the 1961 forecasts, the two equations were adjusted in I_i and X, so that correct values were obtained for the starting quarter of each simulation. New tax equations were determined for the simulation periods, and the changes in revenue laws during 1954 required the use of different tax equations for the quarters of 1953 and of 1954. The results are given in Table 4.

TABLE 4

ACTUAL AND SIMULATED VALUES OF X, 1953–54 AND 1957–58
(billions of 1954 dollars)

Quarter	1953–54		1957–58	
	Actual	Computed	Actual	Computed
I	334.72	334.72	371.90	371.90
II	338.87	337.64	373.03	369.82
III	335.69	332.65	373.24	367.90
IV	329.64	331.29	366.76	368.94
I	326.43	328.18	353.72	365.98
II	325.35	341.27	355.02	378.10
III	327.40	343.62	360.25	388.62
IV	335.33	349.23	370.89	397.91

Computed output turns up one quarter earlier than output in 1954, and the recovery is stronger. In 1958, the timing is coincident, but the downswing started earlier and was interrupted by a temporary advance in the fourth quarter of 1957. The sharpness of the 1957–58 recession is not duplicated in the computed data. The fall is not as great as the actual output decline, and the revival is stronger. The revival is also stronger in the computed than in the actual output for 1954.

The time paths of other variables can be seen in the tables and charts of the JEC study paper referred to earlier. The policy application of the model made in the study paper can be summarized by noting that if inventory fluctuations are autonomously reduced in amplitude, fluctuations in output, employment, and other variables are also reduced. The model results show that if inventory fluctuation (deviations above and below zero inventory investment) can be reduced by a factor of one-quarter, output fluctuations are moderately reduced. At the cycle troughs, we estimate multiplier values of four to five, i.e., the trough of the production cycle is raised by four or five dollars (1954 prices) for every dollar reduction in the absolute value of inventory investment at the trough. If inventory stabilization is much greater, say, a dampening of fluctuations by a factor of three-quarters, the ordinary business cycle in computed output vanishes.

SELF-CRITICISM

This is only another one in a series of American models. There will be more to come. The ancestors of this model have been used to make a number of helpful forecasts, provide a setting for computational experiments, and provide tailor-made subjects for critical doctoral dissertations. They have all had a measure of intellectual attack. In anticipation of some points of attack on the present system, the system might be appraised here and now. This will set the stage for work on the models to come.

By the time data are collected, parameters are estimated, and models are tested for performance, ideas about the detailed structure of the economy can change drastically. At the end of this time-consuming process (about three years in the present case) we usually decide that we would have built the system differently if we were starting the project freshly. The price and interest rate equations are the poorest of the lot in the model, and these need revision.[10] It would be possible to use the present price and interest rate equations in a more essential way in forecasting from the present model, but a good and simple computing routine for coping with the nonlinearities caused by th ese is not fully prepared.

As in past models, we have looked for a balanced estimate of equations as a whole and systems as a whole. Goodness of fit, randomness of residuals, signs of coefficients, approximate magnitude of coefficients, and standard errors have all been used together in deciding whether to accept or reject estimated equations. In these decisions many candidates are accepted for which individual coefficients do not meet some standard test—say a t-test for significance at the 5 per cent level. Some of our standard errors are large. If the

---

[10] In a joint project supported by the work of many scholars, and sponsored by the Social Science Research Council, a new model is being built which appears to be much stronger on the side of price estimation. The price formation equations are quite different.

model were brought up to date and re-estimated with twelve more observations, some of these insignificant results might be changed.

In specific equations there are definite possibilities for improvements. Population might be directly introduced in the consumption equations by expressing all variables in per capita terms. The empirical relation between P_c and P can be improved by extracting dividend and interest income from P, estimating that component separately by some simple autoregressive scheme, and relating only entrepreneurial elements of P to P_c. This relation can be refined even more if farm entrepreneurial income is taken out of P as well.

Inventories should be subdivided by farm and nonfarm category. In addition the nonfarm category should be disaggregated by stage of process and type of holder (seller versus manufacturer). These disaggregations all call for a substantially larger model. Many of these things are already being done in the Social Science Research Council model referred to in note 10. In the equation for residential construction, housing starts are an important variable. Starts are not really independent in their relation and certainly not for as many time periods ahead as we have tried to use them in applications. In fact, construction expenditure series are prepared by the phasing-in of starts data, using an average construction lag. We should have an equation explaining starts, another showing how construction data are built from starts data, and another on unit structure value.

Similarly, investment intentions and consumer buying plans are not really independent data in our system, although we use them in that way. We need separate equations explaining these expectations, in addition to equations showing how expectations are transformed into realizations.

The government sector is purely exogenous except for the simple tax-transfer equations used in applications of the model. There is much useful work that can be done in distinguishing between induced government expenditures like those for highways and education and purely autonomous categories like defense. Some equations can be developed for the induced parts, and some realization functions associating expenditures with budget appropriations can be constructed. Many more things can be done on the side of government receipts. Tax equations using income distribution and internal revenue reports can be greatly improved. Major transfer items could be usefully separated from taxes and estimated in new equations.

All these improvements require substantial research work, but they are all feasible and can easily be added to the basic framework presented here.

COMMENT

EDWARD F. DENISON, Brookings Institution

This meeting on models of income determination stemmed in part from a compelling need to strengthen communication between members of this conference who are concerned with national accounting and related economic statistics, on the one hand, and econometricians, on the other. The Program Committee, in accordance with the objective, gave the econometricians who are presenting papers a strong injunction to translate their mathematics as best they could into the verbal language of the econometrically illiterate. The main sanction available to the Program Committee was assignment of a member of the latter group as a discussant. For Lawrence Klein's paper, the Program Committee took no chances at all, but assigned from its own ranks the only member clearly possessing the desired qualification of innocence of mathematical or econometric knowledge.

Let me first, therefore, fill my assigned role as appointed spokesman for the ignorant by stating that Klein has done an exceptionally good job of translation and explanation of his model. Anyone who merely looked at his list of thirty-four equations would not agree. But there is very little difficulty in understanding the individual equations if they are examined in conjunction with the text description. It becomes immediately apparent that the terms that appear most formidable are simple numbers we are all accustomed to using, such as the net stock of plant and equipment, or the average level of consumption during the past two years. I hope these revelations do not cost Klein his license to practice.

The groupings of equations Klein provides are also very helpful in understanding the approach and general structure of the equations. However, while I think I can follow the individual equations, I am sure I do not understand their interrelationships and the structure as a whole in more than a rudimentary sense. This is no criticism of Klein; I feel I am well ahead of where I was before reading the paper.

From the standpoint of those of us who are accustomed to worry about the relative merits of particular economic series, it would be useful to specify in the definitions of the variables the exact series used—for example, for employment and hours worked. The particular notation used is not always as easy to remember as it could be. But these are small defects, easily remedied. Viewed as a description of his model, Klein's paper is an unqualified success.

Now for the model itself. Without questioning his choice of economic variables in his individual equations, let me raise first a few questions about the particular series used to represent the economic phenomena he wishes to represent. These are quarterly series, seasonally adjusted in most cases.

I believe the labor force and employment series used are from the *Monthly Report on the Labor Force*. Quarterly fluctuations around the trend in these series, and in the private employment subtotal, are dominated by irregular fluctuations in the agricultural component. These fluctuations clearly are irrelevant to the quarterly behavior of either total or agricultural GNP. Even nonagricultural employment in the MRLF series is rather erratic, and I would expect the series derived from establishment reports to be much more closely related to short-term GNP behavior. It is also far more relevant to the derivation of the average wage series which enters Klein's system of equations because of its greater statistical consistency between employment and earnings. Now it is true that erratic fluctuations may roughly cancel in deriving the equation, and may cause little trouble in forecasting when the employment and labor force figures are derived rather than observed. But this is not the case when the model is used, as Klein has used it, to study patterns in past periods. I think most persons who follow employment and payroll data closely will be troubled by the use of MRLF rather than establishment series. It may be heretical, but I suspect that little of relevance to income determination would be lost, and something would be gained, if the incompleteness of the establishment data were surmounted by so crude a device as defining the labor force as nonagricultural employees from the establishment series plus unemployment from the MRLF.

A current minor controversy among economic statisticians concerns seasonal adjustment of labor force data. The Labor Department seasonally adjusts the labor force, employment, and unemployment independently; thus, employment plus unemployment does not equal the labor force. A widely used alternative obtains seasonally adjusted unemployment as a residual from the seasonally adjusted labor force and employment data. Inadvertently, rather than by deliberate choice, Klein uses a third alternative that has no apparent advantage. He obtains seasonally adjusted employment as the residual. Klein needs to obtain employment or unemployment as a residual to avoid introducing an additional variable, but unemployment is the better choice and especially so since it follows the logic of his equations.

Indexes of net capital stock and gross stock differ when the average age of capital changes. Klein uses net stock to measure changes in fixed capital input. My own, and I think the more common, view is that gross stock provides the more logical index of capital input; and I wonder whether Klein disagrees.

Use of housing starts rather than building permits in the estimation of residential construction seems questionable, if the model is to be used more than one quarter in advance. Permits are less erratic and have a longer lead time than the new Census series for starts.

Equation 4 for the estimation of plant and equipment expenditures is interesting. The SEC-OBE projection based on the quarterly antic- ipations survey is used, but as only one term in the equation rather than directly in percentage-change form.

Is the equation primarily an attempt to adjust plant and equipment as defined in the SEC-OBE survey to include farm and other compo- nents excluded from the survey but included in private GNP expen- ditures for producers' durables and nonresidential construction? This seems unlikely. The other variable in the equation, the level of the capacity utilization index, hardly seems appropriate to represent the missing components. Moreover, it appears to be about as im- portant as the anticipations figure in determining Klein's estimate. This greatly exceeds the relative weight of the missing components.

Or, as seems more likely from Klein's preliminary comments on the introduction of anticipations data and on the significance, in equation 4, of the capacity variable, is this equation an attempt to improve on the government plant and equipment anticipation esti- mates? Does it do so? The government agencies themselves correct for systematic past biases in reported anticipations. However, these adjustments do not take account of the unemployment position of the economy. Klein's does, but with no distinction between the upward and downward phase of the cycle. If the equation can be shown conclusively to furnish better forecasts than the government adjustments, as presently applied, this is an interesting and useful discovery. It warrants exhaustive analysis. I would like to know exactly what anticipations data were used in deriving the equation.

38

Also, I wonder at what level of unemployment the implied adjustment of the anticipations series switches from plus to minus.

The preceding comments refer mainly to the choice of statistical series to represent the economic variables, like employment, used in the equations. A thorough critique would consider the choice of economic variables themselves, but I cannot attempt this. However, I am sufficiently surprised at the extensive use of the division of personal income between labor and other income to ask why. Is it perhaps serving as a proxy for something else?

Estimation of corporate profits from nonlabor personal income, which is the sum of farm and nonfarm proprietors' income and of private and government interest, dividends, and rental income of persons, is surprising. In the text, Klein suggests a shift to proprietors' income, presumably confined to the nonfarm sector. Since he now has no equation for proprietors' income, this would seem to lead nowhere. There is, to be sure, a relationship between profits and proprietors' income. The Office of Business Economics, insofar as it can, bases the movement of noncorporate business income on corporate profits. But what Klein would seem to need, if he changes his model in the way indicated, is a method of forecasting both corporate and noncorporate profits, which he now lacks.

In applying his model to forecast 1961, Klein did not actually use all of his equations. He used assumed or independently estimated values for prices, interest rates, and exports. Although Klein indicates he was not too unhappy about this, because he lacks confidence in the price equations anyway, the main reason was inability to solve the system of equations quickly when they lost linearity. This would seem to raise questions concerning the practical value of completeness in a short-term forecasting model. Incidentally, my instincts suggest that the definitional relationships among changes in productivity, unit costs, and prices could cause real trouble if prices are predetermined. Other things equal, the larger the productivity gain, the smaller the price increase.

Although Klein's paper is, in general, commendably lucid, I would appreciate more extended discussion of the procedure to tie in the model calculations with the most recent period for which actual figures are available. In the 1961 projection, Klein adjusted the constants in the key equations to force the most recent observation to fall on the regression line. Would it be quicker and about equally good to solve the equations for the most recent "actual" quarter and future quarters, and base the forecast on changes? Might not this also minimize the problem of getting the GNP components to add up to the total? I do not know the answers to these questions.

How good is the model? Klein compares forecasts from the model with actual data for three time periods. Two are past periods, each extending over eight quarters, encompassing the 1953–54 and 1957–58 recessions. The other is a forecast for the quarters of 1962. The past comparisons show rather poor agreement between actual and calculated GNP values, even though they fall within the period upon which the model is based, and use actual data for exogenous variables, and actual tax rates, which could not have been known in advance. It is true, however, that in both cases a recession and recovery is predicted, two of the four turning points are correctly calculated, one is off by only one quarter, and one by two quarters. I am not clear whether this degree of success depends upon the use of anticipatory data not available at the beginning of the periods.

The 1961 forecast shows rather good agreement, even though the exogenous variables were estimated and the values of many of the endogenous variables were simply assumed rather than obtained from the model.

My greatest doubt about Klein's whole system is an obvious one, and I am a little surprised he did not discuss it more. It is generally recognized that structural changes that accompany a given change in GNP or employment while unemployment is excessive are quite different from the structural changes that occur when the economy is growing under high-employment conditions. This raises the question whether one system of equations can describe both situations accurately.

If it can, I should suppose it to be only by systematic inclusion in the model of some such variable as the unemployment rate in order to distinguish the two situations. Even then I doubt it could be done with functions like Klein's, in which the difference between 3 per cent and 4 per cent unemployment has the same effect as that between 6 and 7, because the change in structural behavior patterns occurs rather abruptly instead of continuously. I suppose it would be possible to work into each equation a variable that would take effect only under depressed conditions, or only under prosperous conditions. Perhaps this might be the arithmetic excess of the unemployment rate above, or below, the postwar low or average, or some carefully selected number. Brown's Canadian model has such a term in the establishment of wage rates. But if done systematically, this is really similar to having two models.

Actually, only a few of Klein's equations explicitly or, I think, even implicitly include any indication of how far from capacity the economy is operating. The current or recent percentage unemployed or the capacity utilization index, the two relevant variables in his system, enter explicitly into only six equations. One of these, that for plant and equipment, I have already mentioned. Four are the equations determining the year-to-year increase in the average wage, average hours of work, the size of the labor force, and unfilled orders. At least equally obvious candidates, such as corporate profits, have no such determinant. Finally, the capacity utilization index enters the private GNP production function, equation 10, but not in the way I have in mind. It enters only as a multiplier for the net capital stock to arrive at capital input.

I presume Klein did not use unemployment or capacity utilization more often because he found they did not improve the estimates. But might this not indicate only that two models or the equivalent are needed, rather than only one?

In short, I wonder whether recession-recovery models such as we have begun to obtain, and companion short-term growth models for periods when the economy is operating at high employment, are not more promising than a single model, both for forecasting and for describing structural relationships.

This reaction to the Klein *model* is that of an outsider and should not be weighed heavily. I am really doing no more than asking questions. My judgment of the Klein paper as an educational document to describe the model for the ignorant, on the other hand, is altogether favorable, and my qualifications for this judgment are solid.

FRANCO MODIGLIANI, Massachusetts Institute of Technology

Over-All Considerations

Before I attempt a critical evaluation of Klein's quarterly model, one in a long string of past and future similar undertakings, I want to make it quite clear that I am a great admirer of his indefatigable labor in this area and that I share with him the conviction that this type of endeavor is very much worthwhile and will contribute with increasing effectiveness to economic forecasting and policy-making, as well as to a basic understanding of the working of our economy. I am, therefore, quite pleased to find that the United States economy decided to encourage his activities by producing in the third quarter of 1961 a GNP within a couple of billion dollars of the forecast made in April 1961, and largely on the basis of information relating only to the last quarter of 1960. The accuracy of the model is even more impressive if stated in terms of change over the last quarter of 1960. On this basis, Klein's forecast is only about 10 per cent over the actual change of some $21 billion. To be sure, this accuracy is somewhat misleading, for it results, in part, from considerably larger offsetting errors. Thus, the change in the price level was understated by 100 per cent, while the change in real private gross national product was overstated by 50 per cent. But even so, I at least feel that the model performed a rather creditable job on this occasion.

I am also quite aware of two difficulties that beset my role as commentator of this paper. The first is that any criticism I might advance is open to the obvious objection: if I claim that Klein's hypotheses should be replaced by better ones, why don't I build my own model? Unfortunately, only in a few instances can I claim that my suggestions have been explicitly tested by myself or others. The second difficulty is that Klein, in presenting the outcome of his labors, could not take the time to tell us how many other things he tried before settling on his final choice. Hence, at least some of my suggestions may have been tried out and rejected as empirically inadequate. Given my assigned role I have no choice but to ignore these difficulties. In setting forth my criticism of Klein's model I do, however, wish to make it quite clear that all of my criticism, right or wrong, is offered in the constructive spirit of advancing a common cause.

Let me, finally, indicate that in trying to assess the strength and shortcomings of the model and in suggesting some promising directions for further improvement I will assume that Klein's construction has also purposes other than that of arriving at accurate short-run forecasts of the course of economic activity. I assume his goal is also to provide an increased empirically supported understanding of the *modus operandi* of our present-day economic system and to develop a tool for testing the effects of alternative economic policies.

From this point of view goodness of fit to historical data and even initial forecasting success, though not unimportant, are clearly not the only relevant criteria for assessing the model and its parts. Other criteria are equally important and, in particular, that the hypotheses on which the model rests make "economic sense" or can be derived from other hypotheses having this property.

In the light of these considerations Klein's latest model strikes me, on the whole, as a very significant improvement over earlier ones. Some of these improvements consist in the incorporation of features that I would have liked to have seen in earlier models; in other words, it comes closer to my own notations, which, of course, I must regard as improvements, although others may not share this view. I am referring here, for instance, to the systematic incorporation of anticipatory variables, to the treatment of the purchase of consumers durables more nearly as a type of investment, and to the increasing attention to monetary phenomena and their interaction with real phenomena. Other improvements reflect, instead, advances in the general state of knowledge, which Klein has been quick to incorporate in his model, e.g., with respect to the inventory equation and the interrelationship of wages and prices. In some cases, as indicated below, I feel that Klein may not have gone far enough; but this is a debatable point; and, in any event, the movement is certainly in the right direction.

My only general complaint is a minor and readily remediable one; I wish he had provided us with a measure of goodness of fit for each of his equations. While such measures must of course be taken with a grain of salt, they are useful in providing an idea of how close we are coming to an explanation of the behavior of the dependent variable. This information is especially valuable where the reader may have serious qualms about the adequacy of the hypothesis.

Let me now abandon generalities and take a closer look at certain major groups of equations.

Comments on Some Specific Components of the Model

THE CONSUMER SECTOR

One feature of the present model is the disaggregation of consumption expenditure into three sectors: durables, nondurables, and services. While I see little point in disaggregation for its own sake, I believe that in the present instance the separation of the three sectors is worthwhile, both because it should help provide a more reliable explanation of total consumption expenditures, and because the behavior of the three components of consumption may be expected to affect differently the rest of the economy.

This separation is especially important in the case of durable goods purchases, since, in my view, this type of expenditure is really in the nature of an investment. It should, therefore, be controlled by somewhat different forces than those controlling other types of consumer outlays and should, in fact, be explainable along the general lines of the "acceleration principle." That is, one might visualize an "optimum" stock of durable goods, the size of which should be controlled by the demand for durable goods *services* and hence, finally, by the level of income and relative prices (although the relevant measure of income might well be something akin to the "permanent income" of the Friedman model or the "total resources" of the Modigliani-Brumberg model, and these might not be too well approximated by measured income in the current quarter). Let us denote this optimum stock by $D = D[Y_t, (p_d)_t]$. The current purchases of durable goods might then be expected to be proportional to the gap between optimum stock and initial stock, D_{t-1}, adjusted for depreciation. In other words, the basic hypothesis I would favor, and with which I have done some encouraging experiments, at least for yearly data, would be of the form

$$C_d = g\{D[Y_t, (P_d)_t] - hD_{t-1}\}$$

where g is the speed of adjustment, presumably smaller than 1.0, and $1 - h$ is the rate of depreciation. The coefficient g might well be a function of certain other variables, while h could probably be approximated by a constant, at least in the short run.

The model actually used by Klein can be regarded as a linear approximation to this hypothesis, except that instead of using initial stock, he uses purchases of the last two years. Since the typical life of durable goods is appreciably longer than two years, this approximation strikes me as inadequate. It might be noted that in Klein's equation 1, the coefficient of past purchases is negative, as expected. It is appreciably larger than 1.0 because the stock is several times annual purchases (in recent years, around four times, according to Goldsmith's estimates).[1] Since estimates of the stock of durables and the depreciation thereof are available at least for part of the period (and can be readily approximated for later years), it would seem desirable to try out the formula suggested here. Eventually, one may

---

[1] Cf. Raymond W. Goldsmith, *A Study of Saving in the United States*, Princeton, N.J., 1955, Vol. III, and *The National Wealth of the United States in the Postwar Period*, Princeton for NBER, 1962, Statistical Appendix.

also want to break out new automobile purchases from the other durables, in view of the importance of this commodity and the availability of promising hypotheses relating specifically to it.

Concerning the remaining consumption equations, I continue to have the most serious doubts about the relevance of cash balances as a determinant of consumption expenditure, except possibly for durable goods, where, however, this variable does not in fact appear (cf. equation 1). I have of course stressed in past and forthcoming writings the importance of consumers' initial net worth as a determinant of consumption. However, in the first place, I believe this variable to be more relevant to the long-run behavior of consumption than to an explanation of quarterly movements, where the effect of this variable can probably be conveniently proxied by other lagged variables, such as Klein's previous consumption. Second, and more important, I do not believe that "cash balances" are an adequate proxy for wealth, especially Klein's total balances, which include a sizable portion of business cash holdings. I am, therefore, not surprised to find that the contribution of this variable to the explanation of consumption is quantitatively negligible in all cases. It is also statistically insignificant, except possibly in the demand-for-services equation, where, however, its relevance is, a priori, most doubtful. I hope, therefore, that Klein will see fit to drop this variable at the next opportunity.

As for the remaining variable common to all consumption equations, P/W, which measures the distribution of income as between labor and property income, I am somewhat bothered by its appearance as a ratio, which creates dimensionality problems. More seriously, I am puzzled because its sign is positive, and, except possibly for durables, this would seem to be contrary to expectation and to some previous evidence. However, this variable, too, contributes very little, and is not significant except in the case of services.

Finally I have some reservations about the way in which the index of buying plans is used in the demand-for-durables equation, but I propose to take up this problem below in connection with the investment equations.

INVESTMENT IN FIXED CAPITAL

The two equations relating to investment in fixed capital, namely, (4) and (5), are notable for the inclusion of anticipatory data, a procedure which, of course, I heartily endorse. However I have some

45

qualms about the specific way in which these data are incorporated in the equations. In my view, Klein's formula does not fully exploit the information such data convey, and also gives rise to hypotheses which, whatever their empirical accuracy, are rather difficult to rationalize.

Take first the case of investment in plant and equipment, which is expressed as a function of anticipations and the rate of utilization of capacity. As I have argued extensively elsewhere,[2] if investment plans are meaningful—a proposition which, of course, cannot be assumed a priori, but is by now supported by a number of empirical investigations—then they embody all the information pertaining to the appropriate level of investment in the current period, as seen at the time the plan is made. This information includes, in particular, all relevant initial conditions and anticipations of future variables, such as sales, profits, availability of funds, etc. If so, actual investment should be expected to deviate from plans only in so far as the actual course of the anticipated variables differs from the anticipations. In other words, the discrepancy between I_p and I_p^e should depend on the error of anticipation. Symbolically, $I = F(I_p^e, A - E)$, where A denotes actual variables and E their anticipation. I have labeled the function F the "realization function." Thus, the realization function should include, in addition to plans, variables measuring the error of anticipations $(A - E)$ rather than the actual course (A), and should not include initial conditions which are already absorbed in plans, unless the initial conditions themselves can be expected to control the extent to which plans are revised in the light of later information.

Now Klein's equation does not include initial conditions (except possibly for the variable X_c), which is in line with my suggestion. However, it includes actual output, X, instead of the error of expectations, $X - X^e$. It is true that he could not very well have used X^e, since this information has not been available on a quarterly basis, at least until quite recently. Nevertheless, I submit that X is a poor approximation to $X - X^e$. A more adequate approximation in terms of readily available observables might be something like the change in sales, on the assumption that, on the average, sales expectations are close to current sales; or one might try to infer quarterly expec-

[2] Franco Modigliani and Kalman J. Cohen, *The Role of Anticipations and Plans in Economic Behavior and Their Use in Economic Analysis and Forecasting*, Urbana, Ill., 1961.

tations from yearly data. Eisner, in a recent paper,[3] has actually tried both approaches, apparently with good results (although I cannot say how they compare with the results obtained from Klein's hypothesis).

An essentially initial condition such as existing capacity may, of course, also play a role, since it is conceivable that the revision of plans might be more responsive to errors of anticipation at high rates of utilization. However, my purpose here is not so much to suggest a specific alternative to Klein's, but rather to indicate the assumptions on which a hypothesis embodying anticipatory data should be based.

Similar considerations apply to the housing equation. This equation again does not contain initial conditions of the type one would include in the ordinary formulation, such as the initial stock of housing. However, the remaining variables that appear here, in addition to the *ex ante* variable "starts," are essentially those that would seem relevant to the explanation of starts rather than to their rate of completion. However, in this instance, my objections are weaker, since starts are in physical units and are, therefore, not the same as planned expenditure. It is certainly conceivable that the actual amount of expenditure per unit, or even the speed of completion and, hence, the rate of expenditure, might be influenced by the variables Klein has used. However, here too I would strongly urge that some attempt be made at reformulating the hypothesis along lines more consistent with the nature of the anticipatory data included in the equation.

THE PRODUCTION FUNCTION

Klein's handling of the aggregate production function, embodied in equations 10 and 11, is quite interesting and ingenious. It has, however, two drawbacks. One of these is of an essentially logical nature, while the other is, I believe, also of considerable practical relevance. Let me first remark that in his model the production function can be looked at as providing a short-run relation between output, X, and equivalent full-time nongovernment employment, $h(N_w - N_g) + N_e$, which I shall, for brevity, denote by E. In time, this short-run relation shifts with the accumulation of capital (the sum of all previous net investment), which I shall denote by K, and with technological progress, proxied in his equation by the time trend. The function of this

[3] Robert Eisner, "Investment Plans and Realizations," *American Economic Review*, May 1962.

relation in the model is essentially that of establishing the employment implication of a given output (since the output itself is largely determined by other mechanisms). Now suppose equation 10 is explicitly solved for X, which in the form stated appears on both sides of the equation. We then obtain

$$\text{(M-1)} \qquad X = \frac{1}{1 - .196(K/X_c)} (91 + 1.76E + .135t)$$

Now, as can be seen from equation 11, X_c is a function of the labor force, N. Therefore, an increase in the labor force will tend to reduce the ratio K/X_c and, hence, the quantity $1/[1 - .196(K/X_c)]$. It follows directly that an increase in the labor force would reduce output, even though employment is kept constant. This is an awkward implication, to say the least, and constitutes my logical objection to the production function.

My second and more practical objection is that, as far as I can see, Klein's production function implies an elasticity of full-time employment with respect to output appreciably below unity. From equation M-1 above it is in fact apparent that the derivative of output with respect to employment—i.e., the marginal productivity of labor—is $dX/dE = 1.7[X_c/(X_c - .196K)]$. From the data in Klein's paper, it can be inferred that, at least in recent years, the expression $X_c/(X_c - .196K)$ is of the order of two (which, incidentally, implies that the proportion of total output imputed to the productivity of capital is surprisingly high, namely, of the order of one-half). Thus dX/dE is of the order of 3.5 (reckoning in thousands of dollars per man-year). On the other hand, the average productivity of labor is much higher, of the order of 6 to 7 (in thousands of dollars per man-year). Thus, the elasticity of output with respect to employment, which is the ratio of marginal to average productivity, is only of the order of 0.6. In other words, according to Klein's equations, a 1 per cent increase in employment would increase output by 0.6 per cent; and conversely a 1 per cent increase in output would increase employment by about 1/0.6, or 1.7 per cent. This very high elasticity of employment with respect to output is in sharp contrast with the results of several recent studies. I might call attention in particular to the results reported by Robert Solow in his paper "Technical Progress, Capital Formation, and Economic Growth," presented in December 1961 at a joint session of the American Economic Association and the Econometric Society. His estimate of the elasticity of output with respect to employment is not far from 1.5, instead of Klein's 0.6; and, consequently, his elasticity of employment with respect to output is about two-thirds, in contrast to Klein's figure which is well above unity. Solow further reports similar results as having been obtained by Arthur Okun.[4]

I am not in a position to say with confidence which of these two widely different estimates is closer to the truth. Perhaps I am inclined to attach somewhat greater credence to Solow's than to Klein's estimates because Solow's analysis was primarily focused on this particular issue, whereas Klein's estimate is unavoidably part of a mass production process. The essential point, however, is that the difference between the two estimates needs to be closely scrutinized and resolved, since an accurate estimate of the responsiveness of employment to short-run fluctuations in output would seem to me one of the essential ingredients of a satisfactory short-run model, whether for purposes of forecasting or of economic policy.

MONEY, INTEREST RATES, AND THEIR EFFECT ON MONETARY AND REAL VARIABLES

A number of equations are devoted to the description of the money market and to the role of interest rates—notably equations 21, 22, 23, and 5. This is, of course, a desirable development, and is in line with the revival of interest in and understanding of the role of monetary policy. Unfortunately, closer examination reveals that, even in this latest model, money plays in fact a very minor role in the short run, at least in the extent of effective interaction between the money markets and the real markets.

It may be noted, first, that interest rates appear in only one of the real markets, namely, in the equation describing investment in housing, which contains i_L, the yield on corporate bonds. But from equations 22 and 23, it can be seen that even this variable is completely determined by exogenous or lagged variables and is completely unrelated to the quantity of money. To establish this point, observe that according to (22), i_L depends on a lagged variable $(i_L)_{-1}$ and on i_s, the yield on ninety-day commercial paper. But from (23), we see that i_s in turn is unrelated to the quantity of money either nominal or real, depending instead on a lagged variable, excess

---

[4] These results are reported in A. M. Okun, "Potential GNP: Its Measurement and Significance," *American Statistical Association, 1962 Proceedings of the Business and Economic Statistics Section*, pp. 98–104.

reserves, R_{-1}, and on an exogenous variable, the Federal Reserve discount rate, i_r. Since (22) and (23) are sufficient to determine both i_L and i_s, it follows that neither rate depends on the quantity of money (L) and, hence, that this variable has no direct short-run effect on investments.

The only other place where L appears is in consumers' demand for nondurable goods and services—a rather unexpected and unconventional vehicle for monetary policy! In fact, however, as pointed out earlier, *even if* Klein's results are taken at face value, the role of L in the consumption equations is quantitatively quite negligible—e.g., a 10 per cent expansion of the money supply in one quarter, implying a rate of 40 per cent per year, would increase consumption in the quarter by well below a billion. Hence, this variable could clearly be dropped out of equations 2 and 3 without appreciably affecting the solution of the system. But if we do so, then, since money appears nowhere else, we must conclude that Klein's system omitting equation 21 is sufficient to determine the value of all the remaining variables, including both real variables and prices, without reference to the quantity of money. Furthermore, the only way in which this solution could be affected by the monetary authority in the short run would be through manipulation of the rediscount rate (which affects the short rate, which affects the long rate, which affects housing expenditure), a conclusion that must certainly come as somewhat of a shock to many Federal Reserve officials.

The above considerations illustrate and support my contention that the description of the monetary mechanism embodied in equations 21, 22, and 23 is exceedingly weak and is in urgent need of mending. Though I cannot enter into details here, let me indicate that this requires at least the following steps: (1) a more careful distinction and specification of the *demand* and the *supply* side of the money market; (2) a more adequate explanation of the short rate and its relation to the quantity of money; (3) a more refined approach to the relation between short and long rates, exploiting recent contributions in this area and, in particular, the very promising line of inquiry opened up by David Meiselman[5] and followed up by, among others, Reuben Kessel.[6]

[5] Cf. his *The Term Structure of Interest Rates*, Englewood Cliffs, N.J., 1962.
[6] "The Cyclical Behavior of the Term Structure of Interest Rates," National Bureau of Economic Research manuscript.

PRICE FORMATION EQUATIONS

The model includes price formation equations for all the major components of GNP. As indicated earlier I regard this as a very desirable development. To be sure, many of these equations are open to criticism on a number of counts. However, I shall not take the time for a detailed criticism, since Klein himself is clearly well aware of the limitations of his current hypothesis, and we also know that the task force now at work under his and Duesenberry's direction for the purpose of constructing an improved model is developing an ambitious and promising fresh approach to this problem.

INVESTMENT IN INVENTORIES

I hold the conviction, which I am sure is shared by most scholars interested in this area and is also strongly supported by the paper of Friend and Jones at this conference, that a reliable explanation of investment and disinvestment in inventories largely holds the key to successful short-term forecasting. Thus, while I have no basic quarrel with Klein's inventory equation 6, I believe it would be particularly worthwhile to pay closer attention to, and provide further scope for, this sector in his model. Once more, it is not possible in this comment to enter into details, but I should like to indicate certain directions for further development which I hold to be very promising, partly on the basis of my own work in this area.

1. We know that, in the short run, inventory changes partly reflect intentional adjustments and partly errors of sales forecasts (and of delivery schedules). The relative importance of the error component will be greater the shorter the period of time over which the change is measured. One should, therefore, try to recognize explicitly this double mechanism—although admittedly the case for doing so is not as strong for a quarterly model as it might be for, say, a monthly model. In order to achieve this goal one has somehow to introduce sales expectations in the model. A good deal of, hopefully, reliable information on short-run sales expectations is now becoming available and should be tried out. For the past, one may have to rely on various kinds of proxy variables, of the type reviewed in Michael Lovell's contribution to this conference.

2. Inventory behavior strikes me as an area where we may stand to gain significantly from disaggregation. There are indications, for

instance, that much of the fluctuation in the postwar inventory cycles has been concentrated in the manufacturing sectors, in the face of relatively negligible fluctuations in sales to final users. One should, therefore, investigate the possibility of separating the retail-wholesale complex from the manufacturing sector. Also, one should explore the possibility of exploiting disaggregation of the consumer sector so as to disaggregate inventory investments in the durable and non-durable goods sectors. While I am fully aware of the "costs" of disaggregation, notably in terms of a considerable enlargement in the number of equations and unknowns, I feel that this is an area very much worthy of further careful exploration.

The Workings of the Model and Its Solution for Short-Term Forecasting

I propose to wind up this already lengthy comment with a few re-marks on the working of the model and its utilization for short-run forecasts. A close examination of Klein's model reveals that its work-ings are fairly intricate, as there is a great deal of genuine interaction between its various parts. Furthermore, recognition of monetary as well as real variables results in a system which is definitely not linear —although it is hard, for a superficial critic like myself, to judge just how essential these nonlinearities are. The nonlinearity shows up most clearly in the equilibrium condition (30), which is, in essence, a glorified version of the standard Keynesian condition that con-sumption demand, investment, and government expenditure must equal gross national product. However, this condition is stated in terms of current values, which are *products* of prices and real vari-ables, which, in turn, depend on both prices and real variables.

In his reported application of the model to the first three quarters of 1961 (and apparently, also, in his later application through the second half of 1962),[7] Klein has, however, disposed of the non-linearity essentially by treating prices as exogenous variables, as-sumed constant or forecasted through *ad hoc* devices. One gathers that this procedure was followed to facilitate the task of solution. While this is an understandable consideration, it should be recog-nized that it amounts to throwing overboard some of the very features that make this latest model a potential improvement over

---

[7] Cf. the release of the Econometric Research Unit, Wharton School, University of Pennsylvania, December 21, 1961.

its predecessors. I should like to suggest that it may be possible and worthwhile to retain, at least in part, both the advantage of simplicity and the richness of the model by having recourse to iterative procedures. That is, having assumed a set of prices and solved the resulting linear system, one goes back and tests how closely the assumed prices and the derived real variables satisfy the various price equations. If the discrepancies are judged unreasonable—which, of course, depends partly on the confidence one is willing to place in the price formation equation—one could change the price assumptions accordingly and iterate. This method should converge to a solution, nor is this an unreasonable hope, if the system makes sense. Although I have not tried out this suggestion, I venture the guess that had Klein followed it, he would have been led to modify his assumption—unwarranted at least *ex post*—that prices would remain constant over the first three quarters of 1961.

Obviously, this comment can in no way do full justice to Klein's paper. For one thing, I have concentrated on the shortcomings of his model. Let me therefore repeat that the only reason for doing so is that there is, on the whole, very broad agreement between Klein and myself on the role of econometric models and on the strategy of model construction and testing, and that, furthermore, the significance and quality of Klein's contributions are so obvious that there is hardly any need for a discussant to point them out.

REPLY by L. R. Klein

I am very fortunate to have such stimulating and constructive comment by my two discussants. I greatly appreciate their remarks. Denison knows his way among Washington figures far better than I do, and I respect his judgment as to the relative accuracy of alternative series where choice is possible. I hope in future revisions of this model to look into his data suggestions.

I have long been bothered about the relationship between corporate and total nonwage income. A rough empirical relation that serves to close the system has been suggested, but in a current revision and re-estimation of the model, we are taking rentier (dividend and interest) income out of nonwage income and forming the relationship between corporate income and nonrentier, nonwage income. We would do better if we were to exclude farm income as well. Rentier income will be treated as a smooth trend corrected possibly for autoregression and possibly for interest rate changes. I disagree, however, with Denison that the relationship being constructed leads nowhere. Profits are treated as a residual in this system, and they are determined in the over-all set of equations. This seems to be reasonable. A separation into corporate and noncorporate profits, however, cannot be made by a rationally constructed equation of behavior. This is a purely institutional relationship that results from some legal distinctions in the functioning of enterprise.

In a completely linear model, the forecasting of *change* (from last period's *estimated* values) in each equation is equivalent to adding last period's error to each equation so that each equation is exactly satisfied if error is unchanged. In our solution process, we did this only after we had reduced the system to two relationships in I_i and X. Our system, after simplification—as explained in the paper—is solved by linear steps. It is not, however, a linear system. Time lags enable us to solve it in linear steps even though it is nonlinear in the variables.

Denison raises some very fundamental questions about reversibility and the use of a single model for different cyclical phases. This system has performed fairly well at both peaks and troughs. There is some plausibility in irreversibility, but much more work needs to be done to establish an empirically sound irreversible model. Eventually, I would like to work on that aspect and revise the model accordingly. For the moment, though, there are a number of other problems to be tackled, and I feel that these have higher priority. I am pleased by the uses we have been able to make so far of capacity and unemployment variables. I am not as disappointed with the results achieved to date as is Denison.

I appreciate Franco Modigliani's suggestions about treating the stock of consumer durable capital in the equation for durables demand. Subsequent to his remarks, we changed the moving average term in this equation to cover twelve past years (forty-eight past quarters) of gross durables expenditure. This gave a better estimate of the stock in consumer hands, but did not improve the equation. We have found only one promising lead for the improvement of this equation, namely, the use of the Survey Research Center's index of consumer attitudes in place of our previous index of buying plans. The attitudinal index shows much higher correlation than buying plans, or almost any other available variable, with durables expenditures. We are now investigating this lead and the interpretation of the attitudinal index more closely.

The coefficient of income in our equation for durables demand seems to be high. Our model in extrapolation has shown some tendency to overestimate durable consumption. In subsequent work on this equation in connection with further testing of the Survey Research Center index, we have, in fact, selected a new equation that has a considerably lower coefficient of income.

All our consumption equations were first formulated on a uniform basis, with liquid assets, factor share ratios, and population as potential variables. Both statistical significance and reasonableness of the whole equation (sign and general size of some coefficients) were used to weed out some alternatives. To my way of thinking there is no a priori basis for choosing between liquid assets and total real wealth as a possible variable. On many occasions, I have considered both of these variables in experimental consumption function calculations. There is no clear-cut empirical case for preferring one or the other. Liquid asset wealth gives us a more direct tie with the monetary sector, and this has been one of our motivations in using this variable. As for the effect of P/W, the factor share ratio, I fail to see how Modigliani arrives at his a priori notions about the effect of this variable. Surely services contain many luxury items (entertainment, travel, personal services, medical services, dental services), so we could not object to the finding of a significant positive effect for P/W. The argument about dimensionality, as far as I am concerned, is pointless. On grounds of elegance, we might want all variables of a linear relation in the same dimension; but elegance, of course, is well known to be a concern of tailors.

Modigliani is extremely rigid and supremely confident of the correctness of his views on the structure of realization equations. We really do not know much about the parametric structure of such subjective relationships. In our experiments, we tried some formulations like those suggested. The change in output or the change in nonwage income was used as a separate variable, together with investment expectations. No formulation looked as good, however, as the version finally selected, with capacity utilization and anticipated outlays as the explanatory variables. There is a good deal of independent evidence that our capacity series is close to what producers call their "preferred" operating level. The ratio of actual output to a "preferred" level of output is a measure of the deviation of actual from desired (not expected) and, in this sense, is a reasonable variable for explaining investment apart from its relation to planned investment.

I have long been an admirer of the time-honored work of Paul Douglas in measuring production functions. I cannot, therefore, feel unhappy about the estimation of production elasticities (w.r.t., employment) in the neighborhood of 0.6. I would regard any alternative figure of 1 5 as utterly ridiculous. There is much evidence against the plausibility of this figure. In earlier models based heavily on observations from the period of the Great Depression, elasticities larger than unity are acceptable. If we think of production functions (in two dimensions) as being of the standard sigmoid shape, we should not be surprised that approximations to sections of the function in the neighborhood of low output values give high elasticities But in the postwar period, our approximations are for a different section of the function and ought to give elasticities less than unity.

My theoretical predilections are very much in favor of a theory of the *real* economy. The monetary economy, if in good housekeeping order, will not have a dominant influence on real affairs. Nevertheless, I have tried hard over the years, in several models, to give the benefit of every doubt to money and interest rates when making statistical estimates. My empirical verdict, thus far, is that little evidence can be found for the actual influence of money or interest on real activity. It is this weak influence that Modigliani finds here, and about which he is concerned.

The links that we have finally tried to establish, and the statistical significance measures, leave much to be desired; they finally boil down to a dependence on the discount rate and excess reserves. Were it not for the weak measures of significance, I would have concluded that these were almost ideal monetary variables to have at the end of a series of relationships tying the real to the monetary sector. These are the variables that the monetary authorities directly control or use as guidelines. In pedagogical models it is assumed for simplicity that the authorities control the money supply; but this is very indirect—through the use of open-market operations, discount policy, and the variation of reserve requirements. What could be a better indication of money supply than excess reserves? What are open-market operations other than means of influencing reserves?

I am not pleased with the sharpness of my coefficients, but I would not want to change the sequence of steps in relating the monetary to the real sector. There are other instruments of monetary action having to do with the regulation of mortgage, share, foreign exchange, and consumer credit markets that ought to be built into a more detailed system, but the broad patterns of the existing scheme ought to be retained. It is hard to see why Federal Reserve officials would be shocked to learn about this pattern, since customary expositions of their lines of influence run just in the terms implied by the model. It would be helpful and constructive if Modigliani would be able to show more explicitly how the real and monetary sectors of the economy are related.

The comments on inventory relations and their importance, on the use of sales expectations, and on the treatment of prices are all well taken. Work is being pursued on all these fronts now, but there are no definite results to present yet. Some iterative and approximation methods have been tried to bring in price forecasts in an endogenous way in the nonlinear model, but the results obtained so far are unsatisfactory.

A Forecast Determination
of National Product, Employment,
and Price Level in Canada,
from an Econometric Model

T. M. BROWN

ROYAL MILITARY COLLEGE OF CANADA

Introduction

A PILOT econometric project was begun in Canada in the summer of 1947 under the direction of Lawrence R. Klein. I was one of those who studied and worked under Klein for three hot and busy but delightful months, nearly fifteen years ago. The work was done within the Department of Trade and Commerce, in Ottawa, to which I am eternally grateful, for facilities provided and interest shown. The results displayed here represent my subsequent research plus results due to S. J. May, who did splendid work on the project from 1949 to 1956, and who has since returned to it. Any opinions expressed in what follows on either analytical matters or policy are solely my own, arising out of my personal research, and the Department of Trade and Commerce is not responsible for them.

The purpose of this paper is to present a snapshot of a model at one stage of the Canadian project; to show how this model could be used to determine national product, employment, and price level; and, finally, to show the results obtained with this model on one experimental prediction of the economy for 1958—a critical year in recent economic history.

Model VIII

This model has evolved out of the original model, designed by Klein to suit Canadian conditions and available data. The evolution has included refinements in the underlying hypotheses—the interaction between hypotheses and observed data—and extensive work on re-fashioning basic data into a form to match the economic hypotheses. In this phase of the work, great thanks are due to the Dominion Bureau of Statistics and other government departments and crown corporations for their help in providing basic series of data. But the processing of these data into the form suggested by theory had to be done within the project, and consumed inordinate amounts of research time. In the field of econometric research one can yearn for the complementarity of highly skilled, resourceful, and painstaking processing of economic data, of the caliber associated with the National Bureau of Economic Research, with the different kinds of specialization required for the econometric research and applications.

In presenting the model I begin with a glossary of the symbols, the shorthand for the economic variables which appear in the model. The variables are presented in the order in which they occur.

GLOSSARY OF SYMBOLS

General notes

1. Symbols for variables which represent flows or stocks of goods and services in real volume terms are in units of billions of constant dollars of 1935–39. (Units for subsequent models have been converted to billions of 1949 dollars.) An exception to this rule is found in the employment and hours-of-work variables, where the units are millions of workers and thousands of hours of work per worker per year. These symbols can be converted to current market or money value by the addition of a subscript, m, or by multiplication by an appropriate price variable.

2. Symbols for financial variables (money, securities, international reserves) express the variable in current market or money value. These symbols can be converted to represent real purchasing power by the addition of a subscript, r, or by division by an appropriate price variable

3. Superscripts d and s are used to designate demand and supply functions. They are often implicit rather than explicit in the model. Superscripts or subscripts a and na are used to designate variables appropriate to the agricultural and nonagricultural private sectors; g, the government sector.

4. The unit of time in the model is one year. Thus, flow variables represent a rate of flow per year. Stocks of goods are year-end stocks. Numbers of workers (in a sense, a stock) are the average over a year.

5. The subscript -1 means that the variable is lagged one time period. Its influence is thus delayed one year in this model.

60

6. Variables marked by an asterisk are endogenous in this model.

Sector A

$C_p^{\cdot}$ = aggregate consumer purchases of new perishable goods C_p, services C_s, house rent paid and imputed C_r*

Y_w = disposable wage-salary income*

Y_π = disposable nonwage or property-enterprise income*
    $= Y_{\pi p} + Y_{\pi n p}$

$Y_{\pi p}$ = disposable nonwage income flowing into household and personal sector*

$Y_{\pi n p}$ = disposable nonwage income not paid to persons (mainly undistributed corporation profits)*

u_1 = unexplained random residual associated with behavior equation 1

C_{sd} = consumer purchases of new semidurable goods*

Y $= Y_w + Y_\pi$*

L_h = liquid asset holdings of households (money, federal government securities, deposits in sundry financial institutions)

K_{sd} = household and individual stocks of semidurable goods

C_{hda} = consumer purchases of new household durable goods and automobiles*

Y_p $= Y_w + Y_{\pi p}$

dp = index of consumer credit conditions, reflecting size of minimum downpayment, and time of repayment

De_1 = consumer debt to finance companies plus personal cash loans of chartered banks, small loan companies, licensed money lenders, and credit unions

K_{hda} = household and individual stocks of household durables and automobiles

Sector B

H = total inventory of firms*

GNP^{na} = gross national product generated in the nonagricultural private sector*

GNP = gross national product = GNE*

GNE = gross national expenditure*

F_1' = imports of goods and services, including payments of interest and dividends to foreign owners of domestic capital*

P^+ = index of price level of $GNE + F_1'$*

N_p = number of paid workers employed, private sector*

h = average hours worked per employed worker during time period (one year)*

w_{ph} = average earnings per hour of paid workers employed, private sector*

$P\cdot$ = price level of gross national expenditure (GNE)*

GI_M = gross investment by firms and nongovernment institutions (private sector) in machinery and equipment

P_1 = price level of imported goods adjusted for import duties and taxes

A_{F1} = shift variable to allow demand for imports equation to adjust to import controls of 1948, 1949, and 1950; in these years A_{F1} is given values of 1.0, 1.0, and 0.5, respectively; in all other years, zero

ΔKS = net inflow of capital for direct investment (K) and for portfolio (S)

P_{F1} = price level of F_1'

N_u = number of unemployed workers*

Sector C

Nh_u = number of unemployed man-hours*

N_1 = labor supply or labor force

N_M = number of personnel in the military, or armed, forces

t = time in years from base = calendar year 1926

Sector D

N_{enp} = number of employers and self-employed (entrepreneurs) plus unpaid family workers

K_{PCM} = stock of producers' fixed capital (plant, construction, machinery, and equipment)*

GNP_{-1}^0 = highest previous level of GNP

Sector E

T_w = direct taxes on wage-salary incomes*

P = price level of net national expenditure (NNE)*

W_m = total wage bill = $w_{ph}N_ph + w_gN_g + w_MN_M$*

Tr_w = transfer payments to wage-salary incomes from government*

Tr_{c1} = charitable contributions of corporations

Tr_{c2} = bad debt losses of corporations to wage sector

$T_{\pi p}$ = direct taxes on nonwage income of persons plus succession duties on personal wealth*

π_p = nonwage income of personal sector*

G_{ip} = total government interest bill paid to persons

$Tr_{\pi p}$ = transfer payments to nonwage personal incomes from government

Tr_{c3} = bad debt losses of corporations to other firms

$T_{\pi np}$ = direct tax on corporation profits, plus withholding tax, plus portion of trading profits of government business transferred to consolidated revenue of government*

Pr_c = net profit of corporations*

$Tr_{\pi np}$ = transfer payments to nonwage nonpersonal incomes from government

T_{i-s} = indirect taxes less subsidies*

F_{1s} = imports of services

P_C = price level of total consumer spending

C = $C_p' + C_{sd} + C_{hda}$ = total consumer spending

GI = gross domestic investment in (producers') new durable capital

 = $GI_{PC} + GI_M = GI_{PCM}$

D_{f1} = provision for depreciation and other capital consumption by firms

P_{GI} = price level of GI

π_{di} = payment of interest and dividends to foreign owners of domestic capital

π_{id} = receipts of interest and dividends arising from domestic ownership of foreign capital

G_i = total interest bill of government sector

Sector F

w_g, w_M = average earnings per year of government civilian and military employees

N_g = number of government civilian employees

π = total nonwage or property-enterprise income in GNP*

D_{f2} = $Tr_{c2} + Tr_{c3}$*

J = capital gains or losses of firms on inventories, arising from price increases or decreases

$\frac{1}{2}R$ = residual error of estimate on income side of national accounts

Pr_f = net profit of all firms*

π_{ip} = interest receipts of resident persons

π_{rp} = rent receipts of resident persons

Pr_{ub} = net profit of unincorporated business*

Pr_{gb} = net profit of government business*

π_{dcp} = dividend payments from corporations to resident persons*

T_d = disposable income of government*

π_{dip} = receipts of dividends from abroad by resident persons

π_{np} = $\pi - \pi_p$*

h_s = standard hours of work per worker per year

D = real depreciation on K_{PCM}

Sector G

GI_d = gross domestic investment in new residential construction (dwellings)

F_2' = exports of goods and services, including receipts of interest and dividends from domestic ownership of foreign capital

GNF^d = $GNE^d + F_1'$, representing demand for all final goods in total economy*

GNF^s = total supply flow of new goods through complete economy*

G_1 = government output or value added = $(w_g N_g + w_M N_M)/P + \pi_{rg}$

π_{rg} = imputed net rent on government buildings and equipment

DESCRIPTION AND DISCUSSION OF MODEL VIII

A macroeconomic structure can be conceived of as the set or matrix of rates at which each aggregative variable in the system is influenced *directly* by all of the other variables in the system. The purpose of an econometric model is to measure this *direct* or *basic* structure, so that it can be used for analysis, prediction, and policy. The common way of proceeding is to express each variable in the system as a function of (or in a functional relationship with) the other variables in the system. In any such equation only those variables are included which deductive theory interacting with observed data indicates to be significant. Thus, the exclusion of a variable from an equation means that its *direct* influence on the variable being explained is believed to be zero. The exclusion of an equation for a variable implies that *no* currently dated variables in the system have any appreciable influence on it. It is accordingly determined outside of the current economic system being studied, and is designated as predetermined—exogenous or lagged. It follows that the predeter-

Model VIII—January 1958

Equations	Method of Estimation

A. DEMANDS FOR FINAL GOODS

(1) $C_p = .1437 + .4485Y_w + .03945Y_\pi + .5250C_{p,-1} + u_1$ — TFML

(2) $C_{sd} = .05756 + .1123Y + .04695L_{hr,-1} - .1016K_{sd,-1} + u_2$ — TFML

(3) $C_{hda} = .02343 + .1499(Y_w + Y_\pi - Y_p^a - Y_{\pi np}) - .06225dp - 1.5104(De_1/L_h)_{-1}$
$- .4759(K_{hda}/Y_p^{na})_{-1} + u_3$ — LS

B. DEMANDS FOR FACTORS OF PRODUCTION

(4) $H^{na} = .1656 + .08124(GNP^{na} + F_1') + .6403H_{-1}^{na} + .5798\Delta P^+ + u_4$ — LS

(5) $N_p^{na}h^{na} = .7139 + .5610GNP^{na} + .1592GNP_{-1}^{na} - 5.4312w_{ph}^{na} + 3.2727P' + u_5$ — TFML

(6) $F_1' = .6501 + .1153(GNP^{na} + F_1') + .5821(H^{na} - H_{-1}^{na}) + .5525GI_M + .6847C_{hda}$
$- .3434P_1 - .2155A_{F1} + .3114\dfrac{\Delta KS}{P_{F1}} + u_6$ — LS

1957	1958

(7) $h^{na} = 2.151 - .2425N_u$ $h^{na} = 2.129 - .2425N_u$

C. LABOR MARKET ADJUSTMENT (SHORT-RUN SUPPLY)

(8) $w_{ph}^{na} = .08994 + .9029w_{ph,-1}^{na} - .03703Nh_u^{na} + .06117\left(.3 - \dfrac{10N_u}{N_1 - N_M}\right)_{+ \text{ or zero}}$
$+ .003941t + u_7$ — TFML

D. PRODUCTION FUNCTION AND SUPPLY

(9) $GNP^{na} = -4.9501 + 1.1579(N_p^{na} + N_{enp}^{na})h^{na} + .1507K_{PCM}^{na} + .3266\overset{0}{GNP}_{-1}^{na} + u_8$ — LS

E. TAX AND TRANSFER EQUATIONS

1957	1958

(10) $T_w = -\dfrac{2.2148}{P} + .2578\dfrac{(W_m - W_m^a)}{P}$ $T_w = -\dfrac{2.1500}{P} + .2375\dfrac{(W_m - W_m^a)}{P}$

(11) $PTr_w = 1.699 + 1.1844N_u$ $PTr_w = 1.946 + 1.2458N_u$
$PTr_{c1} = .033; PTr_{c2} = .016$ $PTr_{c1} = .030; PTr_{c2} = .017$

(12) $PT_{\pi p} = -.7230 + .2424P(\pi_p + G_{ip})$ $PT_{\pi p} = -.7572 + .2368P(\pi_p + G_{ip})$
$PTr_{\pi p} = .3640; PTr_{c3} = .0100$ $PTr_{\pi p} = .3640; PTr_{c3} = .0110$

(13) $T_{\pi np} = \dfrac{.2560}{P} + .6031(Pr_c - Tr_{c1})$ $T_{\pi np} = \dfrac{.2560}{P} + .5938(Pr_c - Tr_{c1})$

$PTr_{\pi np} = .2060$ $PTr_{\pi np} = .2020$

(14) $T_{i \to s} = \dfrac{m_0}{P} + m_1\left[\left(\dfrac{P_{F1}}{P}\right)_{\text{Exog.}}F_1' - \dfrac{F_{1s}}{P}\right] + m_2C_p$
$+ m_3\left(\dfrac{P_C}{P}\right)_{\text{Exog.}}C + m_4\left[\left(\dfrac{P_C}{P}\right)_{\text{Exog.}}C + \dfrac{1}{3}\dfrac{P_M}{P}GI_M\right]$
$+ m_5\left[(GNP - D_{f1}) + \dfrac{P_{GI}}{P}D_{f1} + \dfrac{\pi_{dim} - \pi_{idm} - G_{im}}{P}\right]$

(continued)

65

MODEL VIII—JANUARY 1958 (concluded)

		Equations					Method of Estimation
	m_0	m_1	m_2	m_3	m_4	m_5	
1957	1.2430	.09788	.01860	.01293	.05700	.01046	
1958	1.3360	.09788	.01860	.01293	.05571	.01046	

F. ACCOUNTING IDENTITIES AND DEFINITIONS

(1) $W_m = w_{ph}^{na} N_p^{na} h^{na} + w_p^a N_p^a + w_g N_g + w_M N_M$

(2) $Y_w = W_m/P + Tr_w + Tr_{c1} + Tr_{c2} - T_w$

(3) $\pi = GNP - W_m/P - T_{i-s} - D_{f1} - D_{f2} + J^{na} - \frac{1}{2}R$

(4) $D_{f2} = Tr_{c2} + Tr_{c3}$

(5) $\pi = Pr_f + \pi_{ip} + \pi_{rp}$

(6) $Pr_f = Pr_c + Pr_{ub} + Pr_{gb}$

(7) $Pr_{ub}^{na} = n_1 Pr_c$

(8) $Pr_{gb} = n_2 Pr_c$

Note that $Pr_c = (\pi - \pi_{ip} - \pi_{rp} - Pr_{ub}^a)/(1 + n_1 + n_2)$ and that n_1, n_2, and n_3 can vary from year to year.

(9) $\pi_p = \pi_{ip} + \pi_{rp} + \pi_{dcp} + \pi_{dip} + Pr_{ub}$

(10) $\pi_{dcp} = n_3(Pr_e - Tr_{c1})$

(11) $\pi_{np} = \pi - \pi_p$

(12) $Y_{\pi p} = \pi_p + Tr_{\pi p} + Tr_{c3} - T_{\pi p}$

(13) $Y_{\pi np} = \pi_{np} + D_{f2} + Tr_{\pi np} - Tr_{c1} - Tr_{c2} - Tr_{c3} - T_{\pi np}$

(14) $Y_\pi = Y_{\pi p} + Y_{\pi np}$

(15) $T_d = T_w + T_{\pi p} + T_{\pi np} + T_{i-s} - Tr_w - Tr_{\pi p} - Tr_{\pi np} = Y_g$

(16) $N_u = N_1 - N_M - N_g - N_{enp}^a - N_p^a - N_{enp}^{na} - N_p^{na} = N_1^{na} - N_{pe}^{na}$

(17) $Nh_u^{na} = N_1^{na} h_s^{na} - (N_p^{na} + N_{enp}^{na}) h^{na}$

(18) $K_{PCM} = K_{PCM,-1} + GI - D$

(19) $Y = Y_w + Y_\pi$

(20) $GNE = GNF - F_1'$

(21) $GNP = GNP^a + GNP^{na} + G_1$

(22) $P^{\cdot} = \dfrac{(P^{\cdot})(NNE) + P_{GI}(D_{f1} + D_{f2})}{NNE + D_{f1} + D_{f2}}$

(23) $P^+ = \dfrac{(P)(GNE) + (P_{F1})(F_1')}{GNE + F_1'}$

G. GLOBAL DEMAND, SUPPLY, AND PRICE LEVEL FORMATION

(1) $C_p^{\cdot} + C_{sd} + C_{hda} + GI_d + GI + \Delta H^a + H^{na} - H_{-1}^{na} + F_2' - \frac{1}{2}R = GNF^d$

(2) $GNP^{na} + GNP^a + G_1 + F_1'^d = GNP^s + F_1'^s = GNF^s$

(3) $GNF^d = GNF^s$

mined variables exert a one-way influence on the system, whereas the other variables are mutually interacting, determined inside the system, endogenous.

The model to be discussed in this paper—Model VIII—is presented above, with numerical estimates of structure. These were derived by fitting the model to the observed Canadian data of 1926–41 and 1946–56.

66

A variable which is theoretically endogenous is not always treated as such in a model. This may be because of lack of data on the casual variables which influence it, or in the interest of keeping the model small.

Each equation in Model VIII aims at explaining one endogenous variable in terms of the direct causal influences on it. There are, however, two exceptions. The demand for labor explains the combined demand for employment and hours as man-hours in one equation, with a separate equation to explain the level of hours. Also, there is no separate equation for the price level variable P. This is because the global market for final goods is assumed to reach an average equilibrium within a year; so the equilibrium volume of output and price level are determined jointly by equating global demand with global supply.

The term "equilibrium" here means that the price and quantity of the solution are taken at the intersection point of the global demand and supply equations. In equation G(1) of the model, GNF^d is a function of P, and GNF^s is also a function of P, through their respective components. Disequilibrium in this context would mean that the solution occurred at some point other than at the intersection of the two global functions. In this case, where $GNF^d \neq GNF^s$ a separate equation would be required for the price level of the form $P^+ = f(P^+_{-1}, GNF^d - GNF^s)$. A *stationary equilibrium* in this system would occur when, if left undisturbed, the system moved to $P^+_{t-1} = P^+_t = P^+_{t+1} \ldots$; $GNF^+_t = GNF^s_t$, etc. Such stationary equilibriums are not likely to last long, because of the many possibilities of changing variables in GNF^d and GNF^s, producing shifts. Model VIII assumes that the *average* condition of the economy over one year is merely an equality of GNF^d and GNF^s for that year only, with a different equilibrium of this kind highly likely in the subsequent year. The model thus expresses a shifting equilibrium, in the sense of the term equilibrium used here. Note that in the labor market for this model, we work with a shifting disequilibrium, indicating the extreme sluggishness of this market.

I return to the point that, in general, each equation aims at explaining one endogenous variable, with the exceptions noted, and can now proceed to count equations and endogenous variables. The equation system contains eight stochastic equations; six equations pieced together by observed ratios and estimated elasticities—B(7) and E(10), E(11), E(12), E(13), and E(14); twenty-three accounting identities; and three equations expressing the annual average equality of global demand and supply. There are, thus, forty equations appropriate to each year. There must correspondingly be forty endogenous variables used as such in the system. These are marked out in the Glossary above by an asterisk placed directly after the explanation of the symbol.

Most of the identities are peripheral to the basic structure of the model, but are useful for building the tabular results.

With regard to methods of structure estimation, Model VIII was partially estimated by the method of truncated full-information maximum likelihood[1] (TFML), with help from an electronic computer. (Cf. equations 1, 2, 5, 8, Sectors A, B, C.) The remaining behavior equations were estimated by the ordinary least squares (LS) method. Computation resources and time were limited, and it was not possible to calculate the usual goodness-of-fit statistics. But all of the equations used passed reasonably good tests on this score in the preliminary screening tests using LS. For example, in the following equations the LS coefficient of variation and coefficient of correlation (n.a. = not available) for the complete equation are: A(1): 1.39 per cent, 0 999; A(3): 3.28 per cent, 0.999; B(4): 2.58 per cent, 0.998; B(5): 1.45 per cent, n.a.; B(6): 2.90 per cent, 0.997; C(8): 3.25 per cent, n.a.; D(9): 2.60 per cent, n.a. Tax and transfer equations were estimated by appraisal of appropriate elasticities for the individual components, based on past behavior and current changes in the tax-transfer structure.

If the detail of Model VIII is now examined, it is observed, first, that *consumer demand* has been disaggregated into three components. The research on this separation was done by S. J. May. Only the equation for perishables and services retained the explicit habit-persistence effect,[2] which seemed quite reasonable. The demands for the other components were influenced by stocks held (with an implicit habit-persistence influence), liquid asset holdings, debt position, and credit conditions, as well as by incomes.[3] The last term in A(3) reflects the important hypothesis that as real incomes rise, consumers

---

[1] T. M. Brown, "Simplified Full Maximum Likelihood and Comparative Structural Estimates," *Econometrica*, October 1959, pp. 638–653.

[2] T. M. Brown, "Habit Persistence and Lags in Consumer Behavior," *Econometrica*, July 1952, pp. 355–371.

[3] Cf. C. F. Roos, and V. von Szeliski, "The Demand for Durable Goods," *Econometrica*, April 1943.

raise their sights on their desired or aspiration levels of stocks of consumer durable goods.

The other major final good category for which there should be a set of demand equations is *gross domestic investment*. In this model only the demand for inventories, within this category, is included. For the fixed capital items, the preliminary data of the annual survey of investment intentions were used.[4] It would have been preferable to have also used demand equations for the fixed capital items, along with the survey, but limited resources and time prevented this. In previous and subsequent models, demand equations for plant, construction, and machinery (*GI*) have been used. Investment plans can of course change through the year as economic conditions change, and the initial survey cannot take this into account.[5] An equation should be able to do this. The equation, on the other hand, always has a large random component (exogenous investment), which, to a considerable extent, may be uncovered by the survey. For these reasons the survey and the equation combined may provide an ideal combination.

The *inventory demand* equation expresses the *transaction motive* and the *speculative motive* for holding inventories. The middle causal term expresses the influence of past inventory holdings, producing a certain inertia or implied speed of adjustment with respect to changing the level of inventories. Subsequent results revealed that this term produced too much inertia.

The demand-for-labor equation was tested in a new form in this model—a linear form. Man-hours is the factor of production on the demand side of the equation (the left-hand side), and the main causal variables believed to influence this demand directly are on the right. These causal variables are deduced, from the theory of the firm, to be the expected level of output (GNP, GNP_{-1}), the average price of the factor (w_{ph}), and the price level of the product (P'). Previous versions had combined some of these variables into the real wage bill on the left side, with the expected level of output on the right side, expressing essentially the same economic theory in a slightly different equation form. The present equation, reflecting as it does

[4] *Private and Public Investment in Canada, Outlook 1958*, Department of Trade and Commerce.

[5] O. J. Firestone, "Investment Forecasting in Canada," in *Short-Term Economic Forecasting*, Princeton for NBER, 1955.

such fine and close agreement between economic theory and economic statistical data, is to me the most beautiful equation of the model. As a matter of further interest, the elasticity of demand for man-hours with respect to the average wage rate calculated from this equation for 1958 is -0.94, $(-0 45$ in 1926, -0.61 in 1947), implying that the demand for labor is inelastic. A reduction in wage rates would reduce the total wage bill (direct effect). This result has important implications for employment theory.

In designing the *import demand equation* the theory of the demand of the firm for a factor of production can again be used, taking into account production effects, factor prices, and product prices. Imports separate functionally into industrial materials, capital goods, and consumer durables, with capital goods tending to be prominent in Canadian imports. Hence, production effects in this equation were interpreted by three causal variables: industrial materials and nondurable consumer goods, by $GNP^{na} + F_1'$, which indicated approximately the total flow of nonagricultural goods through the economy; capital goods, by GI_M; and durable consumer goods, by C_{hda}.

The price of the factor of production is accounted for by P_1, but the price of the product (P^+) was not statistically significant, suggesting a low proportion of competitive imports. The inventory variable represents the import content of inventory stocks. A_{F1} is a shift variable to account for the import controls applied in Canada to counter the balance-of-payment difficulties of 1948–50.

The final term in the equation attempted to reflect the impact on imports of the capital inflow for direct investment (K) and portfolio investment (S). This inflow reduced the exchange rate cost of imports, already reflected in P_1, and provided ample international liquidity for imports. (This liquidity was used, for Canada's international reserves held fairly steady through 1950–60, with only a modest upward trend.) In addition, the inflow for direct investment would usually be intended for specific capacity expansion projects, much of the capital goods for which would be imported.

The *demand-for-hours-of-work* equation reflects a long-term downward trend in standard hours of work per week (reflected in the constant term); and the well-known variability of hours over the business cycle. When demand slackens the average production time of the whole plant must decrease; given the degree of complementarity of workers and the downward sluggishness of wage rates,

70

short-time and layoffs follow. Short-time permits a firm to retain its trained workers and is much preferred to layoffs.

Conversely, as demand steps up and passes the normal capacity level in any plant, it is better to increase the time of operation of plant and workers for the short run than to overcrowd the plant with additional facilities and workers. This also eliminates the need to train extra workers, who may then be lost on the next downswing.

The *labor market adjustment* equation follows closely the original design of Lawrence R. Klein,[6] except that it is now in terms of average hourly earnings, with unemployment in terms of man-hours To this design, May added the third explanatory variable. Without this term the average wage rate is equally sticky upward as well as downward. May's hypothesis was that when demand brought the labor market from a region of near full employment to over-full employment the average wage rate would start to climb at an accelerating rate. The third term in the equation interprets this nonlinearity by giving the equation a corner point at a threshold rate of unemployment of 3 per cent. Should the rate of unemployment be greater than 3 per cent, the third term is negative but is given the value zero. When this rate is less than 3 per cent, the term is positive, and its value is allowed to stand.

The interpretation of C(8) in terms of labor market demand and supply curves is shown in the chart. $(Nh)^s$ is the long-run supply of labor, which I assume to be a function of the real wage. (A change in prices would shift this function.) Assume that a stationary equilibrium has formed at A_0 at 3 per cent unemployment. If now demand drops back to $(Nh)_1^d$, equation C(8) says that the market position will not move directly to B, but will move to A_1, because of wage viscidity. At A_1 excess supply is A_1L; given time this may gradually drag the market position down to B. Should demand increase, still in the short run, to $(Nh)_0^d$ and beyond, the market would move along the line A_1A_0, and then along A_0C as May's term comes into play.

A_1A_0C is the short-run, very elastic supply curve of labor posited by Keynes,[7] and clarified by Klein.[8] It follows that C(8) is the Keynesian short-run supply curve of labor.

[6] *Economic Fluctuations in the United States, 1921–1941*, New York, 1950, pp. 51 and 121. Klein's original design for the Canadian model included the first, second, and fourth terms of C(8), in terms of number of people unemployed.

[7] John M. Keynes, *The General Theory of Employment, Interest and Money*, London, 1947 (reprint), p. 8.

[8] Lawrence R. Klein, *The Keynesian Revolution*, New York, 1947, p. 74.

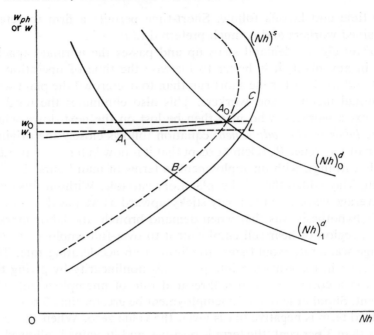

Equation D(9) shows the combination of the major factors of production into a *production function*. When the levels of the factors have been determined by demand and supply in their markets, this technological relation gives the global output, and hence supply, of final goods. The production function presents a difficult estimation problem, since it shifts upward from time to time as the *joint* or *total productivity* of the factors of production increases. This gain in productivity arises from the discovery of new knowledge and its application to production. If it could be assumed that such gains occur regularly over time, a time trend could be added to the equation to shift it upward a systematic amount each year. This is the easiest and perhaps the best solution. But if the shifts occur in a way which is not regular with respect to time, the time trend gives an imperfect result.

In Model VIII an hypothesis was tested which, it was hoped, would let the statistical data decide when productivity shifts occurred. The hypothesis was that the level of the production function depends on the highest previous level of output obtained, $\overset{0}{GNP}_{-1}$. This hypothesis is defective in that it does not take into account changing quantities of factor inputs in the highest previous levels. However,

72

it should allow for the broad changes in total productivity as they occur. Also, it assumes that knowledge once gained is never lost, hence, that the production function ratchets upward and that its level never slips downward.

The resulting parameter estimates seemed reasonable and the fit was good. The elasticity of production with respect to labor in this equation was 0.55 for 1958, and 1 07 for 1926. In 1926 the effective constant term is -1.42. By 1958, the function had been shifted upward by the lagged term and the growing stock of capital; consequently, it had an effective short-run constant term of $+5.96$. Further research and experience are needed to reveal whether this is a reasonable portrayal of reality. The use of a linear form for this function may prove to be a serious shortcoming.

The *tax and transfer equations* were built from elasticity estimates and assumptions for the individual major taxes and transfer payments. It was necessary here to attempt to portray the drastic changes in fiscal policy which the government had quickly put into effect to stem the swelling tide of recession. It is felt that the estimates for this sector need considerable refinement.

In the aggregate, i.e., in the equation on the *global market for final goods*, it is assumed that equilibrium, in the sense discussed above, is reached within yearly periods, a condition which might be much less likely for quarterly or monthly time periods. The equations of GNF^d and GNF^s in this "market" permitted the determination of both GNF and the equilibrating variable. The latter was the price level P^+, which included P, the unknown deflator variable used throughout the model.

Technique of the Forecast

Known or estimated predetermined data for 1957, and predicted predetermined data for 1958 were assembled. The 1957 data were inserted in the model, and a solution vector of endogenous variables Y_{c57} was calculated. Through this solution the model determined national income, employment, and price level, taking into account simultaneously the estimated economic structure and all of the interactions and feedback effects among the endogenous variables.

The model was solved simultaneously through the elimination of variables by substitution, until finally an equation in only one endogenous variable was obtained. In the procedure used for this model the final equation was a fourth-degree polynomial in N_p^{na}. (Note the various nonlinearities throughout the model.) That root of the quartic which was close to the current economic situation was localized, and a solution for it was made by Horner's method. This was followed by a back solution for all of Y_{c57}, and a final check.

This solution vector was now compared with the best available estimates of the corresponding observed data for 1957, Y_{57}. The discrepancies ($Y_{57} - Y_{c57} = u_{s57}$) were assumed to be due to random causes, unless they appeared to represent some known structural change. In the latter case an alteration of the structure involved might be made, and a new 1957 solution derived.[9] The approach to such alteration may be outlined as follows. Let the original estimated model of direct economic structure be

(1) $Y_t = F(Y_t, Z_t) + u_t$, where Y_t, Z_t and u_t are respectively the vectors of endogenous, predetermined, and direct structural residuals of the model. F is a vector of functions. The structural reduced form of the system is derived by solving (1) for Y, with u omitted, giving

(2) $Y_c = R(Z)$; $Y = Y_c + u_s =$ the observed values of Y.

Where u_{s57} indicated that structure revision was needed for say the ith and jth equations of (1), u_{i57} and u_{j57} were calculated from (1). These values were then added to the structure of (1) as a vector $e = (0, 0, \ldots, 0, u_{i57}, 0, u_{j57}, 0, 0, \ldots, 0)$, thereby producing a revised structure.

(3) $Y = F(Y, Z) + e + u^r$.

(3a) $Y = F^r(Y, Z) + u^r$.

This structure was now solved again for 1957, omitting the residuals u_{57}^r, to obtain a revised structural reduced form

(4) $Y_{F57} = R^r(Z_{57})$. The structure (3a) was likewise used to compute the forecast solution vector

(5) $Y_{F58} = R^r(Z_{58})$.

It is Y_{F57} and Y_{F58}, as derived from (4) and (5), that are used in Tables 2–5, which follow.

This solution vector could now be compared with Y_{57} or Y_{c57}. If the latter is used, only the movements of the *systematic* part of the model can be considered, i.e., only purely economic movements based on the systematic structure of the model. If on the other hand a comparison is made of Y_{F58} with $Y_{57} = Y_{c57} + u_{s57}$, the systematic

---

[9] See Lawrence R. Klein, and A. S. Goldberger, *An Econometric Model of the United States, 1929–1952*, Amsterdam, 1955, pp. 77–78, for a systematic way of making many of these adjustments.

movement from 1957 to 1958 is mixed with one random vector. Such mixing has, in the past, produced anomalous economic predictions, when a large random element in $u_{s,t-1}$ has been in the same direction as the corresponding systematic movement in $Y_{Ft} - Y_{c,t-1}$.

Ideally, what we would like to forecast is $Y_{58} = Y_{F58} + u_{s58}$, and compare it with $Y_{57} = Y_{c57} + u_{s57}$, showing movements $Y_{i58} - Y_{i57}$ or, in percentage form, $(Y_{i58}/Y_{i57} - 1) \times 100$. This comparison involves *two* random disturbances. Do we help our cause any by comparing Y_{F58} with $Y_{57} = Y_{c57} + u_{s57}$, involving only *one* of these two random components? Is there some advantage in knowing that our forecast contains only the movements evolving from the systematic structure?[10]

These questions require more study, but the forecast with Model VIII presented below consists of a comparison of Y_{F58} with Y_{c57}. Both of these solutions involved one or two adjustments of structure based on a study of disturbances and other very current information. Inventory demand was the main case in point, where the lag effect and the price effect seemed to give the equation too much trend inertia. Improved structure specification is clearly called for here.

Forecast Results

THE EXTERNAL CAUSES

Once the structure of the model has been decided upon, the keystone of the forecast becomes the *exogenous demands*. The period of forecast was one of uncertainty, and I made three sets of assumptions about these demands, and tested them all. One set involved large declines; another, small declines; and the third took an intermediate position. This intermediate forecast seemed the most plausible to me in January 1958, and is the one presented here. The main components of this part of the forecast are in Table 1.

In this table the assumption of deteriorating world economic conditions can be seen, as well as domestic prospects for fixed investment. At the same time, a part of government fiscal policy can be seen as coming to the rescue with an increased spending program, and with increased mortgage money for housing.

The total assumed decline of 5.3 per cent in exogenous demands was very serious from the point of view of output and employment. With a growing labor force and productivity, the economy must

---

[10] See Klein and Goldberger, pp. 76–77, for an alternative interpretation of such a comparison.

TABLE 1

FORECAST OF VOLUME CHANGES IN EXOGENOUS DEMANDS, 1956–58
(percentage changes)

	1956–57	1957–58
G = government spending	+1.0	+2.9
$GI + GI_d$ = gross private investment in fixed capital	+5.1	−10.3
GI_d = residential construction	−12.5	+10.7
GI_{PC} = nonresidential construction	+21.8	−12.8
GI_M = machinery and equipment	−1.9	−15.6
F' = exports of goods and services	−1.0	−6.5
Total exogenous impact	+1.8	−5.3

grow at a rate of 4 or 5 per cent to maintain full employment at current hours of work. Of course the built-in stabilizers of the modern economy, reflected in the tax and transfer equations of the model, would ameliorate this decline to some extent. But something more than these would be needed to overcome the serious fall in exogenous demands.

Late in 1957, as the economic situation worsened, various changes in the government fiscal program were put into effect. Various tax rates were decreased, and transfer payment rates were increased. Presumably, this was a second wave of attack against the recession. The impact of these changes can be observed in the tax and transfer equations of Model VIII for 1957 and 1958. One assumes that the objective on this front was to increase the disposable incomes of the lower income groups because of their need and because their marginal propensity to consume is highest. Consumer demand is the largest single employment-producing demand. Income tax exemptions were increased, and rates were reduced in the lower brackets. On the transfer side, allowances to war veterans and dependents were increased, old age pension rates were stepped up by something like 37.5 per cent, and family allowance rates were increased about 4 per cent. Unemployment insurance was extended to cover a longer period of unemployment.

Taxes were also reduced on nonwage incomes through the reduction of personal income tax rates; through extension of the lower range of corporation profits covered by a lower tax rate; and through elimination of the estate tax on smaller estates. On the indirect tax side, a special excise tax on automobiles was reduced, to stimulate sales and employment in this industry.

The exogenous demands and government policy constitute the main external or exogenous influences on the economy for a forecast period. The lagged variables cause inertia in the short run, but of course generate trends or cycles over the longer run. In the forecast solution there is a struggle between declining exogenous demands on one side, and the expansionist government policies and the inertias of the model on the other. To the outcome of this struggle I now turn.

THE INTERNAL OR ENDOGENOUS EFFECTS

The results of the forecast solution are presented in Tables 2, 3, and 4 which follow directly. Table 2 shows the forecast outcome with respect to the national accounts. Table 3 gives the all-important prediction of the results in the labor market. Table 3 also shows the changes in the stock of producers' durable capital, movements in the price level of GNE, and finally the government surplus or deficit and its main components. In Table 4, the outputs of the three major producing sectors of the model—private nonagriculture, agriculture, and government—are shown. Then, a section is devoted to the disposable incomes of the wage, nonwage, and government sectors of the economy, all of which add up to GNP. Finally, the predicted savings ratio is presented.

It is not necessary to discuss here all of the detail of these tables. What will be attempted is to draw the broad picture of the results which are found in the tables and the causal analysis given by the model.

The labor market

To go first to the heart of the forecast, we examine the outcome in the labor market in Table 3. The battle between declining exogenous demands on one side and the inertias, automatic stabilizers, and direct government policy on the other is there revealed to have been lost. Unemployment increased from 5.3 per cent of the civilian labor force (311,000 people) to 7.4 per cent (448,000 people), an increase of 44.1 per cent in the number of unemployed. At the same time, the model predicted an increase in the average wage rate of 3.0 per cent. This was produced mainly by the inertia of past upward shifts in the

TABLE 2
ECONOMETRIC PROJECTIONS OF NATIONAL PRODUCT
AT MARKET PRICES, MODEL VIII, 1958
(millions of current dollars)

	Model Solution 1957	Forecast for 1958	Percentage Change 1957 and 1958		
			Value	Volume	Price
INCOME					
Salaries, wages, and supplementary labor income	15,107	15,261	+1.0	+0.2	+0.8
Military pay and allowance[a]	475	499	+5.1	+4.3	+0.8
Corporation profits	2,803	2,461	−12.2	−12.9	+0.8
Other property enterprise or non-wage income	5,110	5,137	+0.5	−0.3	+0.8
Net national income at factor cost	23,495	23,358	−0.6	−1.4	+0.8
Indirect taxes less subsidies	3,799	3,773	−0.7	−1.5	+0.8
Depreciation allowances and similar business costs[a]	3,393	3,664	+8.0	+8.0	0.0
Gross national product	30,687	30,795	+0.4		
GNP less inventory profit	30,617	30,895	+0.9	+0.1	+0.8
EXPENDITURE					
Personal expenditure on consumer goods and services	19,261	20,047	+4.1	+2.5	+1.5
Government expenditure on goods and services[a]	5,545	5,789	+4.4	+2.9	+1.5
Gross home investment in durable assets:[a]	7,311	6,624	−9.4	−10.3	
Housing	1,386	1,533	+10.6	+10.6	0.0
Plant and construction	3,233	2,819	−12.8	−12.8	0.0
Machinery and equipment	2,692	2,272	−15.6	−15.6	0.0
Total producers' durables	5,925	5,091	−14.1	−14.1	0.0
Change in inventories (book value)	+104	−380			
Nonagricultural business[b]	251	−239			
Agriculture and grain[a,b]	−217	−41			
Capital gain or inventory profit[a]	70	−100			
Exports of goods and services[a]	6,379	5,844	−8.4	−6.5	−2.0
Imports of goods and services	7,913	7,129	−9.9	−9.9	0.0
Gross national expenditure	30,687	30,795	+0.4		
GNE less inventory profit	30,617	30,895	+0.9	+0.1	+0.8

[a] Exogenous.
[b] Value of physical change.

78

TABLE 3

LABOR MARKET, PRICE LEVELS, AND OTHER PROJECTED MATERIAL,
MODEL VIII, 1957–58

	Unit	Model Solution 1957	Forecast for 1958	Percentage Change 1957 to 1958
Labor market[a]				
Civilian labor force (LFS)[b]	1,000's	5,914	6,015	+1.7
Total civilian employment (LFS)		5,603	5,567	−0.7
Employment of paid workers, nonfarm		3,897	3,855	−1.1
Unemployment		311	448	+44.1
Unemployment as per cent of civilian labor force (LFS)	%	5.3	7.4	
Average hourly earnings of paid workers, private nonagricultural sector				
Current market value	Current $	1.558	1.605	+3.0
Real value	1935–39 $	.708	.724	+2.3
Average hours worked per week, private nonagricultural sector	1 hour	39.8	39.2	−1.5
Total man-hours worked, private nonagricultural sector	Millions of man-hours	9,195	8,930	−2.9
Real output per man-hour, private nonagricultural sector	1935–39 dollars	1.310	1.340	+2.3
Stock of durable producers' capital in private nonagricultural sector	Millions of 1935–39 dollars	17,228	18,486	+7.3
Prices	1935–39 average equals 100.0			
Price index of *GNP*		223.4	225.1	+0.8
Price index of gross national supply flow (*GNE* + imports)		225.4	226.7	+0.6
Price index of net national product		220.0	221.7	+0.8
Government	Millions of current dollars			
Disposable income (government tax revenue less transfer payments)		5,349	4,610	−13.8
Expenditure on goods and services[b]		5,545	5,789	+4.4
Surplus (+) or deficit (−) (on transactions relating to the national accounts)		−196	−1,179	

LFS = Labor Force Survey concepts, which exclude Yukon and Northwest Territories.

[a] Includes remote areas, Yukon and Northwest Territories.
[b] Exogenous.

TABLE 4

ECONOMETRIC PROJECTIONS OF PRODUCTION, DISPOSABLE INCOME,
AND THE SAVINGS RATIO, MODEL VIII, 1958

	Model Solution 1957	Forecast for 1958	Percentage Change 1957 to 1958		
			Value	Volume	Price
PRODUCTION BY SECTORS (millions of 1935–39 dollars)					
Gross output, private nonagriculture	12,041	11,961		−0.7	
Gross output, agriculture[a]	693	775		+11.8	
Output of government services[a]	973	987		+1.4	
Gross national product	13,707	13,723		+0.1	
DISPOSABLE INCOME (millions of current dollars)					
Wage and salary	16,020	16,630	+3.8	+3.0	+0.8
Personal, nonwage	4,874	4,951	+1.6	+0.8	+0.8
Total personal sector	20,894	21,581	+3.3	+2.5	+0.8
Total nonwage					
Net of depreciation	5,951	5,919	−0.5	−1.3	+0.8
Gross of depreciation	9,318	9,555	+2.5		
Private sector					
Net	21,971	22,549	+2.6	+1.8	+0.8
Gross	25,338	26,185	+3.3		
Government	5,349	4,610	−13.8	−14.5	+0.8
Taxes less transfer payments					
Wage and salary	−393	−828			
Nonwage	1,943	1,667			
Indirect taxes less subsidies	3,799	3,771	−0.7	−1.5	+0.8
Gross national product (private sector plus government)	30,687	30,795	+0.4		
SAVINGS RATIO (personal disposable income)					
	0.0782	0.0711			

[a] Exogenous.

short-run supply curve of labor, reflecting a trend which arose out of the postwar strengthening of the trade unions, and the postwar demand inflation.

Average hours of work (nonfarm) declined by 1.5 per cent, as the economy ground to a halt and unemployment grew. Productivity (real output per man-hour) increased by 2.3 per cent as the production function shifted upward under the influence of its trend and of the growing stock of producers' capital. The latter increased at the spectacular rate of 7.3 per cent, despite the slowing down of investment.

Global real output

The next most vital area of the forecast is the level of total output. This volume remained substantially unchanged (Table 2). The explanation provided by the model from the demand side is as follows. The demand for investment in producers' durables fell heavily (-14.1 per cent), with a substantial decline also in exports (-6.5 per cent). The decline in inventory investment (from investment to extensive disinvestment) was the final major contributor to recession.

Consumer demand was one of the main strengths opposing the decline. By far the largest single component of total demand for final goods, it increased by 2.5 per cent (volume), under the influence of previous standards of consumption, the built-in fiscal stabilizers, and the expansionist fiscal policy of government. Personal disposable income increased by 2.5 per cent in purchasing power, and the savings ratio (personal) in the model declined from 0.0782 to 0.0711 (Table 4).

Government spending was a second force standing against the recession, and advanced 2.9 per cent. A third spearhead of the attack was the provision by the government of considerable extra funds to its Central Mortgage and Housing Corporation for providing insured mortgages and direct mortgage loans for new residential construction. This component of final demand increased strongly, by 10.6 per cent (Table 2).

A final defense against the recession came from another kind of built-in stabilizer, the level of imports. With the investment program falling off, and an assumed decline in the capital inflow as conditions also deteriorated in the United States, imports fell rapidly in the model—by 9.9 per cent.

The net outcome of the struggle between the forces of decline and the forces of defense and attack against the decline was an even balance. The level of total final demand (*ex post*) barely changed. Corresponding to this, on the supply side of the economy, an increase in nonfarm productivity of 2.3 per cent was partly offset by a decline in hours of 1.5 per cent, but the residual effect fell on employment. Demand for paid nonfarm workers fell by 1.1 per cent (*ex post*).

As a result of this prediction of almost no change in output, but of rising labor costs, the model predicted that total nonwage income would decline by 4.0 per cent in money terms, with the heaviest impact in this sector on residual profits (Table 2).

The price level

No attempt was made in this forecast to analyze the shifts in the global demand and supply functions as functions of the global price level. But the forecast solution suggests the following hypothesis. There was only a slight shift in the demand curve, of unknown direction. The supply curve was shifted forward by the gain in productivity (+2.3 per cent) and backward by the increase in average wage rates (+3.0 per cent). The price level increased by 0.8 per cent, suggesting that the net shift was a slight backward shift of supply. The "inflation" would then be produced by cost rather than demand forces. This hypothesis is reinforced by a calculation, from Table 3, that labor cost per unit of output (average wage divided by productivity) increased by 0.7 per cent.

SUMMING UP

Within the framework of analysis of the model, the battle of the recession was nearly won, but was in fact lost. The evidence reveals a valiant attack on a variety of fronts, plus some well-placed defenses. The combined tactics raised the deficit of all three levels of government by $1 billion. But the model indicates that it would take more demand for final goods, or a shortening of hours of work, to close the employment gap. This demand could be carefully aimed at the industries of greatest unemployment. The government deficit need not increase if government policy created further expansion, since government revenues become increasingly elastic with respect to output at full-employment and boom levels of output.

But one problem still remains. Expansion of demand in the model would undoubtedly cause the price level to increase. By the time the economy reached full employment the price level might have increased by 3 or 4 per cent. This is not too great a price to pay for full employment, but it typifies a troublesome defect in modern Western economies. Apparently, it is becoming impossible to reach full

82

employment without inflation.[11] This inflationary problem may inhibit some Western governments from pursuing full-employment policies steadfastly, until complete victory is won. The problem seems to stem from the ability of large firms and associations of all kinds, including labor unions and professional bodies, to administer their supply prices, instead of having these determined by the impersonal demand and supply forces of perfectly competitive markets. The solution of this problem is of vital importance to the Western democracies.

A Brief Post-Mortem

In the above analysis we were discussing the picture of the economy as projected into 1958 by the model. It is now possible to look at the outcome in the real economy, as it actually happened four years ago.

TABLE 5

COMPARISON OF MODEL VIII FORECAST OF 1958
WITH SUBSEQUENT OBSERVATIONS

	Percentage Changes, 1957 to 1958	
	Predicted	First Revised Observation[a]
Input of selected exogenous data		
G	+2.9	+3.8
$GI + GI_d$	−10.3	−7.8
F_2'	−6.5	+0.9
Total exogenous demand impact	−5.3	−1.4
$N_1 - N_M$	+1.7	+2.2
Output of selected endogenous variables		
N_p^{na}	−1.1	−0.2
$N_p + N_{enp} + N_g$	−0.7	−0.4
N_u	+44.1	+57.6
w_{ph}^{na}	+3.0	+2.4
GNP	+0.1	+0.5
C	+2.5	+2.6
F_1'	−9.9	−6.3
P'	+0.8	+1.8
Y_{pm}	+3.3	+7.1
π_m	−4.0	+4.3

[a] *National Accounts, Income and Expenditure, 1958*, Ottawa, Dominion Bureau of Statistics, 1959. Underlying values are in 1949 constant-dollar units.

[11] T. M. Brown, "Unemployment or Inflation—Economic Dilemma of the West," *Queen's Quarterly*, Summer 1961.

In Table 5 a comparison between forecast and observed outcome is made for selected items.

How good or how bad was this forecast? What guidance can it give us for future forecast work? In comparing the forecast with what subsequently happened we must recall that, in the forecast, we are presenting movements of the systematic part of the model only, whereas in our observations of the real world we are studying movements of a systematic and random component combined.

In the first place, I was overly pessimistic in predicting exogenous demands, and made a considerable error in the total exogenous impact. The exogenous variables are by their nature difficult to predict.[12] This is because they emanate from noneconomic areas of causation containing their own laws of behavior and random components. However, this error could have been gradually corrected in the first quarter and first half of the forecast year as more information became available.

Taking into account this error in the exogenous forecast, the model might be expected to predict a greater decline in employment than occurred, and a smaller increase in the total volume of output. Unemployment, however, actually increased more than the model predicted, because the labor force grew at a higher rate than was predicted.

Many of the other errors in the forecast can be largely traced to errors in the exogenous demands. For example, imports would have been closer to the mark but for this error. The error in the price level also reflects the weakness in the assumptions about exogenous demands. On the global supply side, wage rates did not rise as much as the model predicted, but neither did productivity (one estimate put it at +1.1 per cent). Hence, the model may have been about right on the supply side, but too weak on the demand side of the aggregate market for final goods.

In the case of personal disposable income it appears that the rather large error cannot be attributed mainly to the exogenous input. It is likely that here the tax and transfer equations are in need of structural correction through more research and more collaboration with experts in the tax and transfer field.

The error in total nonwage income reflects the volatility of this

---

[12] H. Theil, *Economic Forecasts and Policy*, Amsterdam, 1958, Chap. 7, observes that "erroneous estimates of exogenous changes were by far the most important sources of the errors of the unconditional forecasts."

variable relative to the level of activity and the error in the average wage rate.

Conclusions

This experimental forecast as well as considerable other experience make me believe that useful models of income determination can be derived by econometric measurement. The model described in this paper has many imperfections, but surely all of these could be corrected by adequate research resources. The inventory equation and the tax and transfer equations especially, including the indirect tax equation, need much more study. Also aggregate production and supply in the model should be reformulated from a GNP to a gross domestic product basis. Solution of the model with the correct exogenous and lagged data would point up many other errors and weaknesses.

In addition to research along these and other lines to improve the structure specification and estimates, we should also be thinking about how to measure the *very current* structure of an economy. If economic structure is slowly evolving, the estimates from a time series may not always be able to sort out the time trends appropriately. Some structure estimates may then be only an average of a changing structure. But we might be able to measure the very current structure of an economy by analyzing a stratified sample of households and of firms which keep complete economic records, and passing these monthly, without analysis, to the Dominion Bureau of Statistics or the United States Department of Commerce. Analysis of these records both as time series and as cross-section samples may reveal the clue to the use of current cross-section samples for estimating the *current* "time series" structure.[13]

Also needed is more excellent data designed to match our hypotheses. In matters of basic economic measurement and in the suggestion of hypotheses to be tested, arising out of study of these data, the National Bureau of Economic Research can be a powerful ally to econometric development in the United States (as I am sure it already is). This is because of its wealth of experience and skill in these vital areas.

With excellent models derived by painstaking, large-scale research

---

[13] Pioneering work in the use of cross-section data in econometrics has been done by Klein and his associates. See Lawrence R. Klein (ed.), *Contributions of Survey Methods to Economics*, New York, 1954; and Klein and Goldberger, *op. cit.* (above, note 9).

we can devise and test rational and accurate alternative policies for maintaining economic health—especially full employment and adequate rates of development and growth.[14]

The economic costs of unemployment and inadequate growth in any country are represented by the value of production lost because of these shortcomings. In Canada in the circumstances of 1958 it would have been necessary to increase real output by about 5 per cent to restore full employment. Roughly $1.5 billion were lost that year as a result of our failure to keep healthy. The United States in similar circumstances in the same year probably lost about $21 billion for the same reason. In both countries the *human* costs of the unemployment to workers and their families must be counted as infinite.

The cost of good quantitative research of all kinds aimed at policy problems would be small indeed in comparison to the above costs of economic ill health. On purely economic grounds investment in these fields should have a very high yield.

But in the world of today something greater than domestic costs and gains is at stake. Our governments must show the world that it is possible for the "mixed enterprise" economy to give high regard and value to the individual, to provide a high degree of general welfare, *and to run and grow smoothly.* To me, the best instrument we have been able to devise to help us regulate the over-all behavior of such an economy by indirect means is the econometric model. It is the only instrument which tries to put everything together, and to study the whole economy as an operating unity.

Let us develop these models to their full potentialities, and use them.

COMMENT

CARL F. CHRIST, Johns Hopkins University

This morning's session, with a paper on a Canadian model by T. M. Brown and a paper on a United States model by Lawrence R. Klein, stands as a testimony to the achievements of economists who have persevered in building and testing and improving aggregate econometric models, including Brown and especially Klein. Both of these models represent real progress, and have led to quite good

[14] Cf. Lawrence R. Klein, "The Use of Econometric Models as a Guide to Economic Policy," *Econometrica*, April 1947.

forecasts. Klein's model, which is two years later than Brown's, incorporates several excellent new features. For example: (1) accounting identities are expressed in money terms, as they should be, and the model is designed to explain both real magnitudes and price levels for the various income and expenditure flows; (2) anticipations data are used at several points; (3) inventory investment is related to new and unfilled orders; (4) a relation between actual and capacity output is introduced.

We are particularly fortunate to have Brown describe the Canadian model, fitted to 1926–41 and 1946–56, for although he and his associates in the Dominion Department of Trade and Commerce have been working on models of Canada for some fifteen years, rather little material has appeared concerning these models. Fragmentary reports have suggested that the work is progressing well. Brown's paper gives us a chance to see for ourselves that this is so, to learn a good deal about the models used, and to offer some comments in a constructive spirit with the same good cause in mind.

Quantitative Results

In January 1958, the model was used, together with forecasts of the exogenous variables, to make unconditional forecasts of the performance of the Canadian economy in 1958. Brown denotes by Y_{C58} in equation A(2) the forecast for 1958 of the variable Y made by the reduced form of the estimated model, on the assumption that the residuals for 1958 are zero. If there is high serial correlation of disturbances, then the forecast may be improved by adding to certain estimated structural equations the corresponding estimated structural residual calculated for the preceding year, to get a revised estimated structure, and then solving this to get a revised forecast. This is what Brown does, and he denotes his actual revised forecast for Y for 1958 by Y_{F58} in equation B(5).

In comparing his forecasts for 1958 with the actual performance of the Canadian economy (as estimated in the national accounts early in 1959) he compares the actual and the forecast *percentage changes*, namely $100(Y_{58} - Y_{57})/Y_{57}$ and $100(Y_{F58} - Y_{F57})/Y_{F57}$ (see his Table 5). The *difference* between these two statistics is a rough indicator of the accuracy of forecast, but it is hard to interpret because it is *not* a simple function of the actual forecasting error $Y_{F58} - Y_{58}$, unless $Y_{F57} = Y_{57}$ (in which case it would be the percentage error of the 1958 forecast referred to a 1957 base, i.e.

$100(Y_{F58} - Y_{58})/Y_{57})$. For the major aggregate variables, real GNP and total civilian employment ($N_{pe} + N_g$), these *differences* were 0.4 per cent and 0.3 per cent, respectively, i.e., the accuracy was extremely good. The GNP deflator and the wage rate were quite well forecast, too, with differences of 1 per cent or less. Certain subcategories of total income and expenditure had differences of up to 8 per cent. Unfortunately for those who want a more detailed assessment, the paper presented the actual and forecast values of only ten of the forty endogenous variables; so the results for the other thirty are obscure.

Four of the eight stochastic equations were estimated by the truncated full-information maximum-likelihood method (TFML), and four by least squares (actually least squares was used for all equations first). For four of the equations we are given the multiple correlation coefficient R obtained from the least squares fit. The four values are all at least 0.997, remarkably high.

Statistical Presentation and Evaluation

For *all* of the stochastic equations, it would be desirable to show the multiple correlation coefficient R. For equations fitted by the TFML method, it would be desirable to show also an analogous measure of goodness of fit, such as the square root of the expression

$$1 - \left(\frac{\text{standard error of estimate}}{\text{standard deviation of "explained" variable}}\right)^2.$$

For each of the estimated coefficients, it would be desirable to show the estimated standard deviation, so that observers could form an impression (whether by classical or Bayesian methods) of the reliability of the estimates of individual coefficients.

In addition to the eight stochastic equations (which can be identified by the presence of a random disturbance variable, $u_1, \ldots, u_8$) there are six equations that have numerically estimated coefficients but no disturbances; these are five of the six tax and transfer equations and the equation relating hours worked per week to the level of unemployment. It would be helpful to know how the numerical values of the coefficients in these six equations were obtained.

Forecasting results for this or similar Canadian models for 1959, 1960, and 1961 would be most welcome.

Brown points out that a large share of his forecasting error is due to errors in forecasting the exogenous variables. It has become common practice in presenting the forecasts made by an econometric model to show both the unconditional forecasts (as Brown did), and also the conditional forecasts given the *ex post* correct values of the exogenous variables (as Brown did not). Had he done so, it would be possible for readers to see how large the forecasting errors would have been in the absence of any errors in exogenous variables, and thus to evaluate the model itself, apart from the forecasting process as a whole, which depends on both the model's and one's own ability to forecast the exogenous variables.

Economic Content of the Model

One of the most conspicuous features of the model which calls for revision is that all investment expenditures except inventory investment are treated as exogenous. Brown tells us that in previous and subsequent models demand equations for plant, construction, and machinery have been used. It would be enlightening to have a report on the alternatives tried and the results obtained with the more important ones.

A number of small questions arise about the treatment of income and wealth in the consumption equations A(1), A(2), and A(3). Why are Y_w and Y_π (labor and property income) separated in the perishables equation, but not in the semidurables and durables equations? Why are Y_p^a and $Y_{\pi np}$ (agricultural income and property income of nonpersons) excluded from the durables equation but not from the perishables and semidurables equations? Why is the stock of consumer capital goods divided by income in the durables equation and not in the semidurables equation?

The model is linear for the most part, but there are several clever nonlinearities. Some of them occur when it is desired to take into account that total man-hours worked is a product of employment and the number of hours worked by the average worker per year, or that the total money wage bill is the hourly wage rate times the number of man-hours of labor used. Others occur with respect to price level variables, when a relation between real and money magnitudes is wanted. Another, simple but ingenious, is in the wage adjustment equation, C(8), which asserts the hypothesis that wage rates become more sensitive to the level of unemployment when that level falls below 3 per cent of the labor force. This is because unemployment enters in two terms in equation C(8), the term containing Nh_u^{na} and the term containing N_u; and N_u responds to changes in unemployment only when the level is below 3 per cent.

The discussion at this conference showed that Brown's treatment of prices in his *use* of the model is somewhat different, and more intelligent, than the explicit statement of the model's equations and the list of endogenous and exogenous variables indicates. The model indicates that the only endogenous price level variables are P, $P^{\cdot}$, and P^+, being respectively the deflators of net and gross national product and of GNP plus imports. The prices of consumer goods, investment goods, and the like appear to be exogenous. Such a procedure would not make sense if adhered to rigidly, for then the levels chosen for these "exogenous" price variables would have to be permitted to affect in an important way the general price level variables P, $P^{\cdot}$, and P^+. Actually, in using the model to make forecasts, Brown and his colleagues relate the value of the consumption deflator to the general price level by means of a separate informal equation, and if I understand correctly they do the same with certain other price level variables. Thus, the equilibrium condition [equation G(3)] equating aggregate demand and supply determines the general price level P, and the other price level variables are determined in relation to that. Therefore, in effect, the number of endogenous variables in the model is forty *plus* the number of price variables thus explained, and the number of equations in the model is forty *plus* the number of price-explaining relationships thus employed.

This means that the treatment of prices in this Canadian model is rather similar to their treatment in the model presented here by Klein, for Klein expresses each of his endogenous sector price levels by means of an explicit equation in terms of either the GNP deflator or the wage rate. The main differences on this score between the two models are that Klein's accounting identities are in money terms, as they should be, while Brown's are in real terms (with the exception of the wage bill identity), and Klein shows the influence of relative prices on the demands for certain classes of goods and services. Brown's model would be improved by following this example, and also by showing explicitly the relationships used among price variables that are handled in an endogenous manner for forecasting purposes.

The model as it stands, with forty equations and forty endogenous variables, is rather hard to apprehend. Its central structure may become more visible if certain reducing or simplifying operations are performed, which make no change in its central content. First, the endogenous variable T_d appears only in equation F(15), so both it and that equation can be dropped without changing the content of the remainder of the model. Second, there are two endogenous variables that are essentially exogenous, since each is determined in an equation that contains no other endogenous variables; they are D_{f2} in equation F(4) and K_{PCM} in equation F(18); hence, these two equations can be dropped and the two variables regarded as exogenous. Third, the six endogenous tax and transfer variables can be expressed in terms of the variables on which they depend, and thus they and their six equations can be removed by substitution. Fourth, the three profit variables other than corporate profits can all be expressed in terms of the latter, and so they and their three defining equations can also be eliminated by substitution. The same is true of some half-dozen variables representing different kinds of income flows; after they are eliminated, property income (π) and disposable labor and property income, Y_w and Y_π, remain. Similarly, the price levels $P^{\cdot}$ and P^+ can be expressed in terms of P, the net national product deflator. Continuing such a process, one can obtain a model of sixteen equations, eight stochastic and eight nonstochastic, in sixteen endogenous variables, as follows:

Equations (*stochastic)	*Endogenous Variables* *Corresponding*
* 3 consumption demands, A(1–3)	3 consumption variables
* Import demand, B(6)	Imports
* Inventory demand, B(4)	Inventory investment
* Labor demand, B(5)	Employment
* Wage equation, C(8)	Wage rate
* Production function, D(9)	Gross private nonfarm product
Hours equation, B(7)	Average hours per worker
6 definitions	Wage bill, property income, disposable labor and property incomes, corporate profits, unemployment
Aggregate equilibrium condition, G(3)	Price level

All these equations are interrelated in an essential way, i.e., there is no way of breaking them up into two subsets such that one of the subsets alone determines the values of a corresponding subset of the endogenous variables in a manner logically independent of the determination of the remaining variables. This is as it should be.

Monetary policy and behavior variables have too limited a role in the equations of this model. They enter through lagged real balances of households ($L_{hr,-1}$) and consumer credit terms (dp) in two of the consumption equations, and through capital inflow (ΔKS) in the import equation. And they affect the model by influencing investment in plant and equipment and housing, which the model treats as exogenous. More explicit treatment of money market variables is desirable if Brown's discussion of the roles of demand inflation and cost inflation is to be evaluated adequately.

WILLIAM C. HOOD, University of Toronto

For rather more than a decade, T. M. Brown worked on the official econometric model of the Canadian economy in Ottawa. He has published several contributions to the theory of estimation and forecasting, and some empirical results, but so far as I know this paper represents the first description of the Canadian model as it was developed by Brown and his associates which has been prepared for publication. Since the work that has been done is of high quality, Canadians will not be alone in their pleasure that it will now be available.

In these comments I shall confine myself to brief remarks on:

1. uses to which the models have been put in the service of the Canadian government
2. selected characteristics of the model that has been presented
3. certain statements and conjectures in the paper.

Uses to Which Models Have Been Put in Canadian Government Service

The Economics Branch of the Department of Trade and Commerce has the principal responsibility within the government service in Ottawa for providing aggregate forecasts of forthcoming developments in the Canadian economy. The methods of forecasting are diverse. Substantial use is made of the regular survey of investment intentions, though the results of that survey are not used without adjustment. Considerable application is made of the analysis of reference cycles, diffusion indexes of movements of deseasonalized data, and similar devices. The definitions of the national accounts and other related identities are used as a framework within which to integrate informed estimates. The econometric model, deriving its forecasts of exogenous variables from other work in the branch, is used as an alternative or supplemental means of organizing the information available into forecasts of the main components of national income, expenditure, employment, and prices.

Users of the model have found it particularly helpful in assessing quickly the likely effects on the main economic aggregates of changes in particular elements of federal government expenditure and tax policies. It has also been found to be particularly useful, I am told, in assessing the impact of the opposing demand and supply forces upon the price level.

Some Characteristics of the Model

While the model has been useful in assessing the effects of particular changes in government fiscal policy, it is not constructed with a view to exhibiting explicitly the requirements of government policies of various kinds. In using the model it has not been the practice to specify explicit targets for national income, employment, prices, and the like, and then seek to determine what policy measures would be required in the circumstances to ensure that these targets will be achieved. Some key variables upon which the government might be expected to operate directly do not appear, at least not explicitly, in the model. For example, the stock of money as such does not appear in the model. The rate of interest does not appear explicitly in the model; it may be reflected in the index of consumer credit conditions (dp), though the definition of that variable does not indicate that it is. The rate of exchange does not appear explicitly in the model, though it is reflected in the price of imported goods.

It is important to emphasize, as Brown does, how strategic is the role played by the exogenous variables in the model. I refer not to lagged variables, but to unlagged ones. The model is designed to forecast the gross national output and expenditure and its main components among other items. The exogenous expenditures, however, account for some 58 per cent of gross national expenditure (GNE) and 48 per cent of GNE plus imports. I do not refer to this fact as a criticism, but it *is* an outstanding characteristic of the model and it shows that as of the date of the model at any rate, formal econometric techniques of this particular kind were being used to predict only about one-half of the total of GNE and this, on the whole, the more stable (and hence more predictable) half.

The absence of equations to explain the demand for new fixed capital helps to explain the relatively small role played by financial variables in the model. In the equations dealing with the demand for consumers' goods, financial variables appear. An explicit place has been found for the increment in the inflow of capital from abroad for direct and for portfolio investment in the import equation. But there are financial variables that presumably are important and that have no place in the model. In any event, all financial variables that appear are exogenous. Consequently, the model is not able to handle questions relating to the impact of monetary, debt management, and exchange rate policies upon the economy. These have been important issues of policy in Canada and will continue to be. Perhaps others will feel with me that in building upon Brown's econometric work we should seek to give much more empirical content to our discussions of financial policies and our predictions of their outcomes.

I shall only take time to comment upon one equation in the model, namely, the demand for imports. This equation has a larger number (seven) of independent variables than any other equation in the model. The interpretation given to the equation by Brown is plausible. I would point out, though, that the first four independent variables in the equation have special relations with each other and with the dependent variable. The first independent variable is nonagricultural GNP plus the dependent variable. The second, the increase in nonagricultural inventories, is a component of the first and itself has a substantial import content. The third, investment in machinery and equipment, is a component of the first, and something over half of it is composed of imports of machinery and equipment. The fourth is a component of the first and also has a substantial import content. Thus, the dependent variable or a part of it appears as a component of each of the first four independent variables; and the second, third, and fourth independent variables are components of the first. The equation was estimated by the least squares procedure. I should be curious to see the variances of the estimates of the coefficients of the first four variables of this equation.

Selected Statements and Conjectures in the Paper

I confess that the brief discussion of the determination of prices left me confused. I refer in particular to the paragraph which reads as follows: "In the aggregate or i.e. in the equation on the *global market for final goods*, it is assumed that equilibrium, in the sense discussed above, is reached within yearly periods, a condition which might be much less likely for quarterly or monthly time periods. The equations of GNF^d and GNF^s in this 'market' permitted the determination of both GNF and the equilibrating variable. The latter was the price level P^+, which included P, the unknown deflator variable used throughout the model."

It seems to me that the equation which determines the price level, equation G(3), is an identity, not an equilibrium condition. In what sense is it thought that an equilibrium price is reached within yearly periods? Is it an equilibrium price in the sense that the market is cleared? Surely not, for inventory accumulation is not zero. Is it an equilibrium price in the sense that its value is expected to persist into and through the next period? Surely not, for then it would only be necessary to forecast next year's price as equal to this year's. Does it make sense in general to speak of the average of the prices of the year as an equilibrium price? Would it not be better *not* to refer to the price level as an equilibrium price but rather to refer to it simply as the level of prices indicated by the equations and identities?

There are two observations in the paper concerning the importance of cost-push inflation. On page 82 it is suggested that the forecast implied that the expected rise in prices would result from forces on the side of cost rather than on the side of demand. On page 84 it is suggested that the forecast erred in underestimating the strength of demand forces and that the greater increase in prices than was forecast was to be attributed to this strength on the demand side of the market. Would Brown now feel that in 1958 the rise in prices in Canada would be fairly described as showing the effects both of cost push and demand pull?

One final comment: The author has indicated that forecasts of endogenous variables may be wide of the mark because of errors in the forecasts of exogenous variables, and he has given qualitative illustrations of this from the experience he reports. It is also possible that errors in forecasts of endogenous variables may be small even with poor forecasts of the exogenous variables because of unsatisfactory specification and estimation of the structural equations. It would have been particularly illuminating if Brown had had the resources to permit him to calculate the prediction his model would have yielded of the endogenous variables had the realized values of the exogenous variables been used rather than their projected values.

Income and Asset Effects on Consumption: Aggregate and Cross Section

JEAN CROCKETT

UNIVERSITY OF PENNSYLVANIA

It is the thesis of this paper that we have so far been unable to measure accurately the effects on consumption either of the predominantly important factor, income, or the secondary—but still important—factor, assets. There are a number of reasons for this, of which three are of primary concern here: (1) inability to measure separately various components of disposable income which may have different effects on consumption (e.g., "permanent" and "transitory" components); (2) inability to measure objectively savings propensities, which differ greatly among families and are highly relevant to asset effects; and (3) failure to take proper account of the interactions between income and asset effects.

The inconsistency between the ordinary time series estimates of consumption function parameters and those based on cross-section data is well known. A simple linear relationship gives a good fit, using aggregate time series data, even after the spurious correlation due to price movements and population growth has been removed. Using real per capita series for the United States with disposable income as the only independent variable, marginal propensities in the range 0.70–0.95 are ordinarily obtained by least squares procedures, the exact value in the range depending on the period covered.[1] Income elasticities are somewhat higher, particularly for postwar income levels.[2]

---

[1] E.g., Robert Ferber obtained 0.78 for 1929–40; 0.79 for 1923–40; and 0.93 for 1923–30, 1935–40 (see *A Study of Aggregate Consumption Functions*, New York, NBER, 1953, p. 65). Goldsmith obtained 0.70 for 1897–1949 and 0.82 for the same period excluding war years. For certain short periods or periods dominated by the depression of the 1930's he obtained much lower values (see Raymond W. Goldsmith, Dorothy S. Brady, and Horst Mendershausen, *A Study of Saving in the United States*, Princeton, N.J., 1956, III, 393). More recently, I have obtained 0.89 for 1948–60 and 0.90 for the longer period 1929–41, 1946–60.

For a comprehensive discussion of other recent results see Irwin Friend, "Determinants of the Volume and Composition of Saving with Special Reference to the Influence of Monetary Policy," to be published under the auspices of the Commission on Money and Credit.

[2] Using 1950 levels of consumption and income, a range of elasticities from 0.74 to 0.99 is obtained for the regressions noted in note 1.

Good fits are also obtained for logarithmic linear relationships based on grouped cross-section data, at least when extreme income classes are eliminated. An income elasticity of 0.78 is obtained from the 1950 BLS data in the income range $1,000 to $10,000, with family size held constant. If the extreme income groups are included, the elasticity falls to 0.67. From the 1935–36 BLS data, I obtained an income elasticity of 0.74, using per capita consumption and income, with all income groups included.[3]

While these cross-section estimates are not too different from the lowest of the time series estimates, it should be noted that the differences become substantial whenever recent years are included or years of deep depression are excluded in time series analyses. It may be that estimates of two different things are obtained from the two types of data and that neither is precisely the one wanted. In other words, two different—but relatively stable—sets of biases are involved in the two kinds of estimates of the income effect.

For a number of purposes what we would like to know is the change in aggregate real consumption for a given change in aggregate real income, with the number of consumer units and all other factors affecting consumption held constant. Other relevant factors here include both the distribution of consumers (and consumer income) according to such characteristics as occupation and age and also variables like "standard of living" and availability of credit, which may cause similar consumers (in terms of the above characteristics) to behave differently at different points of time. For prediction, we would also like to know the effects on consumption of these other relevant factors and to have some idea of what changes in them are likely to occur.

Sources of Bias in Estimates of Income and Asset Effects

The shortcomings of both time series and family budget data in providing estimates of the desired income parameter have been widely discussed. Single-equation least squares relationships based on aggregate time series must yield biased estimates since, in the aggregate, income depends on consumption as well as consumption on income. To the extent that income changes are due to shifts in a two-dimensional consumption function, as distinguished from autonomous shifts in investment or government expenditures, the least squares estimate would be expected (for a sufficiently large sample) to lie

[3] See regressions 1, 2, and 3 in the Appendix.

98

somewhere between the desired value and unity.[4] This difficulty is presumably avoided by the use of a complete system, though at the expense of subjecting the estimates of consumption function parameters to the vagaries of other less well-behaved functions in the system.

CONSUMPTION-INDUCED INCOME

The problem of two-way causation is reduced when we turn to cross-section data, though even here there is some presumption of mutual dependence, to the extent that people with high consumption desires make efforts to increase their income in order to fulfill those desires. Some indication of the importance of the resulting bias might be obtained by comparing Engel curves for single-earner families with those for multi-earner families of equal size and for both types combined. One obvious way for a family to raise its income in order to meet consumption needs is for a secondary earner to enter the labor force. Consumption-induced income might therefore be expected to be more important among multi-earner families than among single-earner families. If this assumption is true and if consumption-induced income results in a biased estimate of the income coefficient, then the slope for the pooled regression should be different (presumably higher) than for the single-earner families considered separately, since in the latter case the association between high income and high consumption desires is reduced though not necessarily eliminated.[5]

[4] Consider the simple model

$$C = a + bY + u$$
$$I + G = k$$
$$C + I + G = Y,$$

where C is consumption, I is investment, G is government expenditure, Y is GNP, k is independent of income though variable over time, and u is a random residual. Shifts in u cause equal changes in C and Y; and if only such changes occurred over time the observed points would fall along a line with unit slope. If changes over time were exclusively due to changes in $I + G$, the observed points would trace out a line with slope equal to b. If both kinds of changes occur, it is reasonable to expect an intermediate slope.

[5] Assume that $C = a + bY' + cY'' + \Phi + v$, where Y' is income due to the primary earner, Y'' is income due to secondary earners, Φ is a measure of tastes which is positive for "high spenders" and negative for "high savers," and v is a random residual independent of Y', Y'', and Φ. Then to the extent that secondary earners are induced to enter the labor market by high Φ, there will be a positive correlation between Y'' and Φ. If a regression is fitted of the form

$$C = a + bY + u,$$

where

$$Y = Y' + Y''$$
$$u = \Phi + v,$$

Furthermore, the level of consumption should be different (presumably higher) for the multi-earner families than for single-earner families with the same income.

A test based on the 1950 data shows that, with family size held constant and age of head under forty, consumption levels are somewhat higher for single-earner families at low incomes and somewhat lower at high incomes than for multi-earner families.[6] In the range from $2,500 to $6,000, which contains about five-sixths of multi-earner families under forty, the consumption levels were very similar for single- and multi-earner families of medium size. There was no difference in income elasticity between families with two full-time earners and no other earners and families with one full-time earner and one or more part-time earners; but expenditure levels for the former were slightly lower, except when family size was large. Families with at least two full-time earners and one or more other earners (either full or part time) showed a much steeper income slope than any of the other groups, but were numerically unimportant in this age range.

Where age of head is over forty, income elasticity is again lower for single-earner than for multi-earner families. There is little difference in level in the income range $2,000–$4,000, except that families with two full-time earners only spent somewhat less than the other three groups.

To the extent that any of the four earner groups is consistently low in consumption, it is the group with two full-time earners only. Spending falls below that for the other two multi-earner groups except for the numerically unimportant case of families under forty with two full-time earners and one or more other earners. Furthermore, spending falls short of that for single-earner families at incomes below $5,000 or $6,000.

The lower income elasticity for single-earner families undoubtedly reflects the fact that a relatively high percentage of families in the two extreme income brackets belong to this earner group (92 per cent of families with income under $1,000 and 65 per cent of families with

---

then some correlation may be expected between u and Y, leading to least squares bias. (This will fail to occur only if Y' is negatively correlated with Y'' in such a way that total income is invariant with respect to Y''.) This source of bias is eliminated if we restrict Y'' to zero by considering only single-earner families, though some bias may remain owing to a correlation between Φ and Y'.

[6] See regressions 4–12 in the Appendix.

income over $10,000 as compared with 57 per cent in the $1,000–$10,000 range). It will be recalled that the inclusion of these income brackets reduced the income elasticity for the 1950 sample as a whole from 0.78 to 0.67, a somewhat larger difference than between single-earner and multi-earner families.

It may also be noted that the lower income elasticity of single-earner families is associated, for both age ranges, with a higher family-size elasticity. Presumably the variance of family size is smaller for multi-earner than for single-earner families (since one-person families do not occur), and conceivably this may result in some understatement of the family-size effect and a corresponding overstatement of the income effect. A similar explanation might be offered for the higher income elasticity and lower family-size elasticity of three of the earner groups with age under forty as compared with the corresponding groups over forty.

Finally, we should not overlook the possibility that the relatively low consumption of multi-earner families at low incomes may indicate that they are less willing or less able to dissave than single-earner families. Then it is relatively strong savings motivation (or aversion to dissaving) which brings the secondary worker into the labor force, rather than strong consumption motivation.

If we confine ourselves to the middle income range where multi-earner families are numerically important, we find no evidence that consumption levels are lower for single-earner than for multi-earner families, except in the case of families with head of household over age forty in the income range above $4,000. Even here, families with two full-time earners only consume less than single-earner families. Thus, there is no strong reason, on the basis of these data, to expect that bias due to consumption-induced income will be substantial in cross-section estimates of the income elasticity.

When the income elasticity for all earner groups combined is compared with that for single-earner families, it is found that the pooled regression gives an estimate intermediate between those for single-earner families under forty and for single-earner families over forty. However, it is slightly above the average of the elasticities for the two single-earner groups; and this suggests that some very small bias may arise from the presence of consumption-induced income among multi-earner families. It should be noted, however, that such income leads to relatively high consumption levels only for families where the secondary earner is part time rather than full time.

101

Omitted Variables Correlated with Income

In addition to problems of two-way causation, bias in the income coefficient, whether estimated by least squares or more complicated methods, may arise from the omission of variables, other than income, which affect consumption and are correlated with income. For an individual consumer unit, other relevant factors include all those which affect either the relative urgency of savings and consumption desires or the ability to meet consumption needs in excess of current income. While the urgency of these desires is not directly measurable, it is clear that a number of variables which are readily determined will have some relationship.

Thus, for given income, a family's consumption needs presumably will be stronger the larger the number of persons in the family and the higher the standard of living to which the family is accustomed. While it may be argued that savings needs also rise for larger family size, an increase in certain categories of consumption expenditure, notably food and clothing, would appear to be more urgent than an increase in savings. Consumption needs will also tend to be stronger at certain stages of the life cycle than at others, with savings needs tending to become relatively more urgent as the family's stock of durables is gradually built up and the period of retirement (or declining earnings) approaches. Certain needs may be stronger in the North than in the South. Family size, past income (and perhaps expected future income), age, and region are therefore all relevant. In addition, the accepted standard of living probably reflects in part cultural factors related to such variables as educational level, occupation, and race, and in part availability of consumption opportunities, which may be somewhat greater for white than for nonwhite families and greater in metropolitan areas than in small towns or rural areas. Certainly the availability of consumption opportunities increases substantially over time with the continuous introduction of new products.

Savings desires, for given income, will be stronger the smaller the existing stock of assets, the greater the variability of income, and the higher the return earned by assets. Thus, asset holdings and occupation are both highly relevant. In particular, entrepreneurs may be expected to have relatively high savings propensities, both because they may be subject to substantial variability of income and because they are probably in a position to earn substantially higher rates of return on their savings than persons in other occupations.

Factors affecting the ability of the family to consume in excess of current income include asset holdings, particularly liquid assets, and the availability of credit.

In the aggregate, therefore, changes in population, in the asset position of households, in the availability of credit, in the availability of consumption opportunities, and in the distribution of income by occupation, age, educational level, race, region, and city size may all be expected to have an effect on consumption.

Most of the factors mentioned are correlated with income to some extent, both cross-sectionally and in the aggregate. In some cases they may be affected by past income (which is highly correlated with current income) in a causal sense—e.g., assets holdings and perhaps family size or total population—or they may affect income in a direct way and not simply via an effect on consumption—e.g., occupation, education, race, and age—or they may be related to a third causal factor also affecting income, or in time series analysis they may simply show a chance correlation with income due to sampling error.

Some of these variables show more substantial variation in the cross section than over time and so distort cross-section estimates of income effects more seriously than time series estimates. Others may show greater variation over time than in the cross section. Many, like standard of living, availability of credit, level of asset holdings, occupational distribution of income, or even the distribution of income by age, education, or city size, show substantial variation both among income groups at a point of time and in the aggregate over any extended period of time. However, the joint distribution of these factors with income may be quite different in the two cases; so we cannot assume stability of bias as we move from one type of data to the other. For example, in the next few years a rise in income is expected to coincide with a reduction in the relative importance of the middle age group—not at all what is found in the cross section.

If an attempt is to be made to reduce bias in the estimate of the income coefficient by introducing some other relevant variables into the regression, there are several reasons for preferring to work with cross-section data for this purpose. In the first place recent cross-section studies make information available on a large number of these other variables, whereas aggregate data may be unavailable over any long time period. Secondly, many candidates for inclusion probably show much greater variance cross-sectionally than over time. While this is a disadvantage of cross-section data in that it exaggerates the bias in a two-variable regression, it becomes an advantage in attempting to measure accurately the separate influence of the secondary variables and thus to distinguish their influence from that of income. Finally, there are, of course, many more degrees of freedom to work with in the cross section.

When family size, age, region and city size, liquid asset holdings, value of owned home, and income change–income expectation pattern are explicitly taken into account, a somewhat lower estimate of the marginal propensity to consume is obtained from the 1950 BLS data than when income is the sole explanatory variable. For white employee families in the income range $1,000 to $10,000 the marginal propensity drops from 0.80 to 0.71 with the inclusion of these variables.[7] The inclusion of the income change variable probably causes the decline to be smaller than it would otherwise be, since values of this variable which tend to be associated with high consumption generally are associated with low income, so that its inclusion in the regression should tend to raise rather than lower the income slope.

"NORMAL" VERSUS ACTUAL INCOME IN THE CROSS SECTION

A third source of bias may lie in the lack of homogeneity of the income variable itself. For example, it may be true that deviations of current income from whatever the consumer unit considers to be "normal" at a given point of time have different—presumably smaller —effects on consumption than "normal" income. As Friedman, Modigliani and Brumberg, Reid, and others have pointed out, there are good reasons to believe that this is so.[8] In this case, assuming the two income components to be uncorrelated, the marginal propensity yielded by a regression of consumption against actual income will be a weighted average of the effects of the two components, with weights depending on their relative variance, and will therefore provide a biased estimate of either effect.[9]

When variables other than income are added to the regression, the

[7] See Jean Crockett and Irwin Friend, "A Complete Set of Consumer Demand Relationships," *Proceedings of the Conference on Consumption and Saving*, ed. Irwin Friend and Robert Jones, Philadelphia, 1960, I, 38.

[8] The term "normal" income is used in this paper, in preference to the Friedman term "permanent" income, to disassociate the concept from certain rigid assumptions made by Friedman and not implied here. Also, any nonrecurring income item would be considered a deviation from "normal" income here, though Friedman might consider some part of such items as "permanent" income.

[9] Let $C = a + bY_N + cY_T + u$, where C is consumption; Y_N, normal income; Y_T, the deviation of actual from normal income, which is assumed to be uncorrelated

weight of the normal component will be decreased if these variables are correlated with normal income and increased if they are correlated with deviations from normal income.[10] Thus, the introduction of such variables as age and family size, which we would expect to be correlated with the former rather than the latter, has two results. While it eliminates the bias which arises when the effects of family size, etc., are erroneously assigned to income, at the same time it pushes the income coefficient closer to an estimate of the effect of the deviational (or transitory) component. If we are primarily interested in the effect of the normal component, use of nonincome variables may simply eliminate one of the two offsetting biases and leave the results worse than before.

There does not seem to be any satisfactory way of obtaining unbiased estimates of the two income effects from the kind of cross-sectional information now available. If Friedman's hypothesis is accepted that the effect of transitory income is zero and, further, that mean transitory income is also zero, then it is indeed possible to obtain an unbiased estimate of the effect of permanent income, as he has shown.[11] It may be noted that if consumer units are assumed to define their permanent income in terms of a three-year average of actual income, then one-third of any nonrecurring income item would be defined as permanent income and two-thirds as transitory income. Effectively, then, such nonrecurring income would have one-third the influence on consumption of normal income. Intuitively, such a figure does not seem unreasonable, but I feel strongly that this should be a matter for empirical determination rather than determination by hypothesis.

Another approach which is sometimes used is to group consumer units according to some characteristic believed to be correlated with permanent income. Assuming that transitory income averages out to zero within groups, a regression of mean consumption against mean

---

with normal income; and u, a random residual uncorrelated with either Y_N or Y_T. Then a regression of consumption against actual income yields the slope coefficient $b = \sigma_{CY}/\sigma_Y^2 = (b\sigma_{Y_N Y} + c\sigma_{Y_T Y} + \sigma_{uY})/\sigma_Y^2$, where σ_{CY} is the covariance of C and Y. Since $Y = Y_N + Y_T$, and $\sigma_{Y_N Y_T} = \sigma_{uY} = 0$ in a sufficiently large sample,

$$b = (b\sigma_{Y_N}^2 + c\sigma_{Y_T}^2)/(\sigma_{Y_N}^2 + \sigma_{Y_T}^2)$$
$$= [b\sigma_{Y_N}^2/(\sigma_{Y_N}^2 + \sigma_{Y_T}^2)] + [c\sigma_{Y_T}^2/(\sigma_{Y_N}^2 + \sigma_{Y_T}^2)].$$

[10] For proof see Jean Crockett, "Biases in Estimating Income-Expenditure Regressions from Cross Section Data," *Proceedings of the Conference on Consumption and Saving*, II, 214–215.

[11] Milton Friedman, *A Theory of the Consumption Function*, Princeton for NBER, 1957, p. 33.

income is then computed, with each group treated as a single observation. This is satisfactory only if the characteristic used for grouping has no effect on consumption in its own right and is uncorrelated with any characteristic (except, of course, permanent income) which does have such an effect.[12] While it is conceivable that an unbiased estimate of the effect of permanent income might be obtained in this way, it is extremely difficult in practice to find a grouping variable which clearly meets the requirements.

The income change–income expectation variable available in the BLS 1950 study permits certain inferences to be drawn as to the direction of deviations from normal income. For example, if a family reported that current income was higher than in the previous year and also higher than that expected in the following year, there is some presumption that family income was above normal, though there is no way of determining the size of the deviation. Similarly, if current income is reported to be below both the previous year's income and the following year's expected income, then there is a presumption that the transitory component is negative. Except for these two rather small groups, however, the inferences are far from clear. While for some families no change in income over the three-year period might signify that current income was approximately "normal," for others the normal pattern may be a continuing rise in income, while for some in the higher age brackets a continuing decline might be considered normal.[13] Furthermore, it is entirely possible that the expected income change indicates more about personal tendencies toward optimism or conservatism than any serious attempt at prediction.

What is needed is some empirical basis for separating the two types of income, so that they may be separately introduced into the consumption function. Relevant information might be derived from continuous cross sections, involving reinterviews of the same families, or even from a single cross-section study which investigated income history and perhaps family attitudes toward specific components of current income.

---

[12] See Crockett, p. 220, for a discussion of the bias which arises from this technique when the grouping variable has an independent effect on consumption.

[13] The group of families with constant three-year income has been analyzed by Irwin Friend and Irving B. Kravis, who find the income slope for these families to be insignificantly different from that for all families, though consumption levels are lower (see "Consumption Patterns and Permanent Income," *American Economic Review*, May 1957, pp. 536–555).

One nonrecurring income item was reported in the 1950 BLS Consumer Survey—the National Service Life Insurance dividend paid to veterans in that year—and its influence on consumption has been studied by Ronald Bodkin.[14] Bodkin finds no significant difference between the effect on consumption of this element of income and that of the remainder of income.[15] However, this finding, while extremely interesting, cannot be considered conclusive evidence as to the relative magnitudes of normal and transitory income effects, for a number of reasons. Bodkin's analysis necessarily deals with an incomplete measure of transitory income, and it cannot be certain that all components of income which may be considered transitory have precisely the same effect. It covers a somewhat abnormal period— the beginning of the Korean War—in which motives for spending may have been unusually high, with incomes initially a little depressed as a result of the 1949 recession, but with strong expectations of rising income, and some tendency to stockpile consumer durables and perhaps other items. The families covered were not, in a number of respects, representative of the entire population. And most important, only the effect of positive deviations from normal income is tested, while a priori arguments and time series evidence are most convincing in the case of negative deviations.

NORMAL VERSUS ACTUAL INCOME IN AGGREGATE TIME SERIES

There is no reason to believe that by turning to time series we may avoid the problems arising from the differential effects on consumption of various components of income. In this context, deviations from normal income take on a somewhat different meaning than in the cross section. Many of the types of deviations from normal income which are important in the cross section average out in the aggregate, and what is left is mainly the result of cyclical variations in entrepreneurial income and employment. Thus, the problem of measuring separately the effect of the normal and the deviation components of income becomes essentially the problem of distinguishing the effects of secular changes in income from the effects of cyclical changes; and it would, of course, be quite useful to be able to do this. It should be noted, however, that the effect of cyclical deviations from

[14] Ronald Bodkin, "Windfall Income and Consumption," *Proceedings of the Conference on Consumption and Saving*, II, 175–187.

[15] In fact, the partial regression coefficient obtained for the insurance dividend is higher than for income excluding the dividend, though not significantly so.

normal income is not necessarily the same as the effect of other types of deviations important in the cross section.

If we examine the time series regression of aggregate consumption, or more particularly its nondurables plus services component, against aggregate disposable income, we observe at once that in such recession or depression years as 1960, 1958, 1949, 1947, 1938, and 1932–34, consumption is unduly high relative to income.[16] Since it is highly probable that consumers on the average felt their income to be below normal in these periods, such a finding is consistent with the belief that the normal component of income has a larger effect on consumption than do cyclical deviations from normal income. Also, consumption tends to fall below the regression, at least when consumer durables are excluded, in 1941 (most notably), 1955–56, 1953, 1950, and 1929,[17] years when consumers may well have felt themselves to be somewhat above their normal income, though the whole concept of normal income becomes rather tenuous in reference to a period like the second half of the thirties and the early forties. Consumption was also low in 1936–37 and 1940, when there is a somewhat weaker presumption that income was above the level then conceived of as normal.

Much of the variation in time series estimates of marginal propensities also may be explained in terms of differential effects of the two income components. When periods like 1929–40 or 1923–40 are considered, a high proportion of the total variance of income is due to the cyclical component, and the income coefficient obtained may therefore be expected to move in the direction of the transitory income effect. In such periods as 1923–30, 1935–40 or 1929–41, 1946–60, the relative importance of the cyclical component in accounting for total income variance is reduced, and the effect of the normal component thus receives a heavier weight in the income coefficient obtained.

It should be pointed out that a number of other plausible explanations have been put forward for the tendency of consumption to lie above the regression line in recession years: a simple lag in adjusting consumption downward as income falls; the continuing influence on consumption of a previously established standard of living (i.e., the

---

[16] I refer specifically to regressions obtained for the period 1929–41, 1946–60, using real per capita variables (see equations 13 and 14 in the Appendix). For 1958 consumption of nondurables plus services is high, but not total consumption.

[17] This is no longer true of 1955, 1953, and 1950 when consumer durables are included.

notion that the consumption function continually shifts upward with each rise in the level of consumption attained);[18] an occupational redistribution of income at the expense of the entrepreneurial group with its relatively high savings propensities, though there is little empirical evidence of such a cyclical redistribution in the postwar period.[19] There may well be some validity in all of these.

The pure-lag explanation would suggest the introduction of the previous year's income or an income change variable into the regression or the use of some average of previous and current year's income. The income change variable may also be taken as an estimate of deviation from normal income if it is assumed that concepts of this year's normal income are largely determined by last year's actual income. However, this approach is relatively unsatisfactory in explaining why consumption falls above the regression line in years like 1934 and 1959, when income was rising, as well as in years like 1932 and 1938, when income was falling sharply.

The explanation in terms of redistribution of income by occupation would suggest the separate introduction of entrepreneurial income into the regression, as has been done by Friend and by Klein and Goldberger.[20] But it should be noted that the differences in savings propensities between entrepreneurs and others may be largely a reflection of the greater variance of the transitory or deviational component of income among the entrepreneurs. Thus, when wage income is separated from entrepreneurial income the normal component may become more important in explaining the total variance of the former, and less important in explaining the total variance of the latter, than when both types of income are combined. If so, the coefficient of wage income may be expected to approach more closely a measure of the effect of the normal component and the coefficient of entrepreneurial income to move toward a measure of the effect of deviations from normal. However, since both types of income still contain both components to a substantial degree, we can hardly expect to

[18] See James S. Duesenberry, *Income, Saving, and the Theory of Consumer Behavior*, Cambridge, Mass., 1949, Chap. 5; Franco Modigliani, "Fluctuations in the Saving-Income Ratio: A Problem in Economic Forecasting," *Studies in Income and Wealth*, Vol. 11, New York, NBER, 1949, pp. 371–443.

[19] Proprietors' income as a percentage of national income shows a downward trend throughout the postwar period, declining more sharply than usual in 1947, 1949, and 1953, largely because of the drop in farm income. In 1958, however, it actually rises because of a large increase in farm income.

[20] Irwin Friend, with the assistance of Vito Natrella, *Individual Savings: Volume and Composition*, New York, 1954, p. 142; Lawrence R. Klein and A. S. Goldberger, *An Econometric Model of the United States, 1929–1952*, Amsterdam, 1955, p. 51.

obtain in this way unbiased estimates of either. Furthermore, there are probably other important reasons for the savings preferences of entrepreneurs; and since these as well as the peculiarities of the income mix will affect the coefficient obtained for entrepreneurial income, this coefficient cannot be treated in any sense as an approximation to the transitory income effect.

The upward shifts in the consumption function as standards of living rise are perhaps quite important sources of bias in time series estimates of marginal propensities, but their effect is rather complicated. The rise in the standard of living occurs not only because higher levels of consumption are continually being attained, and once attained tend to alter tastes, but also—and perhaps more important—because the availability of consumption opportunities is continually being increased with the introduction of new products. The second effect may be represented reasonably well by a time trend, and in periods of normal income growth the first effect may also be approximated by such a trend. The introduction of a time trend into the consumption-income regression reduces the marginal propensity substantially in periods when income is highly correlated with time, though only slightly in other periods. Ferber finds a drop from 0.93 to 0.88 in his real per capita relationship for the period 1923–30, 1935–40, as compared with drops from 0.78 or 0.79 to 0.77 in periods more heavily affected by the depression years.

Thus the standard-of-living effect, unless explicitly taken into account, pushes up consumption for high levels of normal income, since this component rises over time, and imparts an upward bias to the income coefficient when income variance is largely due to the permanent component. On the other hand, when income variance largely reflects cyclical factors, the standard-of-living effect is to push up consumption at low, though not at high, incomes and thus impart a downward bias to the income coefficient. It is difficult to devise a critical test to distinguish between (1) the hypothesis that consumption is high (relative to income) in recession because normal income is above actual income and (2) the hypothesis that consumption is high because of the effect on tastes of consumption levels attained in the preceding period of prosperity. There are very few cases where consumption is below its previous peak without income at the same time being somewhat below normal. The immediate postwar years of 1946 and 1948 are perhaps such an instance; but here the issue is hopelessly confused by such other factors as consumer reaction after a long period of artificial wartime restraints and the abnormally high level of consumer liquidity. However, the standard-of-living effect (as distinct from a pure-lag effect) is not helpful in explaining why the consumption of nondurables and services lies below the regression in a number of highly prosperous years; and some kind of normal or permanent income hypothesis is more useful here.

My own over-all preference lies with the hypothesis based on differential effects of the two income components, partly because I feel that it offers a slightly better explanation than any of the others of deviations from the aggregate consumption-income regression, and partly because it offers a much better explanation of the differences between time series and cross-section coefficients, with the latter reduced by the greater variance of transitory income in the cross section. This hypothesis does fail, however, to explain one point Why is it that consumption is not much higher relative to income in the years of deep depression, when (at least viewed from hindsight) actual income was vastly below normal, than in such years as 1960, 1958, and 1949, when the deviations from normal were much smaller? In part, this could mean that consumers' concepts of normality had shifted downward drastically by, say, 1932, though it is hard to explain 1930 or even 1931 (which actually lie below the regression) in these terms. In part, the purely mechanical explanation applies that the depression years themselves largely set the low end of the regression and so cannot greatly depart from it. In part, it may be that while small negative deviations from normal income are largely smoothed out in their effects on consumption, this is no longer true for large deviations. In other words, the effect of transitory income need not be linear and may approach the effect of the normal component for very large negative values, if only because asset and credit resources for consuming in excess of income are limited. This line of reasoning suggests that the size of asset holdings in relation to the size of negative income deviations conditions the effect of such deviations. A second kind of asset effect may also be significant in the early thirties. This is one of very few cases of really significant shifts in aggregate asset position over a short period of time. It seems inconceivable that the loss of homes through foreclosure and of bank accounts through bank failures, to say nothing of stock market losses and defaulted bonds, can fail to have had powerful effects in depressing consumption below what it would otherwise have been.

It is my conclusion that an adequate explanation of this period can only be obtained by disentangling the income mix effect from two types of asset effects: (1) a permissive effect which enables consumers to spend in excess of current income, when they wish to do so either because current income is below normal or for other reasons; and (2) an asset disequilibrium effect resulting from deviations of the actual level of assets from the level considered to be appropriate.

OMITTED VARIABLES CORRELATED WITH ASSET HOLDINGS

With respect to the measurement of asset effects on consumption, the record of cross-section data is even less promising than in the case of income effects. Two asset items were studied in connection with the 1950 BLS data—liquid assets and value of owned home. While high-asset families clearly spent substantially more at low incomes than did low-asset families (due in part no doubt to their presumably higher levels of permanent income), the situation was reversed at high incomes for certain types of consumption items and, within certain subgroups of families, for total consumption. Furthermore, if income is held constant, the effect of liquid assets sometimes appears to be parabolic.

These strange findings presumably arise from a failure to hold savings preferences constant. To a considerable degree, persons with high assets (particularly those with high assets in relation to income) are persons who *want* to have high assets because their taste for accumulating assets is relatively strong. Thus, by selecting a high-asset group, in effect we select "high savers." The downward pressure on consumption exerted by this trait tends to conceal the upward pressure which large asset holdings should exert for given savings preferences.

To the extent that consumer units are "high savers" or "low savers" by reason of their life-cycle status or their occupational stability of income or locational or racial limitations on consumption opportunities, this problem may be handled by including in the regression such variables as family type, occupation, race, and city size. However, it seems clear that substantial differences among families remain even after all these factors are taken into account. It is this residue, related to such considerations as attitudes toward uncertainty and degree of preference for current over future consumption, which I shall refer to as differences in savings preferences; and with current techniques they are not, for practical purposes, measurable. However, continuous cross sections would permit them to be held constant; and thus, an improved estimate of asset effects could be reached, if it can be assumed that these preferences are fairly constant over time. While an experience like the Great Depression may have shifted quite a few savings propensities, and while there seems to have been a reverse shift in the postwar period, still we may hope for considerable stability over short and relatively normal periods, and in this case continuous cross sections may be of real assistance.

A further difficulty in measuring cross-section asset effects arises because families with high assets in relation to income sometimes may be, not high savers, but persons suffering negative deviations from normal income.[21] The high consumption of such persons (relative to income) may reflect the deviation of actual from normal income, rather than asset position, or it may be a result of the interaction of the two effects, which is probably much more powerful than the sum of the two taken individually. High assets in the absence of the motivation provided by negative deviations from normal income may have a fairly small tendency to increase consumption, while an income mix involving negative transitory income may do little to raise consumption (relative to actual income) in the absence of means to finance dissaving. However, the coincidence of high assets, particularly liquid assets, and negative transitory income may have powerful effects.

Thus, we are led again to consider two types of asset effects: a permissive effect, which becomes much more important in the presence of negative transitory income and so cannot be properly estimated until this interaction is taken into account; and an independent causal or motivating effect, which occurs only in the presence of asset disequilibrium and cannot be properly estimated until savings propensities can be measured, or at least held relatively constant. Until this can be done, high assets are at least as likely to imply high savings preferences, which are conducive to relatively low consumption, as they are to imply an asset disequilibrium favorable to high consumption.

The concept of asset equilibrium or disequilibrium perhaps needs

[21] A third difficulty may be mentioned for completeness. This arises from the possibility of two-way causation between consumption and liquid asset holdings—i.e., liquid assets may have been accumulated with the intention of purchasing consumer durables or with the intention of making a downpayment on a house. While the purchase of a house is not in itself consumption, it may well be associated with certain abnormal consumption expenditures. Questions on purchase intentions may be useful in identifying such cases.

a little further clarification. It is assumed here that each family has some idea of the level of assets which it considers appropriate in view of its level of income (presumably normal income), life-cycle status, and savings preferences. The marginal utility of acquiring a dollar of assets, which must, of course, be balanced against the marginal utility of a dollar of consumption, will depend on the gap between the actual and equilibrium level of assets, being relatively high when actual assets are below desired assets and relatively low when actual assets are above desired assets. Thus, an excess of assets will be used up in raising consumption levels, presumably over several years, while an asset shortage will gradually be made up by lowering consumption levels over a period of time.

For individual consumers such asset disequilibriums may occur for a number of reasons—for instance, inheritances, business losses, changes in the market value of assets, the dissipation of assets in periods of abnormally low income or abnormally high consumption needs, recent changes in normal income to which asset position has not yet become adjusted, or asset buildups due to artificial restraints on consumption, as during the war. In the aggregate, asset disequilibriums of substantial proportions are much less likely to occur.

It is the conclusion of this section that with current techniques income effects cannot be accurately estimated, either in the cross section or in the aggregate, because the two income components cannot be separated. We are, therefore, unable to estimate the permissive effect of assets, since this is dependent (particularly in the aggregate, but also in the cross section) on the income mix. Finally, the effect of asset disequilibriums cannot be accurately estimated in the cross section, where they are relatively frequent, because savings preferences cannot be held constant, and in the aggregate because they so rarely occur and perhaps also because aggregate savings preferences may sometimes change. There is good reason to believe that continuous cross-section data may help us, at least to some extent, with all of these problems.

A Suggested Model of Consumer Behavior

The considerations of the previous section lend interest to the following microeconomic model of consumer behavior:

$$C = a' + b'Y_N + cY_T + d(A - \overline{A}) + u'$$

or

$$C = a' + b'Y_N + c(A, Y_N)Y_T + d(A - \overline{A}) + u',$$

114

where C is consumption, Y_N is normal income, Y_T is the deviation of actual from normal income, A is the actual level of asset holdings, $\overline{A}$ the desired level, and u a random residual. The coefficients of these variables are constants, except in the case of negative transitory income, when c is a (decreasing) function of assets and perhaps permanent income.

The linear form is chosen partly for simplicity of exposition and partly because it was found in analyzing the 1950 data that when extreme income classes are eliminated and certain family characteristics—notably assets and occupation—are held constant, the linear form generally provides a reasonable approximation to the data.[22] For purposes of this discussion I shall neglect the effects of family size and other readily measurable characteristics affecting consumption. At the microeconomic level they are easily handled by inserting additional variables in the regression. In the aggregate, the distribution of these variables ordinarily remains relatively constant over short periods of time, say, five or ten years (and remains entirely constant if we wish to consider different hypothetical levels of aggregate income at a given point of time).

If we make the reasonable assumption that $\overline{A}$, the desired level of assets, is a function of normal income, say, a stochastic linear function

$$\overline{A} = j + k Y_N + v,$$

the above relation becomes

$$C = a + b Y_N + c Y_T + dA + u$$

where $a = a' - dj$
  $b = b' - dk$
  $u = u' - dv$

For certain consumer units (high savers) both j and k will be higher than for other units (low savers); so a and b will be relatively low for high savers.

If, for simplicity, it is further assumed that c is a decreasing linear function of assets and normal income when income falls below normal, so that

$$c(A, Y_N) = c' - c''A - c'''Y_N,$$

we obtain

$$C = a + b Y_N + c' Y_T - c''A Y_T - c'''Y_N Y_T + dA + u$$

[22] See Crockett and Friend, pp. 8–10.

for families below normal income. The role of both cross-product terms is, of course, to express the permissive effect of assets or of high normal income in financing consumption levels which are high relative to actual income. At low levels of Y_N, where saving is ordinarily small, assets or the availability of credit are required to maintain consumption when Y_T is negative. At high levels of Y_N, where saving is ordinarily substantial, consumption may be maintained simply by reducing savings when actual income is not too far below normal. Thus, the savings cushion, which exists at high levels of normal income, plays much the same permissive role as assets in moderating the effect on consumption of negative deviations from normal income.

The above considerations lead to the presumption that distinctly different patterns of consumer behavior occur in the following situations: (1) transitory income greater than or equal to zero, combined with high savings preferences; (2) transitory income greater than or equal to zero, combined with low savings preferences; (3) negative transitory income combined with high savings preferences; and (4) negative transitory income combined with low savings preferences. Since savings preferences are presumably a continuum, finer savings classes could be distinguished, if desired, but for present purposes I have confined myself to two classes only. If it is assumed that within the above four categories (or some extended group of categories) consumer behavior is essentially similar—i.e., the same values of the parameters apply—we may aggregate within these categories. We have then for the four groups the following relationships, where the variables now stand for group means:

1. $C = a_1 + b_1 Y_N + c Y_T + dA$
2      $C = a_2 + b_2 Y_N + c Y_T + dA$
3. $C = a_1 + b_1 Y_N + c' Y_T - c'' A Y_T - c''' Y_N Y_T + dA$
4. $C = a_2 + b_2 Y_N + c' Y_T - c'' A Y_T - c''' Y_N Y_T + dA.$

Note that $a_1 < a_2$ and $b_1 < b_2$ It is also possible that c, c', and d may differ as between groups 1 and 2 and groups 3 and 4; but there is no compelling reason to assume this in advance.

If the above model in fact represents a reasonable rough approximation to reality, then the ideal procedure would be to estimate the parameters from cross-section regressions for each group separately, insert the appropriate values of the explanatory variables for each group, and aggregate by applying weights based on the number of families in each group and adding.

While it is likely to be a long time before accurate measures of savings preferences and of the normal and transitory components of income are obtained, either from continuous cross-section data or other sources, it is not too much to hope that ways may be found to separate families into the four groups discussed above, or preferably into six groups, with cases of very small transitory income segregated from cases where deviations from normal income are significantly positive or significantly negative. Since the income mix within each group is then fairly stable, separate regressions may be fitted within each group, using actual income and assets as explanatory variables:

$$C = a_i + b_i Y + d_i A.$$

Aggregate consumption may then be treated as a function of aggregate income and aggregate assets, where each coefficient is a weighted average of the corresponding coefficients for individual groups, the weights depending on the relative importance of the groups, in terms of the number of families and the proportion of aggregate income and aggregate asset holdings represented by each. Since the suggested method omits interaction terms in the regressions actually computed even for groups with income below normal, larger asset effects may be expected for these groups than others,[23] as well as different income effects.

While the relative importance of high and low savers may remain fairly stable over short periods, cyclical variability in the relative importance of families above and below normal income may be expected, causing variation in the aggregate coefficients of both income and assets. Determining the appropriate weights to apply in a particular situation is a ticklish problem at the moment, but one with which continuous cross sections may help by permitting the development of cyclical patterns in the relative importance of the various groups. So long as mean income and mean assets vary in about the same way for all groups over time, the major problem is to determine the proportion of families assigned to each group at various time points.

The income coefficients obtained within each group are still, of course, weighted averages of the effects of normal and transitory in-

---

[23] Under appropriate assumptions, the asset coefficient becomes $d - c'' Y_T$, where Y_T is mean transitory income for the group and is, of course, negative.

come. However, the variance of transitory income is greatly reduced relative to that of normal income. More important, if the groups are defined by restricting the ratio of transitory to normal income, the relative variance of the two types of income will be much the same in the cross section as in time series movements of group aggregates. The cross-section regression will then provide a reasonably good estimate of time series movements of group consumption in response to changes in group income. If, within a given group, mean transitory income represents the same proportion of mean normal income for all income classes in the cross section and also for all variations in aggregate group income over time, then the cross-section regression based on grouped data would be entirely adequate for time series purposes. While this assumption may hold approximately true in the cross section for groups at or above normal income (and for all groups over time, to the extent that changes in group income simply represent changes in the number of families assigned to each group), it is less realistic for groups below normal income in the cross section.[24] Furthermore, unless a finer breakdown by transitory income is used than that contemplated here, a recession may involve a decline in mean transitory income within groups, as well as a redistribution of families among groups, and this will cause the relative weights of the two income effects to be different over time than in the cross section, weakening the relevance of the cross-section relation for estimating aggregate consumption.

From the model certain inferences can be drawn as to the relationship of the income and other coefficients among the six regressions. These are of some interest in themselves, and they may then be tested to some extent against available data. We have already observed that income slopes should be steeper for low savers than for high savers with comparable income mix and that the constant term should also be higher. For given savings preferences, I now compare groups whose transitory income is significantly positive, close to zero (say, less than 5 per cent of normal income), and significantly negative. If we can assume that within each group the breakdown between normal and transitory income is about the same in all income brackets, then it follows that the group with incomes above normal will show a lower income slope than the group with normal income, while the group with income below normal will show a higher slope. Under this assumption, for each family in the group with $Y_T > 0$

[24] See the discussion of this point below.

$$Y_T = mY_N + w$$
$$Y = Y_N + Y_T = (1 + m)Y_N + w,$$

while for families in the group for which $Y_T < 0$

$$Y_T = -nY_N + w$$
$$Y = (1 - n)Y_N + w,$$

where m and n are positive and w is a random residual uncorrelated with Y. Ignoring interaction terms for the moment, the following microeconomic relations are obtained for the three groups:

1. $Y_T > 0$: $C = a + bY_N + cmY_N + dA + \epsilon$
   $$= a + [(b + cm)Y/(1 + m)] + dA + \epsilon'$$
   $$= a + \{b - [(b - c)m/(1 + m)]\}Y + dA + \epsilon'$$
2. $Y_T = 0$: $C = a + bY_N + dA + u$
   $$= a + bY + dA + u$$
3. $Y_T < 0$: $C = a + bY_N - c'nY_N + dA + \epsilon''$
   $$= a + [(b - c'n)Y/(1 - n)] + dA + \epsilon'''$$
   $$= a + \{b + [(b - c')n/(1 - n)]\}Y + dA + \epsilon'''.$$

Here ϵ, ϵ', ϵ'', and ϵ''' are all linear functions of u and w and so, uncorrelated with Y. Thus, under the reasonable assumptions that both c and c' are less than b and $Y > 0$, so that $n < 1$, the coefficient of income obtained in a regression of consumption against actual income and assets for the first group, is an estimate of $b - [(b - c)m/(1 + m)]$, which must be less than b. When such a regression is fitted for the third group, the coefficient obtained for actual income is an estimate of $b + [(b - c')n/(1 - n)]$, and therefore greater than b. If we now consider the effect of the omitted interaction term $-c'''Y_N Y_T$ on the income coefficient obtained for the third group, the latter conclusion is strengthened, since this term pushes up consumption by an amount which in all probability rises as actual income rises.

While it is reasonable to assume a constant relation of Y_T to Y_N for each income bracket in the first group, where both terms are positive, this is not so in the third group, where Y_T is negative. Variation in the relationship is, of course, limited by the group requirement that Y_T (in absolute value) exceed a certain percentage of Y_N. Still we may expect the relative importance of Y_T to decline as Y rises, because for the sum of a positive and a negative component we find that large values of the positive component and numerically small values of the negative component are both conducive to large values of the sum. Our expectation of a high income slope for the group below normal income is therefore weakened. With respect to the low income slope expected in the group above normal income there is no similar reservation.

The interaction term $-c''AY_T$ tends, as I have already indicated, to increase the asset slope obtained in fitting a regression of the form $C = a + bY + dA$ to the third group, since it adds to consumption a positive amount which rises as assets rise.

While it is not possible on the basis of the 1950 BLS data to separate families according to savings preferences, an attempt has been made to distinguish three groups for which some inference can be drawn as to transitory income. The first group, which reported 1950 income as above both 1949 income and expected 1951 income, was presumed to be above normal income. This is not necessarily true, of course. Their normal pattern may have involved continually rising income, but they may have had some reason to expect below-normal income in 1951. The second group, which was assumed to be close to normal income, contained families reporting their 1950 income to be the same as both their 1949 income and their expected 1951 income and also families with 1950 income above 1949 income and expecting a further rise in 1951. These two components of group 2 showed generally similar behavior, and by combining them erratic fluctuations were reduced. The third group, which reported 1950 income as below both 1949 income and expected 1951 income, was assumed to be below normal income. Again, this is not necessarily true, since 1949 income might have been abnormally high, while the expected increase in 1951 may have represented normal income growth or simply an optimistic temperament. Thus, the device used for forming the groups is admittedly an imperfect one.

Within each group weighted linear regressions of consumption on income were fitted to grouped data for white employee families in the income range $1,000 to $10,000, with family size less than ten. No attempt was made to include assets in the regression, since the asset coefficient was not expected to be meaningful without separation of high from low savers. However, separate regressions were computed for families with low liquid assets (cash and deposits less than $500) and for families with higher liquid assets. For the high-cash families, groups 1 and 3 each contained only about 100 families;

so substantial sampling error may be expected. In all other cases, the number of families exceeded 250. The following marginal propensities were obtained.[25]

	Low Liquid Assets	High Liquid Assets
Income above normal	.806	.609
Normal income	.874	.799
Income below normal	.907	.911

We observe that for both asset classes the first group—families above their normal income—clearly has a lower marginal propensity than the second group, for which income is presumably close to normal. This is as expected. However, for the third group—families below normal income—the marginal propensity is only slightly larger than for the second when assets are low; and while it is much larger when assets are high, this result is suspect because the regression is based on a small number of observations and because the slope is considerably influenced by one extreme observation.[26]

When assets are low, there is little difference in level among the three groups at low incomes, though the third group (below normal income) rises above the other two at high incomes. When assets are high, however, consumption levels are higher throughout the entire income range for families below normal income than for families close to normal income. This tends to confirm the importance of the interaction between assets and transitory income for this group. An unexpected result is that at low income levels, high-asset families above their normal income also consume more than those in the normal group. It appears that at low incomes the high initial cash position, in conjunction with positive transitory income, is peculiarly conducive to purchases of consumer durables. Durables expenditures run much higher for this group than for the high-asset normal income group at incomes up to $5,000. The difference runs as high as $300 per family in the income range $2,000–$4,000.

When family size is included as an additional variable in each of the six regressions marginal propensities are lowered, but the general pattern remains much the same. However, for low-asset families, the discrepancy is widened between families with normal and those with

---

[25] See equations 16a–16c and 17a–17c in the Appendix.
[26] When one family is omitted the marginal propensity drops to 0.858.

below-normal income, while families with income above normal move closer to the normal group.[27]

It will also be observed that marginal propensities are substantially lower for high-asset than for low-asset families within a given group, except the third (and even here, too, if one extreme observation is omitted). This is in agreement with other results obtained from the 1950 data. For example, linear regressions that are fitted to un-grouped data for white employee homeowners in the income range $1,000 to $10,000, and that relate consumption to income and to dummy variables reflecting family size, age of head, income change–income expectation pattern, and several other family characteristics, yielded the following marginal propensities for different asset groups:

Asset Group	Marginal Propensity	Standard Error
Low cash and deposits, low value of house	.812	.018
Low cash and deposits, high value of house	.691	.029
High cash and deposits, low value of house	.690	.030
High cash and deposits, high value of house	.571	.033

There are, of course, several reasons for expecting lower income slopes for the high-asset groups: (1) At low incomes (though not at high) the possession of high assets creates some presumption that families are below normal income. While my attempt to segregate such families on the basis of their income change–income expectation pattern may reduce the importance of this consideration, it is not likely to eliminate it entirely. (2) At low incomes (though not at high) the possession of high assets creates some presumption of an asset disequilibrium favorable to consumption. (3) At low incomes, assets are more important than at high incomes as a permissive factor enabling families to achieve high consumption relative to current in-

---

[27] The marginal propensities, with family size held constant are

	Low Liquid Assets	High Liquid Assets
Income above normal	.759	.528
Normal income	.773	.721
Income below normal	.884	.869

The figure of 0.869 is reduced if the extreme observation mentioned in note 26 is omitted.

come, if they wish to do so either because current income is below normal or for other reasons. At high incomes the normal savings cushion serves as an alternative permissive factor, so that in general consumption may be substantially increased without touching assets. (4) High-asset groups probably contain a predominance of families with high savings preferences, and these, on the basis of the model, will have low marginal as well as low average propensities to consume.

To the extent that the first explanation is accepted, the finding (that marginal propensities are low for high-asset groups) may be taken to confirm the differential effects of the normal and transitory components of income. To the extent that the second explanation is accepted, the importance of asset disequilibriums, as distinct from asset level, is confirmed. (If asset level were the important thing the entire curve would rise as assets increase, without a change in slope.) To the extent that the third explanation is accepted the importance of the two interaction terms when income is below normal is confirmed. To the extent that the fourth explanation is accepted the correlation between high savings preferences and high asset holdings, and therefore the need to segregate families according to savings preferences in estimating asset effects, is confirmed. Thus, while several explanations of the finding may be given, each tends to confirm some aspect of the model.

An alternative device for separating families into those above, close to, and below normal income has been applied to the 1956 consumer expenditure data collected by *Life* magazine. Here families with below-average ratios of value of house to current income were taken to be above normal income, families with average ratios were taken to be close to normal income, and families with above-average ratios were taken to be below normal income. There is some reason to believe, however, that the first group may also contain a disproportionate number of low spenders and the third group a disproportionate number of high spenders, to the extent that expensive houses are conducive to high expenditures on durables, household operation, and perhaps other items. On both grounds the model would lead us to expect a low marginal propensity for the first group and a high marginal propensity for the third. Linear regressions were fitted to ungrouped data for white employee homeowners in the income range $1,000 to $10,000, relating consumption to income and to dummy variables reflecting family size, age of head, and other family characteristics. Income in this case was measured before taxes. For this and other reasons the marginal propensities are somewhat lower than for the BLS data.

	Marginal Propensity
Income above normal	
(low ratio of value of house to income)	.566
Normal income	
(average ratio of value of house to income)	.595
Income below normal	
(high ratio of value of house to income)	.852

Again the differences lie in the expected direction, but in this case, as in the case of families with low liquid assets, when family size is held constant, the income slope for the first group is not significantly lower than for the second group.

While these pieces of evidence are not in any sense conclusive, I feel that they are sufficient to indicate the desirability of attempting to group families in cross-section studies on the basis of both savings preferences and the relation of actual to normal income. I further suggest that it may be possible to develop a useful aggregate consumption function with parameters which are weighted averages of the corresponding group parameters by appropriately shifting the weight for each group in accordance with cyclical (and perhaps other) changes in its relative importance.

An Attempt to Segregate the Normal and Transitory Components of Aggregate Income

As an interim device, pending the development of cross-sectional data of the type discussed in the previous section, I have attempted to fit time series regressions of the form

$$C = a + bY_N + cY_T$$

by using an artificial procedure to separate aggregate income into the desired components. I have fitted a semilogarithmic time trend to real per capita disposable income and found a fair degree of stability for different time periods, so long as the depression years are not given too much weight. I have taken this time trend to represent normal income and have defined transitory income as the deviations from trend. While the trend may give a poor approximation to normal income in the latter half of the thirties, being perhaps somewhat above the concept of normality held by consumers at that time, I feel that it is a reasonable enough approximation at other times.[28]

The regression used was based on the period 1929–30, 1940–41, 1946–60 and is

$$\log Y = 3.13486 + .003762t,$$

with t measured in half-years and $t = 0$ at the end of 1944. The slope is very close to that obtained for the longer period 1926–30, 1936–41, 1946–60, but the slightly higher level gives a much better fit in the postwar period. The slope is intermediate between those obtained for the two postwar periods 1946–60 and 1947–60.

Consumption functions have been fitted only for the nondurables plus services component of consumption, in part because this component appears to be considerably more sensitive than consumer durables to the income mix and in part because some kind of stock variable and perhaps other variables which are not of major concern here are considered necessary to obtain a good explanation of durables expenditures. Actual income is used as one explanatory variable, rather than the time trend estimate of normal income; and transitory income, computed as the deviation of actual income from the time trend, is the second. The coefficient of actual income, Y, is then an estimate of the effect of Y_N, while the coefficient obtained for Y_T is an estimate of the difference in the two effects, $c - b$, and is therefore expected to be negative.[29]

The following regression was obtained (in 1954 dollars) for the period 1929–41, 1946–60:[30]

---

[28] My preference for this approximation to normal income over Friedman's device of a weighted average of actual income for a number of previous years is largely a matter of taste. I feel that normality is better represented by some persisting pattern of past behavior than by a mechanical average—that is, such abnormalities as the deep depression years and the war years should receive much less weight than years conforming more closely to the secular pattern.

Mincer associates normal income with that resulting from normal employment levels and, in one of his variants, approximates this, as I have done, by a long-term time trend of real per capita income (see Jacob Mincer, "Employment and Consumption," *Review of Economics and Statistics*, February 1960, pp. 24–25).

[29] This may introduce some upward bias into the estimate of b by least squares procedures, under the reasonable assumption that Y_T is more highly correlated with the consumption residual than is Y_N. However, the form used here facilitates comparison with alternative regressions.

[30] The implied effect of normal income is considerably lower and that of transitory income a little higher than those obtained by Mincer. The differences may reflect in part Mincer's inclusion of depreciation on consumer durables in the dependent variable. This presumably correlates better with the time trend of income than with deviations from the trend. In part, the differences may be due to a different choice of time trend, mine having been chosen to minimize the effect of the 1930's.

$$C_{N+S} = 104 + .752\,Y - .153\,Y_T, \quad \overline{R}^2 = .9924.$$

Comparable regressions, using disposable income only and both disposable income and change in disposable income as explanatory variables, gave slightly lower income slopes: 0.711 and 0.720, respectively. For the postwar years 1948–60 the slopes for the three regressions were 0.732, 0.708, and 0.708, with the implied effect of normal income again slightly higher than the income slopes in the other two regressions. However, the estimate of $c - b$, the difference between the two income effects, is much larger numerically, -0.458, in the postwar regression, suggesting that the higher liquid asset level after the war substantially reduced the effect of transitory income. The regression using change in disposable income yields a slightly higher correlation than that using transitory income for 1929–41 plus 1946–60, though this is no longer true of the postwar regressions. Even when the longer period is considered, the transitory-income variable performs much better than the alternative in the first half of the thirties and also slightly better in the most recent years. Its inferior over-all performance is chiefly due to very large residuals in 1941, 1946, and 1947, which may reflect some war-related factors. Of particular interest is the relative performance in years of cyclical upturns. When income rose, while remaining substantially below normal—i.e., 1934 and 1939—the regression using transitory income was markedly superior. When income rose to about normal—1948 and 1959—the transitory-income variable was still somewhat superior. In 1950 and 1955, when income rose above normal, the income change variable gave somewhat superior results.

An interaction term, taking the value $L_{-1}Y_T$ for negative Y_T and zero for positive Y_T, was next introduced, where L_{-1} represents deflated per capita liquid assets at the end of the previous year. The choice of asset variable was largely conditioned by the availability of data and is unsatisfactory in a number of respects as a proxy for total assets. Because of the substantial decline in prices after 1929, the liquid asset variable rose continuously through 1932, though it seems unlikely that total assets behaved in this way. Furthermore, there is some indication of cyclical shifts in individuals' liquid asset holdings which may simply represent portfolio switches and thus have no implications for movements in total assets. However, increasing liquidity, in itself, may well have some effect on consumption even in the absence of any change in total assets.

When both Y_T and the interaction term were used simultaneously,

126

a positive coefficient was obtained for Y_T. While this is more than offset by the large negative coefficient of the interaction term, even for minimum asset levels, when income is below normal, it is meaningless when income is above normal. When Y_T is omitted, the following regression is obtained:

$$C_{N+s} = 101 + .762Y - .000272Z; \bar{R}^2 = .9938$$

where $Z = L_{-1}Y_T$ when $Y_T < 0$ and zero otherwise.

Again, a relatively high effect is attributed to normal income, while the implied effect of negative transitory income falls below this by about 0.18 for minimum liquid asset holdings (1929) for the period and by almost three times as much for maximum holdings (1946).

Next, an attempt was made to approximate "normal" or "equilibrium" liquid asset holdings in terms of a function of normal income and time, so that the deviation of actual holdings from this norm might be introduced into the consumption regression. Equilibrium holdings, as of the beginning of the year, $(L_N)_{-1}$, were estimated from the following regression, based on the years 1929–41, 1951–60:

$$L_{-1} = -190 + .956Y_N + 6.028t; \bar{R}^2 = .984$$

where Y_N is calculated from the semilogarithmic time trend previously shown and t is measured in half-years with origin at the end of 1944. The immediate postwar years, as well as the war years, were omitted because they were obviously abnormal; if included, they greatly distorted the relationship obtained. The variable $(L - L_N)_{-1}$ was added both to the regression using transitory income and to that using income change, with the following results:

$$C = 75 + .766Y - .238Y_T + .083(L - L_N)_{-1}; \bar{R}^2 = .9961$$
$$(.014) \quad (.045) \quad (.017)$$

$$C = 163 + .716Y - .219\Delta Y + .027(L - L_N)_{-1}; \bar{R}^2 = .9958$$
$$(.009) \quad (.045) \quad (.017)$$

Again, the estimated effect of normal income is significantly higher than the marginal propensity with respect to actual income, and the effect of transitory income considerably lower than that of normal income. The inclusion of the asset variable makes the correlation coefficient virtually the same for both equations. The equation using Y_T now performs as well in 1946 and nearly as well in 1941 and 1947 as the ΔY equation. It remains superior in the first half of the thirties, though inferior in 1935–36 and in 1950. Neither of these regressions performs as well in 1959–60 as that using the interaction term involving actual assets and transitory income.

Summary

I have indicated my reasons for believing that biases exist in the ordinary time series and cross-sectional estimates of income and asset effects on consumption. In particular I have been concerned with (1) the failure to measure separately the presumably different effects of normal income and deviations from normal income, (2) the failure to distinguish between differences in asset holdings which reflect differences in desired holdings (based on income level and, perhaps, other considerations) and those which reflect asset disequilibriums, and (3) the failure to take account of interaction between asset effects and the effects of deviations from normal income.

Two approaches are suggested for obtaining more accurate estimates of consumption function parameters. The preferred approach, which should be feasible in the near future, involves cross-section analysis, with families grouped both by savings propensities and by the relationship of actual to normal income. Reasons are given for expecting income and asset effects to differ among such groups; and some empirical evidence of these differences is offered, based on admittedly imperfect grouping criteria applied to the BLS 1950 and the *Life* 1956 data. If cross-section data can be adequately grouped and regression functions estimated for the individual groups, the aggregate income and asset coefficients may be computed by weighting the corresponding coefficients for the individual groups in accordance with the relative importance of each group, and averaging.

The second approach, which is actually demonstrated in the paper, utilizes time series data and makes a crude attempt to separate the normal and transitory components of aggregate income by defining the latter as the deviation of actual income from a semilogarithmic time trend. A further crude attempt is made to estimate the deviation of actual from equilibrium liquid asset holdings. In this case, the equilibrium level is based on a linear regression of liquid assets against normal income and time. The dependent variable analyzed is the consumption of nondurables plus services. Use of the artificial transitory-income variable raises the income slope significantly, suggesting that, even for aggregate data in a period when the variance of normal income was undoubtedly very large, the effect of normal income is somewhat understated by the marginal propensity as ordinarily computed, while the effect of transitory income is only about two-thirds that of normal income. In terms of the correlations obtained, the transitory income variable, though considered preferable on theoretical grounds, performs no better than an income change variable. The deviation of actual liquid assets from the estimated equilibrium holdings performs slightly better than an interaction term involving actual liquid assets and transitory income.

Appendix: Regressions Mentioned in the Text[31]

1. 1950 BLS data, grouped by income and family size, incomes between $1,000 and $10,000:

$$\log C = .7111 + .785 \log Y + .130 \log n$$

2. 1950 BLS data, grouped by income and family size, all income classes:

$$\log C = 1.1068 + .670 \log Y + .169 \log n$$

3. 1935–36 BLS per capita data, grouped by income class, all income classes:

$$\log \frac{C}{n} = .6496 + .7391 \log \frac{Y}{n}$$

4. 1950 BLS data, grouped by income class and family size, age of head under forty, one full-time earner and no other earners:

$$\log C = .899 + .733 \log Y + .130 \log n$$

5. 1950 BLS data, grouped by income class and family size, age of head under forty, two full-time earners and no other earners:

$$\log C = .675 + .799 \log Y + .090 \log n$$

6. 1950 BLS data, grouped by income class and family size, age of head under forty, one full-time earner and one or more part-time earners:

$$\log C = .704 + .799 \log Y + .055 \log n$$

---

[31] C is family consumption, Y is family income after taxes, n is family size in all cross-section regressions. In time series regressions C_{N+S} is real per capita consumption of nondurables and services, C_D is real per capita consumption of durables, C is $C_{N+S} + C_D$, Y is real per capita disposable income, Y_T is the deviation of Y from a semilogarithmic time trend, and L_{-1} is real per capita liquid asset holdings of persons at the end of the previous year. Numbers shown in parentheses just below the regression coefficients are standard errors.

7. 1950 BLS data, grouped by income class and family size, age of head under forty, two full-time earners and one or more other earners:

$$\log C = .376 + .865 \log Y + .202 \log n$$

8. 1950 BLS data, grouped by income class and family size, age of head over forty, one full-time earner and no other earners:

$$\log C = 1.129 + .658 \log Y + .217 \log n$$

9. 1950 BLS data, grouped by income class and family size, age of head over forty, two full-time earners and no other earners:

$$\log C = .930 + .721 \log Y + .135 \log n$$

10. 1950 BLS data, grouped by income class and family size, age of head over forty, one full-time earner and one or more part-time earners:

$$\log C = .878 + .738 \log Y + .150 \log n$$

11. 1950 BLS data, grouped by income class and family size, age of head over forty, two full-time earners and one or more other earners:

$$\log C = 1.014 + .709 \log Y + .092 \log n$$

12. 1950 BLS data, grouped by income class and family size, all earner groups combined:

$$\log C = .9437 + .717 \log Y + .158 \log n$$

13. Time series data, 1929–41 and 1946–60, per capita, 1954 dollars:

$$C_{N+s} = 169 + .711 Y; \bar{r}^2 = .991$$
$$(.004)$$

14. Time series data 1929–41 and 1946–60, per capita, 1954 dollars:

$$C_D = -100 + .190 Y; \bar{r}^2 = .955$$
$$(.003)$$

15. Sum of regressions 13 and 14:

$$C = 69 + .901 Y$$

16. 1950 BLS data, grouped by income class, white employee families, incomes between $1,000 and $10,000, family size less than ten, cash and deposits less than $500:

a. 1950 income above both 1949 income and expected 1951 income

$$C = 692 + .806 Y$$

130

b. Constant or continuously rising income over the three-year period 1949–51

$$C = 367 + .874\,Y$$

c. 1950 income below both 1949 income and expected 1951 income

$$C = 438 + .907\,Y$$

17. 1950 BLS data, grouped by income class, white employee families with incomes between $1,000 and $10,000, family size less than ten, cash and deposits $500 or over:

a. 1950 income above both 1949 income and expected 1951 income

$$C = 1903 + .609\,Y$$

b. Constant or continuously rising income over the three-year period 1949–51

$$C = 813 + .799\,Y$$

c. 1950 income below both 1949 income and expected 1951 income

$$C = 870 + .911\,Y$$

18. Time series data, 1929–41 and 1946–60, per capita, 1954 dollars:

$$C_{N+S} = 104 + .752\,Y - .153\,Y_T; \quad \bar{R}^2 = .9924$$
$$\phantom{C_{N+S} = 104 +} (.020) \quad (.058)$$

19. Time series data, 1929–41 and 1946–60, per capita, 1954 dollars:

$$C_{N+S} = 161 + .720\,Y - .239\Delta Y; \quad \bar{R}^2 = .9956$$
$$\phantom{C_{N+S} = 161 +} (.003) \quad (.014)$$

20. Time series data, 1948–60, per capita, 1954 dollars:

$$C_{N+S} = 135 + .732\,Y - .458\,Y_T; \quad \bar{r}^2 = .9925$$
$$\phantom{C_{N+S} = 135 +} (.018) \quad (.090)$$

21. Time series data, 1948–60, per capita, 1954 dollars:

$$C_{N+S} = 180 + .708\,Y - .229\Delta Y; \quad \bar{r}^2 = .9838$$
$$\phantom{C_{N+S} = 180 +} (.026) \quad (.089)$$

22. Time series data, 1929–41 and 1946–60, per capita, 1954 dollars:

$$C_{N+S} = 101 + .762\,Y - .000272Z; \quad \bar{R}^2 = .9938$$
$$\phantom{C_{N+S} = 101 +} (.018) \quad (.00025)$$

where $Z = L_{-1}Y_T$ when $Y_T < 0$, and zero otherwise

131

23. Time series data, 1929–41 and 1946–60, per capita, 1954 dollars:

$$C_{N+S} = 75 + .766Y - .238Y_T + .083(L - L_N)_{-1}; \ \overline{R}^2 = .9961$$
$$\qquad (.014) \qquad (.045) \qquad (.017)$$

where $(L_N)_{-1}$ is computed from a linear regression of L_{-1} on normal income and time

24. Time series data, 1929–41 and 1946–60, per capita, 1954 dollars:

$$C_{N+S} = 163 + .716Y - .219\Delta Y + 0.27(L - L_N)_{-1}; \ \overline{R}^2 = .9958$$
$$\qquad (.009) \qquad (.045) \qquad (0.17)$$

where $(L_N)_{-1}$ is defined as in (23).

COMMENT

DANIEL B. SUITS, University of Michigan

It cannot be asserted too often that economics is a science in the same sense as physics. The immediate objective of any scientific enquiry is to develop a system of relations among observable variables that enables us to use information about one set to predict the behavior of others. The ultimate purpose may be to forecast or control behavior, or merely to provide intellectual satisfaction.

The difference between economics—or social science in general—and other sciences lies in the nature of the research techniques that can be applied. The tremendous gains of the physical sciences arise from the possibility of experimenting with one variable at a time in a controlled laboratory environment in which other factors can be closely regulated. In the laboratory world there is seldom confusion between cause and effect. There is rarely doubt as to whether observed results derive from the spurious influence of some other variable. This is not to say that mistakes cannot arise, but that when they do they are generally traceable to poor technique, rather than experimental material.

But the world of the laboratory is closed to the social scientist. He cannot pop a family into a test tube and inject a controlled dose of income, nor raise and lower the price level with a Bunsen burner. On the contrary, the economist must use observations made in the full, uncontrolled complexity of the world, in his effort to estimate relationships embedded in one of the most complex systems known. Under the circumstances, it is hardly surprising that economics has gotten no farther forward than it has, nor that we can control—

nearly to eradication—the plague of smallpox, but not the plague of unemployment.[1]

The substitute for laboratory control takes three forms: Observation and estimation can be restricted to cases in which the values of extraneous variables happen to be relatively fixed. This might be considered a kind of natural laboratory experiment. The second way is to make the estimates or observations in such fashion that the impacts of other factors are randomized and tend to average out. Finally, if neither of these can be done, measurements must be made in such a way as to take explicit account of the impacts of extraneous variables. Failure to make such explicit allowance yields results that are distorted by hidden correlations and unrecognized interactions among the independent variables.

Mrs. Crockett's excellent paper can be viewed in this light. She enumerates a number of variables that she believes have been inadequately controlled or allowed for. To assess the influence such variables may have on estimates, she attempts to control or allow for them. Her separation of families into six groups on the basis of liquid asset holdings and according to whether income is above or below "normal" constitutes a rough laboratory control. Her exploration of other groups can be similarly interpreted. Nobody—least of all Mrs. Crockett—would assert that this is tight control, but that fact only makes the group-to-group divergence in results that much more impressive; and on this score the paper is a pronounced success.

There is, however, a more fundamental problem that, while briefly mentioned in the paper, is worth more discussion than it received. In an experimental environment the concept of cause and effect has experimental meaning. One variable can be manipulated and its consequences for another observed. But in an operating social system, causality is by no means so simple. It is often multilateral, and even changes direction, depending on circumstances. For some people, or under some circumstances, the desire for more consumer goods leads to greater exertion of effort and higher income. For other people, or under other circumstances, the availability of greater income leads to greater consumption outlays. For some people, or under some circum-

---

[1] Of course, social sciences have no monopoly on this problem. For example, much of meteorology is likewise without direct access to laboratory control. It was amusing to note recently that while the performance of rockets and satellites could be forecast with enough precision to send a man into orbit and bring him safely home, the weather at Cape Canaveral could not be forecast a few hours ahead accurately enough to avoid several false starts.

stances, income and consumption standards are mutually determined by education, background, and social status. The force of this fact is clear if three broad classes of income change are contemplated:

1. Income changes naturally over the life cycle of the family. A young man begins his career at a low income and works his way up in seniority, experience, skill, and economic value. At a certain age, he quits work and his income declines to a retirement level.
2. Income changes from forces outside the control of individuals. A job is lost, or the value of service rises or declines owing to shifting demand. Injury and sickness occur. Tax laws vary. Some of these changes are temporary; some are permanent or semipermanent.
3. Income is sometimes deliberately changed. A worker moves from one job to another. The wife works or not. Overtime, vacations, and taking additional jobs permit further flexibility in income.

On the most elementary consideration it is clear that these different sources of income variation will have widely different implications for consumer behavior.

The problem of change in liquid assets and its interaction with income is probably even more severe. The meaning of liquid asset possession and its relation to the marginal propensity to consume is surely different for a family whose income is characteristically highly variable—and whose liquid asset holdings are intended to tide them over the low spots—and a family with characteristically steady income that has been saving to buy a new house, a new car, a trip around the world, or to establish or expand the family business.

In view of the complexity of the causal relationships, it is hardly surprising that measurement of the "effect" of income or liquid assets gives widely differing results, depending on the circumstances in which the measurement is made and the kind of data employed. We would do better in general, I think, to avoid the question, "What is the effect of X on Y?" in favor of the question, "Under what circumstances does X affect Y, and how does its effect vary with circumstances?"

The receipt of income and the acquisition of liquid assets are no less a *result* of human behavior than is consumption expenditure; we cannot expect to get far with a theory that treats income or liquid assets as lottery winnings, visited, willy-nilly, on the household and sweeping all behavior before it. I suspect that the best place to attack the relation of income to consumption is via a basic reformulation of the entire theory of household behavior rather than more sophisticated ways of manipulating data to explore an inadequate theory.

I am not prepared to propose such a reformulation—at least, not one that is operational—and so far as I know, neither is anybody else. There is, however, a method of allowing for the peculiarities of individual households as they affect economic relationships that goes somewhat beyond what Mrs. Crockett has done, at least in one direction. The nature of the method can best be understood by paraphrasing her model of consumer behavior. The Crockett model can be generalized as a formula

$$C = (a_0 + a_1 h + a_2 S) + (b_0 + b_1 h + b_2 S) Y_N \\ + (c_0 + c_1 h + c_2 S) Y_T + \text{(other variables, interactions, etc.)}$$

where C is family consumption expenditure, Y_N is normal income and Y_T is transitory income, h is a dummy variable that takes on the value 1 when transitory income is above zero, and S measures the thriftiness or saving attitude of the family. Mrs. Crockett's results show that the coefficients of h are negative—i.e., the marginal propensity to consume is lower for families whose incomes are above normal. Clearly, savings-oriented families should have lower consumption than others. The research procedure was to attempt to sort families into groups containing high concentrations of particular kinds of families—e.g., different levels of transitory income or different aspirations to save. The sorting was done by reference to external evidence, such as past and expected income change and ratio of assets to income.

The technique we have been experimenting with in the Research Seminar in Quantitative Economics employs a similar philosophy and model, but a different method of allowing for peculiarities of individual families, and of separating the influence of normal from transitory income. The technique requires a moving cross section of data. The analysis, which involves two stages, will be illustrated as applied to durable goods expenditure in an unpublished dissertation by Lewis Shipper. In the first stage E_{jt}, durable goods expenditure of the jth family in the tth year is fitted as a regression:

$$E_{jt} = .12 Y_{jt} - .040 Y_{jt-1} + .042 L_{jt-1} \\ \quad (.06) \quad\quad (.045) \quad\quad (.037) \\ \quad\quad\quad\quad\quad\quad - .66 D_{jt-1} + .17 S_{jt-1} + d_j + e_t \\ \quad\quad\quad\quad\quad\quad\quad (.09) \quad\quad (.04)$$

where Y = income

L = end-of-year liquid assets

D = end-of-year consumer debt

S = discretionary saving

135

Note that the latter three variables are measured as of the preceding year. In particular, the formulation indicates that the amount of current expenditures for durables varies directly with the amount of discretionary saving done the previous year. All peculiarities and correlates of the jth family are captured in the d_j terms, which are constant over time but vary over families. These terms include the impact of such factors as the normal income of the family, and its attitude toward saving; all peculiarities and correlates of the tth year are absorbed in the term e_t. The equation says, in brief, that after taking account of peculiarities of family and year, durable expenditure varies significantly with (transitory?) income, with (transitory?) saving of the preceding year and with (abnormal?) indebtedness, but does not appear to be significantly associated with (abnormal?) liquid assets. It also varies strongly with d_j, the peculiarity of the family.

The second stage of the analysis attempts to resolve the several peculiarities of the individual families by regression of the d_j on family attributes, including the averages over time of family income, liquid asset holdings, etc. The result is

$$d_j = .07(\bar{Y}_j) + 1.26(\bar{D}_{-1})_j - .012(\bar{L}_{-1})_j - .24(\bar{S}_{-1})_j$$
$$ (.04) \qquad (.10) \qquad\quad (.019) \qquad\quad (.05)$$
$$- 238P_1 - 115P_3 - 284P_4$$
$$ (99) \qquad (93) \qquad (84)$$

Here the barred variables represent family means over time. P_1, P_3, P_4 are dummy urbanization variables representing, respectively, metropolitan area, small town, medium-sized town, as compared with suburban areas.

The equation shows that d_j, the normal level of durable goods expenditure, is significantly related to (normal?) income. In addition, a normal syndrome in which there is habitual durable expenditure is associated with high debt and low saving.

The technique is in an experimental stage and is presented here for its interest as such. It appears, however, that the findings in this particular case substantiate those of Mrs. Crockett. Note, for example, that the marginal propensity to spend on durables is 0.14 for transitory income and only 0.07 for normal income. Superficially, this is the reverse of the Crockett result, but when account is taken of the difference between durable and nondurable expenditure the two are quite compatible.

Capital Expenditures, Profits, and the Acceleration Principle

ROBERT EISNER

NORTHWESTERN UNIVERSITY

The Problem

CAPITAL expenditures and their fluctuations have long been recognized as of critical economic importance. This importance is underscored today as our interest in investment as a support of high levels of employment is reinforced by our concern for a growth in capital that may contribute to increases in output.

An understanding of the determinants of capital expenditures has been troubled by inability to choose between two apparently competing hypotheses. One, for which support may be found in work of Tinbergen, Klein, Meyer and Kuh,[1] and others, argues that past or current profits are significant in determining capital expenditure. Another hypothesis, consistent with work of J. M. Clark, Manne, Chenery, Koyck, Modigliani and Kisselgoff, and

NOTE: The long-term research of which this paper is a preliminary partial report has been supported by the Social Science Research Council, Ford Foundation, Guggenheim Foundation, National Science Foundation, Commission on Money and Credit, and Graduate School of Northwestern University. The McGraw-Hill Publishing Company has furnished most of the unpublished basic data. Margaret K. Matulis, of the McGraw-Hill Department of Economics, is to be credited with coding and putting together the McGraw-Hill survey responses and related accounting data. A variety of computational facilities has been used, but the Federal Reserve Board and Robert M. Steinberg of its staff should be singled out particularly for generous recent assistance. Among many other individuals who have aided in data gathering and processing and computation are Jack Barnes, Betty Benson, Robert Coen, Louise Cowan, Lloyd Orr, Jerith Saxton, and Patricia Wishart.

[1] Jan Tinbergen, "Statistical Evidence on the Acceleration Principle," *Economica*, May 1938, pp. 164–176; Tinbergen, *Statistical Testing of Business Cycle Theories*, Vol. I, *A Method and Its Application to Investment Activity* and Vol. II, *Business Cycles in the United States of America, 1919–1932*, Geneva, 1939; Lawrence R. Klein, *Economic Fluctuations in the United States, 1929–1941*, Cowles Commission Monograph 11, New York, 1950; Klein, "Studies in Investment Behavior," *Conference on Business Cycles*, New York, NBER, 1951, pp. 233–277; Lawrence R. Klein and A. S. Goldberger, *An Econometric Model of the United States, 1929–1952*, Amsterdam, 1952; J. R. Meyer and Edwin Kuh, "Acceleration and Related Theories of Investment; an Empirical Inquiry," *Review of Economics and Statistics*, August, 1955, pp. 217–230; Meyer and Kuh, *The Investment Decision: An Empirical Study*, Cambridge, Mass., 1957.

Eisner,[2] points to more or less sophisticated versions of the acceleration principle and the pressure of demand on capacity as a fruitful way of explaining investment. At least some versions of this explanation have in turn been criticized by Kuznets and Hickman,[3] *inter alios.*

Since profits and demand or pressure on capacity have tended to move in rough synchronization over time one may wonder whether we do have two meaningfully separate hypotheses. It is important, however, both for understanding and for possible policy purposes, to ascertain parameters of correctly specified structural relations. For one thing, the implications of a profits explanation as against those of an acceleration explanation would be quite different for various proposals for the stimulation of business investment. A profits explanation might imply that a reduction in the corporate profits tax rate, with total expected tax revenues maintained by increases in other rates, would bring about an increase in investment spending. The acceleration explanation would suggest that unless the reduction in the corporate tax rate increased demand, no additional investment would be forthcoming. To greater or lesser degrees, other proposals for reducing corporate tax incidence and increasing business after-tax profits, such as accelerated depreciation or investment tax credits, may also receive differing evaluations depending upon one's underlying explanation of investment.

The historical correlations are indeed indisputable; periods of high

[2] J. M. Clark, "Business Acceleration and the Law of Demand: A Technical Factor in Economic Cycles," *Journal of Political Economy*, March 1917, pp. 217–235, reprinted in American Economic Association, *Readings in Business Cycle Theory*, Philadelphia, 1951, pp. 235–254; A. S. Manne, "Some Notes on the Acceleration Principle," *Review of Economics and Statistics*, May 1945, pp. 93–99; Hollis B. Chenery, "Overcapacity and the Acceleration Principle," *Econometrica*, January 1952, pp. 1–28. L. M. Koyck, *Distributed Lags and Investment Analysis*, Amsterdam, 1954; Avram Kisselgoff and Franco Modigliani, "Private Investment in the Electric Power Industry and the Acceleration Principle," *Review of Economics and Statistics*, November 1957, pp. 363–380; Robert Eisner, "Expectations, Plans and Capital Expenditures, A Synthesis of *Ex Post* and *Ex Ante* Data," *Expectations, Uncertainty and Business Behavior*, ed. M. J. Bowman, New York, 1958, pp. 165–188; Eisner, "A Distributed Lag Investment Function," *Econometrica*, January 1960, pp. 1–29; Eisner, "Investment: Fact and Fancy," *American Economic Review*, May 1963, pp. 237–246.

[3] Simon Kuznets, "Relation Between Capital Goods and Finished Products in the Business Cycle," *Economic Essays in Honor of Wesley Clair Mitchell*, New York, 1935, pp. 248–267; Bert G. Hickman, "Capacity, Capacity Utilization, and the Acceleration Principle," *Problems of Capital Formation: Concepts, Measurement, and Controlling Factors*, Princeton for NBER, 1957, pp. 419–449; Hickman, "Diffusion, Acceleration and Business Cycles," *American Economic Review*, September 1959, pp. 535–565.

138

capital expenditures have been periods of high profits and periods of low capital expenditures have been periods of low profits. The workings of the acceleration principle have been far less obvious, and attempts to observe it empirically have had mixed success. For my part—and I do have some company—I prefer economic explanations that fit into the main body of the maximization principle in economic theory. In accord with this theory, I would suggest that capital expenditures are undertaken in the pursuit of profits, or perhaps in order to reduce the risk associated with expectations of profits. Setting aside the second aspect of the explanation, I would view the rate of investment demand as related to the expected profitability of investment, something which is quite different from past or current profits. A firm or economy may be enjoying high profits and yet find little profitability in adding additional plant, equipment, or inventories. Similarly, a firm or economy may be enjoying low profits and may have expectations of future demand in relation to current capacity such that substantial increases in capital stock seem profitable. The fairly good association over time between capital expenditures and profits would then be explained in large part, if not entirely, by the fact that profits have served as a "proxy variable." Periods of high profits have tended to be periods when demand was high relative to capacity; and, since there is some tendency, well observed in the past, for entrepreneurs to expect tomorrow to be like today, high-profit periods have also tended to be periods where expected demand was high relative to current capacity. Periods of high profit have, hence, frequently, but not necessarily always, been periods when the expected profitability of investment was high. If, however, profits have served as a proxy variable for demand (and perhaps other) factors, it may be possible by a multivariate analysis to isolate the roles of profits and the other factors for which it has been serving as a proxy in many previous studies.

In undertaking this task of distinguishing between the role of profits and demand factors it will be important to recognize that the response of capital stock to changes in demand cannot be expected to be immediate. The business decision-maker must judge first the extent to which any experienced change in demand is likely to be permanent or long run and, hence, influence his expectation of future demand. He may then be expected to react gradually over time to the changed expectation of future demand brought about by the experienced change in past demand. It should be appropriate, therefore, to attempt to explain investment in terms of a sufficient number of lagged sales variables.

This indeed will be critical to my approach. Previous published studies have frequently "tested" the acceleration principle by the use of variables measuring change in demand over merely one or two relatively short intervals of time. But if my view is correct, such tests would provide no direct measure of those major effects of changes in demand which could only be realized after sufficient time had elapsed for business decision-makers to become confident that the changes had been permanent and, also, for them to effectuate the consequent decisions to alter the amount of capital stock. Hence, in such tests a proxy variable that might capture some of these otherwise unmeasured forces of demand would be left considerable scope. To the extent that all of the role of demand factors can be included in the analysis, the effect of past or current profits should be expected to be sharply reduced, if not entirely eliminated.

The last hedge as to whether we should expect the apparent effect of past profits to be eliminated *entirely* should be explained. For one thing, if capital markets are imperfect, firms with low profits may find it more difficult to raise funds required for desired capital expenditures. Where this is so, it might be manifest most among relatively smaller firms which, it should be noted, would account for only a minor portion of aggregate investment. It might also be argued that this effect, to the extent that it does operate, might loom larger in the cross section than in movements over time or in the underlying structural relation we seek to estimate. Imperfect capital markets might induce allocation of a given amount of funds to firms enjoying high profits at the expense of those enjoying low profits, without seriously affecting the total amount of funds individuals are willing to invest.[4] A second reason why the apparent role of profits may not be entirely eliminated is that our past sales change variables may not "capture" entirely the expected demand-capacity relation, and some of this "uncaptured" element may be picked up in profits. Finally, we must note that factors other than those of aggregate demand must be included in any complete state-

---

[4] This point is discussed further in Robert Eisner and Robert H. Strotz, *Determinants of Business Investment*, Research Study Two in *Impacts of Monetary Policy*, prepared for the Commission on Money and Credit, Englewood Cliffs, N.J., 1963, Part II, section 3.

ment of the determinants of capital expenditures. Alterations in the composition of demand and in locations and methods of production, for example, account for a substantial portion of capital expenditures. Past or current profits might serve as a proxy for these factors as well. If they do, the relation, in including a fuller measure of total demand factors, will indicate a reduced, but not nonexistent, proxy role for profits.

The Data

This paper will offer a preliminary report of analysis of a very substantial and, in many ways, unique body of data collected in relation to the McGraw-Hill Publishing Company capital expenditure surveys. Raw material for the present study comes from surveys of 1954, 1955, 1956, 1957, and 1958, as well as related quantitative data collected from company financial statements. The McGraw-Hill data have been made available to me on an individual firm basis by code number in order to preserve the confidential character of the survey responses. The financial and accounting information has been tied to the individual (coded) firms participating in the surveys. I have data for over 700 firms, only a subset—although a large subset—of the entire McGraw-Hill sample. They tend to include the largest firms, which account for the bulk of capital expenditures, as indicated by the fact that their aggregated gross fixed assets in 1953 were over $160 billion. Data utilized in the analysis underlying the present report include responses to only a portion of the McGraw-Hill questions as well as only some of the separate financial information. These are: capital expenditures, capital expenditure anticipations, depreciation charges, gross fixed assets, sales, expected percentage sales change, profits, and actual and desired rates of utilization of capacity.

While some work has been done with undeflated data, the current analysis involves regressions of price-deflated variables wherever such price deflation was appropriate. In particular, sales have been deflated by one of eight sets of price indexes constructed from Bureau of Labor Statistics indexes and relatives on the basis of the broad product or industry classes into which I was informed the McGraw-Hill firms could be categorized. Capital expenditures and profits were deflated by a capital expenditures price index constructed from an average of the implicit GNP price deflators for "other new [nonresidential] construction" and "producers' durable equipment" weighted by the constant dollar volumes of these aggregates. Capital expenditure anticipations were deflated by the capital expenditures price index for the point of time, presumed to be the fourth quarter, at which the anticipations were indicated. Thus, for example, anticipations of 1957 capital expenditures made known at the end of 1956 were deflated by the capital expenditures price index for the fourth quarter of 1956. This may be rationalized by the assumption that businessmen during this period, in anticipating future capital expenditures, made their calculations on the basis of current prices.

Depreciation charges and gross fixed assets were taken at their accounting values without price deflation. It should be pointed out in this regard that depreciation charges have only been introduced into the present analysis as a ratio of gross fixed assets. Inasmuch as the complicated weighting factors that it would have been necessary to introduce for appropriate price deflation of each of these two variables would have been virtually the same, the value of the ratio of depreciation charges to gross fixed assets would have been little affected by price deflation. Since the capacity and expected sales change variables were, implicitly or explicitly, in physical terms they were not deflated for price changes.

In addition to price deflation, a number of transformations were performed on the basic variables to put them in forms with desirable statistical and economic properties. In particular, since the main focus of this study has been cross-section analysis, it was desirable to transform the variables in such a way as to eliminate the extreme heteroscedasticity that might have been expected because of variance in the size of firms. Without appropriate transformation of data from firms of vastly different sizes, of course, the absolute size of error terms or the scatter around the regression line would be positively related to the values of the independent variables. Firms with high sales, high profits, and high capital expenditures, that is, large firms, would be firms with high absolute values (or squares) of error terms.

Both to meet this problem and to fit the underlying economic relation which I believe to be operative, capital expenditures and capital expenditure anticipations were expressed as ratios of gross fixed assets, and sales changes were expressed as ratios of sales. Capital expenditures divided by gross fixed assets, a measure of capital stock, may be taken, after subtraction of a term to reflect depreciation or scrapping of capital equipment, as a measure of the relative change in capital stock. The change in sales divided by sales is a measure of the relative change in output. With variables in this form, a capital stock adjustment or acceleration relation, implying that capital stock would be kept more or less proportionate to output at least in the long run, can be estimated efficiently without disturbances introduced directly by differences in firm size or in capital-output ratios.

Profits have been measured gross of taxes and deflated by gross fixed assets and, also, net of taxes and deflated by net worth. Either procedure gives a measure, however crude, of the rate of profit on existing capital. Depreciation, taken as a ratio of gross fixed assets, constitutes essentially a measure (in inverse form) of the durability of capital.

Last, it should be reported that some effort has been made to eliminate observations with extreme values. Thus, observations were included in regressions only if all of the sales change (or capacity) and gross profit variables had absolute values less than unity (less than 0.4 for net profits, where they were used) and if the variables measuring depreciation, capital expenditure anticipations, and capital expenditures were less than 0.4. Earlier work with a similar body of data indicated that only a small number of observations are likely to be eliminated by these bounds.

The Model

Our underlying hypotheses have perhaps by now been made clear. Capital expenditures are seen as stemming from the demand to replace worn-out or depreciating plant and equipment and from the adjustment of capital stock to changed expectations of demand. The adjustment, as well as the development of the demand expectations, is seen as occupying substantial periods of time. Thus, an increase in the rate of sales from period $t - 1$ to period t will, if sales are maintained at the new level of period t, develop gradually over, say, m periods, the view that this higher level of sales is permanent. Capital stock may be expected to adjust, with the additional lags introduced by the nature of the decision-making and expenditure process, to the gradually changing view of expected demand resulting from the initial change in sales. Reverting to a formulation I have used earlier,[5] and denoting output by Y and capital stock by F (gross fixed assets), this may be written

[5] "A Distributed Lag Investment Function," *Econometrica*, January 1960, p. 6.

$$\Delta Y \rightarrow \Delta F$$

However, noting again that investment is likely to be induced over a number of periods, this may better be written

$$\Delta Y_t \rightarrow \Delta F_t^t + \Delta F_{t+1}^t + \ldots + \Delta F_{t+m-1}^t,$$

where the subscripts indicate the period in which the indicated changes occur. And then the change in capital stock in any one period, ΔF_t, may be thought of as gross capital expenditures, I_t, minus replacement requirements; and these would equal the sum of the increments of capital stock ascribable to changes in output in a number of past periods, or

$$\Delta F_t^t + \Delta F_t^{t-1} + \ldots + \Delta F_t^{t-m+1}.$$

After some manipulation and utilizing the assumption of a constant ratio of sales to output, we derive finally,

$$\frac{I_t}{F_{t-\tau}} = b_0 + \sum_{n=1}^{m} b_n \left(\frac{S_{t-n+1} - S_{t-n}}{S_{t-\tau}} \right).$$

With a number of further assumptions, such as constancy and linear homogeneity of the production function, constant factor proportions, full (or constant) utilization of capacity, lack of "curbs" to the operation of the accelerator due to bottlenecks or inability to disinvest as rapidly as falls in demand would require, and lack of bias due to transitory elements in sales changes, the sum of the sales change coefficients, that is, the sum of b_n in the last equation, should equal unity. If, in fact, they do not equal unity, part of the explanation may be in the inaccuracy of one or more of the assumptions indicated.

Previous experimentation has shown that profits, measured as a ratio of gross fixed assets, show fairly high collinearity with their lagged values in cross sections. It has, hence, seemed best, by way of testing the role of past or current profits, to include only one profits variable in the linear regressions. On the basis of a priori considerations and results of previous empirical investigations, profits lagged one year were used in the various regressions involving capital expenditures.

The proportion of capital stock which firms might be replacing in any year would relate very largely to the average durability of their capital stock. Also, under current United States accounting rules, depreciation still reflects in large part expected lives of plant and equipment. Therefore, the ratio of depreciation charges to fixed assets has been introduced into the model to account for the inter-firm variance in capital expenditures that may relate to the interfirm variance in durability and replacement requirements.

The basic relation estimated may hence be written,

$$\frac{I_t}{F_{53}} = b_0 + \sum_{j=1}^{7} b_j \left[\frac{S_{t+1-j} - S_{t-j}}{\frac{1}{3}(S_{52} + S_{53} + S_{54})} \right] + b_8 \frac{P_{t-1}}{F_{53}} + b_9 \frac{D_{53}}{F_{53}} + u,$$

where I = gross capital expenditures
$\quad\quad F$ = gross fixed assets
$\quad\quad S$ = sales
$\quad\quad P$ = profits
$\quad\quad D$ = depreciation charges, and
$\quad\quad t$ = year of the dependent variable, capital expenditures.

In the abbreviated symbols used in the tables presenting the estimates of parameters, the preceding equation is

$$(1) \quad\quad i_t = b_0 + \sum_{j=1}^{7} b_i \Delta s_{t+1-i} + b_8 p_{t-1} + b_9 d_{53} + u.$$

It was found convenient, in collecting the underlying data and in the computation and analysis, to keep a constant deflator for sales, capital expenditures, and profits variables of different years. The year 1953 was selected in part because it was roughly centered in the period to which the variables related and in part because it offered a desirable deflator of depreciation charges of 1953, the last year before accounting depreciation began to reflect the changed practices encouraged by the 1954 revisions of the tax law. In deflat-ing sales changes it was felt advisable to use an arithmetic mean of sales of three years, 1952, 1953, and 1954, so that the distribution of 1953 and 1954 sales change variables in particular, and others in general, would not be distorted unduly by low values of sales of 1953 alone. This first or "basic" relation was also used with coeffi-cients of various of the lagged sales changes constrained to be zero.

A second relation estimated includes two sales expectations vari-ables. One is the expected percentage change in the physical volume of sales in 1959 indicated by McGraw-Hill respondents at the end of 1958. The other is the expected percentage change per annum in the physical volume of sales from 1959 to 1962, also indicated by respondents at the end of 1958. I have presented this latter variable, however, in a transformation from its original form on the questionnaires, where the response ostensibly indicated the percentage change in the physical volume of sales expected from 1959 to 1962. This variable actually was used in the regressions; but to put it in a form consistent with the other annual rate of sales change variables, it has been redefined as one-third of the indicated figure, and the regression statistics have been rewritten accordingly.[6] In this second relation, which involves only 1958 capital expenditures, capital expenditures and depreciation were deflated by 1957 gross fixed assets. I deflated sales changes by the arithmetic mean of 1956, 1957, and 1958 sales; measured profits after taxes, designated P^*; deflated profits by net worth, denoted by W; and used 1957 depreciation charges. The relation estimated may hence be written,

$$\frac{I_{58}}{F_{57}} = b_0 + b_1 \left[\frac{\frac{1}{3}(S_{62}^{58} - S_{59}^{58})}{S_{59}^{58}} \right] + b_2 \frac{S_{59}^{58} - S_{58}}{S_{58}}$$

$$+ \sum_{j=3}^{9} b_j \left[\frac{S_{58+3-j} - S_{57+3-j}}{\frac{1}{3}(S_{56} + S_{57} + S_{58})} \right] + b_{10} \frac{P_{57}^*}{W_{57}} + b_{11} \frac{D_{57}}{F_{57}} + u,$$

or, again in abbreviated notation,

$$(2) \quad i_{58}^* = b_0 + b_1 \Delta s_{59-62}^{58} + b_2 \Delta s_{59}^{58} + \sum_{j=3}^{9} \Delta s_{t+3-j}^* + b_{10} p_{57}^* + b_{11} d_{57} + u.$$

A third relation estimated, involving 1957 capital expenditures only, used responses to questions on utilization of capacity as well as expected sales changes, which appeared in the 1956 McGraw-Hill questionnaires. My capacity variable in this relation was a combination of responses to two McGraw-Hill questions. The first was, "At the end of 1956, how much of your capacity were you operating? _____%." The second question was, "What do you consider a desirable operating rate at the end of the year in your industry? _____%." We therefore defined

$$\Delta c = \frac{\dfrac{S}{C} - \left(\dfrac{S}{C}\right)_d}{\dfrac{S}{C_d}}$$

$$= \frac{\text{actual minus desired utilization of capacity}}{\text{desired utilization of capacity}}.$$

---

[6] Such a transformation of the parameter estimates is, of course, permissible with linear transformations of the variables. It would not have been possible had I executed the more precise transformation involved in translating the expected three-year percentage change into annual rates which, when compounded, would give the original total.

This variable, taken from 1956 responses, hence, at the time 1957 capital expenditures were undertaken, described the relative amounts by which firms had felt recently existing demand (sales) left them short of desired capacity.

This third relation also includes the expected percentage change in the 1957 physical volume of sales indicated at the end of 1956 and actual sales changes of 1957, 1956, and 1955, measured as percentages of previous sales. (These sales change variables, unlike those used in the other relations, were taken from reports of sales made in McGraw-Hill responses. The other sales change variables were derived from sales data taken independently from financial statements.) The third relation may hence be written,

$$\frac{I_{57}}{F_{53}} = b_0 + b_1 \frac{\left[\left(\frac{S}{C}\right)_{56} - \left(\frac{S}{C}\right)_d\right]}{\left(\frac{S}{C}\right)_d} + b_2 \frac{S_{57}^{56} - S_{56}}{S_{56}}$$

$$+ \sum_{j=3}^{5} b_i \frac{S_{57+3-j} - S_{56+3-j}}{S_{56+3-j}} + b_6 \frac{P_{56}}{F_{53}} + b_7 \frac{D_{53}}{F_{53}} + u,$$

or

$$(3) \qquad i_{57} = b_0 + b_1 \Delta c + b_2 \Delta s_{57}^{56} + \sum_{j=3}^{5} b_j \Delta s_{57+3-j}^{**} + b_6 p_{56} + b_7 d_{53} + u.$$

Finally, I have examined briefly the role of capital expenditure anticipations. For this purpose I have estimated parameters of a relation expressing capital expenditure anticipations as a function of six current and previous sales changes, previous profits, and depreciation charges. I have then compared this relation with an analogous one for actual capital expenditures, and I have also expressed capital expenditures as a function of capital expenditure expectations and the sales change, profits, and depreciation variables previously used. Employing i_t^{t-1} to denote anticipations at the end of the year $t - 1$ of capital expenditures of the year t, divided by 1953 gross fixed assets, these relations may be written,

$$(4) \qquad i_t^{t-1} = b_0 + \sum_{j=2}^{7} b_j \Delta s_{t+1-j} + b_8 p_{t-1} + b_9 d_{53} + u,$$

$$(5) \qquad i_t = b_0 + \sum_{j=2}^{7} b_j \Delta s_{t+1-j} + b_8 p_{t-1} + b_9 d_{53} + u,$$

147

and

$$(6) \qquad i_t = b_0 + b_1 i_t^{t-1} + \sum_{j=2}^{8} b_j \Delta s_{t+2-j} + b_9 p_{t-1} + b_{10} d_{53} + u.$$

Findings

Parameters of the "basic" relation, (1), were estimated for equations involving capital expenditures of 1955, 1956, 1957, and 1958. The computation procedure involved the inclusion of capital expenditure anticipations in constructing the underlying moment matrices. Complete observations hence required that a firm had reported its capital expenditures in a given survey and had also reported its anticipations of capital expenditures for that year in the survey of the previous year. They also required complete accounting data with regard to 1953 depreciation charges and fixed assets; profits of the preceding year; and sales of the year of capital expenditures and seven preceding years. Since incomplete observations were rejected, this reduced the number of firms included in the regressions in each year to more or less than half of the 700-odd for which data had been received. Some of the detailed results, presented in Tables 1 and 3, may repay careful study. I shall only call attention now to some of the highlights.

First, sales change coefficients of all years in all regressions are positive. In most cases, the coefficients, particularly those of the current and first three lagged sales changes, are significantly different from zero (in a statistical sense) by reasonable tests, usually at the 0.01 probability level. The sums of sales change coefficients for the regressions for the four years were, respectively, beginning with 1955, 0.470, 0.587, 0.525, and 0.564. It would thus appear that one or more of the conditions I have suggested as necessary for the sum of these coefficients to equal unity were not being met.

Coefficients of the profits variable were also positive in all four regressions, but were small. In the case of 1957 and 1958 capital expenditures, these coefficients did not differ significantly from zero. Of more direct bearing on my hypothesis with respect to the proxy role of profits are the relative sizes of the simple and partial correlation coefficients of capital expenditures with profits. It is to be noted that the simple correlations of capital expenditures with profits varied from 0.381 to 0.189, thus accounting for between 14.5 per cent and 3.5 per cent of the variance of the capital expenditure variable. The low partial correlation coefficients, ranging from 0.202

TABLE 1

CAPITAL EXPENDITURES AS FUNCTION OF SEVEN LAGGED SALES CHANGES,
PREVIOUS PROFITS, AND DEPRECIATION CHARGES, 1955–58

	REGRESSION COEFFICIENTS AND STANDARD ERRORS Capital Expenditures, i_t, of				SIMPLE AND PARTIAL CORRELATION COEFFICIENTS Capital Expenditures, i_t, of			
	1955	1956	1957	1958	1955	1956	1957	1958
Constant term	.025 (.008)	.030 (.008)	.047 (.008)	.039 (.007)				
Δs_t	.105 (.022)	.116 (.025)	.058 (.024)	.063 (.025)	.209[a] .274[a]	.277[a] .236[a]	.199[a] .122[b]	.230[a] .142[b]
Δs_{t-1}	.058 (.023)	.106 (.022)	.104 (.025)	.108 (.025)	.221[a] .156[a]	.273[a] .237[a]	.233[a] .204[a]	.283[a] .237[a]
Δs_{t-2}	.074 (.025)	.101 (.022)	.096 (.022)	.108 (.024)	.242[a] .179[a]	.182[a] .230[a]	.196[a] .216[a]	.254[a] .244[a]
Δs_{t-3}	.104 (.027)	.100 (.026)	.106 (.021)	.038 (.023)	.308[a] .225[a]	.169[a] .195[a]	.203[a] .245[a]	.066 .095
Δs_{t-4}	.035 (.026)	.086 (.027)	.120 (.025)	.117 (.025)	.033 .082	.151[a] .160[a]	.244[a] .233[a]	.294[a] .254[a]
Δs_{t-5}	.020 (.028)	.050 (.027)	.020 (.027)	.082 (.027)	.027 .043	.095 .093	.068 .038	.220[a] .169[a]
Δs_{t-6}	.074 (.027)	.029 (.027)	.021 (.026)	.048 (.030)	.307[a] .166[a]	.081 .054	.034 .041	.246[a] .090
p_{t-1}	.052 (.019)	.073 (.018)	.009 (.017)	.011 (.018)	.381[a] .162[a]	.373[a] .202[a]	.189[a] .027	.243[a] .034
d_{53}	.803 (.122)	.792 (.144)	.777 (.132)	.758 (.134)	.509[a] .374[a]	.379[a] .274[a]	.344[a] .285[a]	.376[a] .306[a]
$\Sigma\Delta s$ coefficients	.470	.587	.525	.564				
n	278	386	402	322				
$\hat{R}^2$	.428	.361	.284	.363				

NOTE: In first four columns, regression coefficients are in upper line of each cell; standard errors, in lower line. In last four columns, simple correlation coefficients are in upper line; partial, in lower line.
[a] Significant at 0.01 probability level.
[b] Significant at 0.05 probability level.

to 0.027, indicate, however, that the proportions of variance of the capital expenditure variables accounted for by profits after inclusion of the seven sales change variables and depreciation range only from 4.1 per cent to less than 0.1 per cent of the total. It is further

149

to be noted that while the partial correlation coefficients generally tend to be less than the simple correlation coefficients, the sharp discrepancies noted in the case of profits are not nearly so apparent in the case of the sales change variables. It is clear that the sales change variables account in the aggregate for a substantial portion of the variance in capital expenditures. And earlier work bringing out collinearity among successively lagged profits variables indicates that little would have been gained by including additional lagged profits variables in the regressions.

The depreciation ratios, as expected, did account for substantial portions of the variance in the capital expenditure ratio variables. The total variance accounted for by all variables, as indicated in the unbiased estimates of the square of the multiple correlation coefficients, were 0.428, 0.361, 0.284, and 0.363 for the successive regressions. These, it may be suggested, are relatively high for cross sections of this kind, where a lot of "noise" may be expected to surround the relation we are trying to estimate.

The data used in all four regressions have been pooled in such a way as to average the estimates of coefficients for each year's regression and to add, to some unspecified extent, the effects of changes in variables over time. To accomplish this I have summed the matrices of raw products and cross products over all of the regressions. The regression coefficients calculated from the sum of these matrices hence reflect variance and covariance about the means of observations for four years (with the exception of depreciation charges, which, as noted, were identically defined in all regressions as 1953 depreciation charges divided by 1953 gross fixed assets). Results, shown in Tables 2 and 3, tend to sharpen the picture already delineated. With a total of 1,388 observations, even the smallest sales change coefficients are more than three times their standard errors. The sum of sales change coefficients, 0.572, is somewhat high relative to the corresponding sums in the individual regressions. This suggests that we are picking up some element in the variance and covariance over time which adds to the role of variance in changes in sales, a matter to which we will return both in this paper and other work. It may also be noted that sales change coefficients show a decided tendency to fall off when lags are extended to five and six years, but that the Koyck-type geometric distribution of coefficients, with a hump for the first lag term, is somewhat marred by the relatively high value of the coefficient of the Δs_{t-4} variable.

TABLE 2

POOLED REGRESSIONS OF 1955–58 CAPITAL EXPENDITURES AS DETERMINED
BY RELATION (1) AND REGRESSIONS ON INDUSTRY-YEAR MEANS

| | Regression Coefficients and Standard Errors | | Simple and Partial Correlation Coefficients | |
	Pooled Data, All Years	Industry-Year Means	Pooled Data, All Years	Industry-Year Means
Constant term	.035 (.004)	.021 (.018)		
Δs_t	.085 (.011)	.094 (.069)	.233[a] .199[a]	.217 .287
Δs_{t-1}	.116 (.011)	.230 (.095)	.272[a] .269[a]	.394[b] .465[b]
Δs_{t-2}	.092 (.011)	.133 (.055)	.168[a] .228[a]	.050 .465[b]
Δs_{t-3}	.085 (.011)	.139 (.054)	.147[a] .206[a]	.078 .493[b]
Δs_{t-4}	.101 (.012)	.144 (.082)	.201[a] .216[a]	.288 .356
Δs_{t-5}	.043 (.013)	−.024 (.078)	.097[a] .088[a]	−.203 −.067
Δs_{t-6}	.052 (.013)	.046 (.084)	.168[a] .109[a]	.403[b] .118
p_{t-1}	.033 (.009)	.015 (.070)	.290[a] .098[a]	.535[a] .047
d_{53}	.771 (.066)	1.056 (.491)	.383[a] .298[a]	.452[b] .425[b]
$\Sigma\Delta s$ coefficients	.572	.761		
n	1,388	31		
$\hat{R}^2$	.351	.605		

NOTE: In first two columns, regression coefficients are in upper line of each cell; standard errors, in lower line. In last two columns, simple correlation coefficients are in upper line; partial, in lower line.
[a] Significant at 0.01 probability level.
[b] Significant at 0.05 probability level.

The coefficient of the profits variable is again significantly positive but clearly small. What is more, the simple correlation coefficient of 0.290 reveals that the profits variable alone accounted for 8.4 per

TABLE 3

MEANS AND STANDARD DEVIATIONS RELATING TO REGRESSIONS FOR
INDIVIDUAL YEARS, POOLED DATA, AND INDUSTRY-YEAR MEANS

	Means and Standard Deviations					
	$t = 1955$	$t = 1956$	$t = 1957$	$t = 1958$	Pooled Data	Industry-Year Means
Δs_t	.097	.078	.030	−.047	.039	.037
	.157	.138	.140	.152	.155	.070
Δs_{t-1}	−.058	.098	.073	.036	.045	.045
	.161	.164	.135	.135	.159	.066
Δs_{t-2}	.074	−.043	.103	.075	.050	.053
	.138	.158	.156	.139	.160	.072
Δs_{t-3}	.051	.069	−.035	.104	.043	.043
	.137	.128	.158	.154	.155	.076
Δs_{t-4}	.069	.052	.063	−.033	.039	.028
	.141	.130	.133	.150	.143	.066
Δs_{t-5}	.071	.071	.044	.068	.062	.057
	.131	.133	.128	.128	.130	.053
Δs_{t-6}	−.055	.076	.067	.038	.038	.033
	.134	.127	.135	.120	.138	.073
p_{t-1}	.239	.251	.263	.239	.249	.221
	.189	.200	.210	.203	.202	.098
d_{53}	.055	.050	.050	.051	.051	.049
	.029	.025	.027	.027	.027	.014
i_t	.098	.120	.114	.096	.108	.108
	.070	.079	.076	.073	.076	.028
n	278	386	402	322	1,388	31

NOTE: Means are in upper line of each cell; standard deviations, lower line.

cent of variance in the capital expenditure variable; but the partial coefficient of 0.098 shows that when other variables are included in the regression, the remaining explanatory power of the profits variable is reduced to less than 1 per cent of the variance not otherwise accounted for.

The means and standard deviations presented in Table 3 offer some light on the relative magnitudes of interfirm, intrayear variance and interyear, intrafirm variance. The successive means in the columns headed "$t = 1955$," "$t = 1956$," "$t = 1957$," and "$t = 1958$" indicate how sales moved over time. Thus, for firms included in the 1955 capital expenditure regression the means of sales changes from the preceding year, measured as ratios of average sales of 1952, 1953, and 1954, were (in percentages): 1949, -5.5; 1950, $+7.1$; 1951, $+6.9$; 1952, $+5.1$; 1953, $+7.4$; 1954, -5.8; and 1955, $+9.7$. The corresponding mean percentage changes in sales from 1956 through 1958, taken from the observations included in the 1958 capital expenditure regression, were $+7.5$, $+3.6$, and -4.7. (The means of sales changes for the same year in different regressions were not identical, because of somewhat differing compositions of the sets of firms included in each regression.) These differences in the mean sales change from year to year are reflected in the tendency for standard deviations of sales changes about the means of all sales changes to be somewhat higher in the pooled data than in the data for individual years. For example, the standard deviations of sales changes lagged two years were, for the successive individual-year regressions, 0.138, 0.158, 0.156, and 0.139. These standard deviations were taken about the means of sales changes for each single year from 1953 to 1956. The standard deviation of sales changes lagged two years in the pooled data was 0.160. This standard deviation stemmed from the variance around the mean of sales changes of all four years. However, the standard deviation for the pooled data was even in this instance not markedly higher than the standard deviations for each of the single years; nor was it, observing as well the statistics for other years, in general larger than the standard deviations in all of the individual-year regressions. Apparently, the major part of variance in all variables was the interfirm cross-section variance rather than intrayear variance.

The pooled data for the regressions of four years, hence, reflect largely the average of the regressions of individual years. It should of course be possible to ascertain this more precisely in a formal analysis of variance and covariance to which we intend to turn in subsequent work.

It may be argued, however, that individual firms, particularly smaller firms, would tend to view their own sales experience as unlikely in the long run to differ markedly from that of the industry or, perhaps, the economy as a whole. In deciding the extent to which to consider changes in their own sales as likely to be lasting or "permanent" rather than temporary or "transitory," they might well be influenced by the degree to which these changes in their own sales were similar to changes in the industry or in the economy. Fluctuations in their own individual firm sales might then be viewed as consisting of two components, industry (or economy) sales fluctuations and fluctuations of individual firm sales about the industry (or economy) levels. In terms of the transitory-permanent dichotomy made familiar in the study of the consumption function, the variance of the firms about the industry (or economy) levels, constituting in considerable part essentially random fluctuations in their own relatively small sample of experience, would be viewed as in smaller proportion permanent than the variance of sales of the industry (or economy). And since transitory fluctuations in sales should be expected to contribute relatively little, if anything, to the explanation of capital expenditures, one should expect higher sales change coefficients and higher coefficients of determination in capital expenditure regressions with observations having a larger "permanent" content.[7]

It has been possible to accomplish a preliminary test of this related set of propositions. This has been done by dividing firms into the "industries" or product classes which were identified for purposes of price deflation. Complete observation vectors were available for eight industries for capital expenditures of 1958, 1957, and 1956, and for seven industries (all of the eight except utilities) for 1955. From these were constructed thirty-one sets of "industry-year" means. Variance and covariance among these observations would therefore reflect a combination of interindustry differences and movements of the economy as a whole over the four years encompassed.

Results, presented in Tables 2 and 3, suggest that this approach may prove fruitful. My estimates of the parameters of (1) with these thirty-one industry-year means as observations include substantially positive coefficients for the first five sales change variables. Even taking the number of independent observations as only thirty-one, rather than the 1,388 from which the means are derived, three of these coefficients differ from zero by more than twice their standard errors. The sum of sales change coefficients, 0.761, is markedly higher than the corresponding sum, 0.572, for the pooled data of individual firms. And standard deviations, as seen in Table 3, are much smaller

---

[7] Cf. Milton Friedman, *A Theory of the Consumption Function*, Princeton for NBER, 1957; and Robert Eisner, "The Permanent Income Hypothesis: Comment," *American Economic Review*, December 1958, pp. 972–990.

for the means than for the original data. These statistics are consistent with my hypothesis that the permanent variance in sales change is relatively more concentrated between industry-years than between firms and that it is this permanent variance which is more closely (if not exclusively) related to the variance in capital expenditures.

The industry-year-mean regression offers, further, even more striking evidence of the proxy role of profits. The regression coefficient of the profits variable is 0.015, differing from zero in no significant fashion, either statistically or economically. While the simple correlation coefficient of the capital expenditure variable with the profits variable is a significant 0.535, the corresponding partial correlation coefficient is only 0.047. It may be noted, finally, that the adjusted coefficient of multiple determination is 0.605, suggesting that we have indeed washed out a relatively large proportion of transitory "noise" with the intraindustry variances and covariances.

We have also estimated relation (1) for individual industries, again pooling the observations of all four years (except in the case of utilities, for which only three years were available). Results of these pooled industry regressions, presented in Table 4, seem generally consistent with what we have argued thus far. Sums of sales change coefficients vary between 0.387 and 1.056. Their simple average is indeed somewhat higher (0.630) than the sums of sales change coefficients for the entire cross sections of each year or for all of the pooled data of all years. But this fact may perhaps be better passed over until appropriately weighted within-industry coefficients are obtained from the analysis of variance and covariance, which remains to be undertaken.

Finally, in regard to relation (1), the effects may be noted of eliminating various of the sales change variables or, put in other terms, restricting the coefficients of various of the sales change variables to be zero. Comparing Table 5 and Table 2 it is seen that estimated parameters remain fairly invariant with respect to inclusion or exclusion of a number of sales change variables. The effect of sales changes does, however, seem to be largely additive. Thus, the sum of sales change coefficients is only 0.257 for the pooled individual firm data and 0.380 for the industry-year means when only three lagged sales changes are included, as against 0.572 and 0.761, respectively, when seven sales change variables are included in the regressions. Further, the adjusted multiple coefficients of determination were only 0.264

TABLE 4
POOLED REGRESSIONS OF 1955–58 CAPITAL EXPENDITURES AS DETERMINED BY RELATION 1, BY INDUSTRY

	Primary Metals	Metal Work-ing	Chemical Process-ing	All Other Manu-facturing	Mining and Petro-leum	Utilities	Trans-porta-tion	Com-merc
	REGRESSION COEFFICIENTS AND STANDARD ERRORS							
Constant term	.034 (.019)	.028 (.010)	.067 (.015)	.023 (.009)	.056 (.015)	0.012 (0.034)	0.021 (0.009)	0.04 (0.01
Δs_t	.064 (.044)	.091 (.017)	.048 (.034)	.096 (.025)	.055 (.037)	−0.009 (0.041)	0.136 (0.045)	0.19 (0.07
Δs_{t-1}	.191 (.044)	.091 (.020)	.163 (.033)	.104 (.023)	.082 (.033)	0.300 (0.083)	0.068 (0.049)	0.07 (0.07
Δs_{t-2}	.154 (.050)	.089 (.018)	.076 (.032)	.040 (.022)	.060 (.032)	0.186 (0.047)	0.179 (0.057)	0.05 (0.07
Δs_{t-3}	.075 (.045)	.115 (.018)	.033 (.033)	.057 (.023)	−.0001 (.042)	0.099 (0.047)	0.110 (0.057)	0.05 (0.07
Δs_{t-4}	.068 (.053)	.108 (.020)	.105 (.037)	.053 (.025)	.116 (.042)	0.133 (0.054)	−0.030 (0.066)	0.28 (0.13
Δs_{t-5}	−.023 (.055)	.048 (.022)	.027 (.047)	.055 (.022)	.050 (.043)	0.125 (0.145)	0.126 (0.070)	0.24 (0.11
Δs_{t-6}	.003 (.049)	.064 (.022)	.042 (.044)	.024 (.021)	.023 (.042)	0.052 (0.084)	0.149 (0.050)	0.15 (0.12
p_{t-1}	.155 (.052)	.066 (.017)	.075 (.029)	.031 (.015)	−.065 (.047)	0.046 (0.051)	−0.153 (0.081)	0.05 (0.04
d_{53}	.477 (.328)	.599 (.140)	.233 (.285)	.762 (.163)	.916 (.232)	1.021 (1.187)	1.354 (0.193)	0.71 (0.23
$\Sigma\Delta s$ coeffi-cients	.578	.608	.492	.428	.387	0.886	0.603	1.05
n	81	343	231	273	104	115	122	11
$\hat{R}^2$	.328	.380	.195	.347	.230	0.324	0.718	0.30
	SIMPLE AND PARTIAL CORRELATION COEFFICIENTS (WITH i_t):							
Δs_t	.105 .171	.245[a] .284[a]	.098 .094	.311[a] .231[a]	.138 .151	.166 −.021	.399[a] .273[a]	.33 .22
Δs_{t-1}	.356[a] .457[a]	.210[a] .244[a]	.330[a] .311[a]	.363[a] .267[a]	.136 .250[b]	.456[a] .334[a]	.409[a] −.128	.30 .09
Δs_{t-2}	.145 .346[a]	.097 .257[a]	.101 .156[b]	.221[a] .109	.117 .191	.402[a] .362[a]	.385[a] .287[a]	.20 .07

(continued)

TABLE 4 (concluded)

	Primary Metals	Metal Working	Chemical Processing	All Other Manufacturing	Mining and Petroleum	Utilities	Transportation	Commercial
t−3	−.134	.155[a]	.008	.246[a]	.026	.203[b]	.317[a]	.176
	.195	.327[a]	.066	.150[b]	−.0003	.201[b]	.180	.069
t−4	.247[b]	.140[a]	.217[a]	.228[a]	.254[a]	.264[a]	.346[a]	.201[b]
	.152	.282[a]	.185[a]	.130[b]	.272[a]	.235[b]	−.043	.203[b]
t−5	−.192	.049	−.010	.140[b]	.193	.206[b]	.284[a]	.252[a]
	−.049	.119[b]	.038	.149[b]	.120	.084	.167	.200[b]
t−6	.239[b]	.141[a]	.165[b]	.100	.078	.022	.351[a]	.242[a]
	.007	.157[a]	.064	.070	.058	.061	.271[a]	.114
−1	.365[a]	.394[a]	.267[a]	.296[a]	−.051	.084	.192[b]	.269[a]
	.332	.209[a]	.170[b]	.130[b]	−.140	.089	−.176	.117
	.109	.324[a]	.174[a]	.379[a]	.375[a]	−.213[b]	.824[a]	.385[a]
	.170	.228[a]	.055	.277[a]	.376[a]	.084	.553[a]	.280[a]
MEANS AND STANDARD DEVIATIONS								
t	.013	.040	.049	.030	.052	.064	.014	.044
	.165	.207	.136	.128	.169	.103	.131	.110
t−1	.031	.024	.046	.044	.068	.105	.025	.055
	.167	.204	.142	.141	.193	.056	.123	.121
t−2	.049	.033	.057	.043	.069	.102	.018	.068
	.169	.207	.143	.145	.194	.093	.102	.115
t−3	.020	.036	.062	.041	.052	.085	−.007	.053
	.193	.201	.138	.141	.149	.088	.100	.113
t−4	−.0002	.069	.037	.035	.025	.064	−.0001	.021
	.167	.192	.124	.133	.145	.077	.099	.064
t−5	.075	.106	.062	.039	.034	.071	.035	.029
	.145	.162	.100	.144	.146	.030	.085	.072
t−6	.027	.055	.039	.021	.050	.081	.0004	.021
	.164	.167	.110	.153	.144	.050	.125	.070
−1	.208	.330	.259	.295	.157	.101	.070	.328
	.116	.217	.163	.229	.135	.079	.054	.201
	.045	.062	.052	.052	.051	.022	.034	.066
	.018	.024	.017	.020	.027	.004	.037	.037
	.102	.116	.122	.088	.111	.119	.064	.146
	.063	.073	.074	.063	.068	.051	.084	.101

NOTE: Regression coefficients, simple correlation coefficients, and means are in upper lines of cells; standard errors, partial correlation coefficients, and standard deviations are in lower lines.
[a] Significant at 0.01 probability level.
[b] Significant at 0.05 probability level.

TABLE 5

CAPITAL EXPENDITURES AS FUNCTION OF SELECTED RELATION (1) VARIABLES,
POOLED REGRESSIONS OF 1955–58 AND REGRESSIONS ON INDUSTRY-YEAR MEANS

| | Regression Coefficients[a] and Standard Errors[b] | | | | | | | | | |
	Pooled Data, All Years					Industry-Year Means				
Constant term	.036 (.004)	.036 (.004)	.037 (.004)	.038 (.004)	.040 (.004)	.018 (.018)	0.021 (0.017)	0.018 (0.015)	.026 (.016)	.03 (.01
Δs_t				.085 (.011)	.090 (.011)	.112 (.011)	0.094 (0.067)	0.086 (0.062)	.164 (.052)	
Δs_{t-1}	.122 (.011)	.129 (.011)	.129 (.011)	.116 (.011)	.120 (.011)	.233 (.097)	0.269 (0.061)	0.277 (0.054)	.269 (.058)	.22 (.06
Δs_{t-2}	.086 (.011)	.090 (.011)	.085 (.010)	.085 (.011)	.074 (.011)	.114 (.055)	0.133 (0.054)	0.137 (0.052)	.159 (.055)	.10 (.06
Δs_{t-3}	.079 (.011)	.081 (.011)	.080 (.011)	.075 (.011)	.063 (.011)	.135 (.055)	0.132 (0.051)	0.130 (0.050)	.092 (.049)	.04 (.05
Δs_{t-4}	.126 (.012)	.096 (.012)	.091 (.012)			.219 (.063)	0.142 (0.081)	0.151 (0.073)		
Δs_{t-5}	.060 (.013)	.037 (.013)				.014 (.074)	−0.023 (0.076)			
Δs_{t-6}	.052 (.013)					.045 (.085)				
p_{t-1}	.030 (.009)	.035 (.009)	.037 (.009)	.040 (.009)	.038 (.009)	−.014 (.069)	0.025 (0.067)	0.020 (0.064)	.073 (.062)	.07 (.07
d_{53}	.797 (.068)	.793 (.067)	.815 (.066)	.845 (.068)	.909 (.070)	1.259 (.477)	1.018 (0.478)	1.054 (0.454)	.696 (.447)	.70 (.52
$\Sigma\Delta s$ coefficients	.524	.518	.474	.387	.257	.760	0.747	0.781	.684	.38
n	1,388	1,388	1,388	1,388	1,388	31	31	31	31	31
$\hat{R}^2$	.325	.344	.341	.314	.264	.589	0.617	0.633	.583	.43

[a] Top lines.
[b] Bottom lines.

and 0.432 for the regressions restricted to three sales changes as against 0.351 and 0.605 for the full regressions presented in Table 2. I take this as further evidence that the acceleration relation may in large part be missed in quantitative studies that do not involve functions which give sufficient time for the full impact of changes in demand to be realized in resultant changes in capital stock.

158

TABLE 6

CAPITAL EXPENDITURES AS DETERMINED BY RELATION (2), BY SIZE OF FIRMS, 1958

	Regression Coefficients and Standard Errors			Simple and Partial Correlation Coefficients			Means and Standard Deviations		
	Smaller Firms	Larger Firms	All Firms	Smaller Firms	Larger Firms	All Firms	Smaller Firms	Larger Firms	All Firms
constant term	.004	0.004	.006						
	(.012)	(0.016)	(.009)						
S^{58}_{59-62}	.038	0.324	.125	0.080	0.363[a]	0.154[a]	.065	.065	.065
	(.087)	(0.131)	(.072)	0.032	0.263[b]	0.103	.048	.038	.045
S^{58}_{59}	.073	0.005	.059	0.078	−0.027	0.044	.112	.081	.102
	(.043)	(0.067)	(.036)	0.123	0.008	0.099	.096	.088	.095
S_{58}	.145	−0.017	.119	0.269[a]	0.212[b]	0.253[a]	−.040	−.034	−.038
	(.027)	(0.049)	(.023)	0.370[a]	−0.039	0.293[a]	.157	.122	.146
S_{57}	.102	0.054	.093	0.209[a]	0.279[a]	0.227[a]	.020	.037	.025
	(.032)	(0.060)	(.028)	0.229[a]	0.098	0.199[a]	.119	.095	.112
S_{56}	.024	0.090	.032	0.094	0.212[b]	0.114	.074	.054	.067
	(.032)	(0.070)	(.029)	0.054	0.141	0.066	.129	.073	.114
S_{55}	.007	0.022	.024	0.044	−0.141	0.008	.090	.088	.089
	(.026)	(0.074)	(.024)	0.019	0.033	0.060	.171	.090	.150
S_{54}	−.018	0.163	.015	0.047	0.313[a]	0.105	−.041	−.021	−.035
	(.028)	(0.058)	(.025)	−0.048	0.297[a]	0.036	.166	.103	.148
S_{53}	.024	0.077	.031	0.119	0.298[a]	0.153[a]	.059	.063	.061
	(.029)	(0.068)	(.027)	0.061	0.123	0.071	.143	.083	.127
S_{52}	.033	0.006	.034	0.095	0.343[a]	0.154[a]	.037	.030	.035
	(.030)	(0.081)	(.027)	0.082	0.008	0.076	.135	.095	.123
7	.288	−0.035	.220	0.309[a]	0.216[b]	0.284[a]	.087	.085	.086
	(.077)	(0.140)	(.067)	0.267[a]	−0.027	0.193[a]	.054	.039	.049
7	.603	1.008	.619	0.293[a]	0.524[a]	0.352[a]	.055	.042	.051
	(.181)	(0.242)	(.140)	0.240[a]	0.417[a]	0.257[a]	.022	.023	.023
				1.000	1.000	1.000	.074	.076	.075
				0.559[c]	0.671[c]	0.548[c]	.061	.057	.060
λs coefficients	.427	0.723	.532						
	194	94	288						
	.271	0.376	.273						

NOTE: Regression coefficients, simple correlation coefficients, and means are in upper lines of cells; standard errors, partial correlation coefficients, and standard deviations are in lower lines.
[a] Significant at 0.01 probability level.
[b] Significant at 0.05 probability level.
[c] Multiple correlation coefficient (unadjusted).

159

We may now turn to brief consideration of estimates of the other relations presented earlier in this paper. Estimates of parameters of (2), involving 1958 capital expenditures and two expected sales change variables as well as the other variables already considered, may be seen in Table 6. In this case I have divided firms into "smaller" and "larger" sets, the line of division being 1953 gross fixed assets of $100 million. First, it may be observed that the coefficients of expected sales changes were generally positive but tended to pick up, apparently, some of the role of past sales changes seen in (1). This is, of course, consistent with the model, which suggests that capital expenditures should depend upon the relation between current capacity and expected demand, with past changes in sales relevant because of their effects on expected demand. The sum of the sales change coefficients in (2), including the coefficient of the expected sales change term, is not more (and is even somewhat less) than the sum of sales change coefficients (for a slightly larger sample) observed in the regression coefficients of 1958 capital expenditures for (1) shown in Table 1. It may also be noted that the coefficient of expected long-run sales change, from 1959 to 1962, was markedly higher (0.324 as against 0.038) for larger firms, whose anticipations of the future might be expected to be more precisely formulated, than for smaller firms. However, it is probably unwise to make too much of this difference in view of the relatively small number of firms and high standard errors attached to the coefficients. It may also be observed, with a similar caution even though the finding fits our theory, that there is a significantly positive coefficient of 0.288 for the profits variable for smaller firms and a significantly positive coefficient of 0.220 for the cross section of all firms; but in the case of larger firms the profits coefficient is −0.035. This is consistent with my earlier suggestion that whatever role might be found for past profits in the determination of capital expenditures would be more likely among smaller firms, where imperfections of the capital market might be relatively more operative. It should, of course, be realized that the coefficient of the profits variable in the all-firms estimate of (2) is higher than the corresponding estimate of the profits coefficient for 1958 capital expenditures in (1) partly because of the different definition of the profits variable: profits *after* taxes divided by *net worth* in (2), as against profits *before* taxes divided by *gross fixed assets* in (1).

However, differences in the two sets of estimates remain somewhat puzzling. They may reflect the tendency of firms to have a view of normal demand from which deviations in current experience are treated as in large part transitory. Hence, those firms which experienced low profits in 1957 or low sales in 1958 relative to other firms tended to expect greater gains relative to other firms in later years in order to get back to the normal line which they had accepted. The inclusion of expected sales change variables in the regression would, hence, pick up this effect that otherwise would contribute to negative relations between capital expenditures and current and recent experience in both sales and profits, which of course are not unrelated to each other. This hypothesis, for what it is worth, gets some support from the estimate of the coefficient of 1958 sales change: the figure is higher in the Table 6 estimate of (2) than in the corresponding estimate of (1) in Table 1, i.e., 0.119 compared to 0.063.[8]

It was possible to estimate parameters of (3), involving the variable for actual minus desired rate of utilization of capacity, with only 138 firms for which responses on this and the other variables in the relation were jointly available (Table 7). The coefficient of the capacity variable was 0.112, just over twice its standard error, in the estimate for all firms. However, the separate estimates for the regressions involving firms manufacturing durables and firms manufacturing nondurables, which comprised almost all of the set of firms for which data were available, differed markedly; the coefficient of the capacity variable for the nondurable firms was −0.116. On the other hand, the coefficient of 1956 sales changes was 0.245 in the case of nondurables manufacturers, a low 0.058 for all firms, and −0.046 for firms manufacturing durables. A possible explanation for the uncertain character of these results may be the negative values for the means of the capacity variable in 1956. One would not expect a clear relation between capital expenditures and the rate of utilization of capacity for those firms whose rates of utilization are substantially below desired utilization. The role of such a capacity variable might better be examined separately for firms operating at or above desired rates of utilization and those operating below such rates. This analysis has, however, not been undertaken and would prob-

---

[8] These coefficients are roughly comparable in spite of different definitions of the variables. While denominators of the sales change variables are centered around 1957 in (2) instead of around 1953 as in (1), capital expenditures in (2) are divided by 1957 fixed assets instead of by 1953 fixed assets, as in (1).

TABLE 7

CAPITAL EXPENDITURES AS DETERMINED BY RELATION (3), FOR DURABLE-
AND NONDURABLE-GOODS MANUFACTURERS, 1957

	Regression Coefficients and Standard Errors			Means and Standard Deviations		
	Durables	Non-durables	All Firms[a]	Durables	Non-durables	All Firms[a]
Constant term	.083	0.005	0.050			
	(.032)	(0.028)	(0.020)			
Δc_{56}	.130	−0.116	0.112	−.036	−.054	−.039
	(.075)	(0.089)	(0.054)	.138	.098	.124
Δs_{57}^{56}	.085	−0.047	0.027	.067	.070	.068
	(.110)	(0.088)	(0.072)	.101	.099	.098
Δs_{57}^{**}	.021	0.092	0.039	.016	.001	.009
	(.080)	(0.086)	(0.057)	.144	.109	.129
Δs	−.046	0.245	0.058	.074	.019	.051
	(.068)	(0.066)	(0.047)	.153	.128	.143
Δs_{55}	.072	0.130	0.111	.126	.093	.108
	(.053)	(0.070)	(0.039)	.185	.128	.163
p_{56}	.039	0.003	0.016	.349	.257	.304
	(.044)	(0.051)	(0.032)	.232	.169	.213
d_{53}	.452	1.705	1.029	.055	.051	.054
	(.503)	(0.545)	(0.332)	.020	.016	.020
i_{57}				.129	.112	.123
				.082	.071	.078
$\Sigma\Delta c$ and Δs coefficients	.263	0.304	.347			
n	79	54	138			
$\hat{R}^2$	.043	0.365	0.132			

NOTE: Regression coefficients and means are in upper lines of cells; standard errors and standard deviations, in lower.

[a] Including five nonmanufacturing firms.

ably, in any event, not be successful with the current small number of observations.

Finally, the role of capital expenditure anticipations is examined by considering estimates of parameters of (4), (5), and (6). The under-lying hypothesis, it may be recalled, is that except for data or in-formation which become available after the time anticipations are

TABLE 8
CAPITAL EXPENDITURE ANTICIPATIONS AND CAPITAL EXPENDITURES AS DETERMINED BY RELATIONS (4)–(6): POOLED REGRESSIONS 1955–58 AND REGRESSIONS ON INDUSTRY-YEAR MEANS

| | REGRESSION COEFFICIENTS AND STANDARD ERRORS | | | | | | CORRELATION CO-EFFICIENTS: SIMPLE (RELATION 4) AND PARTIAL (RELATION 6) | |
| | *Pooled Data, All Years* | | | *Industry-Year Means* | | | *Pooled Data, All Years* | *Industry-Year Means* |
	Antici-pations (Rela-tion 4)	Expenditures (Rela-tion 5)	(Rela-tion 6)	Antici-pations (Rela-tion 4)	Expenditures (Rela-tion 5)	(Rela-tion 6)		
Constant term	.036 (.004)	.036 (.004)	.010 (.002)	.031 (.016)	0.018 (0.018)	−0.010 (0.008)		
Δs_t			.048 (.007)			0.081 (0.030)	0.167[a] 0.180[a]	0.057 0.521[b]
Δs_{t-1}	.143 (.012)	.122 (.011)	.015 (.007)	.243 (.085)	0.233 (0.097)	−0.013 (0.048)	0.294[a] 0.055[b]	0.539[a] −0.059
Δs_{t-2}	.097 (.011)	.086 (.011)	.019 (.007)	.142 (.048)	0.114 (0.055)	−0.012 (0.028)	0.174[a] 0.076[a]	0.066 −0.093
Δs_{t-3}	.081 (.012)	.079 (.011)	.024 (.007)	.141 (.047)	0.135 (0.055)	−0.003 (0.027)	0.137[a] 0.092[a]	0.103 −0.021
Δs_{t-4}	.134 (.013)	.126 (.012)	.015 (.008)	.191 (.055)	0.219 (0.063)	−0.037 (0.040)	0.196[a] 0.049	0.233 −0.203
Δs_{t-5}	.063 (.014)	.060 (.013)	.004 (.008)	.035 (.064)	0.014 (0.074)	−0.053 (0.034)	0.095[a] 0.014	−0.211 −0.335
Δs_{t-6}	.062 (.014)	.052 (.013)	.007 (.008)	.093 (.074)	0.045 (0.085)	−0.048 (0.037)	0.183[a] 0.024	0.554[a] −0.276
η_{t-1}	.017 (.010)	.030 (.009)	.019 (.006)	−.007 (.060)	−0.014 (0.069)	0.018 (0.030)	0.264[a] 0.092[a]	0.464[a] 0.133
I_{53}	.902 (.072)	.797 (.068)	.130 (.044)	.956 (.415)	1.259 (0.477)	0.129 (0.232)	0.388[a] 0.079[a]	0.323 0.123
$t-1$	d		.723 (.016)	d		1.000 (0.103)	1.000[a] 0.776[a]	1.000[a] 0.908[a]
t		d	d		d	d	0.851[a] 0.862[c]	0.944[a] 0.975[c]
Δs coefficients	.579	.524	.133	.846	0.760	−0.085		
	1,388	1,388	1,388	31	31	31		
R^2	.336	.325	.742	.668	0.589	0.927		

NOTE: Regression coefficients and simple correlation coefficients are in upper lines of cells; standard errors and partial correlation coefficients, in lower.
[a] Significant at 0.01 probability level.
[b] Significant at 0.05 probability level.
[c] Multiple correlation coefficient (unadjusted).
[d] Dependent variable.

formed or plans are made, capital expenditures and capital expenditure anticipations are functions of the same variables. This seems amply confirmed in the findings presented in Table 8. Where capital expenditures and capital expenditure anticipations are both related to sales change variables current with or preceding the points of time at which anticipations were indicated, the estimates of parameters are found to be strikingly similar. This is true both for the pooled data of individual firms for all years and for the regressions on industry-year means.

In (6), capital expenditures are made a function of capital expenditure anticipations and sales changes current at the time of capital expenditures, but anticipations are postdated, as are the lagged sales changes, profits, and depreciation variables. Here, interestingly, the coefficients of sales change variables known at the time capital expenditure anticipations were indicated were close to zero, but were still significantly positive in a number of cases, in the regressions of pooled individual-firm data. Most, but apparently not all, of the variance of sales changes affecting capital expenditures was picked up in capital expenditure anticipations. The coefficient of the sales changes which were subsequent to capital expenditure anticipations is, however, a distinctly larger and significantly positive 0.048. Results in the case of industry-year means were similar with regard to the positive coefficient of Δs_t in the regression including capital expenditure anticipations as an independent variable. But coefficients of the lagged sales variables, while low in absolute amount, were persistently negative. These results would seem to suggest that capital expenditure anticipations, as a forecast of actual expenditures, rather underreflect the intra-industry variance in actual sales changes but somewhat overreflect the interindustry variance. Be that as it may, these sets of estimates seem essentially consistent with the concept of a realizations function that I have discussed at greater length elsewhere.[9]

Conclusion

While closer study of these and other data is in order and will be forthcoming, the preliminary report I have made here seems to confirm the operation of a distributed lag accelerator in the determination of capital expenditures. It similarly offers further evidence that the apparent role of past or current profits (as distinguished

[9] "Investment Plans and Realizations," *American Economic Review*, May 1962.

from the expected profitability of investment) is in large part if not entirely a proxy role which can be accounted for by introducing properly into the quantitative analysis variables more truly related structurally to capital expenditures. This is indicated both by the regression coefficients of sales change and profit variables for capital expenditures of four successive years and in the comparison of simple and partial correlation coefficients of capital expenditures with profits. These findings are given added support by examination of the role of sales change expectations. In this latter analysis, conducted separately for large and small firms, there is evidence that whatever role does exist for past profits is confined to smaller firms (where imperfections of capital markets may be more relevant). Some sketchy but uncertain further support of the operation of a demand-capacity relation is found in examination of the role of actual minus desired rates of utilization of capacity as indicated in 1956 McGraw-Hill survey responses. Regressions involving capital expenditure anticipations prove consistent with the underlying model of the determination of capital expenditures as well as with the role of anticipations suggested by the concept of a realizations function.

Most interesting and suggestive of fruitful work in the future is the comparison of findings from regressions of pooled individual firm data for regressions of all years and regressions of observations composed of industry-year means. In the latter case the sum of sales change coefficients was markedly higher than in the former; and the proportion of variance in the capital expenditures variable accounted for by the regression, decidedly large. It is suggested that this is strikingly consistent with application of a "permanent income hypothesis" to the theory of investment. For in any quantitative analysis one should expect the variance of capital expenditures around its mean to be related to variances of sales changes around those means which are viewed as relatively long run or "permanent" rather than those that are considered temporary or "transitory." And there is reason to believe that the variance of sales changes around industry-year means includes in larger proportion a permanent component than the variance of sales changes between firms. But definitive and rigorous evaluation of these findings, as suggested earlier, calls for a formal analysis of variance and covariance—and another paper.[10]

[10] Some of this formal analysis has now been reported upon in "Investment: Fact and Fancy," *American Economic Review*, May 1963, pp. 237–246.

COMMENT

BERT G. HICKMAN, Brookings Institution

I find myself in an enviable position for an invited discussant, since I have been asked to comment on a paper which is both important and impressive, but in which I nonetheless find considerable area for disagreement. The bulk of my discussion will be concerned with Robert Eisner's empirical work on the investment function, but first I want to comment briefly on certain aspects of his introductory statement which require qualification if misunderstanding is to be avoided over the points at issue between critics and defenders of the acceleration principle and over the implications of Eisner's empirical analysis.

To begin with, Eisner uses the terms "acceleration principle" and "pressure on capacity" interchangeably. It is clear from his own explicit formulation and from his citations to other authors that when he refers to the acceleration principle, he has in mind a model in which allowance is made for excess capacity and reaction lags when sales increases are translated into investment decisions, and in which curbs on the time-rate of disinvestment in response to sales declines are recognized. Now, for those who identify theories by their predictions, the acceleration principle as originally formulated and still widely understood means at least a strong tendency for net investment to vary with the rate of change of output and to lead fluctuations in the level of output, and for gross investment to fluctuate more widely than output. However, as Chenery emphasized, a capacity formulation of the capital stock adjustment process "has a more fundamental effect than merely making the accelerator flexible. It changes the simple dependence of investment on the rate of change in demand, it alters the phase relationship between investment and output over the cycle, and it does not require that the amplitude of fluctuations in gross investment be larger than those in output."[1] Thus, even if Eisner's results were accepted as providing

---

[1] Hollis B. Chenery, "Overcapacity and the Acceleration Principle," *Econometrica*, January 1952, p. 14. Chenery tests his "capacity principle" against the "acceleration principle." L. M. Koyck also takes the position that the acceleration principle posits a close short-run relationship between net investment and the *rate of change* of output (as in the models of Harrod, Samuelson, and Hicks), and contrasts that situation with one in which the adjustment of capacity to output is slow as a consequence of the distributed lag, making net investment a function of the *level* of output in the short run (as in the Kalecki and Kaldor models). Cf. L. M. Koyck, *Distributed Lags and Investment Analysis*, Amsterdam, 1954, pp. 72–73.

full verification of the operation of his version of the accelerator mechanism, it would be important to remember that this would not constitute verification of the predictions about investment-output relationships historically associated with the acceleration principle and embedded in much of cycle and growth theory.

On another point, Eisner's statement that he espouses the acceleration principle because it fits in with the main body of theory based on the maximization principle must have an ironical ring to those who were critical of the principle in the past precisely because of its disparagement of economic determinants in the investment decision. Eisner does not himself argue that the capital-output ratio is invariant in either the short or the long run for technological reasons, but many distinguished economists have done so. Moreover, even though he implicitly recognizes the relevance of product and factor prices, they do not enter his investment function as explanatory variables. In this sense, the acceleration principle has been abstracted from, rather than fitted into, a maximizing theory of investment.

Nor should Eisner's implication that profits from past or present operations cannot be fitted into the main body of a maximizing investment theory go unanswered. I turn now to a discussion of his empirical findings, in the course of which I will show how profits may enter the investment equation through rational structural relationships derived from maximizing premises.

First for some comments on Eisner's data and deflation procedures. It will be recalled that his basic regression includes as independent variables a set of lagged sales changes, a profits term, and a depreciation term. The dependent variable is gross capital expenditure. Each sales change is expressed as a ratio to average sales in 1952–54, and all other variables are divided by the 1953 value of gross fixed assets. Sales, capital expenditures, and profits are corrected for price changes, whereas depreciation allowances and gross assets are not.

The ratio of depreciation to gross fixed assets is intended to measure the average durability of capital. The data on depreciation and fixed assets are for 1953 and are gross of Korean War accelerated amortization. This means that the useful lives will be considerably distorted in defense-related firms but not in others, introducing a spurious source of variation in the durability measure. Similarly, the 1957 values of fixed assets are involved in his second regression, with distorting effects on apparent useful lives owing to the uneven incidence of methods of curvilinear depreciation under the 1954 tax code.

Another source of spurious variation is Eisner's decision to forego price deflation of fixed assets and depreciation allowances. Whereas it is true, as he states, that the ratio of depreciation to fixed assets would be little affected by price deflation, the same cannot be said of the ratios of capital expenditures and profits to fixed assets. Both capital expenditures and profits are deflated by an index of capital goods prices, but each is expressed as a ratio to fixed assets at original cost. If fixed assets were converted to constant dollars by a weighted average of capital goods prices over the useful life span of assets for each firm, the result would be to alter the capital stocks unevenly as among firms with differing lives and time patterns of past investment. Thus, price deflation of fixed assets would alter the distributions of both the investment-to-assets and profits-to-assets variables.

The foregoing problems concerning biases in the data are troublesome because they have unknown effects on the regression results, but my strongest reservations about the significance of the findings stem from another source. They relate to certain deficiencies in Eisner's formulation of the role of profits in the investment decision. Profits may affect investment by influencing either the cost of funds or the marginal efficiency of investment. Let us deal first with effects on the cost of funds.

Eisner concedes that profits may play an independent role if capital markets are imperfect, but suggests that capital rationing is apt to influence only a small portion of total investment because it is a problem primarily for small firms. However, Duesenberry has shown that the imputed cost of funds may rise abruptly for amounts of investment in excess of internal funds from current operations because of the increased risk associated with higher debt-earnings ratios.[2] Debt aversion is not confined to small firms: rather, it will be strongest for firms subject to high risks from cyclical or competitive factors. Similarly, the cost of equity funds will vary with the degree of risk of the business and its growth prospects. Thus, for many firms, the cost of external funds may be considerably higher than the opportunity cost of internal funds. These considerations suggest that the volume of internal funds may be a significant determi-

[2] James S. Duesenberry, *Business Cycles and Economic Growth*, New York, 1958, Chap. 5.

nant of investment expenditure within a profit-maximizing framework.

How could one test for the influence of internal funds in a multiple regression of the type used by Eisner? The relevant variable would be profits after taxes and dividends plus depreciation. It would be included for either the year preceding or the year concurrent with the investment expenditure to be explained, or for both years, since its principle a priori effect is to cause the firm to increase or decrease the current rate of adjustment of desired to actual capital stock. Depreciation allowances and retained earnings would be entered at their accounting values after deflation by an index of current prices of capital goods. Finally, their combined value would be deflated by gross fixed assets in the same units used to deflate capital expenditure.

Eisner's formulation differs in several respects from the foregoing suggestions. Thus, although profits are included with a one-year lag and are deflated by capital goods prices, they are entered before taxes and dividends. The inclusion of taxes probably makes little difference, since the correlation of before-tax and after-tax profits with investment would be virtually the same,[3] but the distribution of retained earnings may be substantially different from that of after-tax profits because of differing dividend policies. Depreciation allowances have also been included, but with a lag varying between two and six years and without deflation by capital goods prices.

I do not know how the regression results would be influenced by the changes I have suggested, and it may be dangerous to speculate on the meaning of the correlation for the present form of the profits and depreciation variables. It does seem likely, however, that the strong influence exerted by the depreciation variable in the present correlation would persist in the new one. In Eisner's view, of course, the depreciation variable is essentially a measure of replacement

[3] Neglecting small corporations and loss firms, profits after taxes should be about one-half of profits before taxes. Decreasing the profits of all firms by one-half would not alter the partial correlation coefficient between profits and investment, although it would double the size of the net regression coefficient. Incidentally, if comparisons are to be made among the regression coefficients of sales, profits, and depreciation, it would be preferable to use beta coefficients, since the variables are expressed in different units and differ in variability. Inspection of the standard deviations in Table 3 indicates that the size of the regression coefficient of depreciation would be substantially reduced if it were expressed as a beta coefficient. The coefficients of profits and the sales change variables would be increased, but would not change much relative to one other. The considerable disparity between the uncorrected coefficients of profits and depreciation, however, would be substantially reduced by the conversion to beta units.

demand. Admittedly, there is a serious identification problem involved in separating the effects of depreciation allowances as a source of investible funds from their role as an index of replacement demand, but until that is done, the interpretation of the results is largely a matter of taste.

There is yet another way by which current profits may enter the investment decision, this time through the investment demand schedule. The marginal efficiency of investment in additional capacity is that rate of discount which equates the present value of the prospective series of annual net yields from the new assets to their purchase cost. One way to estimate the average annual net yield is to multiply the expected physical volume of sales per year by the expected gross profit margin (profits after taxes plus depreciation) on each unit sold. In view of the uncertainties which confront the decision-maker with respect to the future path of product demand, factor prices, and technical progress, it would not be unnatural or irrational for him to extrapolate the current gross margin into the future, just as he might rationally extrapolate the current level or rate of change of sales.

Thus, one way to introduce price-cost influences explicitly into Eisner's regression would be to include the gross profit margin as a variable. That is, after-tax profits plus depreciation would be entered in the numerator of the variable; and deflated sales of the same year, in the denominator. In order to take into account the decision and gestation lags stressed by Eisner, the profit margin variable would be entered with the same sort of distributed lag as changes in deflated sales. Since the dependent variable is real capital expenditure, each lagged value of the margin variable would be divided by the capital goods price index for that year.

One may speculate tentatively about the possible statistical problems of a regression containing a series of lagged sales changes plus a series of lagged gross margins. Total profits are so highly autocorrelated that Eisner included only one profits variable in the regressions. Autocorrelation of gross margins on current sales should be much smaller. Unfortunately, however, the collinearity between the sales change and profit margin variables would probably be high. This is because there is a strong positive correlation between gross profits margins and levels of capacity utilization. Also, the correlation between sales changes and levels of capacity utilization will be high in periods such as that covered by Eisner, during which there are no deep contractions and full capacity utilization is closely approached at cyclical peaks.

The high simple correlation between sales changes and profit margins implies two things. First, in Eisner's regressions, the sales change variables may be "carrying" part of the influence of the omitted margin variables. Secondly, however, a regression containing both sales change and margin variables might be so strongly affected by collinearity as to provide inconclusive results about the separate influence of the two kinds of variable.

But how essential is it to separate the two variables? Eisner argues that the main task is to distinguish between the role of profits and demand factors. In my opinion, the problem should be defined instead as that of distinguishing between factors affecting the cost-of-funds schedule and those affecting the investment demand schedule, since there are a priori grounds for expecting profits to affect both sides of the investment decision. A step in this direction, given data such as Eisner's, might be made by formulating a regression with the following properties.

A demand variable would be defined which was the product of (1) the change in deflated sales between one year and the next and (2) the gross profit margin in the second year, after correction for changes in capital goods prices.[4] It would be included with a distributed lag. It may be observed in passing that this formulation would be akin to, though less complete than, those capital stock adjustment theories in which the desired level of capital stock is made a function not only of the level of output but also of product and factor prices and interest rates. The cost-of-funds variable would be the one previously suggested: retained earnings plus depreciation allowances at original cost, both deflated by capital goods prices of the same year and expressed as a ratio to gross fixed assets. Once again, however, even if this regression were as successful as the wildest optimist could expect, the "internal funds" variable could be identified as a supply variable only if some way were found

---

[4] This formulation depends on the assumption that the gross profit margin in the second year is a better approximation to the margin at an optimum rate of capacity utilization than would be the margin of the preceding year. This appears reasonable, given the prevailing view that marginal cost is virtually constant until the firm is operating at nearly its maximum short-run output, since the sum of variable costs per unit and overhead costs (excluding depreciation) per unit should then fall throughout most of the observed utilization range. Similarly, profit markups over variable cost are apt to be shaved when substantial excess capacity exists and increased when output is near full capacity.

to control for the relationship between depreciation allowances and replacement demand. Perhaps some discrimination between the two aspects of depreciation could be achieved by retaining Eisner's variable, in which depreciation at original cost is divided by gross fixed assets at original cost, along with the new variable—but this attempt, too, is likely to founder on intercorrelation between the two depreciation variables.

In conclusion, I do not believe that Eisner has proved that realized profits and internal funds are insignificant factors in investment decisions. This does not mean, however, that I am advocating the "profits principle" to the exclusion of the "sales principle" or urging that profits are necessarily more important than the capacity-output relationship in determining the volume of investment. What all of us want to know is the relative importance and elasticities of the various investment determinants; and this can only be established within the framework of a complete model in which all relationships are identified and collinearity is reduced to manageable proportions. We are all in debt to Eisner and other economists who are tackling this formidable task head-on.

REPLY by Robert Eisner

Bert Hickman's attempt to credit me with a novel, flexible formulation of the acceleration principle is all too flattering. J. M. Clark, many years ago, argued against confusing the complex relation between investment and changes in demand with the "mechanical law" which he has employed as an heuristic tool.[1] But since Hickman questions my view of the acceleration principle as an "abstraction from" the broad canvas of economic theory, it may be useful to rise to the issue.

In accordance with hypotheses of profit maximization, one should expect a business firm to incur capital expenditures, when such expenditures would increase the mathematical expectation of profits (or reduce the mathematical expectation of loss).[2] But it must be

---

[1] "Business Acceleration and the Law of Demand: A Technical Factor in Economic Cycles," *Journal of Political Economy*, March 1917, pp. 217–235, reprinted in American Economic Association, *Readings in Business Cycle Theory*, Philadelphia, 1951, pp. 235–254, with "Additional Note," written in 1936, pp. 254–260, especially pp. 256–257.

[2] I do not doubt that business behavior is influenced by more than the goal of maximization of the mathematical expectation of future profits. For one thing, one might certainly wish to take into account, for many purposes, other parameters than the mean of the probability distribution of expected profits, thus allowing, for example, for desires to reduce the risk of major loss or bankruptcy. But I doubt that Hickman really means to challenge the hypothesis of profit maximization suggested above.

clearly understood that this has nothing to do with incurring capital expenditures when profits are expected to be high, let alone incurring capital expenditures when profits have been high. Thus, in my model, a firm would wish to purchase additional plant and equipment when such purchase would add to its profits, whether it is currently making higher profits or not and whether it was expecting to make higher profits or not. Similarly, a firm earning high profits or expecting to earn high profits would not purchase additional plant and equipment unless the additional plant and equipment were expected to *add* to its future profits. This judgment, however, is subject to modification to the extent that imperfections of capital markets affect the ability of firms to finance their desired expenditures.

My theoretical model is thus based on profit maximization, but not on profits. In accordance with it, and with almost any reasonable production function, one should expect increases in demand sooner or later to generate capital expenditures, and profits to be associated with capital expenditures only to the extent that they themselves were associated with the pressure of demand on capacity. Capital expenditures would be associated with profits per se only where imperfections of capital markets were likely to be significant, and we might expect that this would normally be true with relatively smaller firms. And this is—remarkably, to anyone accustomed to the frustration of trying to fit treacherous data to a theoretical mold— what the data do reveal. I am confident of the wisdom of my theoretical formulation and happy to argue in theoretical terms on its merit. But I do regret that Hickman, commenting on an essentially empirical paper, does not note that the empirical data do indeed argue for the usefulness of the theory.

Hickman's only criticisms bearing on the empirical results relate to the possibility that depreciation will indeed measure other things than durability, and to my failure to deflate depreciation and gross fixed assets for price changes. With a better measure of durability presumably I would have gotten higher coefficients of determination. But there is no *apparent* reason—and Hickman has advanced none— why the failure of the depreciation variable to pick up all of the "noise" relating to interfirm differences in durability of capital should lead us to reject the estimated coefficients of the other variables with which we are concerned. Similarly, a better measure of the real value of gross fixed assets should have eliminated some of the "noise" or unexplained variance in the regression. But unless the imperfection of the measure of capital stock has contributed consistent bias, and again Hickman has not argued that it has, one cannot see why this imperfection should obscure any really significant role of profits.

Hickman's preference for beta coefficients to standard regression coefficients in comparing roles of profits and depreciation is surely not justified. According to his theoretical model, apparently, depreciation, like profits after taxes and dividends, should, by affecting the flow of funds, generate investment. A dollar of funds should then generate the same amount of investment, whether called by the accountant depreciation or profits. The decided difference between the coefficients of the depreciation variable and the profits variable is indeed very strong evidence that the element affecting the flow of funds, presumably common, by Hickman's argument, to both profits and depreciation, is not the factor affecting investment. Hickman is certainly cavalier in his comment, on my evidence on this point, that "interpretation of the results is largely a matter of taste."

The variables that Hickman would define and the relations that he would estimate are subject to serious reservations. First, he would take as a measure of the "flow of internal funds" profits after taxes, minus dividends plus depreciation charges. It should, of course, be pointed out that neither profits nor depreciation is a direct measure of funds. As any small businessman can testify, profits need not accrue in any liquid form. All too frequently they are tied up in accounts receivable, inventories, and plant and equipment. But further, whatever Hickman's reservations about the perfection with which depreciation charges measure durability and replacement requirements, it is surely improper to act as if they do not measure them at all and to use a variable involving depreciation charges to indicate the influence of internal funds. As suggested above, if depreciation charges and profits after taxes really do measure the role of internal funds, the coefficients of these two variables should not differ substantially when introduced independently in a multiple regression. Yet my own findings demonstrate that the regression coefficient of profits was small or not significantly different from zero when the depreciation coefficient was substantially positive and highly significant. Nor could I accept profits after taxes, less dividends, as a measure of the influence of internal funds on capital expenditures. If any positive relation were found between capital expenditures and profits after taxes minus dividends, one would be hard-pressed to identify

174

the relation. It would appear at least as reasonable to argue that firms anticipating or incurring high capital expenditures would keep dividend payments low in order to retain funds, as it would be to infer that those firms with a record of low dividend payments decide to use their excess funds to incur capital expenditures, rather than increase dividend payments or use the funds in some other fashion.

One can hardly judge the variable

$$\frac{\text{profits after taxes, plus depreciation}}{\text{sales}}$$

as a measure of price-cost influences. A spurious (replacement factor) element in depreciation charges has already been made clear. But what is more, firms with high ratios of profits to sales would tend, to some extent, to be firms operating at high rates of capacity. It would therefore be quite unjustified to infer that any positive association between capital expenditures and the ratio of profits to sales relates to "price-cost influences" rather than to the pressure of demand upon capacity.

The demand variable defined by Hickman as a product of the change in deflated sales and the subsequent gross profit margin is a queer one, and I would be hard-pressed to interpret his estimated coefficients. (I fail to understand Hickman's argument that the gross profit margin "in the second year is a better approximation to the margin at an optimum rate of capacity utilization than would be the margin of the preceding year.")

That these issues are important and loaded with economic and policy significance is made clear currently (April 1962), when leaders of the United States steel industry argue that they should have higher prices for steel in order to enjoy higher profits, which are in turn necessary to bring about capital expenditures. These would then enable the American steel industry to produce more cheaply and "competitively."

If internal funds and profits really were critical, the steel industry leaders might be correct. If, however, it is the expected profitability of investment that determines its amount, and if this depends largely upon the relation between expected product demanded and the current capacity to produce, then the United States steel industry leaders are unfortunate victims of their own mythology. An increase in prices, far from bringing about higher capital expenditures, might be expected to have the effect of reducing the quantity of steel de-

175

manded, and hence lowering the amount of capital stock required. It would be particularly important that *economists,* not trapped in the business mythology regarding the role of profits, make no similar mistake in *their* analysis of the determinants of business capital expenditures.

Determinants of Inventory Investment[1]

MICHAEL C. LOVELL

CARNEGIE INSTITUTE OF TECHNOLOGY

Introduction

THE crucial role of inventories in the generation of fluctuations in economic activity stands in marked contrast to the limited attention that economists have devoted in their empirical research to the study of inventory behavior. Of course, Jan Tinbergen [62], Lawrence Klein [33] [36], and Colin Clark [11] included inventory equations in their econometric models. Such studies as those of Edwin Mills [48] [50] [51], P. G. Darling [14] [15] [16], Franco Modigliani and Owen H. Sauerlander [52], Nestor E. Terleckyj [59], Jack Johnston [31], Murray Brown [8], and my own [40] [41] [42] have involved somewhat more extended econometric analysis of the behavior of inventories. Nevertheless, relative to the voluminous literature on consumption and fixed investment behavior, the area of inventory investment has barely been touched in econometric investigations.[2]

A convenient touchstone for appraising recent econometric investigations of aggregate inventory behavior is provided by the acceleration principle. In its most elementary form, the accelerator principle involves the assumption that entrepreneurs succeed in maintaining their stocks at an equilibrium level, H_t^e, which is linearly related to sales X_t.

[1] I am indebted to Richard Day, Ruth P. Mack, and Edward Mansfield for valuable suggestions and constructive criticism. Frederick Demming, James Keaten, Seong Y. Park of Yale, and E. Myles Standish of the Wesleyan University computation laboratory assisted with the computations. Research time for this paper was provided through the generosity of the Cowles Foundation for Research in Economics at Yale University and the National Science Foundation. The figures in brackets [ ] indicate references following the paper.

[2] Abramovitz [1, Chap. 21] presented a detailed analysis of the contribution of inventory investment to cylical fluctuations during the interwar period; for example, he contrasted peak-to-trough movements of GNP with the magnitude of inventory disinvestment during the downward half of the reference cycle; Thomas M. Stanback [58] presents a similar analysis of inventory movements during the post-World War II period. I have contrasted [40] the behavior of actual GNP with a hypothetical series derived by subtracting an estimate of the *gross* contribution of inventory investment to cyclical fluctuations, using the multiplier in order to compute the volume of consumption generated by inventory accumulation.

177

(1.1) $$H_t^e = \alpha + \beta X_t$$

This assumption concerning the behavior of the inventory stock implies that actual inventory investment, ΔH_t, is proportional to changes in sales volume.

(1.2) $$\Delta H_t = \beta \Delta X_t$$

Estimates of the parameters of this elementary model have been derived by D. J. Smyth [56] from annual deflated national income data for the United States covering the years 1948 through 1958.

(1.3) $$\Delta H_t = -.86 + .30\Delta Y_t + 0.07t \qquad R^2 = .87$$
$$ (.06) \qquad (0.24)$$

The change in inventory is explained by ΔY_t, the change in gross national product; the coefficient of time is not significant.[3]

Complications have been introduced into the basic accelerator concept in an attempt to obtain a more adequate framework for the econometric investigation of inventory behavior. The simple accelerator model does not explain the *timing* of inventory investment. Moses Abramovitz [1] pointed out in his path-breaking study that in contrast to the implications of the simple accelerator hypothesis, actual inventory investment is *not* proportional to changes in output. Modifications of the basic accelerator model which provide an explanation of why inventory investment does not lead cyclical changes in gross national product are discussed in the second part of this paper.

Errors made by firms in anticipating future sales volume constitute another problem that must be considered in the econometric investigation of inventory behavior. The buffer-stock versions of the accelerator principle of Eric Lundberg [44] and Lloyd Metzler [47] incorporate expectational errors in the analysis of the inventory cycle. The difficulties involved in introducing either data on actual sales anticipations or suitable surrogates are discussed in detail in the third section of this paper.

Other factors in addition to sales and output may influence the volume of inventories that firms desire to hold. Several investigators

---

[3] The contrast between the small trend coefficient in the inventory investment regression with a trend parameter of 1.48, reported by Smyth for fixed investment, suggests that plant and equipment expenditures may be much more important than changes in business inventory as a generator of secular expansion and growth. On the other hand, the fixed investment accelerator coefficient is only 0.17, little more than half the estimated value of the inventory relation.

have attempted to explore within the context of accelerator models the possible effects of monetary policy upon inventory investment [7] [39] [42] [46]. The possible role of "speculative" or "price-hedging" purchases of stocks has also been considered [9] [36] [39] [41]. I have presented rough estimates of the impact of Department of Defense procurement upon inventory investment [42]. In the last part of this paper, I review these interesting questions concerning the structural determinants of inventory investment.

Equilibrium Inventory and Adjustment Lags

The lag of inventory investment behind changes in output might be taken into account by a slight change in the dating of variables. Kalecki [32] found that a closer fit was achieved with annual data for the United States for the period 1930 through 1940 by regressing inventory investment upon the change in output lagged six months; he reports a correlation of 0.913 for the lagged regression as opposed to 0.828 when the lag was not taken into account.[4]

An alternative procedure, frequently employed in econometric investigations of plant and equipment as well as inventory investment, involves the flexible accelerator complication suggested in a theoretical paper by Richard Goodwin [25]. With this approach it is assumed that the typical firm attempts only a partial adjustment of its inventory toward the equilibrium level within a single period. It is assumed that actual inventory investment is only a fraction of the discrepancy between last period's stock and the current equilibrium level.

$$(2.1) \qquad \Delta H_t = \delta(H_t^e - H_{t-1}) + \epsilon_t$$

Here H_t^e represents the equilibrium level of stocks, an unobserved variable possibly determined by sales according to equation (1.1), but more likely influenced by additional variables as explained later in this paper. Only if δ, the reaction coefficient, is exactly equal to unity is an attempt made to adjust inventories fully to the equilibrium level. Consequently, an increase in sales volume or other determinant of equilibrium inventory may lead to a discrepancy between actual and equilibrium stocks which will only gradually be reduced with the passage of time.

---

[4] This evidence is not conclusive, however, for Smyth [56] reports that he achieved a closer fit with the unlagged rather than with the lagged regression.

As is well known, another expression equivalent to (2.1) is the Koyck [37] transformation

$$(2.2) \quad H_t = \delta H_t^e + \epsilon_t + (1 - \delta)(\delta H_{t-1}^e + \epsilon_{t-1})$$
$$+ (1 - \delta)^2(\delta H_{t-2}^e + \epsilon_{t-2}) + \cdots$$

Stocks are a weighted average of past equilibrium inventory levels. Robert Solow has explored an alternative scheme in which the weights are not restricted to simply successive terms in a geometric progression [57]. In his application of this procedure to inventory investment, which involves adding H_{t-2} as an additional explanatory variable to equation (2.1) above, only limited success was achieved, although quite interesting results were obtained with fixed investment [7]. It should be observed, however, that other investigators who have added lagged inventory investment to their inventory equation [16] [17] [39] have in effect followed the Solow rather than the Koyck procedure.

Several factors may account for the inertia of businessmen in adjusting inventories to equilibrium. Time may be required before orders placed to replenish stocks of purchased materials can be filled. Even if items are ordered promptly so as to maintain the sum of purchased materials inventory plus outstanding orders for additional items—what Ruth P. Mack calls "ownership position," adjusted to changes in sales volume—the physical magnitude of inventories actually on hand would still lag because of delays in delivery. Economies involved in large quantity orders may make it advisable for the cost-conscious firm to preserve only an imprecise relation between ownership position and sales volume. Because stocks are generally a conglomeration of heterogeneous items, the firm may find that considerable time is required in liquidating a surplus of a particular item, even though only a moderate excess in its aggregate inventory position is involved. When sales increase, a concomitant expansion of inventories may require enlarged warehouse capacity, and procuring this requires time. When sales of items produced to meet a seasonal pattern of demand prove disappointing, stocks may have to be carried over slack seasons before they can be liquidated. Such factors as these explain why firms are willing to suffice with a considerable departure of inventories from their equilibrium level.

Although most recent econometric investigations have involved a flexible accelerator principle, no attempt has been made to examine empirically possible determinants of the speed of adjustment. In studies of fixed investment behavior it is sometimes argued that there exists a maximum rate at which capital can be liquidated.[5] It might well be asked whether the speed with which inventories are adjusted toward the equilibrium level, the coefficient δ in equation (2.1), may not depend upon the sign as well as the magnitude of the discrepancy between actual and equilibrium inventory. The Goodwin formulation might be derived by assuming that the cost of adjusting inventories is related to the square of the discrepancy between equilibrium and actual inventories.[6] On the other hand, if costs of adjustment are simply proportional to the size of the discrepancy, firms may attempt an immediate adjustment to large departures from equilibrium but not respond at all when inventories are only slightly out of alignment.[7]

Several alternative formulations of equation (2.1) may be employed in econometric studies of inventory behavior. Instead of utilizing inventory investment as the dependent variable, one may fit an expression for the total stock of inventory

$$(2.3) \qquad H_t = \delta H_t^e + (1 - \delta)H_{t-1} + \epsilon_t$$

This is obtained by adding H_{t-1} to both sides of (2.1). With this procedure, the method of least squares yields precisely the same parameter estimates as before, although the correlation coefficient may be expected to be somewhat larger. Another procedure, most appropriate in the study of finished goods inventory, is to utilize the definition of output $Q_t \equiv X_t + \Delta H_t$ in conjunction with (2.1) to obtain:

$$(2.4) \qquad Q_t = X_t + \delta(H_t^e - H_{t-1}) + \epsilon_t$$

This approach has been employed by Modigliani and Sauerlander [52], by Edwin Mills [48] [50] [51], J. Johnston [31], and others in the analysis of the production decision. Observe that the error term ϵ enters equations 2.1, 2.3, and 2.4 in precisely the same form. This means that the application of least squares estimation procedures to any one of these three formulas will yield identical estimates of the

---

[5] Hicks [27] made the one-way accelerator play a prominent role in his model of the trade cycle. Leontief [38] also employed the construct in his generalization of the Hawkins multisector dynamic input-output model.

[6] In an interesting review by Charles Holt and Modigliani [29] of the contribution that the Carnegie quadratic decision rule approach can make to our understanding of inventory investment, the relationships between several alternative cost structures and the implied decision rule are considered.

[7] See Edwin Mills [48] and Martin Beckmann [4] concerning the details of this process.

parameters of the model and the same standard error of the estimate. On the other hand, the multiple correlation coefficient is sensitive to the particular form chosen for the regression; since generally $\sigma^2_{\Delta H} < \sigma^2_H$, we may expect

$$\frac{\sigma^2_{\Delta H} - \sigma^2_\epsilon}{\sigma^2_{\Delta H}} < \frac{\sigma^2_H - \sigma^2_\epsilon}{\sigma^2_H}$$

In certain other formulations of the same model the residual term enters in an essentially different form from the way it appears in (2.1). This is true of both the Koyck transformation and the expression for inventory investment obtained by first differencing equation (2.3).

$$(2.5) \qquad \Delta H_t = \delta \Delta H^e_t + (1 - \delta)\Delta H_{t-1} + \Delta \epsilon_t$$

This procedure has been followed by Mills [48] [50] in an attempt to reduce problems created by autocorrelated error terms. A final possibility is to divide both sides of (2.3) by sales volume in order to have an expression for the inventory sales ratio

$$(2.6) \qquad \frac{H_t}{X_t} = \delta \left(\frac{H^e_t}{X_t}\right) + (1 - \delta)\frac{H_{t-1}}{X_t} + \frac{\epsilon_t}{X_t}$$

For purposes of parameter estimation this last equation might be appropriately employed when one is concerned with the problem of heteroscedasticity, as when cross-section data can be utilized in the study of inventory behavior.

Whatever the form chosen for the regression, a problem is created by the fact that equilibrium inventory, H^e_t, is an unobserved variable.[8] If equilibrium inventory is regarded as a function of anticipated sales,

---

[8] Of course, the Munich business test surveys, the *Fortune* Business Roundup Survey, and the new Office of Business Economics survey of manufacturers' inventory and sales expectations provide some information on equilibrium inventory. But the data are often reported only in terms of the proportion of respondents reporting inventory "high," "low," or "about right." Even here, the validity of the response may be open to question. Thus, Murray Foss [21, p. 29] reports that "over the three-year period covered by the survey . . . relatively few firms have classified their stocks as 'low,' despite some sizable increases in inventories. At the moment it is too early to say whether the comparative absence of 'low' designations is an accurate portrayal of business sentiment regarding inventory conditions over this period, or whether it is the inevitable result of business thinking which always attempts to keep stocks as small as possible and thus classifies stocks as 'about right' so long as they are obviously not 'high.'" Foss also found it necessary to transform the raw anticipations series in order to obtain a relatively good predictor of actual inventory movements. Conceivably, an application of the "realization function" procedure, such as has been attempted by Murray Brown [8] on other data, would prove helpful here.

as with equation 1.1, substitution into (2.3) serves to eliminate the unobserved variable from the regression equation to obtain

$$(2.7) \qquad H_t = \delta(\alpha + \beta \hat{X}_t) + (1 - \delta)H_{t-1} + \epsilon_t$$

Since the coefficient of H_{t-1} provides an estimate of δ, the coefficient obtained for $\hat{X}_t$ may be unscrambled to obtain estimates of α and β, the parameters of the equilibrium inventory equation. Alternatively, the expression for equilibrium inventory could be substituted into (2.1) or (2.5) and utilized to explain investment in inventories. An estimate of the parameters of the equilibrium inventory equation can also be obtained by substituting into equation (2.4) the expression for production. In actual practice, of course, equilibrium inventory probably depends upon other variables in addition to sales, but this does not really introduce any new difficulties. Indeed, recognition of the distinction between equilibrium and observed inventory provides insight into the appropriate form in which additional variables should be introduced into the regression as well as a priori restrictions upon the magnitudes of parameters to be expected in empirical analysis.

Lawrence Klein [33] pioneered the application of the flexible accelerator to inventory data. Least squares estimates derived from deflated annual data for the period 1921–40 are presented by Klein.

$$(2.8) \qquad H_t = 1.06 + 4.66p_t + 0.13X_t + 0.48H_{t-1} + e_t,$$
$$ (1.15) \quad\;\; (0.02) \quad\;\; (0.08)$$

where X_t represents final sales (GNP less inventory change) and p_t is a price index.[9]

Later in this paper I shall show that utilization of actual sales rather than anticipated sales in the regression is equivalent to assuming that errors made by firms in anticipating future sales volume are randomly distributed. Klein's reaction coefficient is approximately 0.5, rather than 1.0, the value implied by the Smyth regression pro-

[9] Klein also estimated the same equation by the method of limited information within the context of a simultaneous equation model. It is interesting to note that the two sets of parameter estimates are practically identical, differing less than alternative parameter estimates of the same equation calculated by Carl Christ [10] from data covering a longer sampling period. There remains some question concerning the accuracy of Christ's data. Nevertheless, in certain applications, parameter estimates may well be more sensitive to the particular years utilized in the regression than to the choice between a simultaneous equation versus a single-equation least squares approach. Klein presented a third set of parameter estimates based on quarterly rather than annual data; a transformation procedure revealed that these coefficients were quite consistent with those derived from annual data.

cedure, equation (1.1); firms attempt to adjust halfway toward equilibrium each year. His regression implies that equilibrium inventories are determined by

$$(2.9) \qquad H_t^e = 2.03 + 8.96p_t + 0.25X_t,$$

an equation suggesting that the level of prices, perhaps because of money illusion, has a pronounced influence on equilibrium stocks.

Paul G. Darling [14] considered the forecasting value of an equation explaining the behavior of the quarterly book value of manufacturing inventory investment.

$$(2.10) \qquad \Delta H = -.387 + .415X_{-1} - .212H_{-2} + .324\Delta U_{-1} + e$$
$$\qquad\qquad\qquad (.044) \qquad (.022) \qquad (.054)$$
$$R = .945$$
$$\frac{\delta^2}{S^2} = 1.85$$

The change in inventory, ΔH, is explained by lagged sales, X_{-1}; stocks lagged two periods, H_{-2}; and the previous quarter's change in unfilled orders, ΔU_{-1}. Data extending from the third quarter 1947 through the third quarter 1958 were utilized in the regression. Darling reports that the lag structure was empirically determined by trial and error. No attempt was made to incorporate explicitly within the regression the impact of errors in anticipating sales volume. In order to determine the equilibrium inventory equation implied by Darling's regression, values of the explanatory variables that would not have led to an attempt to change the level of inventories must be determined. Setting $\Delta H = 0$ and solving the implicit equation thus obtained for H yields

$$(2.11) \qquad H^e = -1.82 + 1.95X + 1.53\Delta U$$

A dollar increase in quarterly sales generates almost twice as large an increase in equilibrium inventory; for every dollar increase in the change in unfilled orders, equilibrium inventory increases by $1.53. The reaction coefficient is 0.212, implying that firms in manufacturing attempt to liquidate roughly one-fifth of the discrepancy between equilibrium and actual inventory each quarter.

Nestor E. Terleckyj [59] has presented an interesting study focused upon the behavior of total inventory holdings in manufacturing and trade combined. Although Terleckyj did not work with deflated data, he did in certain of his regressions subtract the inventory valuation

184

adjustment from the change in book value inventories in order to eliminate the accounting effect of revaluating the existing inventory stock. The percentage quarterly change in the book value of trade and manufacturing inventory, less the inventory valuation adjustment, was explained by the lagged inventory sales ratio, I_{-1}/X_{-1}; the ratio of new orders to sales, N_{-1}/X_{-1}; and the unfilled orders-sales ratio, U_{-1}/X_{-1}.

$$(2.12) \quad \frac{\Delta I}{I} = -14.59 - 11.26 \frac{I_{-1}}{X_{-1}} + 30.75 \frac{N_{-1}}{X_{-1}} + 1.88 \frac{U_{-1}}{X_{-1}} + e$$
$$\quad\quad\quad\quad\quad\quad (2.23) \quad\quad\quad (5.52) \quad\quad\quad (.57)$$

$$R^2 = .78$$

The adjustment mechanism implied by Terleckyj's analysis is somewhat more complicated than that usually utilized in most studies of inventory investment. In order to see exactly what is involved, it is first necessary to determine the equation for equilibrium inventory. The level of inventory implying zero investment for given levels of sales and new and unfilled orders is obtained by setting $\Delta I = 0$ in equation (2.12) and then solving the resulting implicit equation to obtain

$$(2.13) \quad\quad\quad I^e = -1.3X + 2.7N + .17U$$

The coefficient of sales, $-1.3 = -14.59/11.26$, has the wrong sign; it is unfortunate that in every one of Terleckyj's regressions the intercept term is negative. It should be positive if the equilibrium level of inventory is to be positively associated with sales. In order to find the nature of the delayed adjustment mechanism, it is only necessary to observe that (2.13) may be rewritten in the form

$$(2.14) \quad\quad\quad \Delta I = 11.26 \left(\frac{I}{X_{-1}}\right)(I^e_{-1} - I_{-1}).$$

The speed of adjustment, $11.26(I/S)$, thus depends upon the current inventory sales ratio. Over the period of the regression the inventory-sales ratio averaged 1.56. Clearly, the parameter estimates presented by Terleckyj do not lend themselves to a simple interpretation in terms of the flexible accelerator concept.

As a final example, consider the following regression derived from deflated nonfarm inventory investment data for the period extending from the second quarter of 1947 through 1959. Nonfarm business inventory investment is explained by gross national product, the

185

change in GNP, and the backlog of unfilled orders, all measured in constant 1954 dollars at quarterly rates (Table 1).

$$(2.15) \quad \Delta H_t = 2.49 + .328X_t - .407H_{t-1} - .137\Delta X_t + .043U_t + e$$
$$ (2.9) \quad (.0405) \quad (.0485) \quad (.0925) \quad (.007)$$

$$R^2 = 0.736$$

In the chart, actual inventory investment is contrasted with the levels estimated by equation (2.15). The regression equation was computed in the summer of 1960. In order to illustrate how the model performs

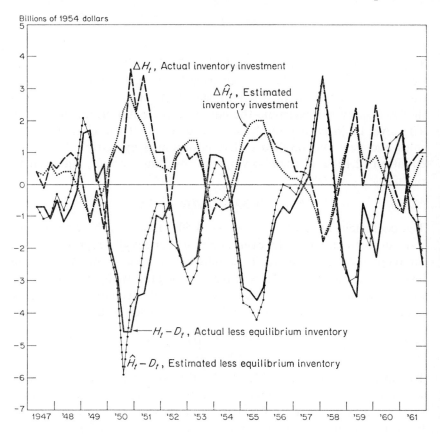

Billions of 1954 dollars

outside the regression period, preliminary Commerce Department data on inventory change, estimates of inventory investment derived by equation (2.15), and the inventory discrepancy are recorded for all of 1960 and three quarters of 1961. Predicted inventory investment clearly tends systematically to fall short of actual inventory accumu-

TABLE 1

NONFARM INVENTORY INVESTMENT AND SURPLUS INVENTORIES, 1947–62
(billions of 1954 dollars at quarterly rates)

		Inventory Investment		Surplus Inventory	
		Actual ΔH_t	Estimated $\Delta \hat{H}_t$	$H_t - H_t^e$	$\hat{H}_t - H_t^e$
1947	I	0.4		1.1	
	II	0.4	0.4	−0.7	−0.7
	III	−0.1	0.3	−1.1	−0.7
	IV	0.7	0.6	−1.0	−1.1
1948	I	0.5	0.3	−0.3	−0.5
	II	0.8	0.4	−0.8	−1.2
	III	1.0	0.4	−0.2	−0.8
	IV	0.8	0.0	0.6	−0.2
1949	I	−0.1	−0.6	2.1	1.6
	II	−1.2	−1.0	1.5	1.7
	III	−0.2	−0.4	0.3	0.1
	IV	−1.4	−0.2	−0.6	0.6
1950	I	0.6	0.8	−2.2	−2.0
	II	1.2	1.4	−3.0	−2.8
	III	1.0	2.3	−5.9	−4.6
	IV	3.6	2.8	−3.8	−4.6
1951	I	2.3	2.2	−3.4	−3.5
	II	3.4	1.9	−1.9	−3.4
	III	2.3	1.2	−1.3	−2.4
	IV	1.0	0.6	−0.6	−1.0
1952	I	1.0	0.5	−0.6	−1.1
	II	−0.8	0.4	−1.8	−0.6
	III	0.8	1.0	−2.0	−1.8
	IV	1.2	1.2	−2.6	−2.6
1953	I	0.8	1.4	−3.1	−2.5
	II	1.0	1.4	−2.7	−2.3
	III	0.4	0.6	−0.9	−0.7
	IV	−1.1	−0.3	0.1	0.9
1954	I	−0.6	−0.4	0.7	0.9
	II	−0.8	−0.5	0.5	0.8
	III	−0.7	−0.2	−0.5	0.0
	IV	0.0	0.5	−2.0	−1.5
1955	I	1.0	1.5	−3.7	−3.2
	II	1.4	1.9	−3.8	−3.3
	III	1.4	2.0	−4.2	−3.6
	IV	1.6	2.0	−3.6	−3.2

(continued)

187

TABLE 1 (concluded)

		Inventory Investment		Surplus Inventory	
		Actual ΔH_t	Estimated $\Delta \hat{H}_t$	$H_t - H_t^e$	$\hat{H}_t - H_t^e$
1956	I	1.6	1.4	−1.7	−1.9
	II	1.2	0.7	−0.6	−1.1
	III	1.1	0.4	0.0	−0.7
	IV	1.0	0.2	−0.1	−0.9
1957	I	0.4	0.2	−0.3	−0.5
	II	0.4	0.0	0.3	−0.1
	III	0.3	−0.3	0.9	0.3
	IV	−0.5	−0.9	2.4	2.0
1958	I	−1.8	−1.7	3.3	3.4
	II	−1.3	−1.2	1.6	1.7
	III	−0.6	−0.2	−0.7	−0.3
	IV	0.5	0.8	−2.5	−2.2
1959	I	1.5	1.5	−3.0	−3.0
	II	2.4	1.8	−2.9	−3.5
	III	0.0	0.8	−1.4	−0.6
	IV	1.0	0.7	−1.0	−1.3
1960	I	2.5	0.9	−0.7	−2.3
	II	1.2	0.3	0.2	−0.7
	III	0.5	−0.2	1.3	0.6
	IV	−0.3	−0.7	1.5	1.1
1961	I	−0.9	−0.9	1.7	1.7
	II	0.6	−0.1	−0.2	−0.9
	III	0.9	0.4	−0.7	−1.2
	IV	1.1	0.9	−2.3	−2.5
1962	I	1.5	1.1	−1.6	−2.0
	II				

lation; much better predictions could have been made by taking advantage of the tendency toward autocorrelated disturbances.[10]

[10] Terleckyj has reported that his model did not perform too satisfactorily as a predictor of inventory investment during this same period. In the 1960–61 recession his equations indicated small amounts of inventory accumulation rather than the substantial disinvestment that actually took place [59, p. 161]. Of course, a test of the predictive ability of a model in this form is difficult at the current time because of the preliminary nature of data currently available on the 1960–61 recession. Judging by past experience, considerable revision in inventory data must be expected. An alternative test is to refit the equation over a subperiod and either observe the stability of the regression coefficients, a test reported by Terleckyj [59, p. 161], or examine the ability of the regression fitted to the subperiod to "predict" the observations excluded from the regression, a procedure I have applied in another connection [42, p. 131].

Regression (2.15) implies the following expression for equilibrium inventory:[11]

(2.16) $$H_t^e = 6.1 + .806X_t + .106U_t$$

The equilibrium inventory-to-final-sales ratio, obtained by dividing both sides of (2.16) by X_t, is

(2.17) $$\frac{H_t^e}{X_t} = \frac{6.1}{X_t} + .806 + .106\frac{U_t}{X_t},$$

not 0.806, the marginal equilibrium sales ratio. Two estimates of excess inventories, the discrepancy between equilibrium and actual inventory, are presented on the chart. The first of the estimated series, $H_t - H_t^e$, was obtained by application of equation (2.16). This series is obviously sensitive to the particular parameter estimates obtained in the regression analysis; it is also sensitive to the implicit assumption that the discrepancy between observed and estimated inventory investment may be attributed entirely to the stochastic term in (2.1), the inventory adjustment equation. There is no basis for assuming that (2.16) is nonstochastic; the observed residuals should be regarded as providing an estimate of the sum of stochastic disturbances in both (2.16) and (2.1). Although there is no obvious way of unscrambling the observed error in the surrogate measurement of excess inventory, a rough estimate of the magnitude of the problem is provided by $\hat{H}_t - H_t^e$; this second set of estimates of the discrepancy between equilibrium and actual inventory differs from the first by the observed residual.[12] The two estimates are quite similar, although $\hat{H}_t - H_t^e$ is subject to somewhat smaller fluctuations.

The provisional nature of the estimates of excess inventory cannot be too strongly emphasized. Single-equation least squares procedures were utilized in estimating the parameters of equation (2.15). Clearly,

[11] In an earlier study [41] I presented estimates of surplus inventory for durable manufacturing.

[12] If the only source of stochastic disturbance were the error made by firms in anticipating future sales volume, equation 2.17 could be regarded as nonstochastic. Such an approach suppresses the role of errors of observation and the possibility that variables have been omitted from (2.17). As long as the residuals of (2.17) and (2.3) are not negatively correlated, the standard error of the estimate may be utilized to obtain an upper bound on the variance of the residual of the equilibrium inventory equation.

Murray Foss has suggested to me that the large discrepancy between desired and actual inventories during the early phases of the Korean War period may have been in part the consequence of governmental controls on the accumulation of strategic materials. The impact of such controls might be interpreted as a disturbance in the speed-of-adjustment mechanism, equation 2.1. A more complicated model might consider the effects of the availability of external funds upon the speed-of-adjustment coefficient.

this is an invalid procedure, for one would expect an increase in aggregate inventory investment, via the multiplier, to influence the level of final sales. Slight comfort with regard to the problem of simultaneity is provided by an examination of results achieved by other investigators who have compared single-equation least squares estimates of inventory-holding equations with those achieved by more complicated estimation procedures. Klein contrasts least square with limited information estimates [33]; Ta-Chung Liu, two-stage least squares with the single-equation results [39]. Although the parameter estimates were only moderately sensitive to the particular estimation procedure utilized, much greater credence could be given to the excess inventory equation if an estimation procedure recognizing the simultaneity problem had been utilized. Quite apart from the question of simultaneity, the presence of the lagged capital stock in the equation contributes to biased if consistent estimates of the reaction coefficient.

In addition to the question of interpretation of the residuals in estimating equilibrium inventory, a serious problem is created by the strong autocorrelation of the observed residuals of (2.15). The Durbin-Watson statistic is an embarrassingly low 0.68, and the serial correlation coefficient is 0.63. The estimates of the parameters of equations 2.16 and 2.17 are sensitive to whatever method is adopted in order to deal with this problem. If, for example, we follow a transformation procedure described by Klein [34] we obtain

$$(2.18) \quad H - .63H_{-1} = 0.9 + .3118(X - .63X_{-1})$$
$$(16.5) \quad (.0653)$$

$$+ .5723(H_{-1} - .63H_{-2})$$
$$(.0733)$$

$$+ .0402(X_{-1} - .63X_{-2}) + .0377(U - .63U_{-1})$$
$$(.0904) \qquad\qquad (.0150)$$

This implies the following equation for equilibrium inventory,

$$2.17' \qquad\qquad H_t^e = 5.7 + .7290X + .0881U$$

where the residual term is again neglected. Comparison of these coefficients with (2.17) reveals that the estimates of the equilibrium inventory equation are moderately affected by the transformation.[13]

---

[13] Although the sign test does not suggest autocorrelated error terms, it would have been interesting to have attempted further iterations with Klein's procedure until the regression coefficients stabilized. Of course, the existence of autocorrelation of the residuals of equation (2.15) does not in itself mean that the parameter estimates of that

In other inventory studies involving the flexible accelerator the problem of autocorrelated error terms has not proved particularly serious. In deriving my earlier estimates of equilibrium inventory for durable manufacturing and component industries the Durbin-Watson statistics were considerably larger. Duesenberry, Eckstein, and Fromm did not encounter a serious autocorrelation problem in their study of aggregate nonfarm inventory based on a more complicated equation.[14]

Derived estimates of unplanned or excess inventories have been utilized as explanatory variables in several regression studies. Klein [33] interpreted the residuals of his inventory determination relation, equation 2.6, as an index of the impact upon inventories of errors made by firms in judging market conditions; these residuals proved to be significant in the equation explaining adjustment in output, where output was defined as final sales plus inventory accumulation. In a recent study, Darling [16] utilized estimates, derived within the framework of the flexible accelerator, of the excess of equilibrium over actual inventory in an equation explaining fluctuations in the manufacturing production index. His significant results are not surprising, for the equivalence between the study of the production decision and inventory investment, as revealed by equation 2.4, means that the flexible accelerator concept itself implies the existence of a relation between excess inventories and production levels. Liu [39] showed cognizance of this relation when he utilized estimates of excess inventories in a price determination equation. The gross national product deflator declines when inventories are excessive, for then producers cut prices as well as curtail production; the effort is frustrated under Liu's assumptions, for the aggregate volume of sales does not respond to the price reductions.

---

regression are biased or inconsistent; it would be possible to retain the original parameter estimates and apply Wold's correction procedure to their standard errors [63, Chap. 13]; Klein's procedure does contribute to efficiency.

[14] The model considered by Duesenberry, Eckstein, and Fromm [17, p. 798] is a complicated equation containing a number of lagged variables. But their empirical results might be the consequence of a much simpler structure of the form

$$\Delta I = \alpha + \beta_1 X + \beta_2 I_{-1} + \beta_3 U_{-1} + \epsilon;$$

for simple calculations yield, for arbitrary ρ,

$$I_t = (1 + \rho)\alpha + (1 - \rho b_1)X + \rho\beta_1\Delta X + [\beta_2(1 - \rho) + \rho]I_{-1} + \rho\beta_2\Delta I_{-1} \\ + \beta_3(1 - \rho)U_{-1} + \rho\beta_3\Delta U_{-1} + \epsilon - \rho\epsilon_{-1},$$

the equation they considered. If the residuals of the first equation are autocorrelated, the second equation will yield a closer fit and perhaps be more satisfactory for prediction purposes; on the other hand, it will not necessarily give a more accurate representation of the determinants of inventory investment.

An explanation of the timing of finished goods inventory investment that is closely related to the flexible accelerator is the concept of production smoothing. This approach emphasizes the costs involved in changing output rather than inventory levels. A firm may systematically accumulate inventory of finished goods during periods of slack demand by having production exceed sales in order to run them off later during periods of peak demand. This practice serves to minimize costs involved in changing production levels and work force; it enables the firm to meet a larger peak demand with given plant capacity, thus economizing on capital. This approach has been employed in empirical studies by Modigliani and Sauerlander [52], Mills [48] [50] [51], and Johnston [31].

The production-smoothing argument implies that the seasonal pattern in inventories (or production) cannot be explained entirely by concomitant seasonal movements in sales. The complication may be suppressed by employing seasonally corrected data, one of several approaches utilized by Modigliani and Sauerlander. An alternative to working with deseasonalized data is to include seasonal dummy variables within the regression equation. This procedure, utilized by Johnston, could facilitate a statistical test of the production-smoothing hypothesis.[15] At a cost of additional degrees of freedom, the regression may be fitted separately for each season; this procedure has been employed by Modigliani and Sauerlander and by Johnston. An advantage of this practice, emphasized by Modigliani and Sauerlander, is provided by a theoretical demonstration that the extent to which changes in sales volume and other explanatory variables affect production levels and planned inventory depends upon whether the current quarter is typically one of seasonally high or low sales volume.

The production-smoothing hypothesis would not be of direct use in understanding cyclical movements in inventory investment if it only provided an explanation of a divergence of the seasonal pattern of inventory from that of sales volume. But the production-smoothing hypothesis may be invoked to explain the cyclical lag in inventory investment behind changes in sales volume that is to be observed in deseasonalized as well as uncorrected data. Mills introduced lagged

---

[15] The appropriate F-ratio for determining whether the addition of the set of seasonal dummies led to a significant improvement in fit was not provided by Johnston. For one model [31, p. 255] fourteen seasonal dummies out of thirty-two computed for eight industries were significant at the 5 per cent level; eight of these were significant at the 1 per cent level. For another model [p. 250], tested on the same data, twelve out of thirty-two were significant at the 5 per cent level; four of these, at the 1 per cent level.

production into equation 2.4; only a partial adjustment of production to the equilibrium level takes place within any one period. In this form, the production-smoothing hypothesis explains a lag of production behind changes in sales volume. Since sales differ from production by the change in inventory, the production-smoothing concept implies that the change in production, ΔQ, should appear in equation 2.1, explaining inventory investment, with a negative sign.[16] Since sales differ from production by the change in inventory, this leads to a lag of inventory behind sales changes over and above that which results from inventory-smoothing considerations. The evidence with regard to the cyclical form of the hypothesis is not conclusive; while lagged production has proved statistically significant in some regressions, in other applications the coefficient of lagged output has consistently had the wrong sign.[17] Additional evidence providing stronger support for the production-smoothing hypothesis is presented below in conjunction with an analysis of problems created by errors made by firms in anticipating sales volume.

Errors in Anticipating Sales Volume

Because production requires time, a firm selling its output in imperfect markets must have decided upon the current level of output on the basis of advance estimates rather than precise knowledge of demand conditions. When sales exceed the anticipated level, the buffer of finished goods inventory carried in order to prevent runouts is depleted; on the other hand, when sales forecasts are unduly opti-

---

[16] If Q_t^* is the level of output required to adjust inventories to the level prescribed by (2.2), the production-smoothing hypothesis implies that $Q_t = \gamma Q_t^* + (1 - \gamma)Q_{t-1}$. But this implies that actual inventory will fall short of the level suggested by (2.2) by

$$Q_t - Q_t^* = [1 - (1/\gamma)](Q_t - Q_{t-1})$$

where $1 - (1/\gamma) < 0$.

[17] When Edwin Mills ran his earlier tests [48] he analyzed his data in first-differenced form in order to avoid autocorrelated error terms. The production-smoothing coefficient inevitably had the wrong sign. In a more recent study [51], based on other data, Mills presents the results of regressions on non-first-differenced observations for four separate industries. In these regressions the lagged production terms generally have the right sign and are significant in terms of the customary tests; although the Durbin-Watson statistic indicates positive autocorrelation of residuals in two cases, it must be remembered that while inefficiency rather than bias is implied by autocorrelation, the standard tests of significance are not valid. I have considered [40, pp. 111–117] a flexibility-of-production term in regressions in which inventories serve as the dependent variable. The results were disappointing, perhaps because seasonally corrected data had to be employed. Approximately half the time the production-smoothing coefficient had the wrong sign; the coefficients were generally small relative to their standard errors.

mistic, unplanned inventory accumulation occurs. Only a firm fabricating goods to specific order escapes the problem. Two essential modifications of the basic accelerator model are required in order to take into account the complications created by anticipation errors in the analysis of finished goods inventory behavior. In the first place, anticipated sales $(\hat{X}_t)$ rather than actual sales must be inserted into the equilibrium inventory equation when the planned level of inventory is being determined. In addition, the impact of errors in anticipating sales volume upon the level of inventory must be taken into account.

These considerations suggest that finished goods inventory behavior is determined by the following equation

$$(3.1) \qquad H_t = \delta\alpha + \delta\beta_1\hat{X}_t + (1 - \delta)H_{t-1} + \lambda(\hat{X}_t - X_t) + \epsilon_{1t}$$
$$= \delta\alpha + \delta\beta_1 X_t + (1 - \delta)H_{t-1}$$
$$+ (\delta\beta_1 + \lambda)(\hat{X}_t - X_t) + \epsilon_{1t}$$

This modification of the basic accelerator may be further complicated if equilibrium inventories depend on other variables in addition to sales, or if production smoothing is introduced.[18] The surprise element $\hat{X}_t - X_t$, the excess of anticipated over actual sales, is preceded by λ, the "production adaptation coefficient," in order to take into account a complication introduced by Modigliani and Sauerlander [52]. If λ equals unity, the equation implies that the firm does not succeed in even partially compensating for errors made in anticipating sales during the period of observation; finished goods inventory falls below the planned level by the full extent of the forecast error. A λ less than unity implies that the firm manages at least partially to offset errors made in anticipating sales volume. At a possible cost of premium wage payments or, alternatively, losses due to idle time, production schedules may be revised on the basis of current sales experience. If $\lambda = 0$, the revision of the production plan is drastic enough to keep inventory at the planned level, a magnitude that may no longer be appropriate for current sales experience. If $\lambda = -\delta\beta$, the firm succeeds completely in compensating

[18] Furthermore, the anticipated sales variable determining equilibrium inventory, the $\beta_1\hat{X}_t$ term in (3.1), may most appropriately refer to moderately long-term expectations; in contrast, the error-of-expectations term, $\lambda(X_t - X_t)$, involves short-term anticipations of sales for the current period. This distinction, emphasized by Holt et al. [28], may be of but secondary importance for econometric studies if firms generally regard sales as having a stable seasonal pattern, so that short- and intermediate-range expectations are more or less proportional, particularly if seasonal dummy variables, deseasonalized data, or separate regressions for each season are employed.

for any errors made in anticipating sales volume.[19] It is apparent that the value of λ encountered in any empirical study would depend in part upon the length of the observation period involved in data collection relative to the duration of the production process; a smaller value of λ should be obtained when quarterly or annual rather than monthly or weekly data are utilized in the empirical study. Furthermore, the concept of adapting production so as partially to eliminate anticipation errors is the converse to the production-smoothing conjecture. If inventories are carried in order to iron out short-term fluctuations in sales, inventory rather than output levels may be expected to bear the brunt of the burden when sales anticipations prove to be incorrect.

UTILIZING ANTICIPATIONS DATA

When suitable data on expectations are available the parameters of the inventory equation may be estimated directly. This approach has been followed by Modigliani and Sauerlander [52], Mills [51], and in my own work [40] with Railroad Shippers' Forecast data. Murray Brown [8] and Peter Pashigian [54] have presented reports of studies based on *Fortune* magazine forecast data and annual Commerce Department–Securities and Exchange Commission anticipation series. T. Thonstad and D. B. Jochems [61] have utilized Munich business test data. None of these sets of data is entirely appropriate for the purpose, either because the data are presented in a form that requires transformation or because the number of observations is inadequate. Furthermore, a controversy continues as to whether the tendency of observed anticipations to regress toward former levels should be interpreted as implying that the data are subject to systematic measurement error or as revealing an important characteristic of actual anticipations.[20]

Consider the following regression derived from quarterly constant-dollar data on manufacturing finished goods inventory for 1948–55:

---

[19] As with δ, there is some question as to whether λ should be regarded as a parameter of the system unaffected by the magnitude or direction of the forecast error. Under the assumption of profit maximization the answer depends upon the costs involved in adjusting the work force and in sufficing with an inventory that is not at the equilibrium level; only if such costs are symmetric would λ be independent of the sign of the forecast error. If the costs are proportional to the square of the discrepancy, λ might be independent of the magnitude of the error.

[20] At one extreme, there is the argument of Albert Hart [26] that the expectations data must be reconstituted. On the other hand, Bossons [5] argues on the basis of cross-section evidence that expectations are actually regressive, and rightfully so!

(3.2a) $\quad H_t = -903.1 + .0746X_t + .1283(\hat{X}_t - X_t) + .7591H_{t-1}$
$$\qquad\qquad (.0195) \qquad (.0262) \qquad\qquad (.0599)$$

$$R^2 = .970$$

These estimates may be transformed in order to obtain a marginal desired inventory coefficient, β, of 0.098; the production adaptation coefficient is 0.054, while the inventory reaction coefficient is 0.24. For total manufacturing durables

(3.2b) $\quad H_t = -515.5 + .0906X_t + .1213(\hat{X}_t - X_t) + .6871H_{t-1}$
$$\qquad\qquad (.0144) \qquad (.0214) \qquad\qquad (.0519)$$

$$R^2 = .978$$
$$d = 1.33$$

For nondurables

(3.2c) $\quad H_t = 38.02 + .0321X_t + .1035(\hat{X}_t - X_t) + .8785H_{t-1}$
$$\qquad\qquad (.0291) \qquad (.0310) \qquad\qquad (.0811)$$

$$R^2 = .953$$
$$d = 1.86$$

In every case the surprise element, $\hat{X}_t - X_t$, appears with a coefficient that is several times its estimated standard error. If these figures could be taken at face value, they would suggest that although manufacturing firms are not prompt about adjusting inventories to their equilibrium level, they are extremely agile in adapting production schedules to unanticipated changes in sales volume.

Another example is provided by regressions obtained with quarterly data on the cement industry, covering 1947–56. Because the data are not deseasonalized, it is possible to subject the production-smoothing hypothesis to further test. It is to be observed that when the seasonal dummy variables[21] are excluded from the regressions (3.3a) and (3.3c), the current sales term has the wrong sign; furthermore, the introduction of the dummy variables leads to a reduction in the unexplained variance which is significant at the 5 per cent level, providing further support for Johnston's formulation of the production-smoothing hypothesis.

---

[21] $d_1 = 1$ in first quarter, zero otherwise;
$\quad d_2 = 1$ in second quarter, zero otherwise; and
$\quad d_3 = 1$ in third quarter, zero otherwise.

(3.3a) $\quad \Delta H = -.4596X + .2429(\hat{X} - X) - .2131H_{-1}$
$\qquad\qquad (.0912) \quad\; (.4313) \qquad\qquad (.1698)$

$$+ 34,439 + e \qquad R^2 = .643$$
$$(4447.8) \qquad\quad \bar{S}_e = 6,944$$
$$n = 39$$

(3.3b) $\quad \Delta H = .0047X + .5753(\hat{X} - X) - .2322H_{-1}$
$\qquad\qquad (.0037) \quad (.1855) \qquad\qquad (.1124)$

$$+ 11,446d_1 - 8,215d_2 - 14,213d_3 + 9,340 + e$$
$$(1,585) \quad\; (2,687) \quad\;\; (1,914) \quad\; (1,824)$$

$$R^2 = .9408$$
$$\bar{S}_e = 2,958$$
$$n = 39$$

(3.3c) $\quad \Delta H = -.2615X + .2203(\hat{X} - X) - .1705H_{-1}$
$\qquad\qquad (.0794) \quad\; (.3281) \qquad\qquad (.1294)$

$$- 1.1652\Delta Q + 22,551 \qquad R^2 = .799$$
$$(.2264) \qquad\; (4,096) \qquad \bar{S}_e = 5,282$$

(3.3d) $\quad \Delta H = .0040X + .5217(\hat{X} - X) - .2713H_{-1} - .3598\Delta Q$
$\qquad\qquad (.0035) \quad\; (.1781) \qquad\qquad (.1085) \qquad\; (.1717)$

$$+ 9,751d_1 - 5,646d_2 - 12,376d_3 + 10,008$$
$$(1,711) \quad\; (2,834) \quad\;\; (2,020) \qquad (1,763)$$

$$\bar{S}_e = 2,813$$
$$R^2 = .948$$

The change-in-quantity variable appears significant and with the correct sign in (3.3d), suggesting that in the cement industry production-smoothing has more than a seasonal influence upon inventory and production decisions.

Unfortunately, the expectational data utilized in all these regressions are an inaccurate synthetic series constructed from suspect Railroad Shippers' Forecast data. A description of the procedure utilized in deriving the $\hat{X}_t$ series may be relegated to the Appendix of this paper. It is necessary to emphasize at this point that since the discrepancy between anticipated and actual sales volume $(\hat{X}_t - X_t)$ is not observed with precision, the least squares procedure may be expected to yield a biased estimate of the production adaptation coefficient. This danger is enhanced if there is a systematic element in the observation error. Suppose that the actual mistake made by the firm in anticipating future sales is proportional to the observed error:

(3.4) $$\hat{X}_t^a - X_t = b(\hat{X}_t^o - X_t) + \epsilon_{4t},$$

where $\hat{X}_t^a$ is the actual level of anticipated sales and $\hat{X}_t^o$ observed anticipations. It has been argued by Albert Hart [26], in connection with the Railroad Shippers' Forecast anticipatory data, that the observed sales anticipations suggest that firms are unbelievably inaccurate forecasters. If this equation is substituted into (3.1), one obtains

$$H_t = \delta\alpha + \delta\beta_1 X_t + (1 - S)H_{t-1} + (\delta\beta_1 + \lambda)b(\hat{X}_t^o - X_t)$$
$$+ (\delta\beta_1 + \lambda)\epsilon_{4t} + \epsilon_{1t},$$

an equation of the same form as (3.1). Clearly, if observed expectational data systematically overstate errors made by firms in anticipating future sales volume, the regression will tend to suggest an excessive degree of flexibility in production plans.[22]

Although considerable improvement in the availability and accuracy of expectational data is currently being made, a number of studies testify to the extreme inaccuracies present in the *ex ante* data currently available. In his recent investigation of inventory investment, utilizing expectational data compiled by the Business Roundup staff of *Fortune* magazine, Murray Brown concluded with the comment that ". . . the *Fortune* ex ante variables provide only marginal gains to the prediction of inventory behavior. However, the anticipations data may become more useful in the future as observation error is reduced." Undoubtedly, expectational data in time series form will prove of increasing usefulness as additional observations become available.[23] While in principle additional degrees of freedom might be obtained by utilizing observations on individual firms, it has not yet proved possible to obtain data in the cross-section form most useful for econometric investigation of inventory behavior.

[22] When, in the summer of 1958, I originally computed the coefficients of equation (3.2), I assumed that production plans were completely inflexible; so the error of anticipations, $\hat{X}_t - X_t$, should enter the equation with a coefficient of unity. When the regression was run with the coefficient of the prediction error forced equal to unity, the fit was grossly unsatisfactory. I was then led, as a result of learning of Albert Hart's [26] attempts to "reconstitute" the basic Railroad Shippers' Forecast data, to the conjecture summarized by equation (3.4). Some time later, I was reminded by Arthur Okun of the Modigliani-Sauerlander [52] point that production plans might have an element of flexibility, permitting their revision when actual sales proved to be developing in a different direction from that anticipated.

[23] The new Office of Business Economics Anticipation Survey [21] should prove particularly useful.

One way of judging both the validity and the usefulness of actual anticipations data is to compare the results obtained when the data are utilized to explain inventory behavior with those provided when proxies for actual anticipations data are used. It is necessary to review various procedures that have been devised in order to circumvent the difficulties created by the meagerness of data on actual sales expectations.

STRUCTURAL PROXIES FOR ANTICIPATIONS

One alternative to the utilization of actual anticipations data is to make some particular assumption about the structure by which anticipations of future sales volume are actually generated. It might be assumed, for example, that the structure explaining the generation of expectations takes the form

$$(3.5) \qquad \hat{X}_t = v_0 + v_1 U_t + v_2 \Delta U_t + v_3 X_{t-1} + \epsilon_{5t},$$

where U_t is the backlog of unfilled orders, and $\Delta U_t = U_t - U_{t-1}$. If we substitute into equation (3.1) because $\hat{X}_t$ is unobserved, we obtain the equation

$$(3.1') \qquad H_t = \delta\alpha + (\delta\beta_1 + \lambda)(v_0 + v_1 U_t + v_2 \Delta U_t + v_3 X_{t-1}) \\ + (1 - \delta)H_{t-1} - \lambda X_t + (\delta\beta_1 + \lambda)\epsilon_{5t} + \epsilon_{1t}$$

More generally, this procedure involves the assumption that actual anticipations are some specified linear function of exogenous or predetermined variables.

$$(3.5') \qquad \hat{X}_t = \sum v_i E_{i,t-1} + \epsilon_{5't}$$

Here the v_i are unknown structural coefficients and the $E_{i,t-1}$ specified predetermined or exogenous variables; $\epsilon_{5't}$ is a stochastic disturbance. If this equation is substituted into (3.1) we obtain

$$(3.1'') \qquad H_t = \delta\alpha + (\delta\beta_1 + \lambda) \sum v_i E_{i,t-1} + (1 - \delta)H_{t-1} \\ - \lambda X_t + (\delta\beta_1 + \lambda)\epsilon_{5t} + \epsilon_{1t}.$$

Once more there is an error of observation connected with an explanatory variable, raising the danger of biased estimates of the parameters of the equation. An additional difficulty with this technique is that its application does not yield an estimate of the marginal desired inventory coefficient, β_1, as the v_i are unknown. Although the application of this procedure might provide some indication about the relative importance of various determinants of expectations, some of the variables thought to be determinants of expectations

199

may actually have a direct influence upon equilibrium inventory, leading to a lack of identification. For example, the backlog of unfilled orders might influence sales anticipations; it might also have a direct influence upon desired inventory, and would therefore belong in equation (3.1) as well as (3.5'). Such influences cannot be disentangled when an expression relating to the structure of expectations is substituted into the inventory determination equation. Consequently, this procedure yields less information concerning the structure of the inventory determination equation than might potentially be gained if good data on actual anticipations were available.

The investigator who wishes to employ this procedure has a host of alternative specifications of equation (3.5') to consider. Alain Enthoven [18] attributed naïve expectations to entrepreneurs in an interesting study of inventory behavior. If $\hat{X}_t = X_{t-1}$, and if it is assumed that both the reaction and production adaptation coefficients are unity, equation (3.1) may be written

$$(3.6) \qquad H_t + X_t - X_{t-1} = \alpha + \beta_1 X_{t-1} + \epsilon_{1t}.$$

By making the total inventory stock plus the change in sales the dependent variable, Enthoven ensured that the reaction coefficient would be unity.[24] Johnston [31] has suggested that for nondeseasonalized quarterly data the expectations function may take the more complicated form

$$(3.7) \qquad \hat{X}_t = X_{t-4} + \nu_1 X_{t-4} \left(\frac{X_{t-1} - X_{t-5}}{X_{t-5}} \right) + \epsilon_{7t}.$$

If this expression is substituted into (3.1), estimates of the marginal desired inventory coefficient may be obtained. Needless to say, valid results will be provided by this procedure only if the structure by which expectations are generated as well as the inventory equation have been correctly specified. Johnston himself has doubts about this particular formula. For one thing, the parameter estimates are not too satisfactory. He considers an alternative, more flexible expectations-generating equation, due to Charles Holt [28], that is

[24] When this equation was fitted to GNP data and to manufacturing and trade figures, an extreme problem of serially correlated disturbances was encountered. Although Enthoven ingeniously applied a correction procedure of Herman Wold [63] in order to test the significance of the marginal desired inventory coefficient, the fact remains that the highly autocorrelated disturbances imply that the lag of inventory investment behind changes in sales is not adequately explained by the assumption of naïve anticipations. A delayed pattern of response rather than a reaction coefficient of unity may be more appropriate.

related to the "adaptive expectations" concept of Marc Nerlove [53] and McGee [45], but more complicated in that both seasonal and trend terms are assumed to be determined by a distributed lag. Johnston proceeds to compute artificial $\hat{X}_t$ series for alternative sets of possible values of the parameters of this second expectations-generating equation, and then fits a production adjustment equation, contrasting the closeness of the fits obtained with alternative values of the expectation parameters.[25] Potentially, the use of such surrogate procedures may eventually yield information concerning the way in which expectations are generated as well as an understanding of the production and inventory decisions.[26]

ACTUAL SALES AS A SURROGATE MEASURE OF ANTICIPATIONS

Edwin Mills [48] [49] [50] [51] has argued that a second alternative to the utilization of anticipations data is to employ *actual* sales (X_t) as a proxy for the anticipated sales volume. This procedure was implicit in the pioneering Klein study [33] based on data for the interwar period. Mills has spelled out its rationale in detail. It is not supposed that firms are clairvoyant. It is assumed that whatever the procedure utilized by the firm in predicting demand, it is not biased and that the errors of prediction are random;[27] hence,

$$(3.8) \qquad \hat{X}_t = X_t + \epsilon_{8t}; \quad \mathbf{E}(\epsilon_8) = 0$$

Substitution of this equation into (3.1) yields an equation equivalent to (2.3):

$$(3.9) \qquad H_t = \delta\alpha + \delta\beta_1 X_t + (1 - \delta)H_{t-1} + (\lambda + \delta\beta)\epsilon_{8t} + \epsilon_{1t}$$

Klein calls the residuals "undesired inventory"; he presents numerica estimates of the disturbances for the sample period [33, p. 111].

---

[25] Johnston cites Ferber's study of the Shippers' Forecasts [19] as partial support for the assumptions he makes concerning the structure of the equation generating expectations; one interesting use of whatever expectations data is available would be in exploring the most fruitful assumptions to make concerning the structure of expectations in studying inventory behavior.

[26] Johnston's evidence is not decisive, as five out of eight regressions yielded a closer fit as measured by the multiple correlation coefficient with functions of form (3.7); this may be seen by comparing Tables IV and V in Johnston's study; on the other hand, the estimated values of the parameters appear somewhat more reasonable with the more complicated regression function. Johnston also makes comparisons in terms of predictive ability, and here again the evidence is not decisive.

[27] It must be noted that this assumption does not involve any particular restriction upon the actual structure by which expectations are generated, equation 3.5'. It does imply, however, certain similarities between the structure generating actual sales volume and the way in which expectations are formed.

201

Mills [50], who worked with a production determination equation, was interested in transforming the observed residuals in order to obtain an estimate of the actual error made in anticipating future sales; the analysis was based on the assumption that production schedules are completely inflexible, i.e., that $\lambda = 1$. Interpretation of the observed residuals of a regression of the form (3.9) in this way involves the implicit assumption that observation errors and the effects of variables omitted from the equation are small relative to the impact of erroneous sales anticipations. The straightforward application of estimation procedures to an equation of the form of (3.9) under the assumptions embodied in (3.8) involves certain other difficulties. The limited information estimation procedure employed by Klein relies on the assumption that the residuals (undesired inventory) of successive time periods are independent. When the procedure of least squares is applied, parameter estimates are necessarily inefficient if the residuals are autocorrelated; customary tests of significance are not valid. Furthermore, the sum of excess inventories over the sample period will necessarily be zero when the least squares procedure is employed. Mills [50] circumvented these difficulties by applying least squares to the equation obtained by first differencing (2.4), a procedure that is appropriate if *changes* in errors made by firms in predicting sales are independent. In order to obtain estimates outside the sample period of errors made by firms in anticipating sales volume, he substituted the parameter estimates obtained with the first-differenced regression back into equation 3.9. There is a difficulty with this procedure: owing to the stochastic element of 3.8, biased estimates will be yielded by the application of least squares to equation (3.9).[28] Furthermore, an inspection of equations (3.2) and (3.3) reveals that the observed forecast error term was significant in those regressions, suggesting that considerable precision may be sacrificed when that variable is excluded.

BIASED EXPECTATIONS

It is possible to examine empirically a more general assumption about the nature of expectations that includes as special cases both Mills' hypothesis, equation (3.8), and the alternative assumption of naïve expectations employed by Alain Enthoven in his empirical work. In

---

[28] If $\sigma_{\epsilon_1} = 0$, it might be appropriate to utilize X_t as the dependent variable rather than I_t, and then translate the equation back into the form of (3.9).

earlier work [40] [41], I hypothesized that expectations, however formed, turn out to be a linear combination of lagged sales and actual developments:

(3.10) $\hat{X}_t = \rho X_{t-1} + (1 - \rho)X_t + \epsilon_{10t}$; $\mathbf{E}(\epsilon_{10t}) = 0$

If the "coefficient of anticipations" ρ equals zero, we have the case considered by Mills. On the other hand, $\rho = 1$ corresponds to the assumption of naive expectations invoked by Enthoven. A value of ρ between these two extremes implies that on the average firms anticipate a definite fraction of actual changes in sales:

(3.11) $X_t - X_{t-1} = (1 - \rho)(\hat{X}_t - X_{t-1}) + \epsilon_{10t}$

Theil's empirical studies suggest that anticipations data have a systematic tendency to understate changes [60]. Since the error made by the firm is

(3.12) $\hat{X}_t - X_t = -\rho(\hat{X}_t - X_{t-1}) + \epsilon_{10t}$,

the coefficient of anticipations is a measure of the bias of forecasts toward last period's sales. $\rho = 1$ implies that firms have no success in anticipating the direction of changes in sales volume; expected sales are randomly distributed about last period's sales. A negative ρ implies that firms have a systematic tendency to overstate changes; $\rho > 1$, on the other hand, corresponds to the perverse case in which the direction of change in sales is generally misjudged, an extreme form of regressive anticipations.[29]

The conjecture underlying equation 3.10 implies nothing about how expectations are actually formed; it says nothing about the structure of anticipations. In the study of inventory behavior, the conjecture does permit the study of a possible systematic tendency for firms to underestimate average changes in sales volume. Substitution of equation (3.10) into (3.1) yields

(3.13) $H_t = \delta\alpha + \delta\beta X_t - (\delta\beta + \lambda)\rho\Delta X_t + (1 - \delta)H_{t-1}$
$$+ (\lambda + \delta\beta)\epsilon_{10t} + \epsilon_{1t}$$

I have reported [41] the following estimates of the coefficients of this equation for quarterly deflated seasonally adjusted data for finished goods inventory of all manufacturers, for 1948–55:[30]

---

[29] If $X_{t-1} = 10$ and $X_t = 15$, then $\rho = -0.5$ implies $\mathbf{E}(\hat{X}_t) = 17.5$, $\rho = 0$ yields 15, $\rho = 0.5$ yields 12.5, $\rho = 1$ yields 10, and $\rho = 2$ yields 5.

[30] When the ΔQ production-smoothing term is included in these aggregative regressions it inevitably has the wrong sign.

$$(3.14a) \quad H_t = -258.2 + .0419X_t - .1315\Delta X_t + .8479H_{t-1}$$
$$(.0203) \quad (.0417) \quad (.0649)$$

$$R^2 = .958$$
$$d = 1.39$$

Data for total durables yield

$$(3.14b) \quad H_t = -325.8 + .0550X_t - .0970\Delta X_t + .8171H_{t-1}$$
$$(.0143) \quad (.0283) \quad (.0523)$$

$$R^2 = .966$$
$$d = 1.33$$

Estimates obtained for the nondurable sector are

$$(3.14c) \quad H_t = 418.7 + .0058X_t - .1695\Delta X_t + .9351H_{t-1}$$
$$(.0292) \quad (.0685) \quad (.0858)$$

$$R^2 = .946$$
$$d = 1.57$$

The coefficients for total manufacturing imply that $\delta = .1521$ and $\beta = .2755$. It is not possible to unscramble the regression coefficients in order to obtain estimates of ρ; the effects of flexibility of production cannot be segregated from the measure of degree of bias of expectations. If it could be assumed that production plans are completely inflexible, i.e., $\lambda = 1$, then the estimates imply that $\rho = 0.1262$ in manufacturing; this figure may be interpreted as the *effective bias* of expectations; although expectations may be much more strongly biased toward last period's sales than this figure suggests, the value of ρ obtained under the assumption of $\lambda = 1$ does indicate the net prediction bias after reductions for a partial readjustment of production plans.[31] Even if a fair degree of flexibility of the production plan is admitted, say $\lambda = 0.5$, then the total manufacturing $\rho = 0.24$, a figure still implying that expectations are, on the average, quite precise. The estimates are consistent with an anticipations coefficient greater than unity only if the flexibility coefficient is less than 9 per cent.

An imprecise check upon the validity of the assumption that actual expectations may be described by equation 3.10 is provided by the

[31] I have also obtained regressions over the same period with inventory data for a number of durable goods industries [41]; purchased materials and goods-in-process inventories are not published separately from finished goods inventory with the industry breakdown. The "effective bias" coefficients range from a low of 0.0283 for transportation equipment to a high of 0.2114 for the stone, clay, and glass industry.

Railroad Shippers' Forecast data. A comparison of the regressions obtained with the observed railroad expectations series, equations 3.2 above, with those obtained under assumption 3.10, indicates discrepancies in the estimates of the underlying parameters of the model. The estimated speed of adjustment is always larger when the anticipations series derived from the Railroad Shippers' Forecast data is employed. The nondurable marginal desired inventory coefficient is particularly sensitive. On the other hand, the differences are no greater than should be anticipated on the basis of a casual interpretation of the standard errors of the regression coefficients. Furthermore, the railroad anticipations series itself involves considerable measurement error, particularly at this level of aggregation. A comparison of the multiple correlation coefficients suggests that the labors involved in compiling the anticipations series are not rewarded by a substantial improvement in fit, although they do provide a rough estimate of λ, the production flexibility coefficient.

A second more direct check of the validity of the assumption that the expectations error is proportional to the change in sales is to regress the observed prediction error $\hat{X}_t - X_t$ upon the change in sales from the preceding quarter in accordance with equation 3.12. The calculations were performed for the cement anticipations data, both with and without seasonal dummy variables. For contrast, the annual change, $X_t - X_{t-4}$, was also utilized as an alternative explanation of the prediction error.

$$(3.15a) \quad \hat{X}_t - X_t = -.0180(X_t - X_{t-1}) - 1,158 + e_t \quad R^2 = .0466$$
$$\phantom{(3.15a) \quad \hat{X}_t - X_t =} (.0218) \phantom{(X_t - X_{t-1}) -} (421.9) \qquad \bar{S}_e = 2,631$$
$$\phantom{(3.15a) \quad \hat{X}_t - X_t = -.0180(X_t - X_{t-1}) - 1,158 + e_t \quad R^2 =} n = 39$$

$$(3.15b) \quad \hat{X}_t - X_t = -.6777(X_t - X_{t-4}) + 1,172.4 + e_t$$
$$\phantom{(3.15b) \quad \hat{X}_t - X_t =} (.0817) \phantom{(X_t - X_{t-4}) +} (381.3)$$
$$\phantom{(3.15b) \quad \hat{X}_t - X_t = -.6777(X_t - X_{t-4}) +} R^2 = .6692$$
$$\phantom{(3.15b) \quad \hat{X}_t - X_t = -.6777(X_t - X_{t-4}) +} \bar{S}_e = 1,539$$
$$\phantom{(3.15b) \quad \hat{X}_t - X_t = -.6777(X_t - X_{t-4}) +} n = 36$$

$$(3.15c) \quad \hat{X}_t - X_t = -.2644(X_t - X_{t-1}) - 660.0d_1 + 11,421.d_2$$
$$\phantom{(3.15c) \quad \hat{X}_t - X_t =} (.0988) \phantom{(X_t - X_{t-1})} (1,152.2) (4,705.9)$$
$$\phantom{(3.15c) \quad \hat{X}_t - X_t =} + 5,734d_3 - 5,130. + e \quad R^2 = .2165$$
$$\phantom{(3.15c) \quad \hat{X}_t - X_t =+} (2,571.6) (1,864.) \bar{S}_e = 2,488$$
$$\phantom{(3.15c) \quad \hat{X}_t - X_t =+ 5,734d_3 - 5,130. + e \quad R^2 =} n = 39$$

$$(3.15d) \quad \hat{X}_t - X_t = -.7242(X_t - X_{t-4}) - 1{,}114.5d_1 + 378.5d_2$$
$$(.0794) \qquad\qquad (673.2) \quad (694.9)$$
$$+ 792.8d_3 + 1{,}319.0 + e_t \qquad R^2 = .7402$$
$$(681.2) \qquad (518.4) \qquad \bar{S}_e = 1{,}428$$
$$n = 36$$

Inspection of the regressions suggests that the forecast error in the cement industry is best explained by the change in sales from the preceding year; even when dummy variables are added in order to net out the effects of stable seasonal influences, it is the annual change that contributes most to an explanation of the prediction error. Equation (3.12) should be modified

$$(3.12') \qquad \hat{X}_t - X_t = -\rho(X_t - X_{t-4}) + \epsilon_t$$

The superiority of this equation, which might well have been anticipated on the basis of Hart's work on the Railroad Shippers' Forecasts [26], may stem from difficulties encountered by firms in correctly judging seasonal movements. Donald J. Daly reports [13, p. 258]: ". . . the practice of using year-to-year changes dated at the end of the period appears to be widely followed by businessmen. Insofar as this practice is widely used, it will contribute to belated recognition of economic changes and perhaps contribute to a distorted view of the recent rates of change with inevitable effects on company expectations." The dummy variable procedure for correcting seasonals utilized *ex post* data not available to the firm at the time that anticipations were formed.

A pragmatic test of the most appropriate proxy to utilize for the error made by firms in predicting future sales is provided by contrasting their effectiveness in explaining inventory investment in the cement industry. In Table 2 each column represents a separate regression. The first four regressions involve the assumption that the anticipations error is proportional to the change in sales from the preceding quarter; the last four utilize $X_t - X_{t-4}$ as the proxy for the forecast error. The four-quarter change in sales again proves to be the best proxy for the error in anticipating sales volume. The estimated marginal desired inventory coefficient has an incorrect negative sign whenever the one-quarter change is utilized as the proxy.[32] Furthermore, the signs of the various parameters of the

---

[32] It might be interesting to rerun the aggregative regressions for total manufacturing and the durable and nondurable components with $X_t - X_{t-4}$, rather than $X_t - X_{t-1}$, as the proxy for the forecast error. Pending such an investigation, it is hard to explain

206

TABLE 2

Inventory Investment in the Cement Industry, 1947–56

X_t							
−.4571	−.0805	−.4322	−.0545	−.4454	.1760	−0.2670	.2151
(.0548)	(.0711)	(.0739)	(.0771)	(.0943)	(.0823)	(0.0847)	(.0831)

$X_t - X_{t-1}$

−.5128	−.5637	−.4707	−.5268				
(.0648)	(.1009)	(.1053)	(.1094)				

$X_t - X_{t-4}$

				−.2673	−.5119	−0.0751	−.5051
				(.3808)	(.1403)	(0.3048)	(.1360)

I_{t-1}

.7447	.1037	.6711	.0271	−.2522	−.3933	−0.2098	−.4987
(.1586)	(.1589)	(.2154)	(.1810)	(.1718)	(.1596)	(0.1363)	(.1667)

ΔQ

		−.1486	−.1510			−1.072	−.2404
		(.2909)	(.1690)			(0.240)	(.1419)

d_1

	8,102		8,140		13,719		13,793
	(2,224)		(2,231)		(2,404)		(2,330)

d_2

	11,281		11,597		−8,641		−5,587
	(4,922)		(4,951)		(2,731)		(3,209)

d_3

	−3,988		−3,822		−15,979		−14,510
	(2,549)		(2,564)		(1,381)		(1,593)

c

11,539	−214.2	11,896	24.93	35,692	3,447	23,986	2,647
(3,925)	(3,381)	(4,029)	(3,402)	(4,457)	(3,033)		

R^2

.871		.872	.961			0.807	.973

S_e

4,175	2,439			6,737	2,165		

n

39	39	39	39	36	36	36	36

model are correct only when the seasonal dummy variables are included; as with the Railroad Forecast data, the proxy procedure supports Johnston's seasonal form of the production-smoothing hypothesis. On the other hand, the ΔQ form of the production-smoothing hypothesis, while of correct sign, is significant only when the rail anticipations data are employed.

Although it appears that suitable proxies for the errors made by firms in anticipating future sales may be employed when accurate expectational data are not available, it is necessary to emphasize certain limitations of the procedure. It is obvious that the presence of the stochastic term means that biased parameter estimates should

why the ΔX_t term is satisfactory at the higher level of aggregation but inappropriate for cement; this may result from the more complex deseasonalizing procedure to which the aggregative series were subjected or from the offsetting of conflicting errors in the aggregation process itself.

be expected whenever the proxy procedure summarized by equation (3.12) or its modified form (3.12') is employed. This in itself is reason for suspecting that even under the assumption of complete inflexibility, the effective bias should not be interpreted in terms of equation (3.13) as an accurate measure of any systematic tendency for firms to underestimate changes in demand.

An additional reason is provided by an identification problem similar to that involved with one of the surrogate procedures discussed earlier. This problem arises once it is admitted that other variables in addition to sales may influence the equilibrium level of inventories. Suppose, for a moment, that equation 3.5 does indeed constitute a correct specification of the structure by which anticipations are generated, so that (3.1') offers a valid description of actual inventory behavior. Comparing this equation with (3.13) we see that certain coefficients of the latter equation are identified only because the backlog of unfilled orders and its change were not included in the inventory-determining equation. Consider next the following nondurable manufacturing regression based on quarterly deflated data extending from the second quarter of 1948 through 1960, where total stocks, H_t, had to be utilized rather than just finished goods inventories because of restrictions on the availability of deflated data stratified by stage of fabrication.

$$(3.16) \quad \Delta H_t = -.1885 - .0755H_{-1} + .0362X_t + .1950U$$
$$ (.5434) \quad (.0522) \quad\quad (.0216) \quad\quad (.0595)$$
$$- .0922\Delta X_t + e_t \quad\quad R^2 = .378$$
$$(.0420)$$

In contrast, when the change in unfilled orders is added to the regression, we have

$$(3.16') \quad \Delta H = -.5084 - .0823H_{-1} + .0426X_t + .2541U$$
$$ (.4090) \quad (.0390) \quad\quad (.0161) \quad\quad (.0456)$$
$$- .0285\Delta X_t - .3557\Delta U + e_t \quad\quad R^2 = .574$$
$$(.0331) \quad\quad (.0581)$$

The order terms were included because earlier empirical work suggested that they have a direct influence upon stocks of purchased materials and goods in process. To maintain the assumption that the change in orders does not influence stocks directly, the first of the reported regressions is identified under the assumption that $v_2 \neq 0$ in (3.5); the estimate of the effective bias is 0.089. If the change in unfilled orders is regarded as having a direct influence upon stocks, certain coefficients of (3.13) are no longer identified because there is now no variable in (3.5) excluded from the structural stock equation. The second set of estimates, which implies a much lower effective bias of expectations, 0.032, would be identified only if (3.5) were replaced by an equation involving the maintained hypothesis that expectations are influenced by other variables in addition to current and lagged orders and sales. The choice between these two alternative estimates of expectational bias can be made only on the basis of a priori knowledge as to the actual structure generating expectations; it cannot be made on the basis of the statistical evidence summarized by equations (3.16) and (3.16′).

The employment of surrogate procedures rather than actual data on expectations has not at this stage provided decisive results. On the one hand, Johnston's analysis has not yet established the preferred assumption, among the alternatives he considers, concerning the structure by which expectations are actually generated. While I have found the ΔX_t term significant in my earlier regressions [41] covering 1948–55, suggesting a bias in manufacturers' forecasts, subsequent regressions [42], using more recent data on manufacturers' inventory holdings as well as equations (2.16), (3.16), and (3.16′) do not yield such strong results. The evidence for the cement industry suggests that $X_t - X_{t-4}$ may be appropriately employed as a proxy when accurate observations are not available on the actual error made by firms in anticipating sales volume.

CONCLUSION

The direct forecasting value of sales anticipations data has frequently been questioned in such studies as that of Modigliani and Sauerlander [52] and, most recently, by Peter Pashigian [54]. It has been argued at the same time that *ex ante* sales observations are chiefly useful in helping to explain changes in such other variables as inventory investment. In terms of this criterion, the reconstituted railroad forecast anticipation data appear to make a significant contribution in (3.2) and (3.3) in explaining the behavior of manufacturers' aggregate inventory holdings and the behavior of cement. Certainly, the regressions offer a substantial improvement in closeness of fit over what would have been achieved if actual sales were employed as a proxy for anticipations. A comparison with those regressions that utilized either the quarterly or annual change in actual sales as an approxima-

209

tion for the forecast error reveals that the reconstituted Railroad Forecast anticipations series offers only a marginal improvement over what can be obtained with suitable proxies. The importance of considering surrogate alternatives in appraising the contribution that data purporting to measure actual anticipations can make toward an understanding of actual inventory movements should not be underestimated.[33]

The review presented here of alternative procedures for analyzing the impact of sales expectations upon inventory behavior suggests that making correct inferences concerning the structural determinants of inventories is extremely difficult. If data purporting to measure actual expectations have a systematic tendency to overstate forecast errors, production plans will appear excessively flexible. Procedures derived by Enthoven and Johnston for circumventing the use of actual anticipations data require strong a-priori judgments concerning the structure by which anticipations are actually generated. On the surface, both Mills' suggestion that actual sales provide a good surrogate measure of anticipations and my generalization that the *change* in sales may be proportional to the error made by firms in anticipating sales appear to circumvent the problem of specifying the structure by which anticipations are actually generated. On closer inspection, however, it becomes apparent that the issue is clouded unless it is assumed that production plans are completely inflexible; furthermore, the unspecified structure of the equation explaining the actual generation of expectations might conceivably be such as to imply that other parameters of the inventory equation are unidentified.

It seems clear from all this that only a limited amount of information about the structure of anticipations may be gleaned from the study of inventories. In particular, the two sets of regressions summarized by equations (3.2) and (3.14) are both compatible with either (1) quite inaccurate, perhaps regressive, anticipations but extremely flexible production plans *or* (2) rather accurate expectations but not much flexibility in production scheduling. A reconstitution of the Railroad Shippers' Forecast data for the cement industry, discussed

---

[33] Although Modigliani and Sauerlander [52] observed that the Railroad Forecasts assisted in predicting cement inventories, they failed to consider possible surrogate measures of anticipations as alternatives. For a more elementary model with output as the dependent variable, Mills found that under the assumption of production inflexibility current sales provided a much better fit then the Shippers' forecasts [51, p. 12a].

in the Appendix of this paper, offers some support for the conjecture that expectations are not as inaccurate as *ex ante* data sometimes imply. However, the investigation of inventory behavior has not established that the expectations of future sales held by individual firms do not have a "regressive" tendency to forecast a reversion toward former sales levels.

Research on inventories and anticipations are clearly complementary rather than competing efforts. It definitely would be worthwhile to test the various alternative assumptions developed by Johnston concerning the structure of anticipations upon actual *ex ante* data as well as to investigate further the extent to which actual anticipations are approximated by my conjecture and that of Mills, equations (3.10) or (3.8). In addition to providing a potential check for determining whether data on anticipations actually help in describing inventory behavior, surrogate procedures facilitate the study of inventory behavior, surrogate procedures facilitate the study of inventory and production movements when concomitant series on sales anticipations are unavailable.

Determinants of Equilibrium Inventory

Other variables in addition to sales influence equilibrium inventory. The role of orders has already been mentioned in this paper. A more detailed study has revealed their importance in explaining stocks of purchased materials or goods in process, although they may have a negligible effect upon finished goods inventory.[34] A tightening of credit conditions might be expected to lead to a reduction in the equilibrium level of inventories. The impact of military procurement upon inventory accumulation has been subjected to preliminary investigation [42]. The influence of speculative considerations upon inventory movements also bears consideration. Here, the conflicting evidence with regard to the possible influence of credit conditions

[34] In [41], where durable and nondurable manufacturing inventories were stratified by stage of fabrication, the orders variable was included in the purchased materials and goods-in-process equation, but excluded from the finished goods regressions. The coefficient of the orders variable in the equation explaining total inventory behavior was only moderately changed from its value in the purchased materials and goods-in-process equation, suggesting that role of orders in the aggregative equation reflects its influence upon inventory in the first two stages of fabrication. When new orders are included in the inventory equation, a problem of collinearity is created because new orders are essentially the sum of sales plus the change in unfilled orders; a more reliable estimate of the role of sales is obtained when the change in unfilled orders rather than in new orders is utilized as an explanatory variable.

and speculative forces will be reviewed within the context of the flexible accelerator principle.

SPECULATIVE INVENTORY HOLDINGS

To the extent that firms accumulate additional inventory in periods of inflation in an attempt to hedge against rising prices they contribute to the inflationary spiral. The evidence with regard to such "price-hedging" or "speculative" behavior is mixed. Klein [36] reports a significant positive association between aggregate inventory investment and the change in the GNP deflator; T. M. Brown [9] also obtains a positive relation in his study of Canadian inventory behavior. On the other hand, two investigations involving a less aggregative approach have not provided strong support for the speculation hypothesis. In a study of manufacturers' holdings of stocks of purchased materials and goods in process, I found [41] the relationship was insignificant in both durable and nondurable regressions, and had the wrong sign for total manufacturing stocks. Darling [15] found that price change, while of correct sign, was insignificant at the 5 per cent level in the equation explaining manufacturers' holdings of purchased materials and goods in process and in regressions for wholesale and retail trade; in other regressions, which constituted the majority, the sign was incorrect. This evidence is compatible with the null hypothesis that firms do not speculate in stocks. Of course, the test is not conclusive; for one thing, firms may simply change the composition rather than the magnitude of their holdings; in addition, they may seriously misjudge price movements. Nevertheless, the negative conclusion is not a complete surprise, for the literature describing current inventory practice does contain some indications that price-hedging is discouraged in most firms.[35]

INFLUENCE OF CREDIT STRINGENCY

Because fluctuations in inventory investment play such a pronounced role in the business cycle, the extent to which the monetary authorities can successfully exert countercyclical pressure depends in part upon the responsiveness of inventory investment to changes in credit conditions. The evidence that has accumulated at this date is not

---

[35] Baumes [3, p. 22] reports that "while most companies say that they do not speculate in the commodity markets, some companies have a policy of allowing forward buying when the price is right. Companies that allow forward buying usually stipulate that purchases above normal requirements be approved by top management."

decisive. Certain regressions have indicated a perverse relationship of incorrect sign between monetary variables and the equilibrium level of inventories, a difficulty that stems in part from problems of simultaneity.

Terleckyj [59] reports on an attempt to include the interest rate on four to six months' prime commercial paper in an equation explaining the percentage change in inventory book value for trade and manufacturing. Although the variable has the correct sign, it is less than one-tenth the magnitude of its estimated standard error. Consequently, Terleckyj excluded this variable from later regressions. He found that corporate liquidity was not significantly correlated with the residuals from his equations.

The study by Brown, Robert Solow, Albert Ando, and John Kareken for the Commission on Money and Credit [7] contains estimates of the effect upon manufacturers' inventory holdings of the interest rate charged on short-term bank loans to business. Undeflated data were utilized; ΔX served as a proxy for errors in anticipating sales volume. One regression suggests that a 1 percentage point rise in the interest rate reduces inventory investment by $1.15 billion in the following quarter; the ultimate impact is a reduction in inventory of $4.86 billion. The authors are rightly cautious about the imprecise nature of their estimates. Although the interest variable was significant at the 95 per cent level in that regression, it was only roughly equal to its standard error in a second equation involving a more complicated lag structure. Furthermore, an attempt to determine a direct link between Federal Reserve policy and inventory investment revealed a perverse negative relation between an availability index (the maximum potential earning assets of commercial banks) and the equilibrium level of inventories.

Three other investigations have failed to yield decisive evidence of a negative relation between credit availability and inventory investment. Paul F. McGouldrick, of the Board of Governors, Federal Reserve System, obtained rather disappointing results in an attempt to determine the influence upon inventory holdings of the ratio of liquid assets to current liabilities, the loan-deposit ratio of commercial banks, and the bank rate on short-term business loans [46]. The interest rate variable had the correct sign in durable manufacturing, but was not significant; the loan-deposit ratio for commercial banks, the measure of availability, was perverse in sign. In trade, either the interest rate variable or the loan-deposit ratio had an incorrect sign.

213

I have also found [42] incorrect signs in regressions involving deflated durable and nondurable manufacturing inventory. Darling [15] reveals in a preliminary report that the coefficient of the bank rate on business loans had a perverse sign in regressions for manufacturing and trade combined and for durable and nondurable manufacturing. Although Darling obtained an appropriate negative relationship between the rate of interest and finished goods inventory as well as various components of wholesale and retail trade stocks, none of the coefficients were significant at the 5 per cent level.

Ta-Chung Liu [39] found the appropriate negative relationship in a study of deflated nonfarm business inventory. He utilized the real rate of interest, the average rate on prime commercial paper less the lagged rate of change in the GNP implicit deflator. Liu reports both single- and two-stage least square parameter estimates; in both cases, the coefficient of the interest rate term is roughly twice its estimated standard error. Liu's regression also contains nonfarm nonfinancial holdings of monetary assets, measured in constant dollars; this term has a positive coefficient, as would be expected, but is not significant.[36]

The evidence accumulated in these studies is conflicting rather than reinforcing. Application of the flexible accelerator to this problem has not established the magnitude of the impact of monetary policy upon inventory investment.

Summary

Although the literature reporting on econometric studies of inventory behavior is quite small relative to the numerous studies on the determinants of other components of effective demand, this neglect may be at least partially explained by the difficulties of the subject. The distinction between actual versus desired inventory and the problem of measuring anticipated sales are but two of a host of hurdles that have confronted the investigator. Techniques have been developed for circumventing the problem created by the fact that both equilibrium inventory and sales anticipations are, for the most part, unobserved variables. But, at this stage, they have not provided decisive evidence concerning the influence of such factors as credit conditions and speculative forces upon inventory investment.

---

[36] It is interesting to observe that Liu includes in his regression several lagged inventory terms, the complication that created trouble for Solow *et al.* Unfilled orders and the rate of change in the wage rate also appear in the regression.

Part of the difficulty may arise from certain weaknesses in the accelerator principle. The model assumes that the impact of erroneous anticipations falls either upon output or inventory, making no allowance for the possibility that adjustments in either price or advertising expenditures may shoulder part of the burden. Although price adjustment models are available, the choice has been between one extreme or the other as typified by the two alternative approaches compared by Mills [51] and by Shozaburo Fujino [23], rather than a successful blend of the two extremes; either a price or a quantity adjustment model rather than a blend of the two polar models is required to do the work. The approach of Liu is a first step in remedying this problem.[37]

A second source of difficulty involves the form in which variables enter the regression equation. Whether or not the desired results are obtained is in part a matter of the persistence of the investigator as well as the validity of the hypothesis. The assumption of profit-maximizing behavior, emphasized by Mills [48] [49] [50] [51], by Modigliani and Sauerlander [52], and by Holt and Modigliani [29] still leaves the empiricist with a wide range of choice. Several alternative modes of behavior have been shown to be consistent with the assumption of profit maximization; what types of behavior are incompatible with it? A second source of a priori knowledge, the assumption that the economy has reasonable dynamic properties, may place further restrictions upon the range of models to be considered. I have argued [43] that the assumption of immediate adjustment is incompatible with stability for reasonable values of the parameters of a multisector model. Further theoretical research may serve to narrow the range of choice that now confronts the empirical investigator.

A final and most serious difficulty is created by the current unavailability of adequate monthly or quarterly cross-section data on the movement of inventories, sales, and related variables at the level of the individual firm. Cross-section data expose movements that are concealed in the process of aggregation. A more complete understanding of the structure of inventory behavior, a prerequisite for successful prediction and hypothesis-testing, will be obtained when suitable cross-section data, a possible byproduct of current statistical

---

[37] It will be remembered that although Liu allowed for an impact of excess inventory upon prices, he omitted the influence of the resulting fall in prices upon demand and, hence, upon inventory.

collection activities of the federal government, become available on a confidential basis for research purposes.

Appendix: A Reconstitution of the Railroad Shippers' Forecasts

Because problems of interpretation arise with any attempt to circumvent the utilization of data on actual sales anticipations in the study of inventory behavior, it is important to interpret correctly whatever information is available on expectations. Here one body of expectational data, the Railroad Shippers' Forecasts, will be considered. This is the set of data utilized in the empirical study of inventory behavior reported in the body of this paper.

The data concern anticipated quarterly shipments by rail broken down into thirty-two commodity groups. A sample of firms contributing a sizable portion of railway freight traffic has provided the data published since 1927 in the *National Forecast* of the Regional Shippers Advisory Boards under the auspices of the Association of American Railroads.[38] The forecasts have proved to be quite inaccurate predictors of actual railroad carloadings, being frequently less accurate than simple naïve projections of the previous quarter's shipments.[39] Nevertheless, they still constitute an important body of anticipations data which has been subjected to repeated analysis.

Albert G. Hart [26] attempted a reconstitution of the Railroad Shippers' Forecast data for the interwar period in order to obtain a series of more accurate carload anticipations, one in closer conformity with the type of expectations entrepreneurs might be expected to hold. Hart found it hard to believe that the actual anticipations held by businessmen could have the "regressive" property of the Shippers' Forecasts, a systematic tendency to predict a movement back toward earlier levels in the face of opposing trends. But arguments concerning the validity of a revised anticipations series based upon their conformity with the way anticipations are expected to behave is inherently a most subjective process. Here, a second attempt to reconstitute the Railroad Shippers' Forecasts, based on post-World War II data, will be described.

Although the traffic manager generally completes the return utilized in preparing the Railroad Shippers' Forecasts of carload uti-

---

[38] For a detailed discussion of the sampling procedures and other aspects of the survey see [19].

[39] Thor Hultgren [30, pp. 364–371, 374–378].

lization, this does not imply that the estimate is derived independently of the firm's sales anticipations. The respondent is asked to state the anticipated percentage increase in carloadings over the corresponding quarter of the preceding year, actual shipments for that quarter of last year, and an anticipations figure in carload units. The respondent may simply assume that carloadings will increase by the same percentage as the increase anticipated by the firm for total sales by all modes of transportation. Firms frequently utilize comparisons with the same quarter of the preceding year as an implicit form of seasonal adjustment. Even if this procedure is not followed explicitly, it seems reasonable to assume that the traffic manager must be aware of the sales forecast and that this figure influences both his planning and the figures he submits in completing the questionnaire on carload shipments. If $\hat{X}_t$ represents anticipated total sales volume and X_{t-4} actual sales in the corresponding quarter of the preceding year, while C_{t-4} stands for actual shipments by rail in carload units for the same quarter of the preceding year, the hypothesis implies that anticipated carload shipments $\hat{X}_t$ were formulated by the respondents by utilizing the equation:

$$(A.1) \qquad\qquad \hat{C}_t = C_{t-4}\left(\frac{\hat{X}_t}{X_{t-4}}\right)$$

This hypothesis cannot be tested directly, for the variable $\hat{X}_t$ is not observed. Furthermore, the other variables are observed at best only in aggregate form. Inaccuracies may result not only from sampling errors but also because the reports of the various firms are weighted by the number of carloadings shipped by the firm in corresponding quarters of the preceding year. Consequently, carload forecasts of firms which ship a relatively large portion of their total output by rail will be overweighted when sales anticipations, the unobserved $\hat{X}_t$, are derived by equation A.1.

A possible test of the validity of the hypotheses is provided by the fact that the Railroad Shippers' Forecasts of carload shipments are not accurate predictors. An inspection of equation A.1 reveals that a sales anticipations series derived from the published rail forecast data could be either more or less accurate than the carload anticipations.[40] If the sales anticipations derived by equation A.1 are

[40] This is the essential difference between the conversion procedure proposed here and that utilized by Modigliani and Sauerlander in a study of the value of the Shippers' Forecasts in the prediction of output in the cement industry. In their study, which covered only the output of firms in the first two quarters of each year, they at first

DETERMINANTS OF INVENTORY INVESTMENT

in fact more accurate, it would offer support for the hypothesis that firms derive their carload anticipations on the basis of this equation and that the derived sales anticipations obtained by solving for the unobserved variable $\hat{X}_t$ is a valid representation of actual sales anticipations. Conversely, if the derived sales anticipations series are less accurate than the carload forecasts it would suggest that the former are not as precise as might reasonably be expected of actual anticipations.

For the cement industry, data on sales in real terms as well as the forecast data in terms of carloadings are easily obtained. A pilot study testing the hypothesis of equation A.1 was made. Although a

TABLE A-1

ACCURACY OF RAIL FORECASTS AND DERIVED SALES ANTICIPATIONS:
CEMENT INDUSTRY, 1947–56

| | | Correlation Coefficients | | |
Period	Number of Observations	Sales and Carloadings	Forecast and Actual Carloadings	Anticipated and Actual Sales
All quarters	40	.8895	.9605	.9866
1st quarter	10	.9589	.4159	.9121
2nd quarter	10	.8345	.4568	.9688
3rd quarter	10	.8523	.6259	.9847
4th quarter	10	.0042	−.0753	.9538

relatively large portion of cement is shipped by rail, an inspection of the first column of correlation coefficients in Table A-1 reveals that for the postwar period the relation between carloadings and sales is not too close and varies considerably for different quarters of the year. The second and third columns of the table present correlation coefficients measuring the closeness of the relation between forecast and actual shipments and between derived anticipations and actual sales. For every quarter of the year as well as for an overall comparison, the sales anticipations series is a much closer predictor than the rail forecasts. For the fourth quarter, the correlation

---

converted carloadings into barrel figures by assuming that firms correctly estimated the number of barrels of cement loaded into a freight car for the particular quarter. Later, deciding this was unrealistic, they in effect averaged the figure given by the above formula with the one obtained by their original assumption. They did not discuss the effects of this procedure upon the accuracy of the anticipatory series. If it is assumed that entrepreneurs derive the carload anticipations by correctly forecasting the ratio of barrels to freight cars, the carload and sales anticipations will be equally accurate when measured in terms of the variance of the percentage error in the forecast [cf. 52, p. 335].

218

between actual sales and carloadings is extremely poor; the correspondingly poor predictive power of the railroad forecasts for this quarter is to be expected under the hypothesis formulated in equation A.1.[41]

It seems safe to conclude that the raw Railroad Shippers' Forecast data constitute a most tenuous form of evidence for judging the accuracy with which business firms actually forecast demand. The conjecture summarized by equation A.1 offers an alternative explanation. While it cannot be concluded with great confidence that expectations are not regressive, the validity of the raw Shippers' Forecast evidence seems open to serious question.

One test of the usefulness of the derived sales anticipation series is obtained by contrasting their ability to predict cement sales with a naïve projection of the sales level realized in the preceding period. The correlation between lagged and current sales is only 0.117; while the fit is improved to $r = 0.979$ when seasonal dummy variables are added, the derived sales anticipations series still provides a somewhat better prediction than that obtained by a naïve projection of last quarter's experience.

Another test concerns the contribution that the anticipations series derived from the Shippers' Forecast can make in predicting the behavior of other operating variables.[42] A preliminary test on the cement industry involved predicting output over the 1947–56 period in terms of anticipated sales and lagged inventory, this is a special case of the model discussed earlier in which it is assumed that there is no production flexibility. With the assumption of static expectations, $X_t = X_{t-1}$, a multiple correlation of 0.646 was obtained; although the addition of seasonal dummies served to raise the multiple correlation coefficient to 0.914, the inventory and lagged sales terms were no longer significant, the dummies carrying the brunt of the explanatory burden. The derived anticipations sales

[41] The same results are apparent when the accuracy of the forecasts is measured in terms of the variance of the percentage error.

[42] Except for the cement industry, a prime difficulty arises from classification complications. The commodity classifications utilized in the preparation of the Railroad Shippers' Forecasts had to be reconciled with the grosser categories of sales data published in the *Survey of Current Business*. This was accomplished by constructing indexes combining the various categories of the rail data with weights in proportion to the value of sales; the ratio of the current figure in the expected shipments index to the value of the index of weighted actual shipments in the corresponding quarter of the preceding year was utilized as the estimate of anticipated change in sales in accordance with equation A.1. Needless to say, the usual problems encountered in index number construction are involved.

series and the alternative provided by Edwin Mills' suggestion that actual sales be utilized as a proxy did equally well, both yielding a multiple correlation coefficient of 0.933; when seasonal dummies were added, the correlation coefficient was raised to 0.951 for the Mills proxy procedure versus 0.946 for the derived sales anticipations series. These studies were conducted under the assumption that the three-month period between successive observations coincides with the length of the planning period; the more promising results reported in the text allowed for a partial revision of production plans within the three-month observation period.

References

[1] ABRAMOVITZ, MOSES, *Inventories and Business Cycles, with Special Reference to Manufacturers' Inventories*, New York, NBER, 1950.

[2] BASSIE, V. LEWIS, *Economic Forecasting*, New York, McGraw-Hill, 1958.

[3] BAUMES, CARL G., *Inventory Management in Industry*, National Industrial Conference Board Studies in Business Policy No. 88, 1958.

[4] BECKMANN, MARTIN J., "Production Smoothing and Inventory Control," *Operations Research*, 1961.

[5] BOSSONS, JOHN D., "Regressive Expectations," paper delivered at August 1960 Econometric Society meetings, as abstracted in *Econometrica*, July 1961, p. 458.

[6] BRATT, ELMER C., "Availability and Reliability of Inventory Data Needed to Study Economic Change," Office of Statistical Standards, Bureau of the Budget, 1961.

[7] BROWN, E. CARY, SOLOW, ROBERT, M. ANDO, ALBERT, and KAREKEN, JOHN, "Lags in Fiscal and Monetary Policy," unpublished paper prepared for Commission on Money and Credit, 1961.

[8] BROWN, MURRAY, "Ex Ante and Ex Post Data in Inventory Investment," *Journal of the American Statistical Association*, September 1961, pp. 518–554.

[9] BROWN, T. M., "A Forecast Determination of National Product, Employment, and Price Level in Canada, from an Econometric Model," above.

[10] CHRIST, CARL, "A Test of an Econometric Model for the United States, 1921–1947," in *Conference on Business Cycles*, New York, NBER, 1951.

[11] CLARK, COLIN, "A System of Equations Explaining the United States Trade Cycle, 1921 to 1941," *Econometrica*, April 1949.

[12] CRAWFORD, C. M., *Sales Forecasting: Methods of Selected Firms*, Urbana, Bureau of Economic and Business Research, University of Illinois, 1955.

[13] DALY, DONALD J., "Seasonal Variations and Business Expectations," *Journal of Business of the University of Chicago*, July 1959, pp. 258–270.

[14] DARLING, PAUL G., "Manufacturers' Inventory Investment, 1947–1958," *American Economic Review*, December 1959, pp. 950–963.

[15] ———, "Tabulations of Quantitative Materials for Report on Regression Analysis of Fluctuations in Inventory Investment," Conference on Social Science Research Council Econometric Models, August 21, 1961 (hectographed).

[16] ———, "Evidence on Postwar Inventory Cycles," paper delivered at December 1961 American Statistical Association meetings.

[17] DUESENBERRY, JAMES S., ECKSTEIN, OTTO, and FROMM, GARY, "A Simulation of the United States Economy in Recession," *Econometrica*, October 1960.

[18] ENTHOVEN, ALAIN CHARLES, "Studies in the Theory of Inflation," Unpublished Ph.D. dissertation, Massachusetts Institute of Technology, May 1956.

[19] FERBER, ROBERT, *The Railroad Shippers' Forecasts*, Urbana, Bureau of Economic and Business Research, University of Illinois, 1953.

[20] ———, "The Accuracy and Structure of Industry Expectations in Relation to Those of Individual Firms," *Journal of the American Statistical Association*, June 1958, pp. 317–336.

[21] FOSS, MURRAY F., "Manufacturers' Inventory and Sales Expectations: A Progress Report on a New Survey," *Survey of Current Business*, August 1961.

[22] FRIEND, IRWIN, and JONES, ROBERT, "Short-Run Forecasting Models Incorporating Anticipatory Data," below.

[23] FUJINO, SHOZABURO, "Some Aspects of Inventory Cycles," *Review of Economics and Statistics*, May 1960.

[24] GOLDE, ROGER A., "Square Root Behavior of Inventories and the Production Distribution Cycle of the Firm," unpublished Senior thesis, Harvard College, 1956.

[25] GOODWIN, RICHARD M., "Secular and Cyclical Aspects of the Multiplier and Accelerator," *Income, Employment and Public Policy: Essays in Honor of Alvin H. Hansen*, New York, Norton, 1948.

[26] HART, ALBERT G., "Quantitative Evidence for the Interwar Period on the Course of Business Expectations: A Revaluation of the Railroad Shippers' Forecast," *The Quality and Economic Significance of Anticipations Data*, Princeton for NBER, 1960, pp. 205–239.

221

[27] HICKS, JOHN R., *Contribution to a Theory of the Trade Cycle*, Oxford, Clarendon Press, 1950.

[28] HOLT, CHARLES et al., *Planning Production, Inventories and Work Force*, Englewood Cliffs, N.J., Prentice-Hall, 1960.

[29] HOLT, CHARLES, and MODIGLIANI, FRANCO, "Firm Cost Structures and the Dynamic Responses of Inventories, Production, Work Force, and Orders to Sales Fluctuations," *Inventory Fluctuations and Economic Stabilization*, Part II, Joint Economic Committee, 87th Cong., 1st sess., December 1961.

[30] HULTGREN, THOR, "Forecast of Railroad Traffic," *Short-Term Economic Forecasting*, Princeton for NBER, 1955.

[31] JOHNSTON, JACK, "An Econometric Study of the Production Decision," *Quarterly Journal of Economics*, May 1961.

[32] KALECKI, MICHAEL, *Theory of Economic Dynamics*, London, George Allen and Unwin, 1954.

[33] KLEIN, LAWRENCE R., *Economic Fluctuations in the United States, 1921–41*, Cowles Commission Monograph No. 11, New York, Wiley, 1950.

[34] ———, *A Textbook of Econometrics*, Evanston, Ill., Row, Peterson, 1953.

[35] KLEIN, LAWRENCE R., and POPKIN, JOEL, "An Econometric Analysis of the Post-War Relationship Between Inventory Fluctuations and Changes in Aggregate Economic Activity," *Inventory Fluctuations and Economic Stabilization*, Joint Economic Committee, 87th Cong., 1st sess., December 1961, Part III.

[36] KLEIN, LAWRENCE R., "A Postwar Quarterly Model: Description and Applications," above.

[37] KOYCK, L. M., *Distributed Lags and Investment Behavior*, Amsterdam, North-Holland, 1954.

[38] LEONTIEF, WASSILY, *Studies in the Structure of the American Economy*, New York, Oxford University Press, 1953.

[39] LIU, TA-CHUNG, "An Exploratory Quarterly Model of Effective Demand in the Postwar U.S. Economy," mimeographed, undated.

[40] LOVELL, MICHAEL C., "Inventories and Stability: An Interindustry Analysis," unpublished Ph.D. dissertation, Harvard University, March 1959.

[41] ———, "Manufacturers' Inventories, Sales Expectations, and the Acceleration Principle," *Econometrica*, July 1961.

[42] ———, "Factors Determining Manufacturing Inventory Investment," *Inventory Fluctuations and Economic Stabilization*, Joint Economic Committee, 87th Cong., 1st sess., December 1961, Part II.

[43] ———, "Buffer Stocks, Sales Expectations, and Stability: A Multi-Sector Analysis of the Inventory Cycle," *Econometrica*, April 1962.

[44] LUNDBERG, ERIC, *Studies in the Theory of Economic Expansion*, London, P. S. King, 1957.

[45] McGEE, JOHN F., *Production Planning and Inventory Control*, New York, McGraw-Hill, 1958.

[46] McGOULDRICK, PAUL F., "The Impact of Credit Cost and Availability on Inventory Investment," *Inventory Fluctuations and Economic Stabilization*, Joint Economic Committee, 87th Cong., 1st sess., December 1961, Part II.

[47] METZLER, LLOYD A., "The Nature and Stability of Inventory Cycles," *Review of Economics and Statistics*, August 1941, pp. 113–129.

[48] MILLS, EDWIN S., "The Theory of Inventory Decisions," *Econometrica*, April 1957, pp. 222–239.

[49] ———, "Expectations, Uncertainty, and Inventory Fluctuations," *Review of Economic Studies*, 1954–1955, pp. 15–23.

[50] ———, "Expectations and Undesired Inventory," *Management Science*, October 1957, pp. 105–110.

[51] ———, *Some Empirical Estimates of Short-Run Price and Output Policies*, Cowles Foundation Discussion Paper No. 123, July 27, 1961.

[52] MODIGLIANI, FRANCO, and SAUERLANDER, OWEN H., "Economic Expectations and Plans in Relation to Short-Term Economic Forecasting," *Short-Term Economic Forecasting*, Princeton for NBER, 1955, pp. 261–351.

[53] NERLOVE, MARK, *The Dynamics of Supply: Estimation of Farmers' Response to Price*, Baltimore, Johns Hopkins, 1958.

[54] PASHIGIAN, PETER, "The Accuracy and Determinants of Sales Anticipations," 1961 (hectographed).

[55] ———, "Sales Anticipations as a Determinant of Inventory Investment," 1961 (hectographed).

[56] SMYTH, D. J., "The Inventory and Fixed Capital Accelerators," *Economic Record*, August 1960.

[57] SOLOW, R. M., "On a Family of Lag Distributions," *Econometrica*, April 1960, pp. 393–406.

[58] STANBACK, THOMAS M., JR., "Cyclical Behavior of Manufacturers' Inventories 1945–1955," Proceedings, Business and Economic Statistics Section, American Statistical Association, Washington, D.C., 1957, pp. 87–95; abstracted in *Journal of the American Statistical Association*, June 1958, p. 592.

[59] TERLECKYJ, NESTOR E., *Measures of Inventory Conditions*, National Industrial Conference Board Technical Paper No. 8, 1960, as reprinted in *Inventory Fluctuations and Economic Stabilization*, Joint Economic Committee, 87th Cong., 1st sess., December 1961, Part II.

[60] THEIL, H., *Economic Forecasts and Public Policy*, Amsterdam, North-Holland, 1958.

223

[61] THONSTAD, T., and JOCHEMS, D. B., "The Influence of Entrepreneurial Expectations and Appraisals on Production Planning: An Econometric Study of the German Leather and Shoe Industries," *International Economic Review*, May 1961.

[62] TINBERGEN, JAN, *Statistical Testing of Business-Cycle Theories*, Vol. II, *Business Cycles in the United States of America, 1919–1932*, Geneva, League of Nations, 1939.

[63] WOLD, HERMAN, *Demand Analysis; A Study in Econometrics*, New York, Wiley, 1953.

COMMENT

RUTH P. MACK, Institute of Public Administration

Michael Lovell's reviews of the efforts of econometricians to build up and "test" inventory models is skillful and to the point. The analysis is ingenious. The material is organized around a systematic progression of important questions.

On many issues Lovell finds results inconclusive because of intrinsic difficulties in salting the tail of *ex ante* concepts, because variables elude econometric identification, or because business adjustments are delayed and incomplete. But much also has been achieved. What is needed, Lovell concludes, is more persevering work, perhaps fewer either-or questions and more combination packages, a better basis for restricting hypotheses, cross-section studies.

Yet though I second his dissatisfactions and find his prescriptions unexceptionable, they miss some of the broad implications of the information that the paper spreads out for examination.

The figures that Lovell assembles and analyzes seem to point to two striking, however highly tentative, conclusions. The first concerns the scope of the sales-linked inventory objective. The data show that sales are a far more ambiguous and less important determinant of inventory investment than generally supposed. The second concerns the role of unfilled orders. It is much too forceful to be explained as a modifying or forecasting adjunct of the sales-linked inventory objective.

These notions involve a judgment about matters of degree. The problem is not, of course, whether businessmen look to other things than sales in formulating their inventory objectives; obviously, they do. The point is rather that as these other matters start to account for as much or more of inventory investment and disinvestment as do sales, the analytic formulation primarily in terms of an accelerator mechanism, however modified, starts to creak and strain. Strained far enough, it falsifies the *essential* dynamics. Feedbacks become innovators of change and innovators become feedbacks.

The evidence that econometric models yield on this matter of relative importance is not discussed by Lovell nor, for that matter, by most of the authors of the investigations to which he refers. It consists of the relative sizes of the contribution of the several measured variables and their relationship to the theoretical requirement; it concerns the economic elements which, paralleling the measured variables, may, in fact, get picked up by them, though anonymously; it involves the likely influence on measured parameters of causality which in fact moves *from* the "dependent" *to* the "independent" variables as well as among the latter. It may be useful to review such evidence as the paper presents on each of the two points in turn—the weak sales-linked inventory objective and the strong role of unfilled orders.

The Sales-Linked Inventory Objective

The studies do not seem to support the notion, central to the accelerator dynamics, that the volume of sales is the primary determinant of inventory investment. Though the subject requires explicit study, the following observations bear on the point:

1. The *wide variety among coefficients* linking inventories to sales, as developed by the several investigators, clouds the significance of each result. Lovell reformulates the analyses to ask what "values of the explanatory variables . . . would not have led to an attempt to change the level of inventories." Three postwar studies of quarterly inventory investment respectively show that an increase in sales of one dollar per month generates changes in equilibrium inventories of the following multiples over a three-month period: −1.30, 1.95, 2.42. An interwar analysis of annual data yields a figure of 0.25, which in terms of monthly average sales would be about 3.0.[1]

---

[1] The quarterly studies are those of Terleckyj, Darling, and Lovell, respectively (see Lovell's paper). As far as I can judge, though all calculations are quarterly, the first two authors use figures in monthly averages for everything except change in stock, which is the total during the quarter. Lovell uses quarterly units. Since the units affect the size of the sales coefficient—the marginal stock-sales ratio—I have multiplied Lovell's coefficient by three to make it comparable. The coverage of the calculation includes deflated data for all manufacturing in Darling, plus trade for Lovell and Terleckyj (not deflated), and all stocks and GNP for Klein.

The size of the equilibrium marginal coefficients also seems to require justification. The size of the actual *average* stock-sales relationships might be one criterion, on the assumption that a situation that would lead to no attempt to change the level of inventories should be one in which that level is somewhat near, though doubtless smaller than, the usual over-all relation. If widely different, it would seem that businessmen were resigned to abject defeat in controlling the size of stocks.[2]

2. *Distributed lags are so large that the notion of a stock intention takes on an equivocal light.* This applies to lags attributed to delayed response, or to the choice to smooth production rather than to adjust stocks, or to failure to predict sales. A "flexible accelerator" implies delayed and often incomplete adjustment of stock, the extent of which is measured by the "reaction coefficient," which was 0.5 for Klein's annual calculations and 0.21 per quarter, or about 0.4 per year,[3] according to Darling's quarterly calculations. But what is the significance of an intention about so volatile a matter as stocks if a business moves only half-way toward its validation in the course of a whole year and only one-fifth of the way in the course of three months? The question answers itself when interest focuses on cyclical dynamics.

In reviewing his own calculations, Lovell does not specifically mention a reaction interval which he has used elsewhere. Nevertheless, the need to anticipate sales causes positive or negative "surplus inventories," and it is notable that they tend quarter by quarter to be larger than either actual or predicted inventory investment (see Table 1). Also, they tend to have the opposite sign (note the inverse pattern in the chart). Again, then, inventory response is pictured as perennially way too little or too late.

3. *Contribution of the sales parameter, which is small relative to the theoretical requirement.* Unfortunately, it is not usual to give partial correlation or beta-coefficients or to graph the contribution of each variable, for this omission makes it awkward to see how the parts of an econometric investigation fit together. However, it seems

---

[2] Post-World War II stocks averaged about 1.9 times monthly sales for manufacturing, and about 1.6 when trade is included. Darling's figure comes close to passing this test, though it is high—the marginal desired ratio should, I would expect, be substantially smaller (because of the inevitable slow-moving items), not larger, than the actual average of 1.6 for all stocks. Lovell's figure is higher still (compare with 1.9 above).

[3] I use the formula $1 - (1 - \delta)^4$, following Lovell in *Manufacturers' Inventories, Sales Expectations, and the Acceleration Principle*, Cowles Foundation Paper No. 169, 1962, p. 300, n. 10 (a reprint of [41] in Lovell's paper).

clear that, stated very conservatively, sales explain less than half of the explained quarterly changes in stocks in the three investigations mentioned before. (The figures discussed below indicate that change in unfilled orders alone accounts for close to or over half.) Moreover, some portion of this gross association in highly aggregative models must reflect the multiplier impact of inventory investment on sales rather than the acceleration impact of sales on inventory investment.

The Forceful Role of Unfilled Orders

Unfilled orders or changes in unfilled orders have been used to explain stocks by Lovell, Darling, and Terleckyj. Beta coefficients that the first two authors very kindly supplied me, some while ago, show that in the first case the unfilled order parameter accounted for more variation in inventory investment in purchased and in-process stock of manufacturers than did any other factor, including sales. In the case of Darling's analysis they were almost but not quite as important as sales; the simple correlation of change in unfilled orders and change in stock is 0.82.[4] Introducing the extreme values in Terleckyj's equations suggests that here, too, the unfilled orders term was the most powerful of the independent variables. Simple correlation with change in stocks in the following three- and six-month period was 0.81 and 0.84, respectively.[5]

Now, if we look at the actual time series, we find that total unfilled orders are dominated by those in the machinery and transportation equipment industries. These two industry groups constitute on the average over 70 per cent of total outstanding orders and also dominate rates of change. Is it then meaningful to say that investment in in-process and materials stocks of all manufacturers (Lovell), in all stocks of all manufacturers (Darling), and in all stocks of all manufacturers and distributors (Terleckyj) are thus heavily influenced by unfilled orders or their rates of change largely in the machinery and transportation industries?

Lovell, in another paper, explains their impact in the following terms:

[4] "Manufacturers' Inventory Investment, 1947–58: An Application of Acceleration Analysis," *American Economic Review*, December 1959, p. 952.

[5] Terleckyj used the ratio of new orders to sales, which must of course virtually parallel change in unfilled orders. The correlation coefficients are quoted from Thomas M. Stanback, Jr., "A Critique of Inventory Forecasting Techniques," in American Statistical Association, *1960 Proceedings of the Business and Economic Statistics Section*.

If unfilled orders represent an established demand, indeed a possible committal to deliver at some future date, entrepreneurs may well consider it advisable to carry additional stocks when unfilled orders are large as a hedge against possible shortage and price commitments. In addition, a rise in the backlog of unfilled orders may be expected to lead to an acceleration of production that is felt first in terms of an increase of goods in process rather than a rise in the output of completed commodities. These considerations suggest that stocks of purchased materials and goods in process should be positively related to the backlog of unfilled orders. Conversely, if unfilled orders were only a surrogate measure of the tightness of the markets on which firms purchase their inputs, a negative relationship between orders and stocks would be revealed . . .[6]

Terleckyj says much the same thing: "One would expect that when new orders are running above sales, and the reservoir of future business is built up, an accumulation of inventories becomes desirable, as the planned production rate rises to fill these orders. The subsequent increase in the actual production rate entails a rise in inventories concentrated in the in-process stocks."[7] Darling originally placed more emphasis on the expectational aspect. He now focuses on industries in which goods are made largely to order. Here "inventory investment is more closely associated in time with receipt of the order, or more accurately with changes in the 'unfilled order' backlog than with the delivery (sale) of the goods to the buyers."[8]

Certainly, influences of the sorts described are at work. The point at issue is merely whether, particularly in view of the overpowering emphasis in the actual data of two groups of industries alone, unfilled orders can reasonably be expected to account for such strong modification of the basic sales-linked inventory objective. The modification, like the camel's head, appears to have taken over the

---

[6] Michael Lovell, "Factors Determining Manufacturing Inventory Investment," *Inventory Fluctuations and Economic Stabilization*, Joint Economic Committee, 87th Cong. 1st sess., December 1961, Part II, pp. 140–141.

[7] Nestor E. Terleckyj, "Measures of Inventory Conditions," in *Inventory Fluctuations and Economic Stabilization*, Part II, p. 185.

[8] "Inventory Fluctuations and Economic Instability" (in *Inventory Fluctuations and Economic Stabilization*, Part III, p. 30). When the theory is incorporated in a regression, the impact of unfilled orders and their rate of change cuts down the impact of sales on *all* stocks, not merely those in made-to-order industries, by about one-half (p. 37). The theory suggests that unfilled orders would be a more important determinant in durable than in nondurable goods. But Lovell's computations suggest the opposite (pp. 129, 143).

premises. It seems likely that backlogs are actually pushing the estimates around with muscle belonging to attributes not recognized by the theory. What might these attributes be?

One set of candidates must be buying prices and other factors that reflect changing short-term patterns of supply and demand. In a different section of the paper from that in which the influence of orders is shown, Lovell summarizes the evidence on "price-hedging" or "speculative" behavior yielded by four studies. His own study yields the only clearly adverse finding. In view of the fact that the price change that he uses involves accurate forecasts of the next quarter's prices, the failure to find it significant is not surprising. A similar requirement for clairvoyance with respect to changes in sales would have shown, no doubt, similarly negative results.

In any event, it seems clear that changes in unfilled orders must reflect a substantial part of the eventual impact of price expectations or other market expectations on stocks. The point is clarified if unfilled orders (reports are for unfilled sales orders) are thought of as outstanding purchase orders of the customer. Also, restrict consideration for a moment to orders for materials rather than for complicated goods including machines. Then, it stands to reason that a large part of the influence of expectations about changing buying prices will be reflected, in the first instance, in a lengthening of the number of weeks' supply on order. By buying more, and thereby fixing prices on the additional supply at an earlier date, the purchaser forestalls the rise. The result is an increase in his outstanding purchase orders or, precisely, the unfilled sales orders of his supplier. But outstanding purchase orders become, in due course, additions to stocks of purchased materials. Thus, changes in outstanding purchase orders act as a vestibule for changes in stock.

But if so, how can a theory that purports to explain change in stocks do so in terms of changes in outstanding purchase orders? One might as well "explain" the number of people just inside the door of a department store by the number outside of it trying to get in. *Obviously, change in outstanding orders must itself be explained,* if any real insight concerning related inventory change is to be achieved.

A second hat that unfilled orders may be wearing is that of the impact of stock on the economy—the feedback unrecognized in the single-equation system. And this may be one reason why a series that is so heavily weighted with machinery helps so materially to "explain" total stock. Change in unfilled orders applies to an earlier date than does the change in stock which it explains. There is some evidence, and certainly it is reasonable to expect, that production schedules will respond to the rate at which backlogs change (or perhaps to the active element in this change, the rate of flow of new sales orders). The association is between change in unfilled orders and change in production, and it may well be almost immediate. The rate of change in production (or its reflection in the rate of change in wages or other income) is presumably a chief determinant of inventory investment. Thus, the causal association could run from changes in unfilled orders to changes in production and income more or less immediately; changes in stocks would then reflect, a bit later, *both* the change in orders and the change in output.

Purport

My difficulty, then, with Lovell's paper is that he has done a better job of review than he is willing to admit. He has arrayed empirical results inconsistent with one another and with the theory. He has uncovered a challenging mystery: unfilled orders and their rates of change explain too much and sales too little of inventory investment.

If I am right in believing that the relative magnitudes rest uncomfortably in the accelerator model, then the theory requires reformulation. The solo theme of sales, however enriched by accompaniment, needs to be recast as a duet in which expectations about market conditions and the entire complex of business choices may have an equal voice.

This will not be easy. For open-end study is required of how businessmen formulate, as well as solve, problems that result directly or indirectly in inventory investment. Economizing inventories have their opportunity costs elsewhere in a business. Does it, for example, make sense to think of the flexible accelerator, production-smoothing, and sales forecast errors as *competing* hypotheses. Are not all necessarily present and substantial? (Lovell himself raises at least part of this question and shows brilliantly how econometric distinction between two of them is virtually impossible.) Are there not, characteristically, cyclical patterns in the relation among the several opportunity costs of changes in stocks? Are errors in forecasts of sales the only ones that motivate changes in stocks or unfilled orders; how about errors in forecasting delivery periods, selling or buying prices, material requirements? Changes in backlogs of

230

unfilled sales orders and in outstanding orders for materials are critically *interrelated* with all these matters.

In short, rather than a better basis for placing "further restrictions upon the range of models to be considered" for which Lovell asks (p. 215) we require, I fear, a better basis for expanding them. Obviously, intense simplification is required, but it must contain rather than amputate the essential bone in business choice. To do so the model will have to penetrate far more deeply into the economic meaning of expectations than any we have used heretofore. It will have to cope with the cumulative social process of the spread of opinion, action, feedbacks, and, particularly, feedins. These are tough assignments, but only tough enough to excite their own solution.

The Federal Sector in National Income Models

WILFRED LEWIS, JR.

BROOKINGS INSTITUTION

Introduction

THE federal budget and the economy interact at many points, with the level of economic activity determining receipts and certain expenditures and being influenced in turn by tax rates and government outlays. This paper attempts to specify some of these interrelationships in the hope of increasing, if only slightly, the precision with which the government sector can be handled in long-term and short-term economic models.

The usual practice is to place a substantial portion of the federal sector in a box called "exogenous." This is as it should be. However much the economic scientist feigns a disinterest in mundane reality, there is usually at the root of his inquiries at least an indirect interest in normative public economic policy. So even if the political scientists offered models in which government behavior was completely determinate, I submit that the economist would decline them. And, of course, there have been few offers of this sort. More than one model-builder has been mildly shocked to find that the government itself does not always know how much it is going to spend within a fairly wide margin of error only a short period ahead.

Having stated the impossibility as well as the undesirability of specifying public sector behavior, I now attempt to make this sector perhaps a little more manageable for the model-builder. In some cases, reasonable quantitative estimates of parameters are possible. In others, identifying if not measuring the parameters may suggest rough limits on the range of permissible values. Finally, certain problem areas are mentioned, where I think further research would pay dividends in pinning down important interrelationships between the federal sector and the rest of the economy.

NOTE: The author was on the staff of the United States Bureau of the Budget when this paper was prepared. However, there is obviously no expressed or implied official endorsement of any of its contents. He is indebted for the perceptive comments of Samuel M. Cohn and Edward F. Denison.

Long-Range Projections for the Federal Sector

FEDERAL REVENUES UNDER CONDITIONS OF STABLE GROWTH AND CONSTANT RATES

A long-run projection of revenues for the federal government conveniently starts from a calculation of yields under existing rates for most taxes, modified in the case of social security payroll taxes, where rate increases are built in under existing law. Subsequently, the effects of additional rate changes can be fed in according to the policy assumptions made or in conjunction with a projection of expenditures.

A yield calculation based on existing rates may appear, on the surface, a rather mechanical exercise, but in practice there is some margin for error. This is particularly the case when both the tax revenues and tax base one is trying to relate are on a national income account basis—presumably the usual situation in economic model-building. Both the base and the tax in national income terms differ conceptually from their counterparts in the tax code. The corporation income tax is an outstanding example.

Corporation Income Tax

On the assumptions that present tax rates are continued, and that profits on the national income definition have been determined elsewhere in the model, what is the best procedure for estimating federal corporate profits tax liability?[1] The ratio of corporate profits tax to corporate profits could be affected by any of the following:[2]

1. Secular drift in the ratio to profits of any of the items which are included in taxable profits but excluded from national income profits, such as intercorporate dividends, capital gains, or profits of mutual financial intermediaries
2. Secular drift in the ratio to profits of items excluded from taxable profits but included in national income profits, such as depletion, state corporate income taxes, profits of Federal Reserve banks, or tax-exempt interest

---

[1] Although five points of the corporate tax are scheduled to expire at the end of this fiscal year, this has been the case each year since 1954, and each year the rates have been extended for another year.

[2] A detailed reconciliation of national income profits and the profits tax and their *Statistics of Income* counterparts is given in one of the supplementary tables to the national income accounts, e.g., *U.S. Income and Output*, Department of Commerce, Table VII-19, p. 230.

234

3. Secular drift in the ratio to profits of items taxed at special rates, such as Western Hemisphere trade corporations or corporations choosing the partnership option under the small-business liberalization enacted in 1958
4. Secular drift in the ratio of losses to aggregate profits, since the effects on tax liability of losses and profits are not symmetrical
5. Secular drift in the proportion of profits accruing to corporations with net profits of $25,000 or less, because of the rudimentary progressivity in the tax structure

It is doubtful that many, if any, of these reconciliation items would appear among the list of variables in a model of manageable size. How much precision is lost by ignoring some or all of them?

Table 1 shows profits and taxes on the two bases over a ten-year period. The bottom part of this table decomposes the ratios of national income profits to *Statistics of Income* profits, of taxes to profits on a national income basis, and of national income taxes to *Statistics of Income* taxes.

Aside from the recession years of 1954 and 1958, the *Statistics of Income* ratio of taxes to profits (T_R/R) has remained between 48.5 per cent and 49 per cent since the current rates went into effect in 1952. With recession years again omitted in order to approximate conditions of stable growth, the ratio of *Statistics of Income* profits to national income profits (R/C) also shows no particular trend. Thus changes in the reconciliation items, averaged over the cycle, are negligible in size or else cancel out against others. However, there is one item for which this is not the case. The major factor in the decline of national income tax relative to *Statistics of Income* tax (T_C/T_R) is for credits against United States liability for foreign taxes paid by foreign branches of United States corporations. These credits, which quadrupled in the period 1948–57 (from $278 million to $1,053 million) while total profits were increasing about a third, are included in liabilities reported in *Statistics of Income* but excluded from the tax on a national income basis. In consequence, the profits elasticity of tax on a national income basis under conditions of stable growth may be as low as 0.91 or 0.92 if foreign taxes paid by United States corporations continue to grow faster than United States taxes. This compares with the approximately unit elasticity of taxes on a *Statistics of Income* liability basis.

TABLE 1

CORPORATE PROFITS AND PROFITS TAX, NATIONAL INCOME BASIS
COMPARED TO STATISTICS OF INCOME, 1948–58
(dollars in millions)

	T_C Federal Corporate Income Tax Liability, National Income Basis[a]	T_R Federal Corporate Income Tax, *Statistics of Income*[b]	R Taxable Corporate Income, *Statistics of Income*[c]	C Corporate Profits Before Tax, National Income Basis[d]
1948	$11,813	$11,920	$32,772	$33,000
1949	9,773	9,817	27,093	26,370
1950	15,711	15,929	40,032	40,628
1951	19,110	19,623	41,150	42,153
1952	17,088	17,597	36,090	36,691
1953	17,806	18,256	37,261	38,311
1954	16,417	16,823	34,859	34,061
1955	20,869	21,741	44,663	44,862
1956	20,195	21,364	44,124	44,683
1957	19,916	20,582	42,369	43,208
1958	17,657	18,814	39,612	37,410

	$\dfrac{T_C}{C}$ =	$\dfrac{T_C}{T_R}$ ×	$\dfrac{T_R}{R}$ ×	$\dfrac{R}{C}$
1948		[e]	.9910	0.9931
1949		[e]	.9955	1.0274
1950		[e]	.9863	0.9853
1951		[e]	.9740	0.9762
1952	.4657	.9711	[e]	0.9836
1953	.4648	.9754	.4876	0.9726
1954	.4820	.9759	.4900	1.0234
1955	.4652	.9599	.4826	0.9956
1956	.4520	.9453	.4868	0.9875
1957	.4609	.9676	.4842	0.9806
1958	.4720	.9385	.4858	1.0589
			.4750	

[a] *Survey of Current Business* and *U.S. Income and Output*, Department of Commerce. Excludes excess profits tax (*Statistics of Income*, Internal Revenue Service) for 1950–54
[b] *Statistics of Income*. Excludes excess profits tax for 1950–54.
[c] Net income, returns with net income, from *Statistics of Income*, less following items (from *Statistics of Income* or Treasury Department): Net operating loss deduction; net income as reported on small business returns (Form 1120-s); 85 per cent of domestic dividends; special credits, life insurance companies; and special credits, Western Hemisphere Trade Corporations.
[d] *Survey of Current Business* and *U.S. Income and Output*.
[e] Tax rates differed from those presently in effect.

Individual Income Taxes

As with the corporation income tax, there are a number of differences between the tax base established in the revenue code and its personal income counterpart in the national income accounts. Differences include both taxable nonincome, such as capital gains, and nontaxable income, such as transfer payments. Progressive rates might also be expected to affect the trend in yields.

Table 2, bottom, records the two components of the trend in taxes as a percentage of personal income. Actual yields have been adjusted for the different rates in effect prior to 1954 to obtain a longer perspective.

Contrary to what might be expected under a system of progressive rates, there is no discernible trend in the ratio of taxes to taxable income. The ratio of taxable to total personal income does, however, rise substantially. It can be shown, although I have not included the data here, that this growth is due to the increasing proportion of personal income in the total of incomes reported in taxable returns, rather than to the other reconciliation items. This confirms that exemptions, rather than progressive rates, are the major source of income sensitivity of the individual income tax.

The combined effects of stable yields relative to taxable income and of growing taxable income relative to total personal income has been a personal income elasticity of taxes at unchanged rates, measured for comparable stages of the cycle in order to approximate stable growth conditions, of 1.25 or more. A faster rate of growth of per capita income than in the period from which this estimate is drawn would mean a still higher elasticity, since exemptions per taxpayer (with no change in law) can reasonably be assumed more or less constant.

Excise Taxes

Table 3 records federal indirect business tax accruals (mainly excises) adjusted for the estimated effects of tax rate changes. It appears that federal indirect business taxes have had a GNP elasticity of slightly more than 0.8 in the period since 1952, aside from changes in rates. This may understate the GNP elasticity for purposes of a stable growth model, since GNP in recent years has been below potential; and there is a relatively high marginal response of the automobile excise tax to cyclical changes in GNP. On the other

237

TABLE 2

INDIVIDUAL INCOME TAX, TAXABLE INCOME, AND PERSONAL INCOME, 1948–53
(dollars in billions)

	Individual Income Tax			TI	Y
	Tax Rate Adjustment Factors		T	Taxable	Personal
	Unadjusted[a]	(1959 Rates = 100)[b]	(Adjusted)	Income[c]	Income[d]
1948	15.44	85.5	18.06	74.7	210.4
1949	14.54	85.5	17.00	71.6	208.3
1950	18.38	89.6	20.51	84.3	228.5
1951	24.23	105.1	23.05	99.4	256.7
1952	27.80	114.3	24.32	107.5	273.1
1953	29.43	114.3	25.75	115.7	288.3
1954	26.67	100.0	26.67	115.3	289.8
1955	29.61	100.0	29.61	128.0	310.2
1956	32.73	100.0	32.73	141.5	332.9
1957	34.39	100.0	34.39	149.4	351.4
1958	34.34	100.0	34.34	149.3	360.3
1959p	38.90	100.0	38.90	167.2	383.3

$$\frac{T}{Y} \quad = \quad \frac{T}{TI} \quad \times \quad \frac{TI}{Y}$$

	$\frac{T}{Y}$	$\frac{T}{TI}$	$\frac{TI}{Y}$
1948	.0858	.242	.355
1949	.0816	.237	.344
1950	.0898	.243	.369
1951	.0898	.232	.382
1952	.0891	.226	.394
1953	.0893	.223	.401
1954	.0920	.231	.398
1955	.0955	.231	.413
1956	.0983	.231	.425
1957	.0979	.230	.425
1958	.0953	.230	.414
1959p	.1015	.233	.436

p = preliminary.

[a] *Statistics of Income*, Internal Revenue Service.

[b] First-bracket rate, current year, divided by first-bracket rate, 1959, times 1.03 (for years prior to 1954) for approximate effect of reduction in liabilities in Revenue Code of 1954.

[c] Joseph A. Pechman, "What Would a Comprehensive Income Tax Yield?" *Tax Revision Compendium*, Committee on Ways and Means, 86th Cong., 1st sess., 1959, I, 257; and *Statistics of Income*.

[d] Department of Commerce.

TABLE 3

FEDERAL INDIRECT BUSINESS TAXES, 1952–60
(billions of dollars)

Calendar Year	Actual[a]	At Constant 1960 Tax Rates[b]	Adjusted Tax as Percentage of GNP
1952	10.52	10.18	2.93
1953	11.19	10.83	2.96
1954	10.06	10.46	2.88
1955	11.04	11.65	2.93
1956	11.60	11.94	2.84
1957	12.21	12.28	2.77
1958	11.88	12.22	2.75
1959	13.04	13.48	2.79
1960	14.00	14.00	2.77

[a] Department of Commerce.
[b] Adjusted for the estimated revenue effects of: (1) the 1954 Excise Tax Reduction Act; (2) the increase in gasoline and highway-user tax rates in 1956 and 1959; and (3) the repeal of the excise tax on passenger transportation in 1958.

hand, tobacco and alcohol, for which income elasticity is probably below unity, account for about half of federal excise taxes. On balance, the GNP elasticity for the system of federal excises under conditions of stable growth and unchanged rates may be taken to be about 0.85.

Contributions for Social Insurance

A calculation of the long-run income elasticity of federal contributions for social insurance—mainly the payroll taxes to finance old age, survivors, and disability insurance—runs into a number of obstacles. Actual data for past years is clouded by changes in coverage, tax rates, and limits on taxable wages, all of which affect the income elasticity of taxes. For related reasons, a projection based only on current rates would be of little use.

For federal employment taxes, unlike other taxes, specific changes in rates already scheduled in the present law are highly likely, and should therefore be put into a projection. The proper treatment of the limit on taxable wages, for which no changes are scheduled under the present law, is less certain.

For given coverage and tax rates, a limit on taxable wages implies an income elasticity of yield of less than unity and a declining elasticity with the passage of time as the mean of the frequency distribution of wages by size in covered industries rises relative to the limit.

239

TABLE 4

CONTRIBUTIONS FOR FEDERAL OLD-AGE, SURVIVORS,
AND DISABILITY INSURANCE, 1951–60

	Limit on Annual Taxable Wages	Actual Contributions (billions)[a]	Combined Payroll Tax Rates	Contributions Adjusted to Tax Rates in First Year of Each Wage Limit (billions)	Adjusted as Per Cent of Total Wages and Salaries
1951	$3,600	$3.32	3.0%	$3.32	1.94%
1952	3,600	3.76	3.0	3.76	2.03
1953	3,600	3.98	3.0	3.98	2.01
1954	3,600	5.14	4.0	3.85	1.96
1955	4,200	5.95	4.0	5.95	2.82
1956	4,200	6.55	4.0	6.55	2.88
1957	4,200	7.87	4.5	6.99	2.93
1958	4,200	7.90	4.5	7.02	2.93
1959	4,800	9.74	5.0	9.74	3.77
1960	4,800	12.05	6.0	10.04	3.70

[a] Department of Commerce.

Table 4 shows, by subperiods in which the taxable wage limit was constant, accrued taxes adjusted for rate changes (but not for coverage). Over each of the two four-year intervals—1951–54 and 1955–58—the elasticity of taxes at constant rates relative to total wages and salaries appears equal to or even slightly greater than unity. This probably reflects the influence of periodic legislative extensions of coverage under the system. Coverage has now reached such high percentages of the labor force that future extensions will perforce be nil or at most at a much slower pace than in the past. On the other hand, the limit has in the past been lifted by legislation at fairly regular intervals. It can probably be safely assumed that this practice will continue with rising productivity and average income. All things considered, an elasticity of yield of approximately unity (aside from rate changes) seems reasonable. To this one would add the effects of scheduled increases in tax rates.

OASDI actuaries duck the problem of a limit on taxable wages in both their benefit and tax calculations by assuming constant average wages in covered employment (contrary to all past experience). From the standpoint of actuarial soundness of the insurance system, this is roughly equivalent to assuming periodic changes to increase the limit on taxable wages to keep pace with rising productivity and wage rates.

TOTAL RECEIPTS

The long-run behavior of federal revenues obviously hinges on the distribution of income shares between corporations and individuals. There is the argument, of course, that the profits share in GNP can be expected to continue declining, as it has apparently been doing over the last decade or so. Because of the high marginal federal tax return from the profits share, such a tendency would reduce the GNP elasticity of the over-all federal revenue system. In passing, however, a counterargument can be noted, which holds that the apparent decline in the profits share is related to the operation of the economy below potential in recent years, and this trend would not occur under conditions of stable growth at unchanged rates of factor utilizations. A continuation of the recent growth in capital consumption allowances, relative to GNP, would also reduce the GNP elasticity of taxable incomes and taxes. Again, however, this may be a phenomenon related to the below-potential operation of the economy. In any event, an analysis of income shares is outside the scope of this paper, and I am content to let this be determined elsewhere in the model.

Table 5 gives an illustrative ten-year projection of federal receipts based on the elasticities discussed above, assuming a 5 and one-quarter per cent annual growth rate in money GNP and assuming that the major income shares—profits, wages and salaries, and total personal income—all move proportionately to GNP. A minor redistribution of relative income shares would not alter the basic conclusions suggested by Table 5, nor are these conclusions seriously affected by my use of actual 1960 receipts as a base rather than a hypothetical high-employment estimate. I have also chosen to ignore in this illustration two relatively minor changes in tax rates—the temporary doubling of the federal portion of the unemployment payroll taxes for two years starting January 1, 1962, and the approximately $150 million increase in highway user taxes on July 1, 1961.

The important points are that the tendency of individual income taxes to rise a good deal faster than personal income, and the increases in OASDI payroll taxes already scheduled in the present law, more than outweigh the effect of less than unit elasticities of the federal excise system and corporation income tax accruals. The GNP

241

TABLE 5

ILLUSTRATIVE TEN-YEAR PROJECTION OF FEDERAL RECEIPTS,[a] 1960 AND 1970
(national income account basis, billions of dollars)

	Calendar 1960 (actual)	Calendar 1970 (projected)
Gross national product	504.4	841.4
Federal receipts		
Corporation income taxes	21.2	33.6[b]
Personal taxes	43.2	81.5[c]
Indirect business taxes	14.0	21.7[d]
Contributions for social insurance:		
OASDI	12.0	31.0[e]
Other	5.6	9.4[f]
Total receipts	96.0	177.2
Total receipts as per cent of GNP	19.0%	21.1%

[a] Assuming 3.5 per cent per year real growth in *GNP*, a 1.75 per cent increase per year in the *GNP* deflator, and unit *GNP* elasticity of corporate profits, personal income, and wages and salaries.

[b] Profits elasticity of tax of 0.92.

[c] Personal income elasticity of tax of 1.25.

[d] *GNP* elasticity of tax of 0.85.

[e] Wages and salaries elasticity of tax of 1.0, plus increases scheduled in present law in combined rate on employers and employees, from 6 per cent in 1960 to 9.25 per cent by 1970.

[f] Wages and salaries elasticity of tax of 1.0.

elasticity of the total system under these assumptions works out to be on the order of over 1.2. Expressed differently, assuming stable growth, constant income shares, and present tax rates (plus the scheduled OASDI increases), federal revenues would rise from 19 per cent of GNP in 1960 to 21 per cent in 1970.

I hope it is clear that I am forecasting neither 5 and one-quarter per cent growth nor unchanged unemployment ratios. The purpose of this projection is to bring out certain features of the federal revenue system—particularly its potentially high GNP elasticity—not to forecast revenues. For forecasting, tax receipts have to be solved for simultaneously with the values for their respective bases. These obviously depend not only on private income-spending relationships, but on the level of federal spending as well.

242

LONG-RANGE PROJECTIONS OF FEDERAL SPENDING

Long-run projections of federal spending are usually done in terms of ranges or alternatives, such as "high," "low," and "medium." The very wide margin allowed for possible error in the form of a difference between the "high" and the "low," typically amounting to several percentage points of the gross national product, has limited the usefulness of some of these projections. In what follows, it will be argued that the usual projections of total federal spending are too timid in this respect—it is possible to forecast with some confidence within a smaller range than is usually done.

The model-builder attempting a long-range projection of government spending is faced with several decisions right at the outset.

In dealing with the public sector, the model-builder should be as explicit as Otto Eckstein was in stating whether he is prescribing what he thinks ought to be or whether he is forecasting what the political process is likely to produce.[3] Although exercises of both types are useful, ambiguous ones are not. While intending no slight to projections of the prescription type, provided they are clearly labeled as such, my following remarks are addressed to the forecast variety.

With defense outlays accounting for half or more of the federal budget, and with nonzero probabilities for both general war on the one hand and disarmament on the other, some explicit assumption about international politics is required. One approach is to make alternative projections based, say, on war, cold war, and disarmament.[4]

Since these probably imply profound differences all through the economy, including the level of nondefense as well as defense spending, the mix of total output and the resultant value per man-hour of input, as well as profit rates in the private economy and the size of the labor force, this approach logically calls for a corresponding number of complete economic models.

Either because there is far less material with which to construct a

---

[3] Otto Eckstein, *Trends in Public Expenditures in the Next Decade*, Committee for Economic Development, April 1959, p. 14.

[4] For example, the ten-year projection of federal budget trends published by the Bureau of the Budget in January 1961 included, in addition to "high," "low," and "medium" projections, which were based broadly on "no marked change in the international situation," a fourth alternative based on the possibility of controlled disarmament.

confident projection of expenditure trends under the general war or disarmament alternatives, or because the forecaster assigns relatively low probabilities to these two alternatives, most projections are based broadly on a continuation of international tension as it has prevailed for most of the years since World War II. Within this broad assumption, however, there would appear ample residual uncertainty in the defense-spending area. That fluctuations in the level of defense spending can be caused by Berlin crises, sputniks, and intervening periods of lesser tension has been amply demonstrated. This uncertainty is typically handled by making a "high," a "low," and a "medium" defense projection sometimes embracing a quantitatively very wide range (e.g., Table 6).

TABLE 6

Selected Ten-Year Projections of Federal Defense Spending,
to 1968, 1970, and 1971

Projector	Defense Concept Used	Year Projected	Range from "Low" to "High" Projections (billions)
Otto Eckstein[a]	Dept. of Defense, military functions	1968	$15
Bureau of the Budget[b]	Major national security[c]	1970	10
National Planning Association[d]	National security[e]	1971	57

[a] Otto Eckstein, *Trends in Public Expenditures in the Next Decade*, Committee for Economic Development, 1959. Both the high and low projections assume that disarmament is excluded and that the world situation will not change in a fundamental way.

[b] *Ten-Year Projection of Federal Budget Expenditures*, Bureau of the Budget, 1961. Both high and low assume no important changes in international conditions.

[c] Department of Defense, military functions, plus military assistance, atomic energy, stockpiling, and defense production expansion.

[d] National Planning Association, 1961 Projection Series. Low assumes a substantial easing of international tensions. High assumes the international situation requires a greatly enlarged program for armaments or civil defense. However, neither disarmament nor war is apparently assumed.

[e] Major national security plus space and civil defense.

A similar dilemma confronts the forecaster in the area of non-defense spending. If a forecast rather than a prescription is desired, the model-builder cannot just total up the "needs" for public spending, but must make a judgment as to what balance Congress and the Executive will strike between the pressures for particular program increases and the pressures for minimizing various tax burdens. He also has to judge what resolution will be made of the sometimes conflicting advice on the proper size of the budget surplus at various stages of the business cycle.

I do not want to minimize the forecaster's problem in sorting through these various uncertainties. But the usual projection allows a larger margin for contingencies than I think is really necessary. At this point, I will simply state those aspects of the usual forecast that give rise to unnecessary imprecision. Subsequently, I will present some historical evidence that argues for a modification of the usual approach.

Almost all the long-range projections I have seen begin by decomposing the federal budget into major functions or program areas, such as defense, agriculture, health, veterans, transportation, etc., and then making for each portion a high, a low, and a medium projection. The high projection for the total budget is then taken as the sum of the individual program highs, etc. However, there is good reason to believe that the pieces so projected are nonadditive. Certainly the high and the low projections are not properly constructed by addition, and perhaps the medium is not as well.

Another mistake, in my opinion, is a tendency to exaggerate the flexibility in the size of the budget available from slight alternation in the political complexion of the legislative and executive branches.

Peacock and Wiseman[5] for the United Kingdom and Kendrick[6] and Cohn[7] for the United States have given very similar descriptions of the growth in central government expenditures. Noting a long-run tendency for such outlays to grow faster than population and prices, all three studies have stressed the unevenness of this growth process. Peacock and Wiseman have put forward an interesting thesis to account for the pattern of alternating increase and stability in government expenditures in democratic societies. The basic propositions in this thesis are that (1) expenditures tend to be broadly conditioned by revenue availability; and (2) unless society is subjected to unusually violent pressures or disturbances, people's ideas about the "tolerable" burden of taxes tend to be fairly stable. A social disturbance, such as war, destroys established conceptions and has a

[5] Alan T. Peacock and Jack Wiseman, *The Growth of Public Expenditures in Great Britain*, Princeton for NBER, 1961.
[6] M. Slade Kendrick, *A Century and a Half of Federal Expenditures*, New York, NBER, 1955.
[7] Samuel M. Cohn, "Economic Policy and the Federal Budget," *Federal Accountant*, September 1959.

lasting impact on expenditures, which Peacock and Wiseman call the "displacement" effect. In the absence of upheaval, differences of opinion about the desirable amount of taxation and expenditure, and the conflict between efficiency through scale economies on the one hand and local autonomy on the other, get resolved in favor of the *status quo*. Any rise in spending during such periods tends to be at rather unspectacular rates.

Major wars are particularly cited not only as leaving a legacy of veterans' pensions and interest on the public debt, but also as changing the notion of the tolerable level of taxation. In theory, Peacock and Wiseman point out, displacements can be negative as well as positive and could be associated not only with wars but with periods of runaway inflation, extraordinary unemployment, or cold war defense outlays. In fact, however, World Wars I and II have been the major displacements in British experience.

In United States experience, major wars—the War of 1812, the Civil War, and the First and Second World Wars—have clearly operated as "displacements" in the sense that Peacock and Wiseman use the term (Table 7). Each of these wars operated to lift the level of spending in the postwar period not only for war-related outlays such as public debt, interest, and veterans' benefits but for civil outlays as well. The Great Depression was also a "displacement" in United States experience, giving rise to a gradual increase in federal cash payments from 2.8 per cent of gross national product in 1929 to 10 per cent in 1940. Displacement effects of smaller wars have generally been less significant. The Korean War was an exception in this respect, leaving a heritage of military outlays substantially higher than prewar. The Mexican War was a minor, but permanent, type of displacement; the Spanish-American War, temporary as well as minor.

In the last century and the first part of this, expenditures in the periods between major displacements probably rose little if any more than could be accounted for by increases in population and prices, and probably less rapidly than the gross national product. Since World War II, however, spending in periods between displacements has risen somewhat faster than the gross national product. A greater income elasticity of the revenue system may well account for this difference.

Long-range forecasts of federal expenditures (e.g., Table 8) are frequently made conditional on the political complexion of the ex-

TABLE 7

DISPLACEMENT EFFECT OF MAJOR WARS ON THE LEVEL OF FEDERAL SPENDING,
WAR OF 1812–WORLD WAR II

	Prewar Five-Year Average	Average of War Years	Postwar, Five-Year Average
War of 1812 (constant dollars per capita, 1926 prices)			
Military	0.71	2.58	1.34
Other	0.77	0.74	1.31
Total	1.48	3.32	2.65
Civil war (constant dollars per capita, 1926 prices)			
Military	1.51	16.34	2.35
Other	1.83	2.47	5.83
Total	3.34	18.81	8.18
World War I (per cent of gross national product)			
Military	0.64	10.37	2.16
Other	1.16	5.76	2.92
Total	1.81	16.12	5.08
World War II (per cent of gross national product)			
Military	2.33	32.94	5.34
Other	8.03	5.70	10.16
Total	10.36	38.64	15.51

SOURCE: M. Slade Kendrick, *A Century and a Half of Federal Expenditures*, New York, NBER, 1955; and *U.S. Income and Output*, Department of Commerce, 1958. Years are fiscal years. Expenditures are federal consolidated cash budget payments to the public.

ecutive and legislative branches, as though to imply that rather abrupt changes in public sector spending might occur as the result of a change in the balance of political power between "spenders" and "nonspenders." For example, Otto Eckstein described his projections as assuming a continuation of the recent balance of political forces with respect to federal spending in his "medium" projection, economy in both Administration and Congress in his "low" figures, and stronger expenditure stress in his "high" figures. The Bureau of the Budget gave a similar explanation of the differences between its high, low, and medium projections. Some hedging by the forecaster on this account is clearly prudent. But it is doubtful if a large range is reasonably required to take care of this source of uncertainty.

TABLE 8

SELECTED TEN-YEAR PROJECTIONS OF TOTAL FEDERAL SPENDING,
TO 1968, 1970, AND 1971

Projector	Federal Expenditure Concept Used	Year Projected	Range from "High" to "Low" Projection as Per Cent of GNP
Otto Eckstein[a]	Consolidated cash	1968	17.3–21.7
Bureau of the Budget[b]	Consolidated cash	1970	15.2–22.0
National Planning Association[c]	National income and product	1971	13.7–18.4

[a] Otto Eckstein, *Trends in Public Expenditures in the Next Decade*, Committee for Economic Development, 1959.

[b] *Ten-Year Projection of Federal Budget Expenditures*, Bureau of the Budget, 1961. (Disarmament alternative disregarded in computing range shown above.)

[c] National Planning Association, 1961 Projection Series. Upper end of range taken from the "high government, low growth" alternative; lower end from the "high con-consumption, fast growth" alternative.

Consider the difficulty a political party would have in justifying significant changes in tax rates. Any such change directly raises the question of the proper allocation of resources between public and private use. A proposed increase of any significant size is likely to arouse accusations of fiscal irresponsibility; and a proposed decrease, complaints of neglect of vital public needs. There are few fighting words more charged than these in our political vocabularies. Attitudes do change, of course, but there can be little doubt of the high degree of sanctity in existing tax rates—the *status quo* raises far fewer political arguments than movements in either direction. Furthermore, attitudes favoring balanced budgets are widespread. Consequently, any proposed reduction that is to be made on the basis of an actual realized surplus in the budget, gets strong support; but it is a clever feat indeed, since a cutback in spending to pave the way for lower taxes would ordinarily be self-defeating. Similar feedback effects may also help to limit changes in the other direction if spending increases are inflationary, or even if they are just thought to be so.

Supporting, although admittedly not conclusive, evidence for the proposition that sudden changes in the balance of power between "spenders" and "nonspenders" are unlikely is furnished by the two most recent changes in national administration. The Eisenhower administration was largely unsuccessful in its announced plan to reduce government spending relative to the gross national product.

Defense spending was reduced from its Korean War peak (Chart 1) but remained well above its prewar percentage of gross national product. Nondefense spending (measured in national income terms)

CHART 1

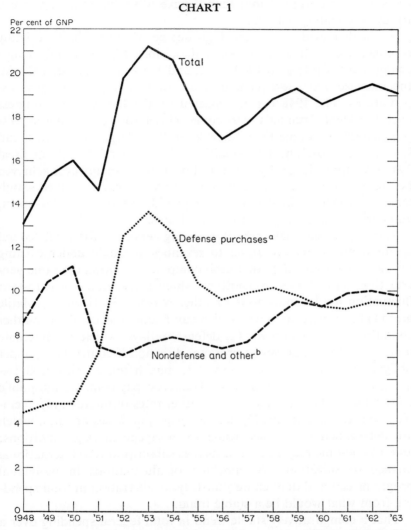

was increased more than GNP the first year in office, slightly less than GNP in 1955 and 1956, and faster than GNP thereafter except for a one-year leveling in 1960.

Expenditures proposed by the Kennedy administration for fiscal 1963 as a percentage of projected gross national product represent a slight decline from fiscal 1962 to about the same percentage as in fiscal 1961.

It must also be remembered that Congress, which is probably still less subject to abrupt change than the executive, has at least as much to say in spending matters.

As further evidence of the high degree of inertia in an existing revenue system, it may be noted that, since 1948, the only major changes in tax rates—in 1950, 1951, and 1954—were associated with the increase and subsequent decrease of Korean War defense expenditures. The 1948 tax cut enacted by the Republican Congress over President Truman's veto comes closer to representing a "displacement" of a domestic political kind. But a large part of the credit is due to a most unusual condition of the federal budget in fiscal 1948—a surplus larger by a factor of over five than any ever achieved before or since, and due more to a fortuitous than a planned simultaneous reduction in defense, foreign aid, veterans' readjustment, and agricultural price support expenditures.

The hypothesis that there is a strong tendency for total federal spending to be set according to revenues available under existing tax rates does not imply that each component follows the same general time path. Some expenditures show considerable year-to-year fluctuation for business cycle or other reasons. Particularly volatile are: (1) farm price supports, which can fluctuate because of weather conditions here or abroad; (2) defense outlays, which can fluctuate quite aside from changes in program direction if contracts let under obligational authority are allowed to bunch up, causing a subsequent bunching of expenditures; (3) interest payments on the public debt, which vary with changes in market rates of interest; (4) unemployment compensation; (5) net mortgage purchases or sales, which are determined largely according to mortgage market conditions; and (6) one-time major outlays, such as subscriptions to international finance organizations. A bunching of fluctuations in individual programs can and does cause year-to-year aberration in total spending from what would be a stable trend.

That a comparatively stable trend in total federal spending over a period of years is consistent with widely divergent movements in major components is illustrated graphically in Charts 1 and 2. In Chart 1, total federal national income expenditures are divided into defense purchases and nondefense. Three points may be noted. First, leaving the Korean War years aside, total outlays as a percentage of GNP appear well represented by a linear upward trend, with deviations around the trend averaging less than 1 per cent of GNP. Second, the impact of Korean War defense outlays on the expenditure total was somewhat dampened by the efforts of the

CHART 2

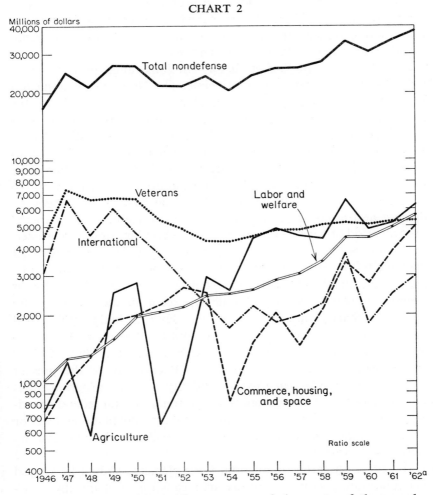

Truman administration to finance part of the costs of the war by holding down nondefense spending. Third, the steady upward trend since the end of the Korean War is the net result of a more rapid upward trend in nondefense outlays and a decline in defense outlays relative to GNP. It is, of course, not surprising that the trend of a total lies between the trends of its components. But it is interesting

251

that the net trend just happens to work out at about the same GNP elasticity as the 1954 revenue code (combined with periodic increases in social security payroll tax rates). This suggests that the "offset factor" operates with respect to defense and nondefense spending, and not just among the nondefense programs, at least when there is no shooting war. Chart 2 suggests the large extent to which fluctuations and divergent trends in major components of nondefense spending have tended to offset one another.

Allowance for an "offset factor" in long-range projections of federal spending is not a new principle. The National Planning Association, for example, in its annual projection series, allows for considerably higher nondefense spending in its "low defense" alternative than in its "high defense" alternative. Similarly, the Budget Bureau's ten-year projection recommended using the "high" nondefense projection as the complement to its disarmament alternative on defense. However, I would recommend even stricter rules. In the absence of disarmament or hot war, a one-for-one offset between defense and nondefense—not year-by-year, certainly, but averaged over a period of years—appears by far the best bet for the forecaster.

In summary, for long-range projections, I would venture a forecast with the following elements: (1) in the absence of a hot war or disarmament, significant changes from current rates of tax for the major sources of federal revenue are unlikely, except for the social security tax rate increases built in under current law; (2) budget policy will continue to aim at small surpluses in years of relatively high employment; (3) total expenditures will rise slightly as a percentage of GNP in line with the greater-than-unity GNP elasticity of the present revenue system; (4) year-to-year volatility in some program areas will produce temporary deviations from trend in total federal spending from time to time; (5) ignoring temporary fluctuations, level or declining trends in some program areas will be offset in time by increases elsewhere.

To repeat an earlier injunction, these elements should be viewed as equilibrium conditions, not as the means for mechanically transforming some assumed growth rate into a forecast of expenditures. The growth rate, the major income shares, revenues, and expenditures must all be solved simultaneously. For many reasons, including three mentioned below, it is obviously not prudent to take 5 per cent or any other growth rate for granted.

Among the implications of the projection outlined above, I would flag three as raising interesting problems for policy-makers as well as model-builders. In the first place, although total spending can, in my opinion, be forecast reasonably well (at least in relation to GNP) the composition of the total as between goods and services purchases, on the one hand; and grants, transfers, and subsidies, on the other, is considerably less predictable. This will depend principally on the trend of defense spending, which accounts for upward of 85 per cent of federal purchases of goods and services but only about 50 per cent of total federal expenditures on income and product account. Nondefense spending largely takes the form of grants, subsidies, and transfer payments. I do not believe the current political process makes much allowance for the probability that, from the standpoint of stable growth at unchanged rates of factor utilization, grants, transfers, and subsidies probably carry considerably lower revenue requirements per dollar of outlay than purchases of goods and services. Moreover, the administrative and consolidated cash budgets, which are the ones used for most decision processes, include loans and mortgage purchases as well—items which are excluded altogether from the national income tabulation and which probably carry still lower revenue requirements from a stable growth standpoint, but not from that of balancing the administrative or cash budget.

A second implication of the tendency toward inertia in the federal fiscal system in the periods between displacements might be labeled, for lack of a more inspired name, the "tired program" effect. More and more economists are moving away from the notion of personal consumption as a simple function of current income, in favor of wealth or, what amounts to much the same thing, permanent income, as the more relevant independent variable. But to my knowledge, the implications of federal spending behavior in the context of a permanent-income consumption function have not been explored.

The "tired program" effect can be illustrated by an example. Suppose a law is enacted according to which every red-headed person becomes eligible for federal transfer payments of, say, $50 a month for the rest of his life. Obviously, the enactment of such a program will release substantial sums for private spending relative to the initial amount of federal outlay. Red-heads would receive not only the first month's benefit check, but also a much larger asset in the form of entitlement to future benefits—an asset in many cases liquid enough to be transformed into a substantial sum of cash at a commercial bank. Subsequent federal outlays under such a program would come close to being capital transfers in a national income sense—an exchange of one liquid asset for another (cash).

Old programs seldom die, and the growth of federal spending during one of our so-called inertia periods between two displacements is likely to be made up much more of the growth of old programs than the initiation of new ones. As a consequence, the total income-generating effects of federal spending during such a period are probably subject to decay, at least relative to potential gross national product.

Something analogous, of course, takes place on the revenue side of the budget. The initiation of a new tax has, through a process of capitalization, negative effects on asset values or permanent income in addition to its effects on current income. These depressing effects on aggregate demand subsequently decay with the passage of time, similar to the decay of the stimulating effects of expenditures under old programs.

Offhand, since the combined income and asset impact decays for both receipts and expenditures during an inertia period, one might be willing to judge that there is no a-priori reason to assume a secular trend one way or the other in the net impact of federal behavior on aggregate demand. However, if I reason correctly, there is one a priori reason for judging that the secular trend during an inertia period may in fact be toward a reduced stimulus to aggregate demand by the federal budget. Suppose the balanced budget multiplier effect, according to which expenditures—at least for goods and services—add more to aggregate demand than is deducted by an equal amount of taxes, applies to the asset as well as the income effects of government activity. Whatever its value, if the balanced budget multiplier is constant, if it applies to asset as well as income effects, and if there is no compensating change in the composition of federal outlays, the multiplier would attach to a successively smaller combined income-and-asset impact from federal spending less federal taxes during an inertia period; and the resulting trend would be toward a lower total impact on aggregate demand.

To what extent the tired program effect may be offset by the influence on expenditures of a greater-than-unity GNP elasticity of federal revenues I am not competent to judge. Of course, the composition effect can be either aggravating or offsetting to the tired program effect.

The third problem I would like to flag is that, while private income-spending relationships probably change slowly, it would be fortuitous indeed if they remained constant for as long as ten years. The expenditure process described above seems less than ideally suited—from the standpoint of stable growth at unchanged rates of factor utilization—to making the federal budget compensate for any such secular trends.

Short-Run Behavior of the Fiscal System— the Built-in Stabilizers

My analysis of the short-run behavior of the federal fiscal system is limited to the part which is fairly predictable—the automatic built-in fiscal stabilizers. Considering their prominent place in the literature on fiscal policy and public finance, there have been surprisingly few attempts at empirical measurement of the built-in stabilizers. I will report here only a brief summary of the results from my own research in this field and some of the problems these raise for fiscal policy analysis.

Mainly because the cyclical behavior of the various tax bases differs widely from the secular behavior, the cyclical GNP elasticities of the built-in stabilizers differ substantially from their secular elasticities. Table 9 records the base elasticity of yield for the major federal taxes during the postwar recessions and recoveries. It also records the marginal changes in federal surplus or deficit on account of these and unemployment transfer payments as percentages of the change in GNP during recession and recovery. In each case, actual data have been adjusted to remove the effects of any legislative changes during the recession or recovery period, so as to measure only the automatic response. For all but the individual income tax, the original data are those from the national income and product accounts. For the individual income tax, two modifications to the data were made. First, collections attributable to individual capital gains were removed. Capital gains are excluded throughout the national income and product statistics. Unless a model includes the flow of capital gains, it seems only logical to exclude the tax on such

TABLE 9

BUILT-IN FEDERAL FISCAL STABILIZERS, POSTWAR RECESSIONS AND RECOVERIES

		Recessions				Recoveries		
Tax	Base	IV-48 to II-49	II-53 to II-54	III-57 to I-58	II-60 to I-61	II-49 to II-50	II-54 to II-54	I-58 to II-59

BASE ELASTICITY OF TAX YIELD[a]

Corporate profit tax accruals	Corporate profits	0.85	0.84	0.90	1.01	0.81	0.88	0.89
Individual income tax accruals	Personal income	1.50	9.71	6.08	−5.80[b]	0.76	1.15	1.56
Indirect business taxes	Gross national product		2.31	1.42	5.71	1.04	1.69	1.00
Contributions for social insurance	Wages and salaries	0.75	0.44	0.96	2.01	0.82	0.76	0.84

CHANGE IN STABILIZER AS PER CENT OF CHANGE IN GROSS NATIONAL PRODUCT[a]

Corporate profits tax accruals	25.3	36.4	29.9	57.1	21.1	13.2	15.6
Individual income tax accruals	2.3	7.5	11.1	17.9	7.4	8.2	8.9
Indirect business taxes		7.1	3.9	16.1	3.3	5.0	2.7
Contributions for social insurance	1.3	1.4	2.2	6.1	1.0	1.3	2.0
Unemployment compensation (sign reversed)	10.5	14.1	9.1	25.0	1.1	2.6	2.0

SOURCE: Department of Commerce and Wilfred Lewis, Jr., *Federal Fiscal Policy in the Postwar Recessions*, Brookings Institution, 1962. "Recession" defined as period from peak to trough in quarterly gross national product. "Recovery" defined as period from *GNP* trough to quarter after which declines in unemployment ratio become minor.

[a] Computed at constant (prerecession) tax rates.
[b] Tax declined while total personal income rose.

gains. Second, refunds and the nonwithheld portion of the tax were placed on an accrual basis, so that the total tax would be as nearly as possible on an accrued liability basis, as is the case with the other taxes in the national income framework.

The fiscal effects of the built-in stabilizers should be distinguished from their economic effects. While the corporation income tax is by far the most important built-in stabilizer in terms of impact on the federal budget, it is by no means clear that this is the case in terms of economic impact.

The major stabilizers obviously differ widely in their effects on disposable personal income. A drop in individual income tax liabilities, or a rise in unemployment compensation, for example, provide direct support to disposable personal income in the sense that they cause disposable income to drop by less than it otherwise would in an economic contraction. A decline in corporate profits tax accruals, on the other hand, affects disposable personal income only insofar as it induces corporations to alter their employment policies or their dividend payments. The indirect stabilizing effectiveness of a drop in corporate income tax liabilities, by way of induced effects on investment, may also be rather minor, at least for brief recessions of the postwar variety in which corporate liquidity is well maintained or actually increases. Employee contributions for social insurance—payroll taxes paid by employees—resemble income taxes and unemployment benefits in having direct consequences for disposable personal income. Excise taxes, on the other hand, resemble the corporation income tax in having only indirect stabilizer effects on disposable income. The employer contributions for social insurance can be argued either way, although I have treated it as a "direct" stabilizer.

The fiscal effects of the direct stabilizers—individual income and employment taxes and unemployment compensation—during postwar contractions have ranged from $1.3 billion to $3.4 billion, measured by changes from peak to trough, or from 14 per cent to 49 per cent of the change in gross national product. They have become more important over the postwar period in their stabilizing effectiveness for three main reasons. First, the increases in OASDI payroll tax rates have increased the cycle sensitivity as well as the level of these taxes. Second, the greater-than-unity GNP elasticity of the individual income tax has caused a secular increase in the average rate of tax and, apparently, has also increased its cycle sensitivity. Finally, there is evidence of a growing responsiveness of consumption expenditures to declines in disposable personal income. This last-mentioned tendency enhances the importance of those factors, like the built-in stabilizers, which cushion a decline in disposable personal income.

The crude response of consumption to changes in disposable personal income is, of course, not reliably measured directly from *ex post* data. Annual data for years in most of which income is rising yield a high marginal propensity to consume, roughly equal to the average propensity, which is no fair indication of what happens in recession. Comparison of actual changes in quarterly data, peak to trough, can be misleading in the other direction, since substantial declines or even increases in gross national product have been ac-

257

companied by small decreases or even increases in consumption, implying an absurdly low or negative marginal propensity to consume. In the absence of a complete model based on underlying behavioral relations for the whole economy, an alternative method of making rough approximations—one I believe is more indicative than a comparison of actual data, whether annual or quarterly—is to compare actual magnitudes at the trough with hypothetical high-employment norms calculated on the basis of a few simplifying assumptions.

Table 10 gives the results of a comparison of this kind. Hypothetical high-employment norms for the trough quarter of each recession were calculated by a linear interpolation of gross national product from prerecession peak to recovery except in 1960–61, where 3 per cent real growth, or 4.4 per cent in current dollars, was projected starting at the peak in the second quarter of 1960. ("Recovery" is defined as the quarter after which further reductions in the unemployment rate became relatively small—I have used II 1950, II 1955, and II 1959 as marking the end of recovery from the first three postwar recessions). Business gross saving, disposable personal income, and consumption are assumed to maintain their prerecession ratios to gross national product under the hypothetical high-employment case. The differences between actual and hypothetical high-employment data are arrayed to show the various offsets to the fall in gross national product that account for the smaller drop in consumption.

At the bottom of the table, the ratios of consumption "shortfall" to GNP shortfall are first calculated as they occurred, and second, as they would have occurred if there were no offset from the direct stabilizers and if the resulting larger drop in disposable personal income were reflected in consumption at the same rate as the actual drop.

As reflected in this table, there has apparently been a growing responsiveness of consumption to shortfalls in gross national product and disposable personal income. Relative to gross national product, the consumption drop has increased from 13 per cent in 1949 to 46 per cent in 1961. Consumption fell short by only 28 per cent of the disposable personal income shortfall in 1949, but reached 100 per cent in 1961.

Whether this growing income sensitivity of consumption reflects the decline in liquid assets (relative to gross national product) in

TABLE 10

EFFECTS OF DIRECT FISCAL STABILIZERS ON CONSUMPTION,
POST-WORLD WAR II RECESSIONS
(dollars in billions)

	II-1949	II-1954	I-1958	I-1961
ACTUAL LESS HIGH EMPLOYMENT AT CYCLICAL TROUGH				
Gross national product[a]	−$12.3	−$22.0	−$27.0	−$22.6
Less: Indirect fiscal stabilizers[b]	−2.7	−5.5	−6.0	−5.3
Gross business saving[c]	−4.3	−2.1	−6.6	−4.1
Direct fiscal stabilizers[d]	−1.5	−3.2	−4.5	−4.2
Other adjustments[e]	+2.0	−4.9	−0.5	+1.3
Equals: Disposable personal income[f]	−5.8	−6.3	−9.4	−10.3
Less: Personal savings	−4.2	−1.8	−0.7	
Equals: Personal consumption expenditures[f]	−1.6	−4.5	−8.7	−10.3
RATIOS AND MULTIPLIERS				
Ratios of shortfalls				
Direct stabilizers to *GNP*	0.12	0.15	0.17	0.19
Consumption to disposable personal income	0.28	0.71	0.93	1.00
Consumption to *GNP* ("*MPC_g*"):				
With offsets from direct stabilizers	0.13	0.20	0.32	0.46
Without offsets from direct stabilizers	0.16	0.31	0.51	0.64
"Multiplier"—$1/(1 - MPC_g)$:				
With offsets from direct stabilizers	1.15	1.26	1.47	1.84
Without offsets from direct stabilizers	1.19	1.45	2.06	2.79

SOURCE: Department of Commerce and Wilfred Lewis, Jr., *Federal Government Fiscal Policy in the Postwar Recessions*, Brookings Institution, 1962.

[a] Hypothetical high-employment obtained by linear extrapolation from peak to recovery, except in 1961, where growth at 3 per cent in real terms (4.4 per cent in current dollars) was assumed starting in II-1960.

[b] Corporate profits tax accruals and indirect business taxes.

[c] Total capital consumption allowances and corporate retained earnings. Hypothetical high-employment value obtained from ratios to *GNP* prevailing at prerecession peak.

[d] Individual income tax accruals excluding capital gains (except 1961, which is on a national income basis), unemployment compensation, and payroll taxes on employees and employers.

[e] Residual, including changes in state-local taxes and transfers, changes in federal taxes and transfers other than built-in stabilizers (including effects of tax rate change), difference between national income and full-accrual basis for recording individual income tax (except in 1961), inventory valuation adjustment, excess of wage accruals over wage disbursements, and statistical discrepancy.

[f] Hypothetical high-employment values obtained from ratios to *GNP* prevailing at prerecession peak.

the postwar period, or the steadily shortened interval between recessions, in which consumers have time to rebuild desired income-debt ratios before the next recession starts, I am none too certain. In any event, this phenomenon has heightened the importance of the direct fiscal stabilizers.

While the ratios shown must be regarded as only crude approximations to the slopes of the underlying analytical consumption functions, their differences from one recession to the next do suggest to me structural change. The significance of this can be interpreted in the following fashion. Suppose, for the sake of argument, that the ratios of consumption shortfall to GNP shortfall were representative of the marginal propensity to consume out of GNP (in Table 10 I have labeled them MPC_g). Then the rate at which initial changes in demand would tend to be multiplied into total changes in gross national product would approach $1/(1 - MPC_g)$.

Calculated values of this multiplier are shown at the bottom of Table 10. The implication of the steady increase in spread between the multiplier values computed with and without the direct fiscal stabilizers is that, while the stabilizers may have been of relatively minor importance in the 1949 recession, they had acquired major importance for the stability of the economy in 1961.[8]

Conclusion

The model-builder looking for precise equations tying the federal sector to the rest of the economy will be disappointed by this paper. While I have suggested a method of approximating equilibrium conditions for a projection of total federal spending over the long run, important questions on the economic implication of these conditions remain unanswered. Similarly, for the short run, the fiscal effects of the built-in stabilizers are far more certain than their economic effects. Finally, some evidence was furnished that the basic structure of the economy—the basic environment in which the fiscal system operates—may have changed significantly over the course of the postwar period. All this serves to remind us that, in the current state of the art, numerical results from our models must still be seasoned with large elements of judgment in drawing conclusions for public policy purposes.

[8] The 1.47 multiplier computed for 1957–58 by this method compares with a quite differently estimated multiplier for that recession of 1.34 as computed by James S. Duesenberry, Otto Eckstein, and Gary Fromm, "A Simulation of the United States Economy in Recession," *Econometrica*, October 1960.

COMMENT

BERT G. HICKMAN, Brookings Institution

Wilfred Lewis has proposed a novel method of measuring consumption propensities in that section of his paper which deals with automatic stabilizers. The purpose of this note is to explore the properties of the new technique and to question the inferences which Lewis has drawn from its application to the postwar recessions.

Lewis believes that his "shortfall" measure provides a better approximation to the true recession value of the marginal propensity to consume GNP (or disposable income) than does the ratio of the actual change in consumption to the actual change in GNP (or disposable income). Let us abstract for the moment from the obvious statistical deficiencies of both methods and assume that the observed values of consumption and income at both peak and trough fall on the underlying behavioral (linear) consumption function for the contraction period. Under that assumption, what is the relationship between the two estimates of the slope of the consumption function?

Lewis's first step is to calculate what GNP would have been at the time of the cyclical trough if the contraction had not occurred and if, instead, GNP had increased at a steady arithmetic rate along a high-employment path from the cyclical peak. In symbols:

$$(1) \qquad Y_h = Y_p + H = Y_p + (Y_h - Y_p),$$

where Y_h is hypothetical high-employment GNP for the trough quarter, Y_p is observed GNP at the peak, and H is the hypothetical increase of GNP between the peak and trough quarters.

Next, Lewis assumes that the average propensity to consume GNP would have remained constant if the economy had moved along the high-employment path; therefore, hypothetical high-employment consumption is given by

$$(2) \qquad C_h = \left(\frac{C_p}{Y_p}\right) Y_h,$$

where C_p stands for observed consumption at the cyclical peak.

Finally, let C_t and Y_t be the observed values of consumption and GNP at the cyclical trough. Then $(C_h - C_t)$ and $(Y_h - Y_t)$ are the recession shortfalls of consumption and income below their high-employment "norms." Lewis uses the ratio of the two shortfalls

261

(3)
$$\frac{(C_h - C_t)}{(Y_h - Y_t)}$$

to estimate the value of the marginal propensity to consume during the contraction.

To facilitate comparison of the ratio of shortfalls with the conventional ratio of actual changes in consumption and income, let us substitute (1) and (2) into (3) and simplify. The result is

(4)
$$\frac{C_h - C_t}{Y_h - Y_t} = \frac{\dfrac{C_p - C_t}{Y_p - Y_t} + \dfrac{C_p}{Y_p}\dfrac{Y_h - Y_p}{Y_p - Y_t}}{1 + \dfrac{Y_h - Y_p}{Y_p - Y_t}}$$

The first term in the numerator of the right-hand expression of (4) is the marginal propensity to consume as conventionally measured. Now, suppose that the marginal propensity $(C_p - C_t)/(Y_p - Y_t)$ were equal to the average propensity C_p/Y_p at the cyclical peak. In that case, it is easy to see from (4) that the shortfall ratio would have the same value as the ratio of actual consumption and GNP changes, namely C_p/Y_p. This is because C_h has been assumed to lie on a consumption function passing through the origin with slope C_p/Y_p; and if C_t also fell on the same function, $(C_h - C_t)/(Y_h - Y_t)$ would necessarily equal $(C_p - C_t)/(Y_p - Y_t)$. But that would mean that the response of consumption to a cyclical decline of GNP was the same as its response to a steady growth of GNP, and that is contrary to both theory and observation. One expects the recession value of the marginal propensity to consume GNP to be smaller than the average propensity at the cyclical peak; that is, one expects the consumption function during a contraction to be flatter than the long-term consumption function passing through cyclical peaks.

Under the normal expectation that the value of $(C_p - C_t)/(Y_p - Y_t)$ is smaller than C_p/Y_p, it follows from equation 4 that the shortfall ratio overstates the value of the marginal propensity to consume during a contraction. The overestimate will be greater, the greater the difference in slope between the short- and long-run consumption function. The degree of overstatement will also vary positively with the ratio of $Y_h - Y_p$ to $Y_p - Y_t$, which means that it will depend on the amplitude and duration of the contraction and on the assumption made about the high-employment growth rate.

One important reason for expecting consumption to fall much less than GNP during a contraction is that automatic stabilizers have a cushioning effect on disposable personal income. Thus, there are really two structural relationships underlying the response of consumption demand to changes in GNP. The first is the relationship between disposable personal income and GNP, and the second is the relationship between consumption and disposable personal income. If the structural functions are assumed to be linear within the relevant range, then

$$(5) \qquad \frac{C_p - C_t}{Y_p - Y_t} = \frac{\overline{Y}_p - \overline{Y}_t}{Y_p - Y_t} \frac{C_p - C_t}{\overline{Y}_p - \overline{Y}_t},$$

where $\overline{Y}$ is disposable personal income and the subscripts have their previous meanings. Exactly the same relationship holds among the several shortfall ratios, as can be seen immediately by substituting the subscript h for p in (5).

Everything that was said earlier about the relationship between the conventional and shortfall estimates of the marginal response of consumption to GNP carries over to the corresponding estimates of the marginal response of disposable income to GNP. That is, the underlying functional relationship between disposable income and GNP should be flatter during a period of contraction than during a corresponding period of steady high-employment growth, because of the operation of both the private (gross business saving) and fiscal stabilizers. The shortfall ratio should, therefore, overstate the marginal response of disposable income to GNP during a contraction.

It is time now to turn to a comparison of the conventional and shortfall estimates of the several marginal relationships during the postwar contractions. Table 1 contains the shortfall estimates and is similar to Lewis's Table 10. The principal difference between my table and his is that my shortfall estimates are corrected for price changes and his are not. It is preferable to deal with deflated figures, since the underlying structural relationships are defined in real terms.[1] The conventional estimates are also based on deflated figures and are shown in Table 2.

---

[1] The use of deflated data introduces a complication into the treatment of disposable income. When the functional relationship between GNP and disposable income is in question, the latter should be expressed in the same prices as GNP. With regard to consumption decisions, however, disposable income should be deflated by an index of consumer prices. When the implicit price indexes of GNP and consumer goods diverge, a corresponding divergence is created between the two versions of "real" disposable income. In Tables 1 and 2, disposable income is deflated by consumer prices. How much difference this makes in the computed relations between disposable income and GNP is shown in the footnotes to the tables.

TABLE 1

SHORTFALL ESTIMATES OF MARGINAL INCOME AND CONSUMPTION
PROPENSITIES, POST-WORLD WAR II CONTRACTIONS
(values in billions of 1954 dollars, seasonally adjusted quarterly totals at annual rates)

	II-1949	II-1954	I-1958	I-1961
ACTUAL LESS HIGH EMPLOYMENT AT CYCLICAL TROUGH				
Gross national product[a]	−$11.9	−$21.9	−$24.7	−$20.2
Less: Direct fiscal stabilizers[b]	−1.7	−3.2	−4.1	−3.6
Other items[c]	−5.5	−11.8	−11.0	−7.3
Equals: Disposable personal income[d]	−4.7	−6.9	−9.6	−9.3
Less: Personal saving[e]	−4.4	−1.9	−0.7	−0.1
Equals: Personal consumption expenditure[f]	−0.3	−5.0	−8.9	−9.2
RATIOS AND MULTIPLIERS				
Ratios of shortfalls:				
Direct stabilizers to *GNP*	0.14	0.15	0.17	0.18
Disposable income to *GNP* (*MPY*):				
With offsets from direct stabilizers[g]	0.39	0.32	0.39	0.46
Without offsets from direct stabilizers	0.54	0.46	0.55	0.64
Consumption to disposable income	0.06	0.72	0.93	0.99
Consumption to *GNP* (*MPC*)				
With offsets from direct stabilizers	0.03	0.23	0.36	0.46
Without offsets from direct stabilizers	0.03	0.33	0.51	0.63
"Multiplier"—1/(1 − *MPC*):				
With offsets from direct stabilizers	1.03	1.30	1.56	1.85
Without offsets from direct stabilizers	1.03	1.49	2.04	2.70
"Multiplier"—1/(1 − *MPY*):				
With offsets from direct stabilizers	1.64	1.47	1.64	1.85
Without offsets from direct stabilizers	2.17	1.85	2.22	2.78

[a] Hypothetical high employment obtained by linear interpolation from peak to recovery, except in 1961 where growth at 3 per cent per annum assumed starting in II-1960.

[b] As in Lewis's Table 10, except deflated by the implicit price index for *GNP* (1954 = 100).

[c] Estimated as residual. In addition to items specified in Lewis's Table 10, includes the difference between disposable income as deflated by the implicit price index for consumer goods and services and what disposable income would be if deflated by the implicit price index for *GNP*. If the latter index were used to deflate disposable income, the successive shortfall estimates would be −5.0, −6.2, −8.5, and −9.3.

[d] As in Lewis's Table 10, except disposable personal income deflated by implicit price index for consumer goods and services.

[e] Residual.

[f] As in Lewis's Table 10, except for conversion to 1954 dollars.

[g] If disposable income were deflated by the implicit price index for *GNP*, as discussed in note c, the successive ratios of disposable income shortfall to *GNP* shortfall would be 0.42, 0.28, 0.34, and 0.46.

TABLE 2

CONVENTIONAL ESTIMATES OF MARGINAL INCOME AND CONSUMPTION
PROPENSITIES, POST-WORLD WAR II CONTRACTIONS
(values in billions of 1954 dollars, seasonally adjusted quarterly totals at annual rates)

	IV-1948 to II-1949	II-1953 to II-1954	III-1957 to I-1958	II-1960 to I-1961
CHANGE FROM PEAK TO TROUGH				
Gross national product	−$7.0	−$13.7	−$18.0	−$10.2
Less: Direct fiscal stabilizers[a]	−1.7	−3.0	−3.2	−2.8
Other items[b]	−4.1	−9.4	−10.0	−5.3
Equals: Disposable personal income[c]	−1.2	−1.3	−4.8	−2.1
Less: Personal saving[d]	−4.2	−1.5	−0.3	0.4
Equals: Personal consumption expenditure[e]	3.0	0.2	−4.5	−2.5
RATIOS AND MULTIPLIERS				
Ratios of changes:				
Direct stabilizers to *GNP*	0.24	0.22	0.18	0.27
Disposable income to *GNP (MPY)*:				
With offsets from direct stabilizers[f]	0.17	0.09	0.27	0.21
Without offsets from direct stabilizers	0.41	0.31	0.44	0.48
Consumption to disposable income	−2.50	−0.15	0.94	1.19
Consumption to *GNP (MPC)*:				
With offsets from direct stabilizers	−0.43	−0.01	0.25	0.25
Without offsets from direct stabilizers	−1.025	−0.46	0.41	0.57
"Multiplier"—$1/(1 - MPC)$:				
With offsets from direct stabilizers			1.33	1.33
Without offsets from direct stabilizers			1.69	2.33
"Multiplier"—$1/(1 - MPY)$:				
With offsets from direct stabilizers	1.20	1.10	1.37	1.27
Without offsets from direct stabilizers	1.69	1.45	1.78	1.92

[a] See note b of Table 1.

[b] See note c of Table 1. If disposable income were deflated by the implicit price index for *GNP*, the successive changes in disposable income would be −1.4, −0.6, −3.8, and −2.3.

[c] See note d of Table 1.

[d] See note e of Table 1.

[e] See note f of Table 1.

[f] If disposable income were deflated by the implicit price index for *GNP*, as discussed in note b, the successive ratios of changes in disposable income and *GNP* would be 0.20, 0.04, 0.21, and 0.22.

The first thing to notice is that the shortfall ratios considerably understate the combined importance of the private and fiscal stabilizers as offsets to the decline of GNP. Thus, according to the shortfall estimates, the marginal response of disposable income to

265

GNP (labeled *MPY*) in the four contractions ranged from 0.32 to 0.46, whereas the conventional estimates lie between 0.09 and 0.27.[2] As expected, the shortfall estimates are considerably larger than the conventional ones. One way to gauge the importance of the disparity is to calculate the corresponding theoretical multipliers for a given marginal propensity to consume disposable personal income. If the latter is assumed to be unity, the marginal response of consumption to GNP (*MPC*) would be the same as the marginal response of disposable income to GNP (*MPY*), as can be seen from equation 5 above. The implied limiting multiplier values under this assumption are shown at the bottom of each table and range between 1.10 and 1.37 on the conventional basis and between 1.47 and 1.85 on the shortfall basis.[3]

Observe also that the shortfall estimates understate the importance of the direct stabilizers alone. As already discussed, the shortfall method is biased toward overestimates of marginal consumption propensities. For exactly the same reasons, the method will tend to underestimate marginal saving propensities. A glance at the tables will show that the shortfall estimates of the marginal response of the direct stabilizers to GNP are indeed smaller than the conventional estimates.

Thus, the absolute importance of the direct stabilizers as income offsets during contractions is understated by the shortfall estimates. This is not true, however, of their importance relative to the combined influence of the indirect and private stabilizers, since the marginal response of the latter to GNP is also underestimated by the shortfall method. Hence, when the theoretical multipliers with and without direct stabilizers are compared under the assumption that the marginal response of consumption to disposable income is unity, it is found that their ratio is about the same under both estimating

[2] The low values for the 1953–54 contraction are misleading. Personal income taxes were reduced about $3 billion at the beginning of 1954. After allowance for the effects of a simultaneous increase in personal contributions for social security and for the treatment of nonwithheld tax receipts in the national income accounts, it appears that disposable income would have been about $1.5 billion lower in the second quarter of 1954 were it not for the tax reduction. When allowance is made for the tax changes, the shortfall and conventional estimates of the induced decline of disposable income per dollar of decline in GNP become, respectively, 0.38 and 0.20—values which are much closer to those for the other contractions.

[3] When corrected for the tax changes discussed in note 2, the values for the 1953–54 contraction become 1.26 and 1.62 on the conventional and shortfall bases, greatly reducing the range of variation between the multiplier estimates for the several contractions.

methods. For the most recent contraction, the multipliers with and without direct stabilizers are 1.27 and 1.92 by the conventional method and 1.85 and 2.78 by the shortfall method. In either case, the multiplier without direct stabilizers is about 1.5 times that with direct stabilizers.

With regard to the relationship between consumption and disposable personal income, it will be recalled that Lewis gives considerable stress to the upward progression of the shortfall ratios during the successive postwar contractions, interpreting the data as evidence of a "growing responsiveness of consumption expenditures to declines in disposable personal income." It is important to remember, however, that the short-term relationship between consumption and current disposable income has displayed considerable instability during the postwar period, although rather more so before than after 1953. It is especially doubtful that the observed consumption-disposable income ratio for the 1949 contraction in either Table 1 or Table 2 has any significance as a measure of the marginal response of consumption to disposable income. Lewis has argued that the progression of his shortfall ratios is strong evidence of a change in the *net* response of consumption to disposable income, on the grounds that nonincome determinants of consumption may be assumed to be constant during each brief recession, even though changing during the long intervals between recessions. In 1948–49, however, real consumption expenditure *rose* $3.0 billion even as real disposable income *fell* $1.2 billion (Table 2). Apparently these contrasting movements were due principally to changes in instalment credit regulations and to the increased availability of new automobiles during the contraction—sales of automobiles were largely supply-determined during the early postwar years, and production was stepped up considerably during the contraction. In any event, it is hard to credit the idea that the net response of consumers to a $1 billion reduction of real income would be a $3 billion increase of real consumption expenditure.

There are similar difficulties with respect to the contraction of 1953–54. As Table 2 reveals, personal consumption expenditure increased $0.2 billion and disposable income declined $1.3 billion between the second quarters of 1953 and 1954. But this peak-to-trough comparison is strongly affected by an upsurge of expenditure during the last few months of the contraction. Real consumption actually fell $2.8 billion as disposable income dropped $1.7 billion between the second quarter of 1953 and the first quarter of 1954. Consumption then rose \$3.0 billion, as disposable income increased only \$0.4 billion during the second quarter of 1954. To view the same facts a little differently, the ratios of the consumption and disposable income shortfalls during the successive quarters of the contraction were 0.938, 1.567, 1.136, and 0.725. Notice that it is only the last of these ratios that looks considerably lower than the trough ratios of 1958 and 1961.

The marginal ratios based on peak-to-trough changes in consumption and income for the contractions of 1957–58 and 1960–61 appear somewhat more reasonable as estimates of the induced response of consumption to decreases in disposable income. At least the consumption and income changes are in the same direction. Notice, however, that the implied marginal propensity to consume for 1960–61 is greater than one. Moreover, again there is evidence of marked variability in the consumption-income relationship during the course of each contraction. For example, the successive quarterly shortfall ratios were 0.673 and 0.927 during the brief 1957–58 recession, and 1.824, 0.880, and 0.989 during the 1960–61 contraction.

With so much variability in the short-term relationship between consumption and disposable income, and with such small movements of disposable income, it is extremely hazardous to rest an estimate of the marginal response of consumption to disposable income on two observations alone, whether by the conventional or the shortfall method. Still less is it justifiable to conclude on the basis of four such estimates that a structural change in the responsiveness of consumer demand to decreases in disposable income has occurred during the postwar years. The 1949 experience is clearly a special case, and the remaining contractions differ much less than is suggested by Lewis's comparison of shortfalls at the troughs.

Suppose, however, for the sake of argument, that the shortfall estimates of the marginal response of consumption to disposable personal income during the successive contractions were entirely accurate. What would such a trend toward greater sensitivity of consumption to changes in disposable income imply about the multiplier effects of autonomous changes in demand? It is easy to calculate the implied limiting multiplier values from a combination of the shortfall estimates of the consumption-disposable income relationship in Table 1 and the conventional estimates of the disposable income-GNP relationship in note 2 and Table 2.[4] The resulting multipliers for the successive contractions are 1.01, 1.17, 1.34, and 1.26. These differences, while not insignificant, are not especially striking. The reason, of course, is that the public and private income stabilizers have exerted such a strong influence during the postwar contractions that disposable income has declined by only a small fraction of the decline in GNP. Under these conditions, even a high marginal response consumption to disposable income can have comparatively little effect on aggregate demand.

To sum up: the shortfall technique does not appear to be a promising method for the estimation of marginal saving or consumption propensities during contractions. It is subject to the same statistical deficiencies as the more conventional comparisons of actual changes in consumption or saving with those in income; and in addition, it is inherently biased toward overestimates of consumption propensities and underestimates of saving propensities. Neither the conventional nor the shortfall method is adequate to deal with the problem of variability in the short-term relationship between consumption and disposable income. This last stricture is less applicable to the more stable relationship between disposable income and GNP, however; therefore, the conventional method may yield reasonably accurate estimates of the marginal response of disposable income to GNP, whereas the shortfall method seriously overstates the response.

JOSEPH A. PECHMAN, Brookings Institution

Wilfred Lewis's interesting and perceptive paper discusses three significant aspects of the federal sector of the United States economy: (1) recent changes in its size and composition; (2) the long-run elasticity of its revenue system; and (3) the contribution of the federal stabilizers to economic stability. On all of these points, Lewis has added a great deal to our knowledge; and my remarks are for the most part only refinements of his major conclusions.

Long-Run Growth of the Federal Sector

Lewis agrees with the Peacock and Wiseman hypothesis that, with the exception of periods of military, social, or economic upheaval,

[4] The reason for using the conventional estimates of the marginal relationship between disposable income and GNP is, of course, that the shortfall estimates give a biased estimate of the response.

government expenditures are broadly conditioned by the availability of revenue. Lewis observes that, since the end of the adjustment following the Korean War, the ratio of federal expenditures to the gross national product in the United States has fluctuated moderately around a trend line which is tilted slightly upward. The upward tilt is explained by two factors: (1) the slight progressivity of the federal tax system that is associated with the growth of the economy; and (2) periodic upward adjustments in payroll tax rates and in the limit on taxable wages. Abstracting from recessions, Lewis's advice to a forecaster of federal expenditures is to estimate federal revenues at present tax rates, make an adjustment for any future statutory payroll tax increases already enacted, and then subtract a small amount (not specified) for the surplus. Needless to say, this advice holds only on the assumption that the forecaster can predict relative income shares ten years hence and that international tensions will remain substantially unchanged.

The available statistical evidence and the history of Executive and Congressional action on expenditures in recent years provide ample support for this hypothesis. The ratio of federal expenditures (national income basis) to gross national product reached its post-Korean low in 1956. Since then, the ratio has increased every year except 1960. Between 1956 and 1963, the federal revenue system remained virtually unchanged, with the exception of increased payroll taxes in 1957, 1959, 1960, and 1962. Substantial deficits were incurred in this period whenever unemployment exceeded about 5 per cent of the labor force; but the rate of growth of revenues at a given level of unemployment has kept pace with the rate of growth of expenditures.

Lewis goes on to point out that the revenue constraint has a substantial impact on the composition of federal expenditures through the "offset factor." If some high-priority programs require increased outlays, other programs will be squeezed. Conversely, as some programs begin to taper off, other programs, which have been held back for budgetary reasons, spurt forward. The offset effect is most apparent between defense and nondefense programs, but it operates among nondefense programs as well.

I have very little to add to Lewis's observations on these points except to lament our continued failure to devise some government machinery for determining the appropriate size and composition of the federal budget. If Peacock and Wiseman and Lewis are right, the revenue-raising capacity of the particular revenue system inherited from the period after the last major war or crisis determines central government expenditures for many years thereafter. It would obviously be sheer coincidence if this particular level of expenditures were the "right" level in the sense that it reflects even approximately the needs and desires of the nation's citizens for government services. I hasten to add that I am not saying that the level of government expenditures determined by the inherited revenue system is either too high or too low. I am saying only that, in all likelihood, this level is wrong and that it is time to devise techniques for making the correct decisions.

I also share Lewis's concern about the relative movements of purchases of goods and services, on the one hand, and grants, subsidies, transfers, and loans on the other. Lewis points out that, from the standpoint of stable growth, grants, subsidies, and transfer payments carry lower revenue requirements per dollar of outlay than purchases of goods and services; loans and other credits carry even smaller revenue requirements. Federal purchases as a percentage of total federal expenditures declined from 65 to 56 per cent between fiscal years 1956 and 1961. Part of this trend is explained by the high level of unemployment that developed during the period. The relative decline in purchases was arrested in fiscal years 1962 and 1963, and the trend will be further moderated if the nation gets back to high employment, but it is doubtful that it will be reversed.

Long-Run Elasticity of the Federal Revenue System

Lewis has shown considerable ingenuity—as well as intimate knowledge of many highly technical details—in his calculations of the long-run elasticity of the federal revenue system. He estimates the elasticities of the major taxes as follows: individual income tax, 1.25; corporate profits tax, 0.92; indirect business taxes, 0.85; and contributions for social insurance, 1.0. He then proceeds to estimate the yield of the present tax rates (plus the scheduled payroll tax increases) in 1970, on the assumptions that (1) the income shares will be the same as they were in 1960, (2) real GNP will grow at an annual rate of 3.5 per cent from the 1960 base and (3) the GNP price deflator will rise at an annual rate of 1.75 per cent. Given these assumptions, it turns out that federal revenues would rise from 19 per cent of GNP in 1960 to 21 per cent in 1970 and that the GNP elasticity of the revenue system would be about 1.2.

271

The following comments and suggestions may be helpful in interpreting and improving Lewis's results:

1. It is obvious that, with the individual income tax having an elasticity of 1.25 and all other taxes having an elasticity no greater than 1, the elasticity for the whole system could hardly be 1.2 unless all the other taxes were of negligible importance. The two elasticities turn out to be almost the same because Lewis has included the scheduled increases in OASDI contributions during the coming decade in his estimate of the yield of the "present" revenue system for the year 1970. Fortunately, he provides the data necessary to correct for the increased contributions. For 1970, it turns out that the payroll tax rates in effect in 1960 would produce contributions of $20.1 billion in 1970 instead of the $31.0 billion shown in Lewis's Table 5.

2. Lewis's estimate that the elasticity of the federal corporate income tax under conditions of stable growth may be as low as 0.92 is not borne out by his own data. This estimate is based on the decline in the ratio of corporate tax on a national income basis to the tax reported in *Statistics of Income* between 1948 and 1958. But he fails to observe that, since 1950, changes in this ratio have been offset by changes in the opposite direction in the ratio of profits as reported in *Statistics of Income* to profits on the national income basis. This explains why there seems to have been no trend during recent years in the effective rate of corporate income tax on a national income basis (see T_C/C in Table 1). Actually, the small variation in effective rates of the corporate income tax in 1952–58—years in which the corporate income tax rate was the same—appears to be related to changes in inventory profits.

In 1960, when inventory profits were negligible, the average effective tax rate on corporate profits was exactly 47 per cent. By contrast, using an elasticity of 0.92, Lewis obtains an average effective rate of 45 per cent in 1970. If this rate is adjusted upward by two percentage points, the corporate profits tax would yield $1.7 billion more in 1970 than the amount Lewis shows in Table 5.

3. I have some doubts about the use of a constant *elasticity* to project individual income tax receipts for a period as long as ten years. What seems to have remained constant in the past twelve years is not the elasticity of the tax, but its built-in flexibility, or dT/dY. Between 1955 and 1959, for example, the individual income tax rose by $1.28 billion for every $10 billion rise in personal income. Now, since dT/dY is larger than T/Y, the latter will keep

rising until it reaches dT/dY. This is what Lewis observes in his Table 2. Note, however, that a dT/dY of 0.128 gives an elasticity of 1.6 when T/Y is 8 per cent, 1.42 when T/Y is 9 per cent, and 1.28 when T/Y is 10 per cent.

Lewis's assumption of an elasticity of 1.25 for the individual income tax works out to be equivalent to a dT/dY of 0.143. I suspect that a rise in the average marginal rate on personal income is in the offing, but it is not clear when it will come and how steep the rise will be. Pending further research into this problem, I would keep dT/dY at about 0.13. This reduces the personal income tax shown in Lewis's Table 5 for 1970 by $3.4 billion.

4. As Lewis suggests, much of the decline in the effective rate of federal indirect business taxes between 1952 and 1960 was the result of the relatively depressed level of automobile sales in the late 1950s. In fact, the average rate scarcely budged between 1957 and 1960, suggesting an elasticity closer to 1 rather than to 0.85. Nevertheless, in view of the heavy weight of the alcohol and tobacco taxes in the excise tax structure, Lewis's present judgment of an elasticity of less than 1 is perhaps justified. Additional quantitative research needs to be done to clarify this point.

5. Collecting the suggested revisions of the yields of the payroll, corporate, and individual income taxes explained above, I find that the yield of the 1960 tax rates in 1970 would be close to $165 billion, as compared to the $177 billion given in Table 5; and the ratio of total receipts to GNP in 1970 turns out to be 19.6 per cent, instead of 21.1 per cent. Thus, the GNP elasticity of the entire revenue system for 1960–70 is reduced from Lewis's estimate of 1.25 to 1.07. In other words, the federal revenue system at present tax rates is only slightly better than proportional (assuming stable growth and constant income shares).

6. It should also be noted that Lewis's projection of federal receipts in 1970 starts off from the base year 1960, when unemployment averaged 5.6 per cent. Consequently, the 1970 projection understates by a substantial margin what receipts would be at full employment, which is now ordinarily assumed to be at the point where unemployment is 4 per cent of the labor force. The shortfall of GNP below full employment in 1960 was probably of the order of about 5 per cent. Applying this to Lewis's GNP estimate for 1970 raises that figure by about $42 billion. At this level of employment, corporate profits would probably be a higher percentage of

GNP than in 1960, say, 10 per cent instead of 9 per cent. On these assumptions, and adding the statutory increases in OASDI taxes scheduled in the period 1960–70, federal receipts in 1970 at full employment would approach $190 billion, assuming an average annual rate of growth in real GNP of 3.5 per cent and an average increase in the deflator of 1.75 per cent per year.

Cyclical Flexibility of the Federal Revenue System

Lewis shows that the fiscal effects of the "direct" federal stabilizers (i.e., individual income and payroll taxes plus unemployment insurance benefits) have increased sharply during the postwar period. At the same time, changes in consumption have come to depend more and more on changes in disposable income—a development that is explained by the sharp reduction in the liquidity of consumers. As a result of the rising sensitivity of consumption to income, the economy might now be highly unstable were it not for the stabilizers.

Although Lewis's multiplier is not the usual one we are accustomed to seeing, I believe his conclusions are essentially correct. What is perhaps equally interesting from a technical standpoint is the manner in which these conclusions were obtained (see Table 10). The heart of the exercise is the assumption that if there were no direct stabilizers, the drop in disposable income would have been reflected in consumption at the same rate as the actual drop in consumption below the high-employment "norm." There is no way of checking this assumption, but it is important to note that the ratio of the shortfall in consumption to the shortfall in disposable income increased so markedly over the four contractions in the postwar period (from 0.28 to 1.00) that any other reasonable assumption would not change the conclusion.

I have considerable doubts, however, about Lewis's finding that the direct stabilizers have been materially strengthened in the postwar period. It is true, as he points out, that payroll tax rates have increased; and this, of course, increased the built-in flexibility of the system somewhat. But individual income tax rates, though higher than they were in 1949, are lower than during the Korean War. Lewis was influenced by the fact that the direct stabilizers accounted for 48 per cent of the change in GNP in the latest contraction; but I believe that, if he were to correct for the degree of shortfall in each of the recessions, much of the difference in the ratio of the direct stabilizers to GNP would disappear, except for the changes in tax rates.

If these observations are correct, I would draw the following conclusions from Lewis's data on the direct stabilizers: First, the fiscal effects of the direct stabilizers have tended to increase over the postwar period, but not significantly. Second, however, since changes in consumption now appear to be more sensitive to changes in disposable income than they were in the early postwar period, the importance of the stabilizers has been greatly enhanced. Third, in view of the possibility that the economy may well be more unstable now than it was, say, fifteen years ago, it is time to devise practical methods of strengthening the stabilizers and of using discretionary fiscal actions more promptly and more vigorously during intervals of economic contraction.

REPLY by Wilfred Lewis

1. Joseph A. Pechman has given us some useful additional facts to be considered in making long-range estimates of federal revenues. He is no doubt right that I have underestimated the elasticity of the corporate profits tax and overestimated that of the individual income tax. For the reason stated before, I am not yet convinced that the elasticity of the profits tax is as high as unity on a national income accounts basis. The 1958 average rate of 0.4720 is certainly an overstatement (this was a recession year); and I would not take too seriously the preliminary national income account estimates for 1960 (which give the 0.47 ratio used by Mr. Pechman) until these can be reconciled with *Statistics of Income* data.

2. The major factor in Pechman's marking down of the GNP elasticity of the over-all system to 1.07 is his unwillingness to label payroll tax rate increases scheduled under present law as part of the revenue "system." While admittedly it stretches somewhat the definition of elasticity to include rate changes, these are a fiscal fact of life that should be kept in mind by policy-makers as well as private forecasters. The tendency to overlook these rate changes just because they take place quietly and outside the administrative budget has, among other things, given rise to misleading descriptions of what went wrong with federal fiscal behavior in early 1960. Accepting Pechman's suggested revisions for corporation and individual income taxes, but not for payroll taxes, the elasticity of the federal

revenue system still works out to be over 1.2. This is a rough measure of the rate at which expenditures will have to grow in order to justify the present revenue system, to say nothing of the matter of working down the unemployment rate. The condition that expenditures will roughly match available revenues can be as easily met at 3 per cent growth as at 5 per cent in the absence of a deliberate policy otherwise.

3. The proposition of structural change toward a more unstable economy, by virtue of a greater marginal response of consumption to recession-induced changes in disposable personal income, can be stated a little more rigorously than was done in my text. For a simple linear consumption function, assuming no shift in the function, the ratios used in Table 10(0.28 in 1949-II, 0.71 in 1954-II, 0.93 in 1958-I, and 1.00 in 1961-I) can be shown to lie between the average and marginal propensities to consume, since they are simply arbitrarily weighted averages of the two. Consequently, the ratios given over-state the marginal propensities in 1949 and 1954, have little bias in 1958, and understate in 1961, implying that the structural change is even greater than indicated in Table 10. The argument that these ratios are not indicative of net regressions of consumption on income because we have not controlled for other variables falls down if we make the not implausible assumption that the change in other variables affecting consumption, such as liquid assets, takes place between recessions but can be regarded as constant for a particular recession. I would conclude either that the consumption function is nonlinear or that the structure has changed frequently enough to make estimation of parameters by ordinary methods troublesome, to say the least. The differences from one recession to the next appear to be mainly in the area of consumer durables.

4. I agree with Mr. Hickman that the shortfall ratios do not measure the underlying marginal propensity and that, because of short-term instability, the ratios should be interpreted cautiously. However, I would point out that the shortfall estimates overstate consumption propensities with respect to disposable income only on the conventional assumption that the marginal propensity to consume during recession is below the average—an assumption which does not appear consistent with the actual behavior of consumption during the two most recent contractions. My basic contention—that there has been an increased responsiveness of consumption to income changes over the postwar periods—is also borne out by actual changes from peak to trough as in Hickman's Table 2.

Combining "conventional" measures of the disposable income—the GNP relationship with the shortfall measures of consumption propensities—Hickman notices no striking differences among the multiplier values for different recessions (1.01, 1.17, 1.34, and 1.26). However, using his method, and computing the multipliers as they would appear without offsets from direct fiscal stabilizers, yields a progression (1.03, 1.43, 1.69, and 1.91) which, while less striking than the ratios in Table 10, still indicates to me an increasing importance of the built-in fiscal stabilizers for the stability of the economy, especially since, for reasons stated before, I think the degree of change in underlying structural relationships is probably understated in these calculations.

Short-Run Forecasting Models Incorporating Anticipatory Data

IRWIN FRIEND AND ROBERT C. JONES

UNIVERSITY OF PENNSYLVANIA

THIS paper represents a preliminary progress report on an attempt to determine the most reliable quantitative tools for short-term forecasting of the gross national product at the present stage of knowledge. Short-term forecasting is considered to cover time periods from about one quarter to one year ahead. The results we have been able to obtain so far are extremely limited, but we have decided to present them anyhow because we consider them useful even though incomplete.

On the basis of our reactions to the existing literature and to the state of the art, we started with the assumption—which we of course planned to test further—that a highly multiequational and multivariate econometric model is not likely at present or in the foreseeable future to give as satisfactory results for short-term forecasting as a simple model. There seemed to be little evidence that otherwise important niceties, such as production functions, demand-for-labor equations, labor market adjustment equations, interest rate and price equations, disaggregated consumption functions, or perhaps even distributive share and financial variables, added significantly to the short-term prediction of the gross national product and its major components. Moreover, it appeared plausible that a simple or small system of relationships would be associated with less proliferation of random and perhaps of systematic errors than a large or complex system. It might also be noted that with n equations in a model of income determination, and an average of m forms which can be fitted or tested per structural equation for each one finally selected, there are a truly impressive number of combinations possible if m and n are at all large,[1] whereas the best combination of a few simple equa-

NOTE: We are greatly indebted to Paul Taubman for his invaluable statistical assistance.

[1] For example, in a system of thirty equations and an average of ten forms per equation, there are, theoretically, 10^{30} possible combinations of the equations.

tions—which concentrate on a small number of basic rather than a large number of marginal variables—should be much more easily determined (and more easily tested). Similarly, it is much easier in a simple model to test the stability of parameters over time and to make any required changes.

This is not to say that eventually large-scale models of income determination may not be highly useful for understanding the broad dynamics of our economic system, for appraising the quantitative effects of changes in economic policies, and for forecasting the level and composition of the national income. We simply doubt that at least for short-run economic forecasting the large models have as yet proved themselves, though we propose to test this skepticism rather than leave it in this ex-cathedra form. Nor do we have any reason to expect that large-scale models will ever be superior to smaller systems for short-run forecasting. Thus, even in the constant dollar models discussed in this paper, it seems quite plausible that in the short run the supply of output accommodates itself to the demand for output. Therefore, production functions and demand-for-labor equations may be unnecessary in explaining short-term fluctuations in the gross national product. On the other hand, it is obvious that the same assumptions about flexibility in productive capacity, or about the existence of at least temporarily expansible capital stock and labor supply, cannot be made in the longer run.

The proof of all this is of course in the pudding, so long as it is a proper and not an ersatz pudding. The only really satisfactory test of the predictive ability of a model is obtained by comparing the forecasts made for some period ahead with the actual values for that period (adjusted, if necessary, for the conditional nature of certain forecasts and for changes in the basic data incorporated in the model). The degree of reliance placed on predictive performance would not only obviously increase with the number of periods so tested but also, normally, with the extent to which accuracy in over-all forecasts (e.g., the gross national product) is a result of accuracy in component forecasts (e.g., consumption, inventory investment, etc.). The difficulties of relying on *ex post* tests of predictive ability are well known. With sufficient resources and diligence, it should be possible to fit a structural equation (or a reduced form) in a model to past data reasonably well if enough forms are tried. Under such circumstances, the usual statistical tests of significance have serious limitations, and a chart or table showing the closeness of observed to predicted values may have no meaning at all. Even the common device of omitting some recent periods from the data used to derive the basic model, and then testing the predicted against the observed values for these periods, is not very satisfactory. If the model no longer "works" in this new situation, the analyst may make a few selective alterations—not to delude anyone, but to ensure that the model presented to the public is the best possible.

There are three additional points which should be made before considering the results presented in the rest of this paper. First, we have attempted a fairly comprehensive investigation of the utility of anticipatory data in the simple models of income determination on which we are concentrating our attention, though as yet only partial results are available. What may appear an excessive preoccupation with anticipatory or expectational data in areas where their performance in earlier studies has been less than remarkable (e.g., durables consumption and inventory investment) is due largely to the availability of new data. But it is also due to a feeling that plans, expectations, and the degree of fulfillment should be useful in short-run income determination, with different types of expectations likely to be useful for different time periods. Second, there is no presumption that the same forecasting model will perform best for various time periods ahead (e.g., the annual rate of activity one quarter, two quarters, or four quarters in the future) or for varying time intervals (one quarter, a half-year, or a year). This is true because of the heterogeneity in both the predictive time span of different variables (e.g., housing starts versus plant and equipment expenditure plans or *ex post* versus *ex ante* variables) and in the relative importance of changes in different components of the gross national product for shorter and longer periods of time. Furthermore, it should be pointed out that if the time interval covered by the forecast is short enough, purely random or nonpredictable elements may predominate. Third, no attention has been paid in this study to the comparative predictive performance of forecasting tools other than quantitative income models.

Some Recent Models

The most recent short-term model which has been made publicly available is a large-scale quarterly model by Lawrence R. Klein, which consists of twenty-nine structural relations plus some accounting identities and tax-transfer payments relations and is fitted to a sample of postwar observations terminating in 1958. This system makes use of some *ex ante* as well as *ex post* variables. The mimeographed announcement of the model itself is dated April 13, 1961; and the initial forecasts—covering the first three quarters of 1961—were publicly released on April 24. A more complete description and discussion of the model has been presented at this conference. It is not possible to tell without additional information and a great deal of work how much influence the different types of structural equations have on the estimated gross national product and whether they better or worsen the forecasting results. However, the first six structural demand equations—i.e., for consumer durables, consumer nondurables, consumer services, investment in plant and equipment, investment in housing, and investment in inventories—are likely to be particularly important in explaining fluctuations in GNP; and it is interesting to examine the respects in which they differ from simple models. First, consumption has been disaggregated into durables, nondurables, and services. There would seem to be good reason for the disaggregation of at least consumer durables from the rest of consumption.[2] In explaining each of these types of consumption, a nonlabor-to-labor income ratio has been added to the usual personal disposable income and lagged consumption variables. In addition, an index of consumer durable goods buying plans has been added to the durable goods equation; a lagged cash balance variable, to the other two consumption equations; and a population variable, to the services equation. Instead of a single lagged consumption variable, there are now three, one each for consumer durables, nondurables, and services. It is difficult to tell what has been gained by these complications either from a theoretical or empirical viewpoint. The coefficients of the nonlabor-to-labor income ratio would appear to be opposite in sign to those obtained by Klein in his more aggregative annual model and incorrect in sign if the cross-section results which he cites there are taken as the basis for justification of inclusion of such a variable into time series equations.[3] The cash balance variable is significant only in the services regression and is omitted completely from the durables regression, presumably because of an incorrect

[2] See Irwin Friend and Robert Jones, "The Concept of Saving," *Consumption and Saving*, Philadelphia, 1960, Vol. II.
[3] See Lawrence R. Klein and A. S. Goldberger, *An Econometric Model of the United States, 1929–1952*, Amsterdam, 1955.

sign, even though this seems to be the one place where a-priori considerations might suggest an important positive influence. The reason for the peculiar cash balance effects may be that the variable used includes corporate as well as personal balances (and corporate cash balances may be inversely correlated with cyclical conditions, while durables consumption is directly correlated); but the question of the justification for such a variable in the other two consumption equations remains. Nor do the regression coefficients of the lagged consumption variable in the three separate consumption equations seem to be as reasonable as the regression coefficient of lagged consumption in a composite consumption function. The separate equations imply surprisingly little difference between short-run and long-run income effects on services expenditure, a more pronounced (and more plausible) difference between these effects on nondurable expenditure, and an apparently strong tendency for the long-run income effect on durables expenditures to be considerably smaller than the short-run income effect. The size of the constant term in the services regression is also troublesome. Thus, there does not seem to be much theoretical justification for the complications introduced in the usual consumption function, and the statistics presented do not permit an evaluation of either the improvement in the goodness of fit obtained or in the reliability of forecasts made.

So far as the three investment equations are concerned, the plant and equipment regression is quite simple and reasonable, though as will be indicated later we feel it can be improved through the substitution of a form which might be considered even simpler. But we are more dubious about some of the complications introduced in the housing and inventory equations, particularly the use of number of marriages and interest rates as explanatory variables in the former and of change in prices in the latter. Again, however, we have no basis for evaluating the statistical improvement, if any, effected.

The record achieved in the second- and third-quarter forecasts for 1961 from the Klein model is presented, in Table 1, by comparing them with the actual values reported subsequently. The first-quarter projections, which are considerably closer to the actual reported values, are not considered here as forecasts in view of their timing and, therefore, are not shown.

It should be noted that the comparative-level values above are not so interesting as the respective changes, since the relevant official

TABLE 1

COMPARISON OF FORECAST AND ACTUAL VALUES, KLEIN QUARTERLY MODEL, 1961
(billions of 1954 dollars except GNP) [a]

	Second Quarter				Third Quarter			
	Forecast		Actual		Forecast		Actual	
	Level	Change[b]	Level	Change	Level	Change	Level	Change
Durable consumption	43.4	2.0	39.8	2.2	47.9	4.5	39.9	0.1
Nondurable consumption	145.4	1.5	142.6	1.0	148.2	2.8	144.5	1.9
Services consumption	116.9	1.4	119.2	1.4	118.7	1.8	120.6	1.4
Residential construction	18.2	0.5	17.6	1.1	19.9	1.7	18.7	1.1
Private plant and equipment	35.4	0.0	36.9	0.6	36.3	0.9	37.8	0.9
Inventory investment	−2.7	1.7	2.9	6.1	0.7	3.4	3.9	1.0
GNP (current prices)	508.8	10.0	516.1	15.3	528.2	19.4	525.8	9.7

[a] Seasonally adjusted at annual rates.

[b] These are changes from preceding-quarter forecasts, which in I-1961 are fairly close to actual values.

national accounts statistics were revised slightly in July 1961,[4] subsequent to these forecasts. Even the earlier national income statistics do not seem to correspond precisely to the base figures used in this model. A comparison of actual and forecast changes in GNP points to a significant understatement of the recovery in the second quarter and an even larger overstatement of the recovery in the third quarter. As a result, the two quarterly forecasts of GNP are not too impressive (though such a statement implies that other methods are available which are at least as reliable or otherwise more appealing); but the change for the two quarters combined is reasonably close to the reported values. It is interesting to observe that simply taking the average increase in GNP in the first and second recovery quarters of all earlier postwar cycles ($5.6 billion and $9.7 billion, respectively, in 1961 dollars) results in a less reliable forecast for the change in the second quarter and a more reliable forecast in the third quarter of 1961. (If these "naïve" forecasts are adjusted for the difference between the average value of government purchases and exports in past recovery quarters and in the relevant 1961 periods, the "predicted" increases in GNP in the second and third quarters of 1961 would

[4] The official statistics were further revised in July 1962. In terms of changes, the new data indicate that Klein's second-quarter forecast was somewhat better than shown here; his third-quarter forecast was slightly poorer; and for the two quarters combined, the forecasted change shows greater deviation from the actual values.

amount to $6.5 billion and $11.4 billion, respectively, without any allowance for further multiplier effects.)

A question which immediately arises, of course, is whether the assumptions made in the essentially conditional Klein forecasts— viz., a steady growth in the government sector, exports steady, and prices almost steady, etc.—account for a major share of the discrepancies between the forecast and actual values. By comparison of the assumed and actual values (available after the forecast was made) of the exogenous variables, and by consideration of the relevant structural coefficients, it is possible to estimate roughly the impact on the forecasts of errors in the assumptions regarding the exogenous variables.[5] The changes from the first to the second quarter in the exogenous variables (the ratio of wage to other personal income, consumer buying plans index, cash balances, population, anticipated plant and equipment outlays, marriages, long-term interest rate, and lagged housing starts) appearing in the consumption and fixed investment equations were rather consistently overestimated; i.e., the second-quarter levels were placed too high. Thus, in view of the generally positive structural coefficients involved, the forecasted changes (in constant dollars) in consumption and fixed investment were too large. Of the other elements affecting the estimation of the gross national product, the major exogenous variables were government expenditures, exports, and the government wage bill (all in current dollars) as well as the set of appropriate price indexes for consumption, investment, and private GNP. Errors in the assumed changes from the first to the second quarter in government expenditures, exports, and the government wage bill were largely offsetting. On the other hand, the assumed constancy of prices (in all but one case) generally represented an understatement of price changes and thus served as a mild offset to the overstatement in real consumption and investment noted above. On balance, it would appear that a "corrected" forecast of change in GNP from the first to the second quarter would result, if anything, in an even greater error than appears in Klein's original estimate. From the second to the third quarter, in contrast, the errors in the assumed change in exogenous variables ran mainly to understatement. The changes in the exoge-

[5] One could, of course, solve the system of equations, substituting the actual values of exogenous variables. Apart from obvious problems associated with the size of the model and data revision, the problems of duplicating Klein's procedures, involving adjustments and selections of predetermined variables, precluded any attempt at "complete" solution.

nous variables appearing in the consumption and fixed investment equations were for the most part understated; the changes in government expenditures plus exports were understated by about $2 billion (current dollars, annual rates); and the changes in prices were again understated. There was little error in the estimate of the change in the government wage bill. Had the actual changes in the exogenous variables been used in the third quarter, therefore, it appears that the forecasted change in GNP would have shown an even larger overstatement.

Thus, the substitution of actual for assumed values of the exogenous variables in the Klein model apparently would have resulted in worse rather than better forecasts for the second and third quarters of 1961 (though not necessarily for the two quarters combined). If the major components of GNP which were forecast separately are examined, it appears that the chief deficiency of the model was in the estimate of inventory investment (and, to a lesser extent, other investment) in the second quarter and in the estimate of durables consumption and inventory investment (and, to a lesser extent, every major component of GNP other than plant and equipment) in the third quarter.

Clearly it is much too early to appraise this model adequately. An appraisal by Arthur Okun of the earlier Klein-Goldberger annual econometric model (see note 6) concludes that the model performed well for 1953 and 1954 but not for 1955, 1956, and 1957 as compared to forecasts by business economists generally.[6] The years of relatively poor performance, not surprisingly, are those appreciably beyond the period on which the model was based.

Another recent, moderately large-scale quarterly model was published by James S. Duesenberry, Otto Eckstein, and Gary Fromm in *Econometrica*,[7] October 1960, though completed considerably earlier. The model contains fourteen equations depicting the interrelationships of the items involved in going from gross national product to disposable income. This system, which is fitted to a sample of observations terminating in 1957, with some observations for 1958 available before the article was completed, is somewhat less complex than the Klein model—with fixed investment as well as government pur-

---

[6] Arthur M. Okun, "A Review of Some Economic Forecasts for 1955–57," *Journal of Business*, July 1959. Okun points out, however, that Daniel B. Suits used this model to predict 1956 with comparative reliability by adjusting the initial 1956 forecast of the model by the amount of the rather substantial 1955 error.

[7] "A Simulation of the United States Economy in Recession."

chases and net exports determined outside the system—has a more specialized nonforecasting purpose, and makes no use of expectational data. For our purposes, it would seem proper to compare the quarterly forecasts implicit in the model and the actual values of changes in GNP for at least 1960 and 1961, except for one complication. These equations were fitted to the official national accounts data prior to their substantial revision in late 1958;[8] so a significant part of the discrepancies between the forecast and actual data may reflect the revision of the basic data rather than pure forecasting deficiencies of the model. As a result, the comparative data will not be presented; but it may be noted that the discrepancies between forecast and actual changes in GNP seem quite substantial, largely reflecting the inventory function used but also, at times, reflecting the consumption function. Thus, of the seven 1960–61 quarters tested, the change in consumption seemed to be overstated by close to $7 billion in the third quarter of 1960 and understated by a somewhat larger amount in the second quarter of 1961, with these two aberrant quarters immediately following cyclical turning points.

The last quarterly model to which we shall refer was presented by Lowell E. Gallaway and Paul E. Smith in the *Journal of the American Statistical Association* in June 1961.[9] Like the Duesenberry-Eckstein-Fromm relationships, the Gallaway and Smith model is fitted to observations terminating in 1957, with observations for 1958 also available before the article was completed; so again the implicit quarterly forecasts and actual values for 1960 and 1961 may be compared. This model is extremely simple, involving essentially only a consumption function, an aggregative gross private domestic investment function, and a composite government expenditure and net foreign investment relation (there are, therefore, no autonomous expenditures), and is based entirely on *ex post* lagged variables. Though only five explanatory variables—all in change form—are involved in the prediction of change in gross national product, viz., disposable income, money supply, prior change in gross national product, property income before taxes, and government expenditures on goods and services plus net foreign investment, the model is surprising in the amount of importance it apparently gives to the money supply and property income. A comparison of the quarterly actual and predicted changes for 1960 and 1961 is presented in Table 2, but it

[8] See *U.S. Income and Output*, Department of Commerce.
[9] "A Quarterly Econometric Model of the United States."

TABLE 2

COMPARISON OF FORECAST AND ACTUAL CHANGES IN GNP,
GALLAWAY-SMITH QUARTERLY MODEL, 1960–61
(billions of current dollars)

	1960				1961		
	I	II	III	IV	I	II	III
Forecast	7.0	7.6	1.6	.2	2.3	0.7	16.7
Actual	13.2	4.9	−1.3	−.6	−3.7	15.3	9.7

should be noted again that the changes in the official national income statistics subsequent to the completion of this model may affect somewhat the original regression coefficients which have been used for projection purposes (though not to a serious degree, since the basic national accounts data used were apparently obtained from *U.S. Income and Output*). The record of performance for this period seems rather poor, especially for the second quarter of 1961 (and is not particularly improved if the actual values of government expenditures and net exports are substituted for the forecast values). The performance was somewhat better on a semiannual than on a quarterly basis, which is consistent with the results obtained from the Klein and the Duesenberry-Eckstein-Fromm models.

Some Preliminary Short-Term Relationships

That inventory investment plays a key role in short-run cyclical movements in the gross national product or generally in the type of relatively minor cycles experienced since the end of World War II will come as a surprise to no one. However, it is of interest to investigate just how important fluctuations in inventory investment have been as compared to fluctuations in other major types of investment expenditure. A rough simple way of doing this is to relate the quarterly changes in gross national product to changes in total investment plus government expenditures, ΔZ, and then separately to changes in this total less changes in residential construction, $\Delta(Z - H)$; less changes in plant and equipment expenditure, $\Delta(Z - PE)$; and, finally, less changes in inventory investment, $\Delta(Z - I)$, all seasonally adjusted at annual rates in billions of 1954 dollars. These results are then supplemented by adding in appropriate form what we consider to be the most relevant additional variables for forecasting plant and equipment expenditures, viz., such expenditures anticipated a quarter

288

earlier *(PE^e)*, and residential construction, viz., housing starts in hundreds of thousands of units, a quarter earlier *(HS_{-1})*, to those relationships in which the current value of these variables is no longer assumed known. The computed regression equations for the period from the third quarter of 1951 to the fourth quarter of 1960 (thirty-seven observations) are shown below, together with the adjusted coefficients of determination, standard errors of the regression line, and standard errors of the regression coefficients. This period is selected in view of the timing of the significant rise in the personal saving–disposable income ratio (i.e., decline in the consumption ratio as measured in the national accounts) from the earlier, relatively depressed, post-World War II level to a new and, comparatively stable, higher level, which suggests that for short-term projection it may be safer to restrict the usual assumptions relating to stability of structural relationships (or at least of the short-run consumption function) to the period starting with mid-1951.

The following four regressions point to the particularly important role played by inventory investment in the quarterly fluctuations of gross national product.

(1) $$\Delta Y = 2.11 + 1.39\Delta Z \qquad \bar{R}^2 = 0.90$$
$$(0.08) \qquad \bar{S} = 1.8$$

(2) $$\Delta Y = 2.31 + 1.45\Delta(Z - H) \qquad \bar{R}^2 = 0.86$$
$$(0.10) \qquad \bar{S} = 2.2$$

(3) $$\Delta Y = 2.22 + 1.37\Delta(Z - PE) \qquad \bar{R}^2 = 0.71$$
$$(0.14) \qquad \bar{S} = 3.1$$

(4) $$\Delta Y = 1.87 + 1.13\Delta(Z - I) \qquad \bar{R}^2 = 0.22$$
$$(0.34) \qquad \bar{S} = 5.1$$

Without positing any direction of causation, it is interesting to observe that changes in total consumption statistically contribute much less to changes in gross national product than changes in investment, of which inventory investment is by far the most important. Thus,

(5) $$\Delta Y = -2.19 + 2.11\Delta C \qquad \bar{R}^2 = 0.72$$
$$(0.22) \qquad \bar{S} = 3.0$$

Incidentally, there is virtually no observable simple relationship between short-term changes in gross national product and those in government expenditures plus net exports.

The above relationships are only slightly modified if the regressions are computed for the period from the second quarter of 1953 to the fourth quarter of 1960 (thirty-one observations). This shorter span, in addition to reflecting a period of comparatively stable savings-income ratios, is selected to minimize the possible economic irregularities associated with the Korean War. For the shorter period the regressions are:

(6) $$\Delta Y = 2.07 + 1.40\Delta Z \qquad \bar{R}^2 = 0.92$$
$$(0.08) \qquad \bar{S} = 1.7$$

(7) $$\Delta Y = 2.24 + 1.47\Delta(Z - H) \qquad \bar{R}^2 = 0.88$$
$$(0.10) \qquad \bar{S} = 2.2$$

(8) $$\Delta Y = 2.15 + 1.46\Delta(Z - PE) \qquad \bar{R}^2 = 0.77$$
$$(0.14) \qquad \bar{S} = 2.9$$

(9) $$\Delta Y = 1.81 + 1.59\Delta(Z - I) \qquad \bar{R}^2 = 0.33$$
$$(0.40) \qquad \bar{S} = 4.9$$

(10) $$\Delta Y = -2.47 + 2.23\Delta C \qquad \bar{R}^2 = 0.75$$
$$(0.23) \qquad \bar{S} = 3.0$$

It can be seen that with one possible exception the regression and correlation coefficients show no appreciable change from those computed for the longer period. The coefficient of $\Delta(Z - I)$ is higher, but not significantly so, for the shorter period; and the $\bar{R}^2$ for this relationship is somewhat higher, as it is also for the other relationships. Again, the results suggest the predominant importance of a satisfactory inventory investment relationship in predicting quarterly changes in gross national product.

Since quarterly data may be subject to large random errors (including estimating errors in the national accounts) which are essentially unpredictable at the present stage of our knowledge, it is desirable to extend all our analyses to semiannual and annual intervals. These results, which cover eighteen observations for the semiannual data and nine observations for the annual data, follow. The semiannual regressions are:

(11) $$\Delta Y = 4.12 + 1.52\Delta Z \qquad \bar{R}^2 = 0.96$$
$$(0.08) \qquad \bar{S} = 2.0$$

(12) $$\Delta Y = 4.56 + 1.60\Delta(Z - H) \qquad \bar{R}^2 = 0.90$$
$$(0.13) \qquad \bar{S} = 2.9$$

(13) $$\Delta Y = 4.30 + 1.65\Delta(Z - PE) \qquad \bar{R}^2 = 0.80$$
$$(0.20) \qquad \bar{S} = 4.2$$

(14) $\qquad \Delta Y = 3.59 + 1.55\Delta(Z - I)$ $\qquad \bar{R}^2 = 0.35$
$\qquad\qquad\qquad (0.49)$ $\qquad\qquad\qquad \bar{S} = 7.6$

(15) $\qquad \Delta Y = -5.58 + 2.40\Delta C$ $\qquad \bar{R}^2 = 0.88$
$\qquad\qquad\qquad (0.21)$ $\qquad\qquad\qquad \bar{S} = 3.3$

These semiannual relationships have higher correlations and lower relative standard errors ($\bar{S}$ divided by the mean absolute value of ΔY) with not too much change in the comparative importance of fluctuations in the different components of gross national product. The corresponding annual regressions are:

(16) $\qquad \Delta Y = 7.48 + 1.65\Delta Z$ $\qquad \bar{R}^2 = 0.96$
$\qquad\qquad\qquad (0.12)$ $\qquad\qquad\qquad \bar{S} = 2.6$

(17) $\qquad \Delta Y = 8.45 + 1.62\Delta(Z - H)$ $\qquad \bar{R}^2 = 0.84$
$\qquad\qquad\qquad (0.25)$ $\qquad\qquad\qquad \bar{S} = 5.0$

(18) $\qquad \Delta Y = 7.47 + 2.02\Delta(Z - PE)$ $\qquad \bar{R}^2 = 0.77$
$\qquad\qquad\qquad (0.39)$ $\qquad\qquad\qquad \bar{S} = 6.1$

(19) $\qquad \Delta Y = 7.52 + 1.28\Delta(Z - I)$ $\qquad \bar{R}^2 = 0.27$
$\qquad\qquad\qquad (0.65)$ $\qquad\qquad\qquad \bar{S} = 10.8$

(20) $\qquad \Delta Y = -7.37 + 2.07\Delta C$ $\qquad \bar{R}^2 = 0.84$
$\qquad\qquad\qquad (0.31)$ $\qquad\qquad\qquad \bar{S} = 5.0$

These annual relationships have correlation coefficients about the same as, or even lower than, the semiannual, though the relative standard errors are somewhat further reduced. Again, there is not much change in the comparative importance of fluctuations of the major categories of investment in explaining fluctuations in gross national product, pointing to the critical role played by inventory investment even in annual changes in over-all economic activity in the postwar period. Also, even on an annual basis, knowledge of the change in total investment plus government expenditures, viz., ΔZ, permits a comparatively reliable estimate of the change in gross national product. This is significantly more reliable than the corresponding estimate associated with knowledge of the change in the much larger figure for total consumption.

It may be noted that adding housing starts (HS_{-1}) and anticipated plant and equipment expenditures (PE^e) to the corresponding quarterly regressions of gross national product on total investment less housing (equations 2 and 7) and on total investment less plant and equipment expenditures (equations 3 and 8) contributes significantly to the explanation of changes in gross national product. For the longer period (thirty-seven observations) the new equations are:

$$(21) \quad \Delta Y = 2.30 + 1.41 \Delta(Z - H) + 1.41 \Delta HS_{-1} \qquad \bar{R}^2 = 0.89$$
$$ (0.09) (0.31) \phantom{HS_{-1}} \qquad \bar{S} = 1.9$$

and

$$(22) \quad \Delta Y = 1.71 + 1.31 \Delta(Z - PE) + 1.44 \Delta PE^e \qquad \bar{R}^2 = 0.77$$
$$ (0.13) (0.46) \qquad \bar{S} = 2.7$$

and for the shorter period (thirty-one observations):

$$(23) \quad \Delta Y = 2.28 + 1.43 \Delta(Z - H) + 1.28 \Delta HS_{-1} \qquad \bar{R}^2 = 0.90$$
$$ (0.09) (0.43) \phantom{HS_{-1}} \qquad \bar{S} = 1.9$$

and

$$(24) \quad \Delta Y = 1.49 + 1.42 \Delta(Z - PE) + 2.12 \Delta PE^e \qquad \bar{R}^2 = 0.86$$
$$ (0.11) (0.47) \qquad \bar{S} = 2.2$$

where ΔPE^e is anticipated plant and equipment expenditures in quarter t (anticipated a quarter earlier) less actual expenditures in quarter $t - 1$; and the subscript -1 is used in the equations as a shorthand expression for $t - 1$.

Some Short-Term Predictive Models

The maximum amount of information about prospective economic activity which is normally assumed known in forecasting models is government expenditures and exports. The first of these variables (or at least the federal government share) may be regarded as a control variable giving rise to conditional forecasts, and no one to our knowledge has yet had much success in projecting the second (viz., exports). We have, therefore, tested a number of very simple quarterly, semi-annual, and annual models in which only government expenditures and, for convenience, net exports are assumed known. Since certain promising bodies of anticipatory data are of recent vintage, and do not cover the entire period for which the basic models have been computed, we shall whenever possible relate residuals from the basic relationships to these anticipatory data in an attempt to determine whether they add to predictive ability.

The best simple set of "structural" equations which we have been able to derive so far for explaining quarterly changes in the total and major components of gross national product over the period from the beginning of 1953 through the end of 1960 is the following:

(25) $\quad \Delta C = 1.04 + .30 \Delta \tilde{Y} + .16 \Delta C_{-1}$ $\qquad \bar{R}^2 = 0.50$
$\qquad$ (.41) (.07) $\qquad$ (.15) $\qquad\qquad \bar{S} = 1.67$

(26) $\quad \Delta H = .14 + .55 \Delta HS_{-1} + .28 \Delta H_{-1}$ $\qquad \bar{R}^2 = 0.60$
$\qquad$ (.09) (.12) $\qquad$ (.12) $\qquad\qquad \bar{S} = 0.47$

(27) $\quad \Delta PE = -.39 + .94 \Delta PE^e + .033(\Delta \tilde{Y} + \Delta Y_{-1})$ $\quad \bar{R}^2 = 0.71$
$\qquad$ (.13) (.17) $\qquad$ (.015) $\qquad\qquad \bar{S} = 0.65$

(28) $\quad \Delta I = 1.96 + .075(\Delta Y_{-1} + \Delta Y_{-2}) - 1.02 I_{-1}$
$\qquad$ (.58) (.053) $\qquad\qquad$ (.16)

$\qquad\qquad\qquad + .69 \Delta O_{-1} + 1.77 \Delta PE^e \qquad \bar{R}^2 = 0.59$
$\qquad\qquad\qquad$ (.19) $\qquad\qquad$ (.72) $\qquad\quad \bar{S} = 2.08$

The identity below completes the model:

(29) $\qquad\qquad \Delta Y = \Delta C + \Delta H + \Delta PE + \Delta I + \Delta G'$

where the new symbols are G', government expenditures plus net exports, and O, unfilled orders. Changes with the subscript -1 (i.e., $t - 1$) are measured from $t - 2$; and all variables are again seasonally adjusted at annual rates in billions of 1954 dollars[10] except for HS, which is in hundreds of thousands of units, as previously noted. The regression coefficients in equations 25 and 27 have been estimated by a two-stage least-squares procedure. A $\Delta \tilde{Y}$ indicates that computed values (from a reduced form discussed subsequently) have been used instead of actual values. No ΔY term has been used in equation 26, since it adds nothing statistically and in a quarterly form may not be needed on a priori grounds once HS_{-1} is included.[11]

The $\Delta \tilde{Y} + \Delta Y_{-1}$ term in equation 27 gives significantly better results than either alone and has the theoretical justification that it assumes that income over a longer time span than a single quarter is relevant to plant and equipment expenditure decisions. It seems to have an informational content not contained in ΔPE^e; and it may be noted that attempts to use accelerator terms (such as $\Delta^2 Y$, $\Delta^2 Y_{-1}$, and more complex accelerators involving average in-

---

[10] Unlike the other variables deflated by the appropriate price indexes drawn from the national accounts, O (and in later regressions the level of sales S and the level of inventories L) were deflated by the wholesale price index, omitting farm products and food, converted to a 1954 base. Deflation by the wholesale price index for all commodities produced no significant differences in the estimated coefficients.

[11] It may be worth noting that the $\bar{R}^2$ presented for change forms would be expected to be substantially lower than for the corresponding level forms; so in comparisons of change and level forms, attention should be directed to the standard errors.

comes) did not help nearly so much as the income term used, even though some of these accelerator terms may also serve as a proxy for unanticipated sales. Attempts to substitute or add other explanatory variables, such as beginning-of-period capacity utilization, lagged profits, and ΔPE_{-1}; or to substitute $PE^e - PE^e_{-1}$ for $\Delta PE^e = PE^e - PE_{-1}$, did not give as satisfactory results.[12] Nor did a direct measure of unanticipated manufacturing sales help to explain residuals from equation 27 for the short period (starting with the third quarter of 1959) for which such data were available.

The $\Delta Y_{-1} + \Delta Y_{-2}$ term in equation 28 again gives better results than either income alone and relates inventory investment to an average of two quarters' income. The substitution of business sales for income gave about the same results; so income was utilized to simplify the model. Lagged change in inventory investment did not help at all. The lags used were obtained by empirical investigation.[13] The explanatory variables I_{-1} and O_{-1} are obvious candidates for inclusion both on theoretical grounds (particularly I_{-1}) and on the basis of earlier studies. However, PE^e is included as a proxy for business expectations (which to some extent of course is already reflected in O_{-1}) and for direct evidence on a type of expenditure which may be associated with inventory investment.

All of the signs of the regression coefficients in these structural equations are in accordance with theoretical expectations; and given the standard errors, even the magnitudes of the coefficients are not too unreasonable. The housing, plant and equipment, and inventory equations give surprisingly good fits for such quarterly relations, though they provide comparatively small lead times for forecasting purposes. The housing equation is further deficient as a structural relation in view of its omission of income and housing stock variables, neither of which was useful. The consumption function, however, is more disappointing; but a number of attempts to improve it did not help, including the substitution of the more theoretically correct disposable income or of more complicated averages of current and past incomes for Y and the addition of cyclical variables.

The residuals from the consumption and inventory equations (equations 25 and 28) were related to two other major bodies of an-

[12] Further work is now in process, substituting a $PE^e - PE^e_{-1}$ for the ΔPE^e variable and using first anticipations data in lieu of second anticipations.

[13] A $\Delta^2 O_{t-1}$ term was also tested in lieu of ΔO_{t-1}, but did not seem to give as good results. Cf. Paul G. Darling, "Manufacturers' Inventory Investment, 1947–1958," *American Economic Review*, December 1959, pp. 950–963.

ticipatory data which have recently been made publicly available—the Federal Reserve Board–Census Bureau quarterly series on anticipated expenditures on consumer durables and the Department of Commerce quarterly series on anticipated inventory investment. In view of the presumed greater importance of explaining inventory fluctuations, for reasons which have been discussed, the comparative absence of previous work in integrating inventory anticipations into models of income determination, and our own time limitations, we have spent more time on testing the utility of inventory than of consumer anticipations.[14] However, the results in both areas are generally negative so far as the explanation of residuals from equations 25 and 28 (or from similar equations tested) is concerned. The residuals from the inventory equation were related to changes in reported and corrected first and second inventory anticipations[15] for each quarter from the third quarter of 1959, when the series started, to the fourth quarter of 1960. The resulting regression was then used to determine whether the information on inventory anticipations helped in the "prediction" of inventory investment (or, more precisely, in the reduction of the residuals between actual change in inventory investment and that estimated from equation 28) in each of the four quarters of 1961 and the first quarter of 1962. Unfortunately, while the correlation between inventory residuals and changes in inventory anticipations is fairly impressive[16] ($\bar{R}^2$ = 0.51, 0.38, 0.84, and 0.54 for the reported and corrected first anticipations and the corresponding second anticipations, respectively), the inventory anticipations data do not seem to help at all in the "prediction" of the quarters noted for 1961 and 1962. On the other hand, the prospects for future utility of inventory anticipations data[17] are enhanced by these posi-

[14] We have not tested at all the utility of the consumer anticipations data compiled by the University of Michigan Survey Research Center, since they are collected only about twice a year, are not conveniently available, and have been and are being analyzed elsewhere.

[15] See Murray F. Foss, "Manufacturers' Inventory and Sales Expectations: A Progress Report on a New Survey," *Survey of Current Business*, August 1961, and later issues of the *Survey* for the basic data used. The data are seasonally adjusted and were further price deflated.

[16] The changes in inventory anticipations are the $\Delta I^{2e} = I^{2e} - I_{-1}$, and $\Delta I^{1e} = I^{1e} - I^{2e}_{-1}$ data reported by Commerce, where the superscript $2e$ refers to the second anticipation and $1e$ to the first anticipation. The attempted deflation of the reported data made the results worse. Further work is now in process, substituting the corresponding $I^e - I^e_{-1}$ and also I^e alone for ΔI^e.

[17] The Department of Commerce finds that inventory anticipations explain short-run fluctuations in inventory investment somewhat better than a regression equation not unlike the one used here, except for the expectational term (see "Factors Influencing

tive correlations between changes in the inventory residuals and in the anticipations series and, also, by the positive simple correlations between changes in inventory investment and in at least the second corrected anticipations series for the entire period from the third quarter of 1959 through the first quarter of 1962 ($\bar{R}^2 = 0.01$ and 0.71 for the corrected first and second anticipations). Surprisingly, there is no indication in this analysis, admittedly covering a very short period of time, that the corrected inventory anticipations data perform any better than the reported anticipations data in explaining deviations from the regressions which relate inventory behavior to *ex post* variables. On the other hand, without *ex post* data, the predictive value of the second anticipations seems to be definitely superior to the first anticipations.

A similar analysis was made of the relationship between the residuals from the computed consumption relation (equation 25) and the Federal Reserve–Census series, starting with the second quarter of 1959, on plans to buy automobiles within twelve months (as reported two months before the quarter in question).[18] The results here were less promising than for the inventory anticipations (with an $\bar{R}^2$ of zero and no help in the "prediction" of consumption in the four quarters of 1961 and the first quarter of 1962).

The reduced form for ΔY which was used to obtain the structural relations presented above is:[19]

Manufacturers' Inventories," *Inventory Fluctuations and Economic Stabilization*, Joint Economic Committee, 87th Cong., 1st sess., December 1961, Part I). However, the Commerce analysis is confined to manufacturing inventories alone (since trade and other inventory anticipations are not yet available) and relates to change in book value rather than to inventory investment as measured in the national accounts. We have attempted to construct a composite inventory structural equation utilizing anticipations for the manufacturing sector and the *ex post* regression for the trade (and other) sectors, so far without much success.

Another *ex post* inventory form, recently derived by Paul G. Darling (*Inventory Fluctuations and Economic Stabilization*, Part III), does not appear to offer any significant improvement in fit or in predictive ability over equation 28. This form, recomputed for the period from the third quarter of 1951 through the fourth quarter of 1960, yields the following result:

$$I_i = 19.41 + .26S_{t-1} + .04O_{t-1} + .51\Delta O_{t-1} - .74L_{t-1} + .13I_{i_{t-1}} - .00009t \qquad \bar{S} = 1.95$$

where L is the level of inventories and t is a linear time trend variable with 1951-III = 0. It is quite possible that the deflators we used, as well as the different time period, account for the somewhat poorer results we obtained with this form as compared with Darling's findings.

[18] See "Quarterly Survey of Consumer Buying Anticipations," *Federal Reserve Bulletin*, May 1961, and later issues of the *Bulletin* for the basic data used. The twelve-month anticipation data were used in an attempt to avoid problems of seasonality.

[19] The *ex post* reduced form for ΔY obtained by solving the structural equations is:

$$\Delta Y = 4.03 + 1.50\Delta G' + 4.06\Delta PE^e + .16\Delta Y_{-1} + .11\Delta Y_{-2} - 1.53I_{-1}$$
$$+ 1.04\Delta O_{-1} + .24\Delta C_{-1} + .83\Delta HS_{-1} + .41\Delta H_{-1}$$

$$(30) \quad \Delta Y = 4.91 + .75\Delta G' + 4.11\Delta PE^e + .53\Delta Y_{-1} \qquad \bar{R}^2 = 0.71$$
$$ (1.36) \quad (.47) \qquad (1.42) \qquad (.26) \qquad\qquad \bar{S} = 3.69$$
$$- 1.55I_{-1} + .94\Delta O_{-1} - .36\Delta C_{-1}$$
$$ (.36) \qquad (.37) \qquad (.63)$$
$$- .25\Delta HS_{-1} + 1.07\Delta H_{-1}$$
$$ (1.29) \qquad\quad (1.16)$$

A ΔY_{-2} term was tested but not used, since the results were somewhat less satisfactory, probably reflecting a relatively high intercorrelation with ΔY_{-1}. Again, attempts to add other explanatory variables, which we discussed in connection with the structural equations, and also to improve the fit by breaking down the entire period into recession and nonrecession periods separately, were not particularly successful.[20] The inventory anticipations help very little and the consumer plans moderately well in explaining deviations between actual GNP and that implied by equation 30 in the "base" period, thus reversing their roles in the relevant structural equations; but, again, neither helps at all in the "forecast" period.

The signs of the coefficients of all the variables in equation 30 are in accordance with theoretical expectations with the exception of ΔC_{-1} and ΔHS_{-1}, which are not statistically significant and are retained because they help considerably and have the correct signs in the structural equations. The unsatisfactory results yielded by ΔC_{-1} and ΔHS_{-1} in the reduced form equation for ΔY are probably explained by the relatively high intercorrelations of ΔC_{-1} with ΔY_{-1} and of ΔHS_{-1} with ΔH_{-1} and of both with the other variables included in the regression. Nevertheless, the standard errors of most of these coefficients are quite high and the magnitudes of the coefficients vary considerably in the different forms tested, with that of ΔC_{-1} generally positive if ΔY_{-1} is omitted and that of ΔHS_{-1} generally positive if ΔH_{-1} is omitted. All the explanatory variables combined are able to explain about seven-tenths of the variance in the quarterly changes in gross national product. Of the six cyclical turning points in the fitted period, the model using computed rather than actual values for the lagged endogenous variables correctly "predicted" five and led one by a quarter (the 1960 downturn).[21] The

[20] However, the adjusted standard error of the regression for the recession period was appreciably smaller than for the period as a whole.

[21] The use of computed rather than actual values for the endogenous variables improved both the "predictions" in the base period and the actual predictions discussed below, a result consistent with expectations if the model correctly represents the true structure and if the serial correlation of the endogenous variables is less troublesome than the random errors. The use of such computed values also is a first step in increasing the forecasting lead time of the model.

TABLE 3

COMPARISON OF FORECAST AND ACTUAL VALUES, QUARTERLY, 1961 AND 1962
(billions of 1954 dollars)

	First Quarter 1961		Second Quarter 1961		Third Quarter 1961		Fourth Quarter 1961		First Quarter 1962		Second Quarter 1962	
	Pre-dicted	Actual	Pre-dicted	Actual	Pre-dicted	Actual	Pre-dicted	Actual	Pre-dicted	Actual	Pre-dicted	Actual
ΔC	1.0	−0.6	3.2	4.3	3.8	3.5	5.7	4.6	3.1	3.3	2.8	3.0
ΔH	−0.2	−1.3	0.3	0.9	0.7	1.4	0.7	0.9	0.3	−1.5	−0.2	1.7
ΔPE	−1.5	−2.1	0.2	0.5	1.0	0.9	1.3	1.1	0.5	0.1	0.8	1.4
ΔI	−2.8	−2.3	3.3	5.0	2.2	1.5	1.5	1.9	−1.3	0.5	1.1	−2.2
ΔY [a]	−0.6	−3.8	6.6	10.0	7.5	6.5	13.2	13.0	3.9	4.0	4.3	3.4

NOTE: All actual figures are as reported in *Survey of Current Business,* July 1962, and in preliminary release OBE 62–69 of GNP data for the second quarter of 1962.
[a] Sum of individual components including actual figures for $\Delta G'$.

model did not clearly signal any false turn, though on one occasion it showed an insignificant decline when the actual change was an insignificant increase.

The "predictions" from equations 25–29 for the four quarters of 1961 and the first two quarters of 1962 are presented in Table 3. They were obtained by substituting computed rather than actual values for the endogenous (lagged as well as current) explanatory variables in these relationships.[22]

The forecasts as a whole seem better than those obtained from the more complex models, though this conclusion is highly tentative, particularly because the lead times involved in this comparison are comparatively small and because these forecasts must be considered largely *ex post* predictions. For GNP as a whole a significant over-statement in the first quarter of 1961 is associated with a correspond-ing understatement in the following quarter, and the directions of movement are correct in both quarters. The GNP forecasts for the next four quarters are remarkably good. The most significant pre-diction errors in the components of GNP consist of the errors for consumption in the first quarter of 1961 and for inventory investment and home construction in the first and second quarters of 1962. The underestimation of inventory investment in early 1962 probably re-flects the anticipated steel strike, and this is more than offset by the overestimate in the second quarter. The first- and second-quarter errors for home construction are also offsetting, which may partly reflect deficient seasonal adjustments in either the actual or predicted

[22] It may be noted that the computed values used included I_{-1}.

values.[23] We have not examined the possibility of other "abnormal" developments which might help to explain the remaining sizable errors. Of the major components, the least satisfactory forecasts are those for housing, largely reflecting the unsatisfactory nature of recent housing starts data; and further work on this relationship is under way, including the incorporation of data on new housing permits and other anticipatory housing series.

Since at least part of our lack of success in explaining quarterly fluctuations in the gross national product and its components may be attributable to erratic changes (including errors of observation) which are to some extent offsetting over longer periods of time, it is quite conceivable that significantly better explanatory and predictive results might be obtained by lengthening the time unit of analysis from a quarter to half a year. Semiannual relationships based on calendar half-years were fitted for the period from the second half of 1951 through 1960 (we went all the way back to 1951 so as to increase the number of observations—to eighteen). The semiannual relationships for explaining changes in the total and major components of gross national product generally turn out to be an improvement over the corresponding quarterly relationships, which is particularly noteworthy in view of the substantially longer lead times involved in semiannual "forecasts."[24] The best structural relationships obtained on a semiannual basis are given by equations 31–34:

(31) $\quad \Delta C = 1.95 + .38\Delta \tilde{Y} + .14\Delta C_{-1}$ $\qquad \bar{R}^2 = 0.77$
$\qquad \quad$ (.71) (.05) $\quad$ (.12) $\qquad\qquad\qquad \bar{S} = 1.82$

(32) $\quad \Delta H = .28 + 1.06\Delta HS_{-1/2}$ $\qquad\qquad \bar{R}^2 = 0.76$
$\qquad \quad$ (.15) $\quad$ (.22) $\qquad\qquad\qquad\qquad \bar{S} = 0.58$
$\qquad\qquad\qquad + .037(\Delta \tilde{Y} - \Delta Y_{-1}) - .16\Delta PE^e$
$\qquad\qquad\qquad$ (.012) $\qquad\qquad\qquad$ (.09)

(33) $\quad \Delta PE = -.81 + .57\Delta PE^e + .072(\Delta Y + \Delta Y_{-1})$ $\qquad \bar{R}^2 = 0.64$
$\qquad\qquad$ (.39) (.26) $\qquad$ (.032) $\qquad\qquad\qquad \bar{S} = 1.21$

(34) $\quad \Delta I = .77 + .12(\Delta \tilde{Y} + \Delta Y_{-1})$ $\qquad\qquad \bar{R}^2 = 0.44$
$\qquad \quad$ (1.18) (.09) $\qquad\qquad\qquad\qquad\qquad \bar{S} = 3.24$
$\qquad\qquad\qquad\qquad - .94I_{-1} + 1.21\Delta PE^e$
$\qquad\qquad\qquad\qquad$ (.27) $\qquad$ (.83)

[23] Offsetting first- and second-quarter errors for 1961 as well as 1962 are found for both home construction and plant and equipment expenditures.
[24] In view of this result, further work is being done on a semiannual forecasting model based on overlapping half-years in a study by Irwin Friend and Paul Taubman.

where the time interval for the subscripts is one-half year: $\Delta HS_{-1/2}$ represents the change from the first to the second quarter of the preceding half year. PE^e was derived by averaging the second anticipation of plant and equipment expenditures for the first quarter of each half year and the first anticipation for the second quarter at seasonally adjusted annual rates. The regression coefficients in these equations have again been estimated by two-stage least squares (from a reduced form presented below). All the coefficients have signs which conform to expectations, and their magnitudes seem generally reasonable.

A comparison of these equations with the quarterly results indicates that the consumption and housing equations are considerably improved on a semiannual basis, since the correlation coefficients are significantly higher, and the standard errors are not too much larger than the corresponding quarterly estimates, though the semiannual errors might have been expected to be nearly twice as large. The consumption function has the same form as the quarterly relation, though, as would be expected, the short-term marginal propensity to consume (i.e., the $\Delta \tilde{Y}$ coefficient) is higher in the semiannual form.[25] The semiannual housing function is different in two respects from the quarterly form: current income is introduced in the form of an accelerator term; and a plant and equipment expectation variable is introduced to reflect credit conditions in the housing market; it is, of course, inversely correlated with accessibility of credit. This ΔPE^e variable has a similar influence in the corresponding equation in the annual model. A different form of the accelerator in the housing equation, where an average of $\Delta \tilde{Y}$ and ΔY_{-1} was used in conjunction with H_{-1} as explanatory variables instead of $\Delta \tilde{Y} - \Delta Y_{-1}$ gave about equally good results.

The semiannual plant and equipment and inventory equations are not quite as good statistically as the quarterly results, though they do have the advantage of a considerably longer lead time for forecasting purposes. The form of equation 33 for plant and equipment is identical with that used in the quarterly relation, but is less satisfactory in view of the relatively low coefficient of ΔPE^e, which would be expected to be close to one. Equation 33 is significantly improved if the first two observations, which were distorted by the Korean War, are eliminated, with the new relation:

[25] It is higher still in the annual form.

300

$$(35) \quad \Delta PE = -.71 + .64\Delta PE^e + .074(\Delta \tilde{Y} + \Delta Y_{-1}) \qquad \bar{R}^2 = 0.80$$
$$\qquad\qquad (.30) \quad (.19) \qquad\quad (.024) \qquad\qquad\qquad \bar{S} = 0.90$$

The semiannual inventory equation is the same as the quarterly form except that no unfilled orders term is included, since neither a ΔO_{-1} nor $\Delta^2 O_{-1}$ term (nor both together) helped.

The reduced form which was employed in deriving the computed values for ΔY used in the above structural equation is:[26]

$$(36) \quad \Delta Y = 6.53 + 1.96\Delta G' + 5.27\Delta PE^e + .50\Delta Y_{-1} \qquad \bar{R}^2 = 0.80$$
$$\qquad\quad (1.36) \quad (.45) \qquad (.83) \qquad (.21) \qquad\qquad \bar{S} = 4.16$$
$$\qquad\qquad\qquad + 2.00\Delta HS_{-1/2} - 3.35I_{-1}$$
$$\qquad\qquad\qquad\quad (1.90) \qquad\quad (.67)$$

A ΔC_{-1} term was tested but not used, since the results were somewhat less satisfactory, probably because of its intercorrelation with ΔY_{-1}.

The cyclical turning points are again reasonably well duplicated by this semiannual model. The "predicted" changes in gross national product (again in billions of 1954 dollars) calculated from equations 31–34 also appear to compare favorably with the actual figures. This comparison is presented in Table 4 (with the data as usual at seasonally adjusted annual rates):

TABLE 4

COMPARISON OF PREDICTED AND ACTUAL CHANGES IN GROSS
NATIONAL PRODUCT, SEMIANNUAL, 1961–62
(billions of 1954 dollars)

	1961				1962	
	First Half-Year		Second Half-Year		First Half-Year	
	Predicted	Actual	Predicted	Actual	Predicted	Actual
ΔC	2.5	1.4	8.9	8.0	10.3	7.1
ΔH	1.0	−1.0	1.7	2.3	0.2	−0.2
ΔPE	−1.6	−1.8	1.0	1.7	2.3	1.4
ΔI	−4.2	−1.0	4.8	5.0	2.3	0.3
ΔY	0.3	0.2	17.5	18.0	18.8	12.9

NOTE: See Table 3 for source of actual data.

The GNP forecast for the first half of 1962 is somewhat too high, with most of this overestimate reflecting consumption and inven-

[26] The *ex post* reduced form for ΔY, obtained by solving the structural equations, is:
$$\Delta Y = 5.55 + 2.53\Delta G' + 4.12\Delta PE^e + .39\Delta Y_{-1} + .35\Delta C_{-1} + 2.67\Delta HS_{-1/2} - 2.39I_{-1}$$

tories. The result for inventories may be due to the threat of the steel strike and its aftermath. In this semiannual model, the use of computed values for the lagged endogenous variables did not improve the predictions as much as in the quarterly model. As a result, the most significant prediction error in the first half of 1961, that for change in inventory investment, would have been considerably reduced and the overestimate of change in gross national product in the first half of 1962 somewhat reduced, by the substitution of actual for computed values of the lagged endogenous variables in obtaining predictions from the structural equations.

In view of the few observations available no test of the inventory and consumer anticipations data in explaining residuals from these semiannual equations was attempted.

On an annual basis, the time period covered by our analysis (viz., 1951–60) is too brief to permit any definitive conclusions. However, it may be useful to present the most interesting relationships obtained for explaining annual fluctuations in gross national product. The best statistical fits were associated with the following system of structural equations:

(37) $$\Delta C = 3.61 + .43\Delta \tilde{Y} + .07\Delta C_{-1} \qquad \bar{R}^2 = 0.90$$
$$(.05) \qquad (.11) \qquad\qquad \bar{S} = 1.69$$

(38) $$\Delta H = .46 + 1.67\Delta HS_{-1/4} - .10\Delta PE^e \qquad \bar{R}^2 = 0.91$$
$$(0.25) \qquad\qquad (.08) \qquad\quad \bar{S} = 0.56$$

(39) $$\Delta PE = .10 + .99\Delta PE^e + .10(\Delta \tilde{Y} - \Delta Y_{-1}) \qquad \bar{R}^2 = 0.95$$
$$(.03) \qquad\quad (.01) \qquad\qquad \bar{S} = 0.75$$

(40) $$\Delta I = .11 - 1.04I_{-1} + .18\Delta \tilde{Y} + .42\Delta PE^e \qquad \bar{R}^2 = 0.92$$
$$(0.17) \qquad (.05) \qquad (.21) \qquad\quad \bar{S} = 1.43$$

where all coefficients except those in equation 38 have been estimated by the method of two-stage least squares.

Before discussing the implications of the above system, we may briefly consider the estimated reduced form for ΔY used in deriving the two-stage least-squares estimates:[27]

---

[27] The *ex post* reduced form for ΔY, obtained by solving the structural equations, is:
$$\Delta Y = 14.76 + 3.45\Delta G' + 4.52\Delta PE^e - .34\Delta Y_{-1} + .24\Delta C_{-1} + 5.76\Delta HS_{-1/4} - 3.59I_{-1}$$

(41) $\quad \Delta Y = 33.02 + 3.92 \Delta G' + 6.80 \Delta PE^e$ $\qquad \bar{R}^2 = 0.97$
$\qquad\qquad\quad (0.90) \qquad (1.19)$ $\qquad\qquad\qquad \bar{S} = 2.28$

$\qquad\qquad + .30 \Delta Y_{-1} - 2.35 \Delta C_{-1} - 3.43 \Delta HS_{-1/4}$
$\qquad\qquad\quad (.26) \qquad\quad (1.45) \qquad\quad (7.52)$

$\qquad\qquad - 5.37 I_{i-1} - .99 \Delta O_{-1}$
$\qquad\qquad\quad (1.22) \qquad (.31)$

In view of the number of observations available, of course, the number of variables barely allows estimate of this relationship. Alternative reduced forms were obtained with lower standard errors (viz., the substitution of ΔHS_{-1} for $\Delta HS_{-1/4}$), but the corresponding structural equations were considerably poorer from both economic and statistical points of view.

The symbols in the above equations are self-explanatory (note that a lag of one period refers to a year) with the exception that ΔPE^e refers to the first differences in anticipated plant and equipment expenditures for the year t (as reported at the beginning of that year), $\Delta HS_{-1/4}$ is the change in housing starts between the last two quarters of the previous year, and ΔO_{-1} represents the difference between unfilled orders at the beginning of years t and $t - 1$.

While the fit is apparently quite satisfactory in the reduced form, there are only nine observations (and only one degree of freedom), the signs of several of the regression coefficients seem incorrect, and the constant term appears unusually large.[28] In the structural equations, on the other hand, the theoretically expected signs are obtained for all regression coefficients, the coefficients seem reasonable and are consistent with the quarterly and semiannual results, and the standard errors are quite low. Although it appears in the reduced form, a ΔO_{-1} term is not shown in the inventory equation, since its coefficient was close to zero and completely insignificant in this structural form.

The housing function again employs ΔPE^e as a proxy variable for credit availability, but neither change in current income nor an accel-

[28] In view of these results in the reduced form, which are probably due, at least in part, to intercorrelations among the exogenous variables, an alternative form with several of the suspect variables removed (and thus with more degrees of freedom) is given below:

$$\Delta Y = 21.86 - .39 \Delta Y_{-1} + 2.64 \Delta G' + 3.83 \Delta PE^e - 4.31 I_{-1} \qquad \bar{R}^2 = 0.85$$
$$\qquad\qquad (.37) \qquad (0.69) \qquad (0.74) \qquad (1.79) \qquad \bar{S} = 4.85$$

Here, the signs are correct except for the ΔY_{-1} term, which is insignificant.

erator term helped. In the annual data an accelerator term in the plant and equipment equation, unlike the case of quarterly and semi-annual data, is of considerable help, probably because of the longer time periods involved. This accelerator term may also serve as a proxy for unanticipated sales. The use of ΔPE_i^e in the inventory equation as an expectational or cyclical indicator also proved to be quite helpful, and the resultant standard error is fairly satisfactory.

It is interesting to note that anticipated plant and equipment expenditure is consistently a well-behaved and important explanatory variable in this annual model. In the housing equation, lagged housing starts proved a much stronger variable than lagged housing investment (ΔH_{-1}), although the appropriate lag for housing starts is, not surprisingly, less than a year.

Equations 37 to 40 were used to "predict" change in gross national product for 1961 and 1962. Actual values of the lagged endogenous variables were employed in the predictions because they seem to give fully as good predictions as computed values and the potential time advantage of computed values is not so important in the annual data. The predicted changes in gross national product and components for 1961 compared with the actual values for 1961 as well as the predicted changes for 1962 (all in billions of 1954 dollars) are presented in Table 5.

TABLE 5

Comparison of Predicted and Actual Changes
in Gross National Product, Annual, 1961–62
(billions of 1954 dollars)

	1961		*1962*	
	Predicted	Actual	Predicted	Actual
ΔC	5.9	6.0	18.0	n.a.
ΔH	−0.3	−0.0	0.2	n.a.
ΔPE	−2.6	−1.1	4.8	n.a.
ΔI	−3.6	−1.6	5.0	n.a.
ΔY	3.9	7.7	32.6	n.a.

NOTE: See Table 3 for source of actual data. $\Delta G'$ is estimated at $4.5 billion (in 1954 dollars) for 1962.

The predicted change in ΔY for 1961 proved to be somewhat too low, owing to consistent underestimates of investment components; but the sign of the change is correct in each case. With data available

304

through the second quarter of 1962, the "predicted" gross national product for 1962 seems reasonably satisfactory, although in all likelihood it will prove too high. Based upon the assumption of modest increases in government expenditures (mainly state and local government) and no change in net exports for the remaining quarters of the year, the predicted change implies a 1962 GNP of $480.5 billion in 1954 dollars, or about $562 billion in current dollars (assuming a 1 per cent increase in prices over 1961).

It may be noted that revised national income estimates as of July 1962 were used in the predictions, although no adjustments were made in the equations. Predictions for 1961 based upon previously released values for the lagged endogenous values were somewhat better. The use of computed values for the lagged endogenous variables also improved the prediction for 1961 but resulted in an increase in the apparent overestimate of GNP for 1962.

While the annual results must be used with particular caution, they suggest that it is no more difficult to explain or "predict" annual than semiannual fluctuations in gross national product. The annual ΔY multiplier for ΔPE^e of over 4 implied by the model, i.e., the change in GNP associated with a unit change in plant and equipment expectations, seems rather high, as do the semiannual and quarterly multipliers for ΔPE^e, and to a lesser extent, the corresponding multipliers for $\Delta G'$. However, ΔPE^e reflects the effects of changing business expectations generally. Finally, it might be noted that limited-information estimates of the coefficients of the annual model were not nearly so satisfactory as the estimates presented.

Supplementary Comments and Tentative Conclusions

For short-run prediction of the gross national product, the most obvious deficiency in the simple models which have been presented is the assumption that government expenditures plus net exports is known. Consequently, these models permit only conditional forecasts. We shall not discuss in this paper the attempts that have been made by others to fill in this gap, of which probably the most important work for short-term forecasting relates to the use of budgetary and related data (as well as the recent trend in outlays) to predict federal expenditures on goods and services.[29] However, it should be noted that the substitution of government expenditures plus gross

[29] See Murray Brown and Paul Taubman, "A Forecasting Model of Government Purchases," *Journal of the American Statistical Association*, September 1962.

exports for the government expenditures plus net exports variable, on the grounds that it is more reasonable to treat the former than the latter as exogenous, does not change appreciably the results of the quarterly analysis.

Another potentially significant deficiency of the models presented here for short-run prediction of the gross national product is the absence of tax variables and relationships. Clearly, the impact of major changes in tax rates may be substantial and should be allowed for if they occur. We have constructed simple quarterly models with consumption related to disposable income and the latter to the gross national product but are not presenting them here, since we plan to do much more with them and so far they offer no improvement over the results presented (in a period, of course, of relatively small changes in tax rates). We also plan to do more with monetary variables.

Turning to the substantive (albeit highly tentative and admittedly inconclusive) results treated in this paper, the simple quarterly model we have tested seems to do at least as well as the more complex models, though much more exploration and testing of this hypothesis is required and planned. Semiannual and apparently also annual models are somewhat more successful than quarterly models, even though they entail forecasts for substantially longer periods ahead. It should be noted that in all of these predictions, at least one and one-half months of the period being projected would normally have elapsed before the forecasts could be made, which is a significant limitation of the quarterly model presented.

Limited tests of the predictive value of key series on business and consumer anticipations within the context of complete short-run models of income determination point to plant and equipment anticipations as the one stellar performer in all of the quarterly, semiannual, and annual analyses carried out. Business inventory anticipations and consumer automobile purchase plans do not seem to contribute significantly to the explanation of fluctuations in gross national product in these simple models, though the former appear to offer somewhat more promise. It should be stressed that apparently significant results can be obtained from these two series, but that these results are not at all stable from one set of regressions to another; equally good results can be obtained by the use of objective *ex post* variables alone. If housing starts and unfilled orders data are also included as anticipatory (though not anticipations) data, it may

306

be noted that they also add to the forecasting ability of the short-run models but, particularly for unfilled orders, not so strongly nor so consistently as the plant and equipment anticipations series.

Obviously, this paper has only scratched the surface in exploring the subject of optimal short-run forecasting models. We are in the process of testing the utility of many other bodies of anticipations data (and of other anticipatory series such as stock prices) and eventually hope to experiment with appropriate models for different time periods when certain types of data may not be available. Even with the anticipatory series tested in this paper, much more work is necessary before reasonably definitive conclusions can be drawn. In the meantime, without too strong preconceptions, we invite a comparison of the predictive ability of these simple models for the period ahead with the alternatives currently available.

LAWRENCE R. KLEIN, University of Pennsylvania

Straightforward forecasting is one among many possible applications of econometric models. It is to be expected that Friend and Jones might find a model of smaller dimension than most major models now being used in this country and throughout the world that forecasts well. Indeed, an extensive empirical effort might uncover one with higher sample correlations and better *ex post* extrapolations than can be found in the models whose usefulness they are questioning.

The objectives of econometric model construction are manifold: (1) to *explain* the structure of the economy, (2) to give empirical content to theory, (3) to try to solve the mystery of the business cycle, and (4) to guide alternative economic policy decisions. A model that has a fine empirical record in sample correlations and *ex post* forecasting may serve these broader ends poorly.

One of the reasons for making models complicated is to try to explain economic events that have no place in the Friend-Jones models. Forecasting *is* one of the objectives, and the forecasting of prices, interest rates, employment, unemployment, factor shares, wage rates, etc., is a problem of great interest. Success has not been uniformly good in these areas, but they certainly warrant a major effort. To do the things that we want to do, it is inevitable that systems will have to be large and complicated, whether we are interested in forecasting or in a wider range of problems. It seems to me that being against the inclusion in models of such things as production functions, demand-for-labor equations, labor market adjustment equations, and interest rate and price equations is like being against motherhood, the family, and all the widely accepted social customs of our world.

Econometric research will actually trend toward just the opposite of simplicity. Bigger, more detailed, and more complex models are being constructed. They will dominate the field because they will give much more information and allow us to tackle a larger number of problems than their predecessors. The econometric model project of the Social Science Research Council's Committee on Economic Stability, drawing upon the combined research efforts of many different econometricians with varying backgrounds, veered immediately in the direction of building a big model with much sector detail. It will dwarf the models considered large in the present discussion. The consensus of professional opinion is clearly the opposite of Friend and Jones's.

Apart from the desire to display or analyze variables that can only be studied in the context of a large model, experience has shown that there is a positive advantage in having a detailed model. An economy as complex as ours shows heterogeneous dynamic movements. Sometimes one sector is strong; sometimes another. In a large, detailed system it is possible to have compensating errors. In fact, our forecasting experience has frequently shown this. It is not accidental that strengths in some sectors are offset by weaknesses elsewhere. Insofar as GNP forecasting is concerned, a detailed model frequently comes out better for these reasons.

Is the Friend-Jones model really so simple? Their model consists of four equations and an identity. These four are the most powerful among those contributing to the explanation of GNP, on the demand side, in my larger model; therefore, I am not at all surprised that the model appears to work fairly well. Surely they will not object to an endogenous treatment of foreign trade, even if exports have to be assigned a predetermined value in forecasting since they depend on overseas variables. Incidentally, the export equation might add much to our understanding of the functioning of the economy without contributing a great deal, as a relationship, to individual forecasts. Surely they will not object to explicit treatment of taxes. Given a few more innocent complications like these, and their model will not be simple any more. These changes ought not to impair forecasting ability and might help. Any number of differences like this between their model and more complex models have this same property; i.e., they should not impair the forecasting ability; they might improve it; they promote economic understanding.

In recent periods the American economy has fallen into the Keynesian pattern in the sense that the short-run "supply of output accommodates itself to demand for output." The American situation has not always been like this since the end of World War II; it was often not like this before the war; and it will not always be this way. A more universal model is needed. The larger United States models parallel similar large-scale efforts in Canada, the United Kingdom, Holland, Japan, and a number of other countries where econometric methods are being introduced for model-building purposes. We are searching for more universal schemes than one like the Friend-Jones model, which has a very limited scope of applicability.

The same anticipatory variables that Friend and Jones find powerful in their forecasting model were already explicitly introduced in models they criticize—orders, housing starts, investment anticipations, and others. These variables are powerful in short-run forecasts but have brief lead times; therefore, Friend and Jones cannot look far ahead in the future; but this is of critical importance in useful forecasting. In at least one respect, my own model is enlarged because of an attempt to make order variables endogenous and to generate them within the system. The work of Robert Eisner (reported at this conference) and Dale Jorgensen hold much promise for the generation of investment intentions. Similarly, Sherman Maisel, in his work on the Social Science Research Council project, has developed equations for housing starts. If Friend and Jones build a more useful model capable of looking further ahead, they will soon find that their imagined simplicity has vanished.

Another limitation of the Friend-Jones model is that it does not lend itself well to simulation studies. The Klein-Goldberger model achieved some very respectable successes in the strict field of forecasting, but I would regard the most significant application of that model to be the Adelman-Adelman simulation.[1] To estimate a model, complicated as it may be, and to *propagate* random shocks through it in a pattern that faithfully duplicates America's 100-year business cycle history gives, in my opinion, great insight into the cyclical process. It deals with important matters of business cycle theory and

---

[1] Irma Adelman and Frank L. Adelman, "The Dynamic Properties of the Klein-Goldberger Model," *Econometrica*, October 1959, pp. 596–625.

suggests possible interpretations. Simple models are not suitable here, especially if they rely heavily on anticipatory variables that cannot be generated over the course of the simulation run.

For my tastes, the Friend-Jones approach has too much of pure empiricism and not enough theory or other a-priori information. Rigid following of the size of correlation coefficients and of *t*-ratios of individual estimates, as well as *ex post* forecasting, are seriously overdone in their paper. Even on the interpretation of signs, I cannot agree. Who is to say what is the correct sign of the factorial income distribution coefficient in the equations of demand for particular components of consumption? There is very good a-priori reason to include interest and demographic variables in equations of housing demand. There will be *genuine* forecasting occasions when they might wish they had such variables in their relationship.

As *ex post* forecasts, the Friend-Jones results are good. As for the standards that they will have to meet in real tests of predictions, the forecasting success of the Klein-Goldberger model and its successor is much better presented in Daniel B. Suits' recent article than in the piece to which they refer.[2] In such references it is hard to bring out the dramatic pressures put on the genuine forecaster who makes a public statement, based on a complicated model result, such as we found in the recession of 1953–54 or the recovery of 1961.

As I mention in my reply to Franco Modigliani at this conference, the marginal income coefficient in the equation for consumer durables demand now appears to be too high. In a re-estimation of the model with revisions of this coefficient, the forecasts of 1961 would be better. The 1962 forecasts, which are only just being checked for the first time, were too high for GNP, but the degree of overestimation (in genuine forecasting) was considerably reduced by changing this coefficient.

These comments have been largely centered around my own models, which come in for criticism by Friend and Jones. I would say that the criticism of the Duesenberry-Eckstein-Fromm model is largely misplaced. That is not a complicated alternative. It has hardly more behavioral relationships than does the Friend-Jones model. Besides the inventory and consumption equations, it has only relationships between personal income and GNP and between personal income and disposable income. In addition to a number of technical

2 "Forecasting with an Econometric Model," *American Economic Review*, March 1962, pp. 104–132.

fiscal relations, the main relations are those dealing with corporate saving, capital consumption, profits, and inventory revaluation. I would classify this model, in terms of complexity, with the Friend-Jones model. The two will be more similar in this respect if the latter introduce taxes and transfers explicitly. As to the Gallaway-Smith model, even Friend and Jones describe it as "extremely simple." How can the main point of the latter authors be demonstrated or proved by reference to this system?

COMMENT

F. THOMAS JUSTER, National Bureau of Economic Research

The paper presented by Friend and Jones is a report on work still in the formative stage. Their preliminary research is based on the premise that highly multivariable models are not likely, at least at present, to predict more accurately than much simpler ones, and that simpler ones have the further advantage that an optimal combination of variables is easier to find and test. This premise implies that a high level of aggregation is desirable in a forecasting model; consumption, for example, is treated as a single homogeneous category in all of their tests. Like most people I would prefer to deal with simple rather than complex model systems, perhaps because it is easier to trace the basic cause of a poor forecast in the simpler models. But I would have thought that the weight of recent empirical and analytical investigations pointed in the other direction—that more, not less, disaggregation is necessary, and that more rather than less complex forms represented a move in the direction of realistic specification of behavior relationships.[1] However, as the authors point out, the proof of the pudding is in the eating.

The appropriate criteria for determining what constitutes a "good" forecasting model are discussed in a brief review of some current models. It seems to me that Friend and Jones have ambiguous feelings

[1] I have added to my comments on the original Friend-Jones paper. Footnotes to my original comments represent additions, and are based mainly on the Friend-Jones Reply.

The evidence I had in mind here is the vast array of cross-section studies, relating both to households and business firms, which suggest rather strongly that disaggregation would improve the explanation of both saving and investment decisions by economic units. It does not follow, of course, that a time series prediction model incorporating these complexities will do better than one that ignores them—certainly not at the present time, and perhaps not in the foreseeable future. My own judgment would be, however, that prediction models will continue to be seriously in error (on occasion) until the models begin to describe decisions with realistic behavioral variables rather than with proxy variables that perform reasonably well most of the time.

311

about this matter. They start by saying quite plainly that ability to predict is the only really satisfactory test of a forecasting model, making appropriate adjustments for conditional forecasts if assumed and actual conditions diverge. In other parts of the paper, I get the impression that improvements in the fit for the base period are of some importance in determining a proper model; and some attention —far too little in my view—is given to the presence or absence of economically satisfactory (i.e., logically tenable) signs for regression coefficients.

At one level, this problem is not particularly interesting. Suppose that forecasting model "A" provides a near perfect fit for the past and that all its terms are consistent with firmly established theoretical preconceptions. On the other hand, "B" shows a worse fit for the past, but its theoretical basis is equally sound. If B persistently forecasts more accurately than A, it seems obvious that B is a better model. The difficulty lies with the word "persistently." Does a better record for the only two available forecast periods constitute a reasonable test? Does it make any difference whether the forecast period involves sharp changes in the level of GNP or no change in GNP? On the whole, I have the feeling that Friend and Jones (in this paper, at any rate) have given far too much attention to the improvement in prediction that results from adding this or that variable, and far too little to testing alternative models that involve competitive but internally consistent hypotheses about behavior.[2] This impression may be incorrect, since their paper is a progress report and, hence, is incomplete. But the tone of the paper is that prediction is what counts; and this position, while correct in the sense of being a necessary condition for virtue in a forecasting model, seems to me essentially misleading. Let me illustrate more specifically what I have in mind.

Friend and Jones contrast two models, identical except that one incorporates the recent Commerce series on businessmen's (subjective) inventory anticipations and the other does not. The inventory

---

[2] In their Reply, Friend and Jones say that "the simple point, which we do discuss at some length (and which, as Juster illustrates, is frequently overlooked), is that it is relatively easy to get good fits and much more difficult to get good forecasts." (Parentheses added.) Agreed, except for the clause in parentheses, but why is this the case? I would be inclined to argue that the basic reason is an unwillingness on the part of model-builders to impose theory on their model, in that variables of obvious relevance and importance are left out if a structural regression with the appropriate sign for them cannot be had. But if the variable is clearly relevant, the real difficulty must be that the structural equation is improperly specified. Having expressed all this in somewhat ex-cathedra form, I freely confess that I have no practical solution to offer.

anticipations variable greatly improves the fit for 1959 and 1960 (a hindcast period) but does not improve 1961 predictions. Their procedure involves regressing inventory anticipations against the GNP residuals from a model (equation 16) that *already* includes actual inventory investment in period $t - 2$ and the change in both unfilled orders and business sales between $t - 1$ and $t - 2$.

Perhaps inventory anticipations really do not improve predictions of the quarterly change in GNP, but I do not see how it can be known by this test. To begin with, the first three quarters of 1961 may not constitute a reasonable test period. I have no real objection to its length, although everyone, including the authors, would doubtless prefer a longer one. But whatever is causing the model to generate numbers different from actual GNP during this period may have nothing to do with inventory change. If the inventory anticipations improve predictions of inventory change (I_i) but knowing I_i does not help much (for this period) in predicting the change in GNP, one can hardly say that the model is not improved.

In the second place, and more important in my judgment, the authors seem to me to have given too much weight to the numbers and too little weight to theorizing in deciding whether the model is improved and which variables are necessary. Inventory anticipations are presumably based on something. To have real content they must be based on implicit forecasts of sales, on production schedules based on these forecasts, and on the current inventory level. If this is the case, why use both inventory anticipations and the combination of actual inventory change, lagged change in orders, and lagged change in sales to explain I_i? The latter are the objective variables most closely associated with I_i, while the former is an alternative (subjective) forecast of I_i. If the anticipations constitute a conditional forecast of inventory change based on assumptions about production and sales, the appropriate model would have the form

$$I_i = f[\hat{I}_i, (S - \hat{S}), (P - \hat{P})],$$

where $\hat{I}_i$ is anticipated change in inventory; $\hat{S}$ is anticipated sales; S, actual sales; $\hat{P}$, production scheduled in the light of current inventory and anticipated sales; and P, actual production. I do not see the point in simply inserting $\hat{I}_i$ into a model that already purports to explain actual $\hat{I}_i$, and, hence, I_i itself.[3]

[3] In their Reply, Friend and Jones argue that the rationale for including both inventory anticipations themselves and the (*ex post*) data on which the anticipations must

313

Somewhat similar treatment is accorded the other recent body of subjective anticipatory data—the FRB-Census survey of automobile buying intentions. Here Friend and Jones find that the intentions data do not help to explain residuals from their GNP hindcast during 1959 and 1960, nor do they improve 1961 predictions. But the only substantial quarterly changes in sales of durables during the 1959–61 period—to which the intentions series ought to be related if it is of any use—occurred in the first and second quarters of 1961. The only noticeable changes in the intentions series during the 1959–61 period are increases between the third and fourth quarters of both 1959 and 1960, followed by declines in the first quarter of the respective years. These are almost certainly seasonal movements; hence, the series shows little actual variation to date. Since it is clearly not possible to explain residuals or anything else with a series which consists (as it should) of essentially random numbers during the period when it has been available, it seems to me that the test must be inconclusive.

The analysis of these subjective anticipations or intentions variables in the Friend-Jones paper is exclusively concerned with examination of time series relationships, presumably on the grounds that a time series model is obviously needed for prediction. My own judgment is that any substantial improvement in forecasting models obtained by including these kinds of variables depends on achieving a much better understanding of the way in which anticipations are related to behavior. And it seems to me unlikely that much will be learned from time series about the interrelationships between actual investment, on the one hand, and business investment intentions, sales expectations, and actual sales on the other—or between purchases of consumer durables and consumer buying intentions, associated expectations, and outcome; or between inventory changes and inventory anticipations, unfilled orders, expected sales, and actual sales. Much more analysis of cross-section data seems essential if any of

---

have been based is that "the *ex post* variables may be necessary to take account of firms that do not do serious jobs of budgeting" while "anticipated inventory investment . . . may very well have an informational content that *ex post* variables do not have." It still seems to me that this procedure serves to introduce a sort of statistical haze over what may be a very useful set of relations. If inventory anticipations mean one thing for firms that undertake serious budgeting and another for firms that do not, fine. But then the appropriate model has a disaggregated inventory function consisting of one structural equation for type A firms and a quite different one for type B firms. What has been gained by getting coefficients that represent averages for both sets of firms combined?

Incidentally, I knew that one of the authors had previously made use of the kind of analysis suggested by my comments. But I had supposed that the comments were to be directed to the paper presented at this conference.

these kinds of relationships are ever to be usefully incorporated into forecasting models. The alternative is to let enough time elapse so that sufficient variance is generated to permit reliable use of time series tests. Many of these variables, especially those relating expectations and outcomes to the fulfillment of plans or intentions, are likely to be of little use most of the time. Their values are typically fairly close to the mean, and it is possible that only substantial departures from the mean are of any consequence for behavior. But if such variables occasionally exhibit extreme values and if they do in fact have an association with behavior, models that fail to incorporate them will perform badly during some periods—even though most of the time such variables will fail to improve predictions. In sum, I would argue that (subjective) anticipatory data cannot be effectively incorporated into forecasting models without extensive use of cross sections to decide whether and how these variables relate to spending decisions. Once we know whether and how, e.g., investment plans are altered when sales diverge from expectations, this relationship can be incorporated into a forecasting model. But the whether and how, as well as adequate tests of alternative hypotheses, are simply not obtainable from time series.

Let me turn now to some specific points in the empirical results. Early in the paper the authors examine the question of which expenditure sectors are most closely associated with changes in GNP. Appropriate classification of GNP into sectors that, in old-fashioned terminology, are mainly induced or mainly autonomous (with respect to GNP) is obviously useful if forecasting is the goal, since the induced sectors do not need to be independently explained. Friend and Jones run regressions that relate ΔGNP to (ΔZ), the latter being the combined change in private investment, government spending, and net foreign investment, and then to

$$\Delta(Z - I_{pe}), \Delta(Z - I_h), \Delta(Z - I_i),$$

and so forth. ΔZ explains some 90 per cent of the variance in ΔGNP for the quarterly data, somewhat more for semiannual or annual series. Removing particular investment sectors from ΔZ always reduces the association with GNP, the biggest drop occurring when $\Delta(Z - I_i)$ is the independent variable; the same pattern is shown by all the series—quarterly, semiannual, and annual.

It is not at all clear to me what these data show. Friend and Jones make two points: (1) these results underline the important role of inventory accumulation in the fluctuations of GNP; (2) knowledge

315

of ΔZ would permit very reliable estimates of ΔGNP, and these estimates would be significantly more reliable than those obtained from knowledge of the (much larger, in absolute terms) change in consumption, ΔC. One is left with the impression—perhaps wrongly —that consumption need not be of much concern in the design of a satisfactory forecasting model. Instead, effort should be concentrated on trying to explain movements in the sectors that traditionally were thought to be the cause of changes in GNP, especially government expenditures, inventory investment, and plant and equipment investment.

Two comments are in order. First, the only clear evidence that changes in a given spending sector may be the cause, rather than the consequence, of a change in income consists of an observed low correlation with income change. If inventory change is uncorrelated with income change it obviously cannot be a consequence of income change; if it is highly correlated no analytical conclusion is possible. By this criterion changes in I_i and G are clearly causes of GNP change, while PE and consumer durables could be either. Secondly, it seems to me that this problem can be investigated with sharper analytical and statistical tools. The procedure, which is described below, grew out of discussions with Gary Becker and Jacob Mincer.

Suppose we divide GNP into a number of component sectors— A, B, and R. Assume that we know on a priori grounds that A is wholly autonomous with respect to GNP; A might be government spending, for example. Also on a-priori grounds, we know or are willing to assume that R is wholly induced by GNP; for example, R might be consumer expenditures on nondurable goods. We are interested in whether the B sector is induced, autonomous, or partly both. The simplest procedure is to estimate coefficients for the following regressions:

(1.0) $$R = b_0 + b_1 A + b_2 B + u_1$$

(1.1) $$A = a_0 + a_1 R + a_2 B + u_2$$

If B is wholly induced by GNP it is completely substitutable for R, which is known to be wholly induced; in that case a dollar increase in B will be associated with a dollar decrease in R, holding A constant, and b_2 will be -1. If B is wholly autonomous, on the other hand, a dollar increase in B will be associated with an increase in R—the amount depending on the size of the multiplier—and b_2 will be positive and equal to $k - 1$, where k is the multiplier. Further, the coefficients of A and B will be the same, because both will be

316

associated with the same amount of change in R and hence in GNP. I am assuming that a dollar change in expenditures that are wholly autonomous with respect to GNP will have the same multiplier regardless of the character of the change. This assumption may not be entirely realistic, although its validity does not depend on the presence or absence of complex interrelationships among the several expenditure sectors. In effect, A and B are perfect substitutes if B is wholly autonomous, while B and R are perfect substitutes if B is wholly induced. If B is partly induced but has some autonomous element, b_2 will be somewhere between b_1 and -1.

Equation 1.1 serves as a check on the b_2 coefficient in equation 1.0, since b_2 will be a biased estimate if u_1 is correlated with any of the other variables. In equation 1.1, a_1 and a_2 will be both positive and of equal size if B is wholly induced, while a_2 will have a value of -1 if B is wholly autonomous. Estimates of a_1 and a_2 supplement the information provided by b_1 and b_2, and facilitate a better judgment as to the relative importance of induced and autonomous elements.[4]

[4] Friend and Jones correctly point out that my criterion for isolating autonomous (my terminology, not theirs) expenditure sectors depends on the proposition that "sectors" have been defined in a meaningful rather than an arbitrary way. If, for example, PE is in fact wholly induced by GNP, "PE in the petroleum industry" may well appear to be autonomous. The problem they raise is a real one, although as a practical matter it seems manageable. In their illustration, to take a case in point, if ΔD really appeared to be autonomous vis-à-vis ΔGNP solely because of the negative correlation between ΔD and ΔN (in which case the appropriate consumption sector is $\Delta D + \Delta N$) this fact would show up quite clearly in a multiple regression of ΔN on ΔD and $\Delta \mathcal{Z}$ (where $\Delta \mathcal{Z}$ is $\Delta GNP - \Delta D - \Delta N$), as noted in my comments. In such a situation the coefficient of ΔD would presumably be -1.

I have no particular quarrel with the reservations expressed by Friend and Jones about the bias in estimates obtained by my suggested procedures. Whether my procedure or theirs is more useful, I leave to the judgment of the reader. Incidentally, my reference to I_i as a cause of income change, given my criteria, may be incorrect, but it certainly was not an oversight! For quarterly data over the period III–1950 to III–1960, the correlation between ($\Delta GNP - \Delta \mathcal{Z}$) and various expenditure sectors is as follows (where $\Delta \mathcal{Z}$ is defined as in the Friend-Jones paper except that consumer durables have been included):

$X_1 = \Delta GNP - \Delta \mathcal{Z}$
$X_2 = \Delta D$ = consumer durables change
$X_3 = \Delta I_f$ = change in gross private investment less change in inventory investment
$X_4 = \Delta I_i$ = change in inventory investment
$X_5 = \Delta G'$ = change in government spending on goods and services plus change in net foreign investment
$b_{12} = .29, r_{12}^2 = .16$
$b_{13} = .32, r_{13}^2 = .17$
$b_{14} = .11, r_{14}^2 = .11$
$b_{15} = .06, r_{15}^2 = .01$

The best candidates for autonomous (vis-à-vis GNP) sectors are clearly X_4 and X_5, that is, change in inventory investment and change in G'.

This procedure essentially constitutes a test of whether a particular component of GNP can be better substituted for that GNP component known to be wholly autonomous or for that component known to be wholly induced. If no a-priori knowledge is available, the test cannot tell us anything except that components A and B are substitutes, C and D are substitutes, and A and B are complementary to C and D. We cannot determine whether A and B are autonomous or induced, and similarly for C and D.

For quarterly data covering the same period as the paper, one such test shows the following results:

(1.0) $\qquad \Delta R = b_0 + .096\Delta D + .134\Delta I + .153\Delta G' + u_1$

(1.1) $\qquad \Delta G' = a_0 + .308\Delta D - .362\Delta I + .644\Delta R + u_2$

where $\Delta G'$ = change in government spending on goods and services plus net foreign investment

$\qquad \Delta I$ = change in gross private domestic investment

$\qquad \Delta D$ = change in consumer durable goods expenditures

$\qquad \Delta R$ = change in $[GNP - (G' + I + D)]$

all in current prices.

I would interpret these results as indicating that there are autonomous and induced elements in both D and I, with the latter having relatively more of an autonomous and less of an induced element. In equation 1.0, the coefficients of D, I, and G' are all positive, indicating that expenditure changes in these sectors, net of each other, are all associated with changes in the same direction for the R sector; hence, all these sectors contain a strong autonomous element. The coefficients of D and I are less than G'; hence, these sectors are apparently not quite so autonomous as G'. In equation 1.1, I and G' are partial substitutes; since G' is known to be autonomous, I must have a strong autonomous component. The D coefficient is positive but is considerably below the coefficient for the (wholly induced) R sector; hence, D appears to be partly autonomous, although evidently not so much so as I. Both equations rank the sectors G', I, and D in that order with respect to the relative importance of autonomous components. In connection with a current National Bureau project, I plan to do additional empirical work on this question.

My final comment relates to the form in which the anticipatory variable ΔPE^e is introduced in the change equations. This variable appears in a long list of equations (3, 16, 19, 24, 27, 28, 29, 32, 34) and represents the only real anticipatory variable—as distinct from lagged forms—that the authors found of much use. Unfortunately, even this variable may not really help, since their regression 3,

$$\Delta Y = 2.20 + 1.37\Delta(Z - PE) + .80\Delta PE^e,$$
$$\qquad\qquad (.14) \qquad\qquad (.39)$$

contains a spurious positive correlation between ΔY and ΔPE^e. The latter is defined as $(PE_t^e - PE_{t-1})$, that is, ΔPE^e is anticipated investment in plant and equipment for period t less actual investment in the preceding period. But, adding and subtracting PE_t, we get,

(2.0) $\qquad\qquad \Delta PE^e = PE_t^e - PE_{t-1} + PE_t - PE_t;$

combining the two terms in the middle,

(2.1) $\qquad\qquad \Delta PE^e = (PE_t - PE_{t-1}) + (PE_t^e - PE_t),$

or

(2.2) $\qquad\qquad \Delta PE^e = \Delta PE_t + (PE_t^e - PE_t)$

That is, the change in anticipated spending on plant and equipment during t is equal to the actual change in plant and equipment expenditures (ΔPE_t) plus the difference between anticipated and actual expenditures in t. Even if the second term in equation 2.2 has a covariance of zero (anticipated and actual being entirely unrelated), ΔPE^e might still be correlated with ΔY if the first term (ΔPE_t) has a strong enough correlation with ΔY.[5] It is hard to tell whether the spurious element in ΔPE^e is strong enough to force a statistically significant relationship with ΔGNP where none really exists—it depends on the relative size of the variances of ΔPE_t and $PE_t^e - PE_t$. I would originally have thought that the spurious element would not be strong enough because PE_t^e is a fairly good predictor of PE_t, but the coefficient of ΔPE^e is barely twice its standard error even with the aid of a spurious element.[6]

[5] I gather from the Reply that Friend and Jones do not agree that their ΔPE^e variable contains a spurious correlation with the dependent variable ΔY. First, the availability of "completely reliable anticipatory data for every sector . . . so that $\Delta Y^e = \Delta Y$" leads to the conclusion, not that the correlation between ΔY^e and ΔY is "entirely spurious," but that $Y_t^e - Y_t = 0$, hence, that there is in fact no spurious element. Second, my objection to the Friend-Jones procedure is that one simply cannot tell whether ΔPE^e is really helping to predict ΔY, because of the way they have chosen to define ΔPE^e. If one explains ΔY by the Friend-Jones variable ΔPE^e, both sides of the equation turn out to contain the common element ΔPE; hence, the observed correlation has a spurious element of unknown strength. If PE_t^e and PE_t are perfectly correlated, the spurious element is nil; if the two are wholly uncorrelated, the spurious element accounts for all of the observed correlation. And if the truth is somewhere between, as it doubtless is, one cannot say anything.

[6] In the revised version of the paper the coefficient of ΔPE^e (equation 22) has grown to where it is now about three times its standard error.

REPLY by Irwin Friend and Robert Jones

A closer reading of the first two pages of our paper should reveal to Klein that we are not "against the inclusion in models of such things as production functions . . . interest rate and price equations" but that we do question their usefulness for short-run prediction of the gross national product and its major components. Nor are we particularly impressed by appeals either to "motherhood" or the "concensus of professional opinion."

We of course do not object to any complications, whether "innocent" or otherwise, which improve the forecasting ability of our model. We simply require that they do in fact rather than as an ex-cathedra proposition.

We must confess that we are confused by two statements appearing in the same paragraph of Klein's comments; viz., our "approach has too much of pure empiricism and not enough theory or other a-priori information"; and in referring to our criticism of his model "Who is to say what is the correct sign of the factorial income distribution coefficient in the equations of demand for particular components of consumption?" Klein has every right to have different theoretical preconceptions from our own but considerably less right to overlook the other relevant and conflicting "a-priori information" from cross-section data which he himself has cited on other occasions. We consider this another example of the weaknesses of large-scale models, which in this case would seem to be based on "too much of pure empiricism."

We agree with Klein and emphasize in our paper that our "good" results must be considered largely as *ex post* predictions and still have to stand up in the crucible of public *ex ante* forecasting. However, it is only fair to point out also that any literate outsider can at any time in the future not only test the usefulness of our model in a few minutes of not too arduous labor but also use the model himself for forecasting—which, of course, is not true of Klein's model. As a matter of fact, a comprehensive and objective test of the predictive ability of a large-scale model by any outside analyst is extremely difficult to perform for a variety of reasons, including the problems raised by frequent adaptations made in the model.

Finally, we do not understand the point of Klein's concluding comments on our brief discussion of the Duesenberry-Eckstein-Fromm model, which we characterize as "moderately large-scale," and the Gallaway-Smith model, which we characterize as "extremely simple." Klein feels that the Duesenberry-Eckstein-Fromm model is not moderately large scale. We disagree, but think it hardly worth arguing about. More important, he apparently also feels that the Gallaway-Smith model is either not relevant to what he characterizes as our "main point" or that if it is, it would be inconsistent with ours in view of the relatively poor results obtained. We of course do not take the position that any model is good because it is simple and assume that Klein does not take the position that any model is good because it is complicated. However, in discussing relevant past models, we believe in presenting them even if they are not corroborative of our "main point."

On reading the comments by F. Thomas Juster, we must confess that we have a vision of Don Quixote tilting at windmills. We are certain there must be some valid criticism contained in his comments and are embarrassed to admit that we have not been able to find it. With the exception of his concluding comment, which we shall consider first because it appears to be the only instance in which he takes issue with one of our substantive results, we shall discuss all of his major strictures in the order in which they appear.

Juster states that change in plant and equipment expectations (ΔPE^e) represents "the only real anticipatory variable—as distinct from lagged forms—that the authors found of much use. Unfortunately, even this variable may not really help . . ." This concluding comment is certainly one of the strangest in his paper. We had to read the reasoning twice and still did not believe what we read. The reasoning goes like this: ΔPE^e is certainly correlated with ΔPE, which is obviously correlated with the change in GNP (ΔY), thus introducing a "spurious" correlation between ΔPE^e and ΔY. Therefore, at the extreme, ΔPE^e might unfortunately be perfectly correlated with ΔPE and thus introduce extremely high spurious correlation with ΔY. Apparently, Juster is confused by the relationship between ΔPE^e and, in turn, ΔPE and ΔY and that between ΔPE^e or ΔPE and $\Delta(Y - PE^e)$ or $\Delta(Y - PE)$. Following his line of reasoning, clearly if we had completely reliable anticipatory data for every sector of ΔY, so that $\Delta YE^e = \Delta Y$, he would arrive at the novel conclusion that this was entirely spurious. This is a surprising dereliction for someone who counsels more theory and less arithmetic.[1]

---

[1] If we may be permitted to indulge in a little more arithmetic, the same point can be made in more precise statistical terms. Assume that Z (which now may be regarded

Let us consider the rest of his comments in order. First, he states that "the weight of recent empirical and analytical investigations" has pointed in the direction of "more, not less, disaggregation" and "more rather than less complex forms." Now, since we indicate in our paper that we are not aware of any such "weight of . . . investigations" and, in fact, are attempting to obtain some relevant empirical evidence, we would have preferred a little less ex-cathedra statement and a little more empirical evidence—as a matter of fact, any at all. In our revised paper, which incorporates other results presented at this conference as well as new results we have obtained, we note further evidence of the unsatisfactory basis of the common implicit assumption that disaggregation and complexity improve forecasting results.

A second criticism seems to be that we place too much stress on the ability to predict as the most satisfactory test of a forecasting model and pay too little attention to improvements in fit for the base period and "far too little" attention to "the presence or absence of economically satisfactory . . . signs for regression coefficients." Juster seems to have completely missed the reason for our stress on ability to predict. The simple point, which we do discuss at some length and which, as Juster illustrates, is frequently overlooked, is that it is relatively easy to get good fits and much more difficult to get good forecasts. Concerning our neglect in failing to point out economically unsatisfactory signs, which seems to be implied in Juster's comments, we wish he would give one example. It is true, as we point out, that an adequate test of predictive performance requires more than the extremely small number (typically two) of forecasting periods we used, and we stress the need for continuing to test in the light of subsequent performance whatever models are adduced. However, Juster does not seem to realize that while a couple of good forecasts may not give strong support to a forecasting model a couple of bad forecasts create grave doubt about its usefulness. This does not mean, of course, that the model which fails in

---

as a generalization of PE^e) is an autonomous variable highly correlated with PE and that $Y = PE + C$, with C, or consumption, largely induced. Then we may write $PE = a_1 + b_1Z + u_1$ or $b_1Z = PE - a_1 - u_1$, and fit the regression $Y = a_2 + b_2Z + u_2$ which may also be written

$$Y = a_2 + \frac{b_2}{b_1}PE - \frac{a_1 b_2}{b_1} - \frac{b_2}{b_1}u_1 + u_2.$$

Clearly it makes little sense to talk of spurious correlation between Z and Y simply because PE is part of Y.

this critical sense may not or should not be resurrected in some modified form but that at the very least some such modification is called for.

Juster's third comment is that our test of predictive utility of inventory anticipations in a GNP model does not permit us to tell whether the predictions have been improved. He states, "If the inventory anticipations improve predictions of inventory change (I_i) but knowing I_i does not help much (for this period) in predicting the change in GNP, one can hardly say that the model is not improved." If he had looked at the discussion several paragraphs beyond the ones he is apparently commenting on, he would have noted that the inventory anticipations data are (as yet) not helpful in explaining deviations between estimated and actual inventory investment.

Next, Juster raises the banner of measurement without theory in connection with our use of anticipations data in forecasting relationships. He raises the question of the use of a large number of *ex post* variables in conjunction with inventory anticipations to explain the level of inventory investment as against the use of inventory anticipations in conjunction with deviations between the actual and anticipated levels of operational variables which entered into the inventory anticipation. We thought we made it clear that we had to rely on the *ex post* variables for the period as a whole because of the small number of observations for which inventory anticipations data were available and that we simply related residuals from the *ex post* regressions to the anticipatory data over the period for which this was possible. Clearly, we would have introduced the anticipatory data in another manner had more data been available. However, in any case, there is another point which Juster seems to miss completely. Anticipated inventory investment can be introduced in conjunction with *ex post* variables (even without, say, a sales minus anticipated sales type of term), since it may very well have an informational content that *ex post* variables do not have. On the other hand, the *ex post* variables may be necessary to take account of firms that do not do serious jobs of budgeting. We plan, of course, to use deviations of other relevant operational variables (such as sales) from expected values in conjunction with anticipated inventories when enough data become available. Not too surprisingly our limited experiment to introduce such a term in this paper was not successful. Probably this was due, at least in part, to the small number of relevant observations but also to the lack of anticipatory inventory and sales data for the trade sector.[2] Juster evidently was not aware that one of the authors, in collaboration with another colleague, was perhaps the first to use the type of analysis which he is recommending here, in a situation, of course, where the data were available.[3]

We have somewhat weaker reservations about his discussion of the inadequacies of the consumer intentions data that we attempted to use for improving predictability. However, when he says that the tests "might be inconclusive," this is really all we said, though we have no objection to its repetition.

Again, we have no strong reservations to Juster's comment that, "much more analysis of cross-section data seems essential if any of these kinds of relationships are ever to be usefully incorporated into forecasting models." However, we might point out the rather obvious point that we relied on other work, cross-section as well as time series, done by ourselves and others in this area. We feel Juster is raising a straw man when he states that he would argue that "anticipatory data cannot be effectively incorporated into forecasting models without extensive use of cross sections to decide whether and how these variables relate to spending decisions." Obviously, we do not disagree, but the ultimate utility of such information must be in the insights it gives us into time series behavior, and it is this that we are testing.

In the rest of Juster's Comment he takes issue with our examination of the relationships between changes in various expenditure categories and changes in GNP, and then proceeds to set up an alternative scheme which he feels is superior. We are afraid that again he misses the rather obvious point of what we were trying to do. We were not attempting a breakdown of GNP components into "autonomous" and "induced" classifications in the section to which he refers, since we had not yet set up the subsequent simple forecasting models which do indicate the assumed flow of causation. Our initial correlations were simply directed to determining which components of GNP had been primarily associated with the short-run changes in total GNP; but, as we were careful to point out, no

---

[2] However, it might be pointed out that the Department of Commerce did not find sales deviations useful in explaining quarterly unrealized inventory investment even for the manufacturing sector, for which both sets of data are available over the limited period covered (see Murray F. Foss, "Manufacturers' Inventory and Sales Expectations: A Progress Report on a New Survey," *Survey of Current Business*, August 1961).

[3] Irwin Friend and Jean Bronfenbrenner, "Business Investment Programs and Their Realization," *Survey of Current Business*, December 1950.

direction of causation was being assumed and the question of which variables were autonomous was not being considered. It is only in our forecasting models that we indicate the nature of our economic assumptions regarding autonomous and induced variables; and, as a matter of fact, we are inclined to believe the stipulation of a complete forecasting model is the only satisfactory way of doing this. Inventory investment may be largely induced but still may be the most important variable whose fluctuations have to be explained if we are interested in accounting for fluctuations in GNP. We are rather hesitant to expatiate on so obvious a point, but we shall do so anyhow. If ΔGNP is not highly correlated with ΔX_i, a component of GNP, then there is a large variance in the residuals of the regression of either of these variables on the other. On the other hand, if ΔGNP and ΔX_i are highly correlated, ΔX_i may be induced with small residuals or may be autonomous and free of negative correlation with ΔX_j. As a matter of research strategy, components of the second type are clearly worth more attention than the first, even though the results cast no light on how "autonomous" or "induced" the different ΔX_i are. In this connection, while it is not greatly relevant to our argument, Juster's statement that "the only clear evidence that changes in a given spending sector may be the cause, rather than the consequence, of a change in income consists of an observed low correlation with income change" seems to be incorrect. A little reflection, for example, would indicate that the correlation between ΔY and ΔD, which is durable consumption, might be close to zero. Juster would, therefore, apparently conclude that ΔD is autonomous, even though in fact ΔD and ΔN, which is nondurable consumption, were highly negatively correlated and even though the relation of ΔD per se with ΔY was not meaningful, whereas that of ΔC and ΔY was. Incidentally, we assume his reference to I_i as a clear cause of GNP change, in accordance with the criteria he sets up, is simply an oversight.

Turning finally to his suggested prescription for determining whether a component of GNP is induced or autonomous, we might point out that we have used a related mechanism for helping to determine the appropriate nature of structural relations.[4] We really do not see its utility, in the context in which Juster is trying to use it, for two reasons. First, no rigorous criteria are used to take care of

[4] Irwin Friend and Robert Jones, "The Concept of Saving," and "Rejoinder," *Consumption and Saving*, Philadelphia, 1960, Vol. II.

the only realistic case, that of partial substitutability (unlike the treatment in the Friend-Jones paper previously referred to); and secondly, in the case of partial substitutability, both his equations would lead to biased estimates of parameters.[5] In any case, we consider vastly preferable the approach we follow in erecting a set of structural relationships.

FURTHER REPLY to Juster

We feel that Juster's supplementary comments (see footnotes to his Comment) do not require any modification of our reply, with two minor exceptions. First, we are happy to correct our erroneous impression that his reference to inventory investment as a clear cause of GNP change was an oversight. Second, and more important, we still consider his treatment of spurious correlation between ΔY and ΔPE^e as mystical, in spite of the modification he has made in his original comments from ΔPE^e *would* still be correlated with ΔY *because* this first term (ΔPE_t) is obviously correlated with ΔY, even if anticipated and actual investment were entirely unrelated, to ΔPE^e *might* still be correlated with ΔY *if* the first term (ΔPE_t) has a *strong enough correlation* with ΔY. We thought we had indicated in fairly precise statistical terms that in writing, as Juster does, $\Delta PE^e = \Delta PE_t + (PE^e - PE_t)$, there is no basis for talking of spurious correlation between ΔPE^e and ΔY simply because ΔPE_t is part of ΔY. We might point out, as a last attempt at clarification, that while ΔPE_t is clearly part of ΔY, it is not part of ΔPE^e, because of the negative correlation between the two terms into which Juster divides ΔPE^e.

[5] It might be useful to point out that in Juster's equations 1.0 and 1.1, even if A is completely autonomous, R and B, holding A constant, may still be positively correlated, ~~CONTRARY TO~~ the assumption Juster makes. To indicate the theoretical rationale, there presumably is implicit in Juster's equations something equivalent to the following model, where t is time, ϵ_1, ϵ_2, and ϵ_3 are random residuals, and $f_1(t)$ and $f_2(t)$ may, of course, be highly complicated functions:

(1)	$A = f_1(t) + \epsilon_1$
(2)	$R = \alpha_2 + \beta_2 Y + \epsilon_2$
(3)	$B = \alpha_3 + \beta_3 Y + f_2(t) + \epsilon_3$
(4)	$Y = A + R + B$

Given A, a negative correlation between R and B is certain only if the residuals are negatively correlated and B has no autonomous part (i.e., $f_2(t) = 0$). But if A is given without t being held constant, then variation in $f_2(t)$ and, hence, in Y may still occur; and the positive correlation of the Y terms in equations 2 and 3 may still outweigh the negative correlation of ϵ_2 and ϵ_3, giving positive partial correlation of R and B, even holding A constant. There is, of course, no obvious reason to assume the negative correlation of residuals which Juster appears to have in mind.

An Empirical Model of United States Economic Growth: An Exploratory Study in Applied Capital Theory

ALBERT ANDO

MASSACHUSETTS INSTITUTE OF TECHNOLOGY

Introduction

RECENT publications in economics, both books and journals, are full of contributions to our knowledge of the process of economic growth.[1] At the same time, anyone who attempts to read through this literature cannot avoid a sense of frustration because of the conspicuous absence either of relevant data or of an adequate theoretical framework, depending upon whether he is attempting to test a theory of his own, or trying to organize a body of empirical information into a coherent system. Upon reflection, the conclusion seems unavoidable that, so far, communication between those whose primary interest is the construction of a theory of the process of economic growth and those who are concerned primarily with the organization of empirical knowledge about the process of economic growth has been poor at best.

We are often reminded that the Keynesian Revolution in economics had the profound impact that it did on the thinking of economists because the theoretical contribution of Keynes coincided with the then new availability of empirical information on aggregative income

NOTE: This paper was written in association with Ralph Beals of the Massachusetts Institute of Technology and David Kresge of Harvard University. The research was partly supported by a grant from the National Science Foundation. I am indebted to a number of my colleagues and students, particularly to Professors Franco Modigliani and Louis Lefeber, Messrs. Stephen Goldfeld, Donald Tucker and Robert Pollack of the Massachusetts Institute of Technology, who have read the entire manuscript and have given me extensive and helpful comments; to Mr. Ronald Teigen of the University of Michigan, who gave me valuable computational assistance; to Mrs. Felicity Skidmore of the Massachusetts Institute of Technology for her expert editing of the manuscript; and to Professor Franklin Fisher of the Massachusetts Institute of Technology, who was patient enough to listen to my incessant complaints.

I also wish to express my gratitude to Professor James Tobin of Yale University, who generously permitted me to see his unpublished manuscript on monetary theory.

[1] See the References at the end of this paper for a list of more recent contributions on this subject. The list is not meant to be exhaustive.

and output that resulted from the painstaking efforts of the group of economists in and around the NBER. It was good fortune for economists and for those who use the findings of economists as the basis of their policy decisions that the concepts used to organize the income and output data and the concepts in terms of which Keynes formulated his theory were sufficiently similar for these two bodies of knowledge to complement each other.

While some of the more important contributions to the current theoretical discussion of the problem of economic growth were made a number of years ago [18] [36] [54],[2] the attempt to estimate parameters in growth models started only in very recent years. Similarly, systematic organization of the data dealing with growth, particularly those relating to accumulation of capital, is very new, as evidenced by the yet uncompleted NBER project on capital formation. It may still be too early to expect these two quite separate enterprises to be well coordinated. However, if we are to increase our knowledge of the process of United States economic growth, such a coordination must eventually be made; and this essay is an attempt to make a modest contribution in this direction.

The model discussed in the first section is a very simple one-commodity model which is a slight variation of the models often used in classroom exercises, and it is presented here briefly to provide motivation for the direction of generalizations undertaken in the subsequent sections. The second section of the paper is addressed mainly to two questions: first, which of the simple, convenient properties of the single-commodity model can be preserved when the model is generalized to contain many commodities, particularly if the production of each commodity is subject to its own distinct rate of technological change? Second, is it possible to define a concept of aggregate capital for which data are likely to be available, and for which a useful interpretation can be given in terms of a less aggregated model? The third and last section of this paper deals with a special case of the model presented in the second section. In this special case only two goods, a consumption good and a capital good, are distinguished. The consequences of the introduction of government and a monetary system into our model are then investigated, and some preliminary empirical findings are presented. In view of the complexity of the model and the inadequacies of the data, these

---

[2] The number in brackets refers to the similarly numbered item in the References at the end of this paper.

empirical findings should not be regarded as anything more than rough consistency checks for the model and an illustration of the use to which the model can be put if more reliable data become available.

I. A Model with a Single Good

Models of growth in which there is only one good have been studied by a number of authors, particularly by Harrod [25] [26], Domar [11], Solow [42], Tobin [46], and Ando and Modigliani [1] [2]. The purpose of reviewing them in this section is to provide a point of reference for later models to be considered in this paper and to facilitate the interpretation of these simple models in terms of a less aggregated model. Solow has shown that the extreme instability of the Harrod-Domar model of growth is due to the fixed coefficient production function that they implicitly assume. Thus, one of the crucial questions that must be faced at the outset is the choice of the production function. In this paper, I shall adopt, in contrast to Harrod and Domar, the Cobb-Douglas production function.

The aggregate production function is at best what Samuelson calls the "Clark-Ramsey Parable" [38], and the capital stock which goes into the aggregate production function cannot represent concrete, physical capital. In the next section of this paper, it will be shown that it is best interpreted as representing the value of existing capital, heterogeneous as it is, valued at reproduction cost, adjusted for changes in the general price level.[3] Even if the capital coefficients are absolutely fixed for production of each specific commodity, the composition of commodities produced varies over time, and there is no reason to believe that the relation between the aggregate value of capital and the value of output must remain constant over time—i.e., that the capital-output ratio should remain fixed. It seems more reasonable to represent this relationship in a somewhat more flexible form. In addition, in growth models we are dealing with a very long-run, broad pattern of economic relationships, ignoring the short-run adjustment problems. In the short run, there may be severe limitations on the way existing physical capital can be combined with labor to produce output. Given enough time, however, the composition and structure of capital can be changed, and the value of capital available per unit of labor can be shifted

[3] More exactly, it should be the market value of the existing capital, but the market value would be the same in the equilibrium as defined in this paper.

much more easily. These considerations suggest that a production function with a fixed capital coefficient is not an appropriate representation of reality. This, however, is not a sufficient reason to adopt the Cobb-Douglas production function, and my reason for doing so is largely the ease with which it can be handled analytically.[4]

I shall work with a production function of the form

$$(1.1) \qquad Y_t = X e^{gt} E_t^{1-\beta} K_t^{\beta}$$

where Y_t = the rate of output per year at time t

$\quad E_t$ = the rate of employment per year at time t (in man-hours)

$\quad K_t$ = the stock of productive capital employed at time t, measured in terms of output

$\quad g$ = the rate of technological change, assumed to be exogenous and constant over time

$\quad \beta$ = constant, relative share of income accruing to capital

$\quad X$ = a scale factor

$\quad e$ = the base of a natural logarithm

I assume either that the depreciation of capital takes place in the declining balance form at a fixed rate, or that capital, once built, never depreciates but has a given probability of becoming unusable, independent of its past history or age. These two interpretations lead to the identical mathematical formulation; so the reader may adopt either of them. In addition, technological change reduces the value of existing capital by making more efficient capital available. For example, suppose that capitals I and II have been produced last year and this year, respectively, at identical costs, but that because of the changes in technology, when combined with the same amount of labor, I produces only 0.8 times as much output as II. In this case an original unit of I is treated as 0.8 unit. Since technological change is assumed to be occurring at a constant rate, this consideration increases the rate of depreciation described above, and no further complication in our analysis is needed. With this interpretation of the meaning of K, the demand for capital and employment can be written as marginal conditions as follows:

[4] Recently, Arrow, Chenery, Minhas, and Solow have suggested a somewhat more general form of homogeneous production function of the first order, which includes both the fixed coefficient case and the Cobb-Douglas case as special cases, and yet is relatively easy to work with [4]. A substantial part of the results reported in this paper appears to be sustained even if the Cobb-Douglas function is replaced by this more general function, though the difficulties of estimation will be increased enormously.

(1.2)
$$r_t + \delta = \frac{\partial Y_t}{\partial K_t} = \beta \frac{Y_t}{K_t}$$

(1.3)
$$w_t = \frac{\partial Y_t}{\partial E_t} = (1 - \beta) \frac{Y_t}{E_t}$$

where w_t = wage rate in terms of output
$\quad r_t$ = rental rate on capital per year, in terms of output
$\quad \delta$ = the rate of depreciation of capital, including the rate of obsolescence, as defined above

The supply of labor is assumed to be given exogenously, and takes the form:

(1.4)
$$L_t = L_0 e^{nt}$$

The market equilibrium condition in the labor market is then:

(1.5)
$$E_t = L_t$$

where L_t = labor supply at time t
$\quad L_0$ = a constant
$\quad n$ = a constant, representing the rate of increase of labor supply

The supply of capital is given by the savings function. It is here that I will depart from Solow [42] and follow the formulation proposed by Ando and Modigliani [1] [2]. Most writers in the past, including Harrod [25], Domar [11], Solow [42], and Tobin [47], have assumed a constant saving-income ratio in their growth models. This is not as unrealistic an assumption as it may sound at first, since work by Goldsmith [20] [21] shows that the saving-income ratio for the United States does appear to be reasonably stable in the long run. Nevertheless, I will adopt the consumption function given below:

(1.6)
$$C_t = \alpha_1 w_t E_t + \alpha_2 A_t$$

where C_t = the rate of consumption per year
$\quad A_t$ = the value of net worth held by consumers, in terms of output
$\quad \alpha_1$ and α_2 are parameters, and assumed to be constant over time

The rationale and the empirical evidence for this consumption function are reported elsewhere [3]. In the context of the present paper, equation (1.6) has the advantage that (1) it is consistent with the stable saving-income ratio in the long run; (2) it provides a more explicit behavioral hypothesis about the consumers' holding of wealth; (3) in the short run, it makes the saving-income ratio move with income; (4) the market equilibrium condition for capital stock can be stated (as in equation 1.8 below), rather than the market equilibrium condition for the increment of capital stock—in my opinion, the former condition is more appropriate as a part of a growth model than the latter.

In this simple model, in which government activities and the existence of money and other financial assets, as well as land, are ignored, the rate of change of A is equal to the rate of output less the rate of depreciation (defined broadly to include the rate of obsolescence as described above) less the rate of consumption. Thus,

$$(1.7) \qquad \dot{A}_t = Y_t - \delta A_t - C_t$$

Again in this simple model, net worth of consumers consists entirely of ownership of the capital good; so the supply of capital is equal to the net worth of consumers. Hence, the market equilibrium condition for capital is given by

$$(1.8) \qquad K_t = A_t$$

As in any general equilibrium system, one of the market equilibrium conditions (in this case, that for output) is redundant. There are eight equations (1.1) through (1.8), in eight unknowns, Y_t, A_t, K_t, L_t, E_t, C_t, w_t, and r_t.

To analyze the behavior over time of this system, let us note that Euler's theorem applied to equation (1.1) gives

$$(1.9) \qquad Y_t = w_t E_t + (r_t + \delta) K_t$$

Appropriate substitutions then result in:

$$\dot{A}_t = w_t E_t + (r_t + \delta) K_t - \delta A_t - \alpha_1 w_t E_t - \alpha_2 A_t$$
$$= (1 - \alpha_1) w_t E_t + (r_t - \alpha_2) A_t$$

$$(1.10) \qquad \frac{\dot{A}_t}{A_t} = k_t + (1 - \alpha_1) \left(\frac{w_t E_t}{A_t} - \frac{k_t + \alpha_2 - r_t}{1 - \alpha_1} \right)$$

where k_t is any number. In particular, we are free to define

$$k_t = \frac{\dot{K}_t}{K_t}$$

We are specifically interested in the existence of a growth path of this system on which k_t and r_t remain constant over time. If such a path exists and is unique, we shall define it as the *equilibrium* path of growth for this system. Equation (1.1) can be rewritten as

(1.11a)
$$\frac{\dot{Y}_t}{Y_t} = g + \beta \frac{\dot{K}_t}{K_t} + (1 - \beta) \frac{\dot{E}_t}{E_t}$$

Equations (1.2), (1.9), and (1.10) indicate that, if k_t and r_t were to remain constant over time, so must the ratio of $w_t E_t$ to A_t, and furthermore the rates of growth of Y_t, $w_t E_t$, and A_t must all be the same. With this consideration, inserting the definition of k_t into equation (1.11a) yields

(1.11)
$$k_t = g + \beta k_t + (1 - \beta)n = \frac{g}{1 - \beta} + n$$

Equations (1.10) and (1.11) imply that if the rate of growth of the labor force is given by n and the rates of growth of A and of Y are both given by k defined by (1.11), the rate of rental on capital, r_t, will remain constant over time, thus defining an equilibrium path of growth. It can be shown that such a growth path in fact exists and that it is stable. To show this, let us define a new variable $a_t \equiv w_t E_t / A_t$. Substitution of this definition and that of k_t into equation (1.10) gives

(1.12a)
$$a_t \equiv \frac{w_t E_t}{A_t} = \frac{k_t + \alpha_2 - r_t}{1 - \alpha_1}$$

In addition, equations (1.2) and (1.3) and the definition of a imply

(1.12b)
$$r_t + \delta = \frac{\beta}{1 - \beta} a_t$$

Equation (1.12) can be solved to yield:

(1.13)
$$r^* = \frac{\beta(k + \alpha_2) - \delta(1 - \beta)(1 - \alpha_1)}{1 - \alpha_1(1 - \beta)}$$

(1.14)
$$a^* = (1 - \beta) \frac{k + \alpha_2 + \delta}{1 - \alpha_1(1 - \beta)}$$

To show that the path defined above is stable, suppose that, by some accident,

$$\frac{w_t E_t}{K_t} = a^* + \Delta a, \quad \Delta a > 0.$$

333

Then, through equation (1.2),

$$r_t = r^* + \Delta r = \frac{\beta}{1 - \beta}(a^* + \Delta a) - \delta$$

$$= \left(\frac{\beta}{1 - \beta}a^* - \delta\right) + \frac{\beta}{1 - \beta}\Delta a$$

$$= r^* + \frac{\beta}{1 - \beta}\Delta a$$

Substitution of these values into equation (1.10) yields

(1.15)
$$\frac{\dot{A}_t}{A_t} = k + \Delta a\left[(1 - \alpha_1) + \frac{\beta}{1 - \beta}\right]$$

Substituting this result into (1.11a) finally gives

(1.16)
$$\frac{\dot{Y}_t}{Y_t} = k + \beta\Delta a\left[(1 - \alpha_1) + \frac{\beta}{1 - \beta}\right]$$

Comparison of (1.15) and (1.16) shows that if a is greater than a^*, i.e., if the ratio of labor income to capital is greater than its equilibrium value, capital is growing at a faster rate than output. But because of equation (1.3), the rate of growth of labor income is identical to the rate of growth of output. Hence, the equilibrium path of growth defined above is stable.[5]

The model analyzed above is obviously too simple, and contains a number of drastic assumptions that are not tenable if it is to be capable of helping us interpret long-run data for the United States. At this point it would be useful to make some observation on the less tenable assumptions underlying the above model in order to determine the directions in which it must be generalized. As in any work of this kind, the adequacy of a model depends on its purpose. As was indicated earlier, the main purpose of this paper is to explain the data relating to the accumulation of capital stock in the United States economy and its relation to the growth of capacity to produce output in the long run, neglecting short-run cyclical fluctuations. It is quite feasible that the short-run fluctuations may have serious effects on the long-run trend of the economy, making it necessary to analyze the short-run fluctuations and the long-run trends of the

[5] It must be added here that the above analysis is valid only to the extent that the parameters in the consumption function, α_1 and α_2, are invariant under changes in r. However, it can be easily shown that, if α_2 is a function of r while α_1 is independent of r (as is likely to be the case), the above analysis is completely unaffected provided that the absolute value of the first derivative of α_2 with respect to r is less than unity.

economy simultaneously; but such an undertaking must be deferred to a future paper.[6]

In the above model, aggregate capital, K, was not clearly defined, and was taken to mean the sum of the value of capital stock, without a justification. This, in turn, was equated to the value of consumers' net worth. The meaning of aggregate capital, and of the aggregate production function that has aggregate capital as one of its arguments, has been the subject of sharp controversy in recent years. We have learned from these controversies that this question can be discussed fruitfully only in the context of a specific model. Accordingly, in the next section, we shall define a model involving many capital goods that are distinct from one another, and endeavor to exhibit a set of assumptions under which the concepts of aggregate capital and aggregate production functions are meaningful. Furthermore, consumers' net worth in reality includes, in addition to the value of reproducible physical capital, the debt of the United States government (a part of money and United States securities), non-reproducible wealth (land), consumer durables, and a few other items. Problems arising from these discrepancies, and the roles of government and of the monetary system will be discussed in the third section of this paper.

Before turning to the task of generalizing the model, let us pause briefly and consider whether the simple model presented above possesses any resemblance to reality in terms of the available data.

I assume the following numerical values for the basic parameters of the system:

$$\alpha_1 = .65 \qquad g = .017$$
$$\alpha_2 = .07 \qquad \beta = .35$$
$$n = .006 \qquad \delta = .04$$

The values for α_1 and α_2 are taken from a study by Ando and Modigliani reported elsewhere [3], and these values, after rounding, appear to be reasonably stable over the period 1910–59, excluding war years. The value of n is the average rate of increase of man-hours per year according to Kendrick [28]. This figure appears to be surprisingly low, particularly since the average rate of increase of the labor force, according to *Historical Statistics* [50], is close to 0.017. However, I believe that the figure given by Kendrick is about as accurate as any that could be found. The figure for g is the aver-

---

[6] Some preliminary analysis dealing with this problem has been reported elsewhere [1] [2].

age of the rate of technological change reported by Solow [45]. The value of β is a problem, since there are a variety of estimates reported in a number of sources. I take the figure of 0.35, a round figure lifted from Solow in the work cited above, to make it consistent with the value of g. These figures imply, through equation (1.11), that the rate of growth of output should be roughly 3.2 per cent per year. The average rate of growth of net national product as implied by the data reported by Goldsmith [21] for 1896–1950 is roughly 3.4 per cent per year, a figure somewhat larger than the one mentioned above. The cause of this discrepancy may be that the periods to which each of the parameters refer do not match exactly. I shall use the figure 3.2 per cent for k for this illustration.

I need to guess at the value of one more parameter, the rate of depreciation. Goldsmith uses various rates of depreciation for different types of capital goods in his *Study of Savings*, and a rough computation to get a weighted average of these rates suggests that the over-all rate is about 4 to 5 per cent per year [21]. For the computation in this section, I accept the figure of 4 per cent for the rate of depreciation. Then, equation (1.13) implies that the rate of return on capital should be roughly 4.5 per cent per year, and equation (1.14) implies that the ratio of labor income to the value of consumer net worth should be approximately 0.16.

The table below shows historical values of ratios of property income to consumer's net worth and of labor income to consumer's net worth, averaged over the periods indicated. It should be clear that the comparison of these figures with the theoretical expectations of r^* and a^* suggested above cannot be more than an encouraging indication that our analysis should be generalized and refined, since there is a great deal of discrepancy at this stage of our analysis between the theoretical concepts used in the model and the definitions forced on us by the empirical data.[7]

[7] Since the model in this section does not allow for taxes and government expenditures, a decision must be made as to whether to use income after or before taxes. The figures reported here are labor income *after* taxes, but the ratio is of nonlabor income *before* taxes to the value of net worth. The choice may appear inconsistent, and the justification must await the results of the later model, involving taxes explicitly. As the model does not allow explicitly for the existence of intangible assets such as securities of the United States government and money and for nonreproducible tangible assets (land), we are also faced with the choice between total net worth of consumers and net worth of consumers less intangible assets and land. The figures in the following table are computed using total net worth. Here again, discussion of the possible bias due to this choice must be postponed until a later section, where I shall deal with a model that explicitly allows for the existence of intangible assets and land.

	$\dfrac{Y - wE}{A}$	$\dfrac{wE}{A}$
1910–17	.054	.16
1921–29	.062	.16
1935–41	.034	.16
1947–58	.058	.17

Even so, the correspondence between the figures reported in the preceding table and the theoretical expectations implied by the figures for the parameters given earlier is reasonably good. The fairly low value of the ratio of property income to net worth for 1935–41 is undoubtedly the consequence of the depressed state of the economy and partial unemployment of capital stock, and suggests that if we are to do serious statistical work using this type of model, we must adjust for underutilization of capital and labor.

On the other hand, for all other periods the actual rate of return is much higher than that implied by the values of parameters through equation (1.15). This is partly because the model does not allow for the existence of uncertainty and of monopoly power, which in the real world tend to make the rate of return somewhat higher. In addition, the actual figures reported, as mentioned above, represent the rate of return before taxes, and the effects of taxes on these rates must be explicitly treated before a meaningful comparison can be made.

In addition, there are reasons to believe that the values of the basic parameters, particularly those for g and n, have changed somewhat during the first half of the twentieth century; and if so, we must allow for these changes in our calculations.

We conclude this section with the acknowledgment that the model presented here is totally inadequate and must be generalized and refined substantially in order to explain the long-run data of the United States economy even approximately, and with the cautious hope that when generalized and refined, this type of model may yield reasonably satisfactory results.

II. A Model with One Consumption Good and Many Capital Goods

In this section, the consequences of recognizing heterogeneity of capital goods will be analyzed in detail, and the conditions examined under which the concept of aggregate capital can be meaningfully defined.[8]

II. A. PROPERTIES OF THE MODEL

The system to be analyzed is given by equations (2.1)–(2.11) below. In all cases, $i = 1, 2, \ldots, J$ and $j = 1, 2, \ldots, J - 1$.

$$(2.1) \qquad O^i = X_i e^{g_i t} \prod_{j=1}^{J-1} K^{ij\beta_{ij}} E^{i(1-\beta_i)},$$

where

$$\beta_i = \sum_{j=1}^{J-1} \beta_{ij}$$

$$(2.2) \qquad p^j(r^j + \delta_j) = \beta_{ij} \frac{O^i}{K^{ij}} p^i$$

$$(2.3) \qquad p^J w = (1 - \beta_i) \frac{O^i}{E^i} p^i$$

$$(2.4) \qquad L_0 e^{nt} = \sum_{i=1}^{J} E^i \equiv E$$

$$(2.5) \qquad K^j = \sum_{i=1}^{J} K^{ij}$$

$$(2.6) \qquad C = \alpha_1 w E + \alpha_2 \frac{A}{p^J}$$

$$(2.7) \qquad C = O^J$$

$$(2.8) \qquad O^j = K^j + \delta_j K^j$$

$$(2.9) \qquad A = \sum_{j=1}^{J-1} p^j K^j$$

$$(2.10) \qquad r = r^j + \frac{\dot{p}^j}{p^j}$$

$$(2.11) \qquad p^J = 1$$

The convention adopted is that indexes $1, 2, \ldots, J - 1$ represent capital goods, and the index J denotes the consumption good. The time subscript is omitted except where any possibility of confusion exists. In the definitions below, $i = 1, 2, \ldots, J$ and $j = 1, 2, \ldots, J - 1$:

[8] It will be assumed that there exists a single homogeneous consumption good. It is possible to generalize the model to cover the case of a number of heterogeneous consumption goods and still keep most of the conclusions unaltered, provided that price and income elasticities of demand for all consumption goods are unity. Cf. the results given by Dhrymes [10].

O^i = the rate of output of ith good, in physical units
E^i = man-hours employed in production of the ith good
K^{ij} = quantity of jth capital employed in production of the ith good, in physical units
K^j = the existing stock of the jth capital good
r^j = the rate of rental accruing to the jth capital good, in terms of the jth capital good
p^i = price of the jth good
w = wage rate, in terms of the consumption good
C = the rate of consumption, in terms of the consumption good
A = net worth of consumers
r = the rate of interest

Equations (2.1) through (2.11) constitute a system of $J(J + 4) + 2$ equations in the same number of variables. With i and j having the ranges noted above, the parameters of the system are:

δ_j = the rate of depreciation of the jth capital good
n = the rate of growth of labor, measured in man-hours
g_i = the rate of technological change in the production of the ith good; assumed to be exogenous in the system
β_{ij} = parameters of production functions
α_1, α_2 = parameters of the consumption function
X_i = scale factors in the production functions
L_0 = scale factor in the labor supply

Equation (2.11) states that the consumption good will be used as the nummeraire in this section.

Equations (2.1) are production functions. As in the case of (1.1), it is assumed that technological change is neutral and constant over time, though the rate (g_i) is *different* for different industries. Unlike the case of (1.1), however, K^{ij} represents the number of machines of the jth type employed in the ith industry. Because of this, one may seriously question the appropriateness of the Cobb-Douglas production function, with its unitary elasticity of substitution. At best, this form of production function can be justified only as an approximate description of the relationship between output and inputs in the long run when everything is optimally adjusted. Equations (2.2) and (2.3) are marginal conditions, and they define the demand conditions for labor and capital stock; (2.4) and (2.5) are market equilibrium conditions for labor and capital stock, respectively. Equation (2.6) is the consumption function, which has already been discussed in Section I, while equation (2.7) is the market equilibrium condition for the consumption good. Equation (2.8) gives the market equilibrium conditions for the capital goods, and states that the supply of each capital good must be equal to the rate of net increase of demand for the stock of that capital good plus the depreciation of the stock. Equation (2.9) defines net worth of consumers. Equation (2.10) represents the well-known proposition that, for the markets for many capital goods to be simultaneously in equilibrium, it is necessary that the rate of rental of each capital good measured in terms of itself plus the rate of change of its price must be equal to the rate of interest.[9]

The condition equivalent to equation (1.7) in the foregoing section I can be derived from the above system, and is exhibited below:

(2.12)

$$\dot{A} = P^J wE + \sum_{j=1}^{J-1} p^j(r^j + \delta_j)K^j + \sum_{j=1}^{J-1} P^j K^j - \sum_{j=1}^{J-1} \delta_j \dot{P}^j K^j - P^J C$$

It will be convenient to define here the following notations:

$$a \equiv \frac{P^J wE}{A}$$

$$\pi_j \equiv \frac{\dot{P}^j}{P^j} \qquad j = 1, 2, \ldots, J-1$$

$$k_j \equiv \frac{\dot{K}^j}{K^j} \qquad j = 1, 2, \ldots, J-1$$

$$\phi_j \equiv \frac{P^j O^j}{P^J O^J} \qquad j = 1, 2, \ldots, J$$

Note that $\phi_J = 1$ by definition.

The behavior of the system defined by equations (2.1) through (2.11) can be analyzed in a number of ways. The analysis presented below concentrates on the situation in which all k_j's are constant over time. It will be shown that a growth path on which all k_j's are constant exists, and that such a growth path (which will be called the "equilibrium growth path" in this paper) exhibits a number of distinctive characteristics.

The reason for the special attention given to this path is that, regardless of the initial conditions, the system will eventually approach the equilibrium path of growth, given enough time.[10] Thus,

---

[9] For a discussion of this condition, see Samuelson [37] [39].

[10] The stability for the general case has not been rigorously proved, but a sufficient number of special cases has been proved; so we feel the conjecture in the text is a reasonably safe one.

if the basic structure of the United States economy bears any resemblance to the system specified by equations (2.1)–(2.11), it may
be expected to fluctuate around the equilibrium path, and the long-
run data for the United States economy should be roughly consistent
with the general characteristics of the equilibrium path, showing
minor deviations at all times and major deviations at some times.
Therefore, in order to see whether or not the long-run data for the
United States confirm in broad outline the predictions of the model
proposed in this paper, it is only necessary to exhibit the characteristics of the equilibrium path of growth—a task much easier than
that of setting down the properties of the model in general. It must
be emphasized that the data should not be expected to conform to
the properties of the equilibrium path in detail; but the long-run
data are very rough in any case, making it impossible to judge
predictions of the model in detail. However, our decision to compare
the data against the equilibrium path does imply that we should
exclude from our consideration observations for years of the Great
Depression and war, and that we should make adjustments in the
data for cyclical underemployment of labor and resources.

If k_j's are to remain constant over time, the equations (2.8) imply[11]

$$(2.13) \qquad \frac{\dot{K}^j}{K^j} = \frac{\dot{O}^j}{O^j} = k_j; \; j = 1, 2, \ldots, J-1$$

Our strategy is to suppose that there exists a set of values of k_j,
π_j, ϕ_j, r^j, r, and a which is consistent with the system (2.1)–(2.11)
and which can remain constant over time, and then attempt to ex-
hibit such a set of values of these variables in terms of the parameters
of the system (2.1)–(2.11). If we can so express them, then we shall
have proved the existence of the equilibrium path on which these
variables remain constant.

From equation (2.2), for any given j and a pair of indexes i and i',
we may write

$$\frac{\beta_{ij}K^{i'j}}{\beta_{i'j}K^{ij}} = \frac{P^{i'}O^{i'}}{P^iO^i} = \frac{\phi_{i'}}{\phi_i}$$

$$\frac{K^j}{K^{ij}} = \sum_{i'=1}^{J} \frac{K^{i'j}}{K^{ij}} = \sum_{i'=1}^{J} \frac{\beta_{i'j}\phi_{i'}}{\beta_{ij}\phi_i}$$

[11] Write (2.8) in the form

$$\frac{O^i}{K^j} = \frac{\dot{K}^j}{K^j} + \delta_j$$

Since δ_j is a constant, $\dot{K}^i/K^i$ is constant if, and only if, O^i/K^i is constant for all t, implying (2.13).

Hence, the relative distributions of capital stocks among industries are given by

$$(2.14a) \qquad \frac{K^{ij}}{K^j} = \frac{\beta_{ij}\phi_i}{\sum\limits_{i=1}^{J} \beta_{ij}\phi_i}; \quad \begin{matrix} i = 1, 2, \dots, J \\ j = 1, 2, \dots, J-1 \end{matrix}$$

Similarly, the relative distribution of labor among industries is given by

$$(2.14b) \qquad \frac{E^i}{E} = \frac{(1-\beta_i)\phi_i}{\sum\limits_{i=1}^{J}(1-\beta_i)\phi_i}; \quad i = 1, 2, \dots, J$$

Equations (2.14) indicate that if the ϕ's remain constant over time, the distribution of factors of production over industries must also remain constant. These constancies, through production functions (2.1) and equation (2.13), imply:

$$(2.15) \qquad k_i = g_i + \sum_{j=1}^{J-1} \beta_{ij}k_j + (1-\beta_i)n; \quad i = 1, 2, \dots, J-1$$

Equation (2.15) can be solved to give values of k_j's, $j = 1, 2, \dots,$ $J-1$, in terms of the g's, β's, and n.

The constancy of the ϕ_j's, through their definition and equations (2.13), implies that

$$(2.16) \qquad \frac{\dot{O}^j}{O^j} = \pi_j + k_j; \quad j = 1, 2, \dots, J-1$$

In addition, from the production function for O^J, we have

$$(2.17) \qquad \frac{\dot{O}^J}{O^J} = g_J + \sum_{j=1}^{J-1} \beta_{Jj}k_j + (1-\beta_J)n$$

When the values of the k_j's obtained from (2.15) are first substituted into (2.17) and the value of $\dot{O}^J/O^J$ so obtained is then substituted into (2.16), the equilibrium values of the π_j's, $j = 1, 2, \dots,$ $J-1$, may be obtained. Thus, the equilibrium values of the k_j's and the π_j's can be expressed in terms of n, the β's, and the g's.

There remains the problem of expressing the equilibrium values of ϕ_j, r^j and a in terms of parameters.

Returning to equations (2.2), using (2.8) and (2.14), the following relations can easily be derived:

$$(2.18) \qquad r^j + \delta_j = \beta_{jj} \frac{\dfrac{O^j}{K^j}}{\dfrac{K^{jj}}{K^j}}$$

$$= \beta_{jj}(k_j + \delta_j)\frac{\sum\limits_{i=1}^{J} \beta_{ij}\phi_i}{\beta_{jj}\phi_j}; j = 1, 2, \ldots, J-1$$

Equations (2.10) and (2.18) yield

$$(2.19) \qquad \pi_1 + \beta_{11}(k_1 + \delta_1)\frac{\sum\limits_{i=1}^{J} \beta_{i1}\phi_i}{\beta_{11}\phi_1} - \delta_1$$

$$= \pi_j + \beta_{jj}(k_j + \delta_j)\frac{\sum\limits_{i=1}^{J} \beta_{ij}\phi_i}{\beta_{jj}\phi_j} - \delta_j; j = 2, 3, \ldots, J-1$$

From equations (2.3) and (2.4), it can be seen that

$$(2.20) \qquad p^J wE = \sum_{i=1}^{J} p^i(1 - \beta_i)O^i$$

Hence, the definition of a can be rewritten as

$$(2.21) \qquad a = \frac{\sum\limits_{i=1}^{J} p^i(1 - \beta_i)O^i}{\sum\limits_{j=1}^{J-1} p^j K^j} = \frac{\sum\limits_{i=1}^{J}(1 - \beta_i)\dfrac{p^i O^i}{p^J O^J}}{\sum\limits_{j=1}^{J-1}\dfrac{p^j O^j}{p^J O^J}\dfrac{K^j}{O^j}} = \frac{\sum\limits_{i=1}^{J}(1 - \beta_i)\phi_i}{\sum\limits_{j}^{J-1}\dfrac{\phi_j}{k_j + \delta_j}}$$

Let us define k_J by

$$(2.22) \qquad k_J \equiv \frac{\dot{O}^J}{O^J} = \pi_j + k_j; j = 1, 2, \ldots, J-1$$

Note that, for any j, on the equilibrium path,

$$\frac{\dfrac{d(p^j K^j)}{dt}}{p^j K^j} = \pi_j + k_j = k_J$$

Hence, it is clear, from the definition of A, that $\dot{A}/A = k_J$.

In view of the definitions of A and r given by (2.9) and (2.10), equation (2.12), after substitution into it of (2.6), may be rewritten as

$$(2.12a) \qquad \dot{A} = p^J wE + rA - \alpha_1 p^J wE - \alpha_2 A$$

343

When both sides of the above equation are divided through by A, and the resulting terms on the right-hand side are rearranged by the addition and subtraction of k_J, it becomes

$$(2.23) \qquad \frac{\dot{A}}{A} = k_J + (1 - \alpha_1)\left(a - \frac{k_J + \alpha_2 - r}{1 - \alpha_1}\right)$$

It is clear from equation (2.23) that A grows at the rate k_J if, and only if, the relation

$$(2.24) \qquad a = \frac{k_J + \alpha_2 - r}{1 - \alpha_1}$$

holds.

We now have equations (2.18), (2.19), (2.21), and (2.24), giving $2J - 1$ conditions to determine $2J - 1$ quantities, $(J - 1)\phi_j$'s, $(J - 1)r^{j}$'s, and a. Since equations (2.15), (2.16), and (2.17) have already determined k_j's and π_j's, it has now been established that there exists a growth path on which the rates of change of prices, π_j, the rates of growth of capital stock, k_j, the relative shares of value of each output to the value of output of the consumption good, ϕ_j, the own rental rates on each capital good, r^j, and the ratio of labor income to the value of consumers' net worth, a, are all constant.

It is easy to show that on the equilibrium path of growth having the properties described above, the over-all share of gross income (defined not to include capital gains) going to labor, denoted by $1 - \beta$, is given by

$$(2.25) \qquad 1 - \beta \equiv \frac{P^J wE}{\sum\limits_{j=1}^{J} P^j O^j} = \frac{\sum\limits_{j=1}^{J} \phi_j(1 - \beta_j)}{\Sigma \phi_j}$$

The ratio of saving to income, denoted by s, is given by

$$(2.26) \qquad s \equiv \frac{\dot{A}}{\sum\limits_{j=1}^{J} P^j O^j} = \frac{\dot{A}}{A} \frac{(1 - \beta)}{\frac{P^J wE}{A}} = k_J \frac{(1 - \beta)}{a}$$

Equation (2.26) states the familiar proposition that the saving-income ratio is the rate of growth of output measured in terms of the consumption good times the asset-income ratio. However, it should be noted that the definition of the saving-income ratio given above is somewhat unusual in that saving is defined to *include* capital gains, while income is defined to *exclude* capital gains.[12]

While, in principle, π_j, k_j, ϕ_j, r^j, and a can all be solved for in terms of parameters of the system, to do so in fact is quite tedious because of the nonlinearity of some of the equations involved. However, it is instructive to write down the expressions for the equilibrium values of these magnitudes for the case in which $J = 2$, i.e., there is only one consumption good and one capital good. Denoting equilibrium values by starred symbols, it can be shown that:

$$(2.27) \qquad k_1^* = \frac{1}{1 - \beta_{11}} g_1 + n,$$

i.e., the rate of growth of the capital stock and of the capital-good production.

$$(2.28) \qquad k_J^* = g_J + \beta_{J1} \frac{1}{1 - \beta_{11}} g_1 + n,$$

i.e., the rate of growth of the consumption-good production.

$$(2.29) \qquad \pi_1^* = g_J - \frac{1 - \beta_{J1}}{1 - \beta_{11}} g_1,$$

i.e., the rate of change of price of the capital good relative to that of the consumption good.

$$(2.30) \qquad \phi_1^* = \frac{(k_1^* + \delta_1)[1 - \alpha_1(1 - \beta_{J1})]}{(1 - \beta_{11})(k_1^* + \delta_1) + \alpha_2},$$

i.e., the ratio of the value of the capital-good output to that of the consumption-good output.

$$(2.31) \quad r^{J*} = \frac{\beta_{J1}\alpha_2 + k_1^*[\beta_{11}(1 - \alpha_1) + \alpha_1\beta_{J1}] - \delta_1(1 - \alpha_1)(1 - \beta_{11})}{1 - \alpha_1(1 - \beta_{J1})},$$

i.e., the rate of rental of the capital stock in terms of itself.

$$(2.32) \qquad a^* = \frac{(k_1^* + \delta)(1 - \beta_{11}) + \alpha_2(1 - \beta_{J1})}{1 - \alpha_1(1 - \beta_{J1})},$$

i.e., the ratio of labor income to the value of consumers' net worth.

The value of k_1^* given by equation (2.27) is very similar to the value

[12] The saving-income ratio in which income is also defined to *include* capital gains, but to *exclude* depreciation, is given by

$$s' \equiv \frac{\dot{A}}{p^J w E + rA} = \frac{k_J}{a + r}$$

for the rate of growth for the single-good model given by equation (1.11). In particular, this expression is independent of any characteristic of the production function for the consumption good. This is because the consumption good does not contribute to the production of the capital good, and the distribution of factors between the two industries remains constant along the equilibrium growth path. The rate of growth of the consumption-good output, given by equation (2.28), indicates that this rate is the sum of the rates of growth of the labor force and technological change in consumption-good production, supplemented by the modified rate of technological change in capital-good production. The factor modifying the rate of technological change in capital-good production takes account of the importance of capital in the production of the consumption good, and the effectiveness of technological improvement in capital good production in the production of the capital good. The rate of change of relative prices, given by equation (2.29), is the difference between the rates of technological change in the consumption and the capital-good-producing industries, modified by the intensities with which capital is used in both industries. The faster the technological improvement in the consumption-good industry and the slower the technological improvement in the capital-good industry, the greater the rate of increase in the price of the capital good relative to the consumption good. This tendency will be stronger the more labor-intensive the production of the consumption good, and the more capital-intensive the production of the capital good.

Since the distribution of factors between the two sectors is constant on the equilibrium path of growth, and the rates of technological change in the two sectors are not the same, the rates of growth of output in physical terms are not the same in the two sectors. However, the system as a whole will generate changes in relative prices such that they insure that the *value* of output will grow at the same rate in all sectors. The expressions (2.29) and (2.30) represent these properties of the model.

Finally, equations (2.31) and (2.32) express the equilibrium rate of rental of capital in terms of itself, and the equilibrium ratio of labor income to the value of consumers' net worth both measured in terms of the consumption good.[13]

---

[13] It may be noted that if there are no consumption requirements, i.e., $\alpha_1 = \alpha_2 = 0$, and there is no nonproducible factor of production, i.e., $\beta_i \equiv 0$ for all i, then the system represented by equations (2.1) through (2.11) reduces to a special case of the von

In abstract theory, the presence of many heterogeneous capital goods will merely make the expressions (2.27) through (2.32) more complex. In principle, it is possible to write down these expressions, and investigate their characteristics for any finite number of capital goods. However, in order to utilize them in empirical studies, the situation is not so simple. We should like to estimate the parameters of the system, g's, β's, α's, and n, and inquire, for suitably selected periods with reasonably full employment without abnormal shocks such as wars, whether or not observed values of k^*'s, π^*'s, ϕ^*'s, r^*'s, and a^* are in fact reasonably close to those given by substituting into equations (2.27) through (2.32) empirically observed values of the parameters. Data needed for such an inquiry are available for very aggregated sectors at best, and even then must be used with extreme caution. I have put together a set of data which may enable us to work with the two-sector version of the above model. But a serious question arises in the empirical interpretation of the aggregated variables in the above model, particularly in the meaning of aggregate capital. It is well known that various indexes of aggregate capital (for instance, on the one hand, the market value of aggregate capital deflated by a single price index such as an implicit GNP deflator; and on the other, the so called "real capital stock" in most of the National Bureau publications, constructed by deflating various segments of capital stock by their own price indexes and then summing) move substantially differently over time. We must make sure, therefore, that the empirical definition of aggregate capital most consistent with our model will be adopted. We shall turn to this question in the next section.

II. B. AN INTERPRETATION OF THE CONCEPTS OF AGGREGATE CAPITAL AND OUTPUT

We require our definition of aggregate capital and output to be such that the relation between them reflects accurately an aspect of the system defined by equations (2.1) through (2.11). Furthermore, we wish the relation between such aggregate concepts to be in the form of the Cobb-Douglas production function. In addition, when such a relation is treated as though it is in fact a production function,

---

Neumann model of growth, and the "equilibrium path of growth" defined above is a von Neumann ray. One indication of this is seen in the fact that, under such conditions, r^{j*} given by (2.31) reduces to k_1^*, a well-known property of the von Neumann ray. On the other hand, under these conditions, a number of other concepts introduced in this section must be modified to remain well defined.

the results should be capable of meaningful interpretation—the exponents of labor and capital should represent the shares of income accruing to labor and capital, and the rate of technological change measured by Solow's method of residuals should be a weighted average of the rates of technological change in the disaggregated functions.

Since, in the system defined by equations (2.1) through (2.11), technological changes are occurring in different industries at different speeds, the relative size of the stocks of different capital goods will be constantly changing. In such a situation it is difficult to define a concept of the aggregate capital stock in terms of physical units of individual capital goods. However, we note that the values of the stocks of all capital goods, $p^j K^j$'s, are growing at the same rate if the system is moving along the equilibrium path of growth. In view of this, it is tempting to ask whether the value of capital can be used as the measure of capital to be introduced into the production function.

Let us, then, consider the following function for any i, where $i = 1, 2, \ldots, J$.

$$(2.33) \qquad O^{i*} = X_i^* e^{g_i t} E^{i(1-\beta_i)} \prod_{j=1}^{J-1} \left(\frac{p^j}{p^k} K^{ij} \right)^{\beta_{ij}}$$

where p^k is some price index. For the moment, all we shall require of $\dot{p}^k$ is that $\pi_k \equiv p^k$ be constant over time if the system is on the equilibrium path of growth. Equation (2.33) is not a production function. It is considered here simply in order to provide a possible clue to the interpretation of aggregate capital. (2.33) may be rewritten as

$$(2.33a) \qquad O^{i*} = X_i^* e^{g_i t} E^{i(1-\beta_i)} \prod_{j=1}^{J-1} K^{ij\beta_{ij}} \prod_{j=1}^{J-1} \left(\frac{p^j}{p^k} \right)^{\beta_{ij}}$$

Now, from the analysis in the preceding section, it is known that $\dot{p}^j/p^j = \pi_j$ is constant on the equilibrium path of growth, and hence, $\pi_j - \pi_k$ is constant also. Therefore, on the equilibrium path of growth, the movements of O^{i*} defined by (2.33) and of O^i given by the proper production function will be strictly parallel if[14]

$$(2.34) \qquad \sum_{j=1}^{J-1} \beta_{ij}(\pi_j - \pi_k) = 0$$

---

[14] A sufficient, but certainly not necessary, condition for (2.34) to hold is that technological changes proceed in all capital goods industries at the same speed.

Let us consider p^k to be defined by the above equation (2.34), i.e.,

$$(2.34a) \qquad \pi_k = \frac{\sum_{j=1}^{J-1} \beta_{ij}\pi_j}{\sum_{j=1}^{J-1} \beta_{ij}}; \frac{\dot{p}^k}{p^k} = \pi_k$$

On the equilibrium path of growth, it is also known that $(p^j/p^k)K^{ij}$ is growing at the rate $k_J - \pi_k$ for all j. Let us write

$$(2.35) \qquad \frac{p^j}{p_k}K^{ij} \equiv K_o^{ij}e^{k^*t}; k^* = k_J - \pi_k$$

where K_o^{ij} is some constant, and substitute this expression into (2.33).

$$(2.36) \qquad O^{i*} = X_i^* e \ E^{i(1-\beta_i)} e^{k^*t \sum_{j=1}^{J-1} \beta_{ij}} \prod_{j=1}^{J-1} K_o^{ij \beta_{ii}}$$

Since $\prod_{j=1}^{J-1} K_o^{ij \beta_{ii}}$ is a constant over time, it may be subsumed under X_i^*; and in terms of time series data, the share of capital will turn out to be approximately $\sum_{j=1}^{J-1} \beta_{ij} = \beta_i$ if (1) the system does not deviate too far from the equilibrium path of growth; (2) O^i is used as the measure of output; and (3) some index which moves parallel over time to $(p^j/p^k)K^{ij}$ is used as the measure of capital. An index satisfying condition (3) is given by

$$(2.37) \qquad K^* = \sum_{j=1}^{J-1} \frac{p^j}{p^k} K^{ij}$$

Thus, one proposition has been established which is important in giving us some guide to the treatment of aggregative data: if some price index, p^k, can be found which satisfies the condition (2.34), then the use of an output index, O^i, and the capital index, K^*, will enable us to estimate g_i reasonably well. The exponent of K^* may be interpreted as the share of capital.

In order to see if it is possible to define and interpret the marginal product of K^*, let us for a moment suppose that an index p^k satisfying (2.34) can be found and that O^{i*} in equation (2.33) is replaced by O^i. Does the partial derivative of O^i with respect to K^* have any interpretation? To obtain some clue to the answer to this question, note first that

349

(2.38)
$$\frac{\partial O^i}{\partial \left(\frac{p^j}{p^k} K^{ij}\right)} = \frac{\partial O^i}{\partial K^*} \frac{\partial K^*}{\partial \left(\frac{p^j}{p^k} K^{ij}\right)}$$

Equation (2.37) implies that $\partial K^* \Big/ \partial \left(\frac{p^j}{p^k} K^{ij}\right) = 1$, and, by direct differentiation of (2.33)

(2.39)
$$\frac{\partial O^i}{\partial \left(\frac{p^j}{p^k} K^{ij}\right)} = \beta_{ij} \frac{O^i}{K^{ij}} \frac{p^k}{p^j}$$

Not only does the expression on the right-hand side of equation (2.39) have a very ambiguous meaning at best because the units are wrong, but this equation fails to define $\partial O^i/\partial K^*$ in (2.38), since (2.39) says that the left-hand side of equation (2.38) has different values depending on j.

The right-hand side of equation (2.39) has a well-defined meaning only when $p^k = p^i$. In that case it is the marginal product of K^{ij} in terms of K^{ij} in the production of O^i. Suppose, then, that $p^k = p^i$, and consider a new concept O^{i**} defined by

(2.40)
$$O^{i**} \equiv O^i + \sum_{j=1}^{J-1} \left(\frac{\dot{p}^j}{p^i} - \frac{p^j}{p^i} \delta_j\right) K^{ij}$$

Then

(2.41)
$$\frac{\partial O^{i**}}{\partial \left(\frac{p^j}{p^i} K^{ij}\right)} = \beta_{ij} \frac{O^i}{K^{ij}} \frac{p^i}{p^j} + \frac{\dot{p}^j}{p^j} - \delta_j$$

$$= r^j + \delta_j + \pi_j - \delta_j$$

Hence, through an equation similar to (2.38),

(2.42)
$$\frac{\partial O^{i**}}{\partial K^*} = r^j + \pi_j = r$$

The above analysis suggests that, if O^{i**} (output less depreciation of capital used in production of O^i in terms of O^i plus capital gains or losses on capital goods used in production of O^i) is used to measure output instead of O^i, then the marginal product of K^* in the production of O^{i**} is equal to the rental on any capital good in terms of itself plus capital gain, $r^j + \pi_j$, the value of which is independent of j.

Equation (2.42) is valid only if p^i is proportional to p^k defined by equation (2.34a). This is equivalent to saying that the marginal product of K^* is well defined only if the rate of technological change in the production of the ith good is equal to some appropriately weighted average of the rates of technological changes in the production of capital goods. This is a reasonable, but not very helpful, result, since such an accidental equality cannot be counted on. However, there is one consolation. Let equation (2.2) be rewritten in the form

(2.2a) $$p^j K^{ij}(r^j + \delta_j) = \beta_{ij} O^i p^i$$

Adding $p^j K^{ij}(\pi_j - \delta_j)$ to both sides gives:

(2.2b) $$p^j K^{ij}(r^j + \pi_j) = \beta_{ij} O^i p^i + p^j K^{ij}(\pi_j - \delta_j)$$

The summation of this expression over j, where $j = 1, \ldots, J - 1$, on both sides, noting that $r^j + \pi_j = r$ for all j, results in:

$$r \sum_{j=1}^{J-1} p^i K^{ij} = \beta_i O^i p^i + \sum_{j=1}^{J-1} p^j K^{ij}(\pi_j - \delta_j)$$

and hence

(2.43) $$r = \frac{\beta_i O^i p^i + \sum_{j=1}^{J-1} p^j K^{ij}(\pi_j - \delta_j)}{\sum_{j=1}^{J-1} p^j K^{ij}}; \quad i = 1, 2, \ldots, J$$

Equation (2.43) says that if the share of capital in the value of total gross output in any industry is adjusted for the total capital gains and losses and for the depreciation on all capital goods used in the industry, and is divided by the value of all capital goods used in the industry, the result should be the same in all industries, and it should be equal to the rate of interest. Furthermore, it is clear from the foregoing analysis that equation (2.43) holds even when the data are aggregated over any number of industries. Thus, in spite of the difficulties of defining the precise meaning of $\partial O^J / \partial K^*$, there is a practical way of estimating the value of r from readily available aggregate data.[15]

We conclude, then, that the measure of aggregate capital stock should be the value of capital deflated by some price index satisfying

[15] At the risk of laboring an obvious point, I shall restate the implication of equation (2.43). Only when the rental rate is redefined to include the rate of capital gain can it be computed through equation (2.43), using aggregative data. This is reasonable in a model such as the one in this paper in which complete certainty and perfect knowledge are assumed, since, under these assumptions, individuals must be indifferent between the gain from the rental paid to them and the gain from the increase in value of the capital good they own.

351

the condition (2.34) as closely as possible. There remains the question of aggregating output, to which I shall now turn.

Suppose that the production function (2.1) is replaced by

$$(2.44) \qquad O^i = X^{i*}e^{\alpha_i t}E^{i(1-\beta_i)}K^{*i\beta_i}; \; i = 1, 2, \ldots, J$$

where K^{*i} is defined in the analogous manner to K^* in equations (2.37) and (2.34). If it is permissible to assume that the price indexes for defining K^{*i} for all i are sufficiently similar so that the movements of K^{*i} over time are also similar (provided that the system is on the equilibrium path of growth), then equation (2.44) would imply the following approximate equalities on the equilibrium path of growth:

$$(2.45) \qquad k_i = g_i + (1 - \beta_i)n + \beta_i k^* = k_J - \pi_i = k^* + \pi_k - \pi_i$$

Let us define the "total output," O^k, of the capital goods industries and the "aggregate" capital, K^k, and "aggregate" labor force, E^k, employed in the capital goods industries by

$$(2.46) \qquad O^k = \sum_{j=1}^{J-1} \frac{p^j O^j}{p_k}; \; K^k = \sum_{i=1}^{J-1} \frac{p^j K^{ij}}{p^k}; \; E^k = \sum_{j=1}^{J-1} E^j$$

and consider the "aggregate" production function of capital goods

$$(2.47) \qquad O^k \simeq X_k e^{g_k t} K^{k\beta_k} E^{k(1-\beta_k)}$$

where β_k is defined, in a manner analogous to equation (2.25), by the aggregate share of gross income originating in capital goods industries going to capital, i.e.,

$$(2.48) \qquad \beta_k = \frac{\displaystyle\sum_{i=1}^{J-1} \phi_i \beta_i}{\displaystyle\sum_{i=1}^{J-1} \phi_i}$$

Since assumptions leading up to equation (2.46) are very severe, equation (2.47) cannot be expected to hold exactly in reality. To remind ourselves of this fact, we have written (2.47) as an approximate equality rather than as an equality. However, to the extent that the underlying system defined by equations (2.1) through (2.11) is moving along the equilibrium path of growth and that equation (2.47) holds, it will exhibit most of the characteristics of a production function; and the usual marginal conditions discussed earlier in this section will apply to equation (2.47). However, one other concept must be clarified, namely g_k.

352

As long as the system defined by equations (2.1) through (2.11) is moving along the equilibrium path of growth, equation (2.47) implies that

(2.49)
$$k^* = g_k + \beta_k k^* + (1 - \beta_k)n$$

Substituting into the above expression definition (2.48) and equation (2.45) and rearranging terms, g_k can be expressed as

(2.50)
$$g_k = \frac{\sum_{i=1}^{J-1} \phi_i g_i}{\Sigma \phi_i} + \frac{\sum_{i=1}^{J-1} \phi_i(\pi_i - \pi_k)}{\Sigma \phi_i}$$

In some sense, it might be argued that the aggregate measure of the rate of technological change should be given by

(2.51)
$$g_k^* = \frac{\sum_{i=1}^{J-1} \phi_i g_i}{\Sigma \phi_i}$$

If the residual method of Solow is applied to equation (2.47), using the aggregate measures of output and capital given by (2.46), the resulting estimate of the rate of technological change is g_k, given by (2.50), rather than g_k^*, given by (2.51). To this extent, this method may be said to give a biased measure of the rate of technological change. Fortunately, however, the last term on the right-hand side of equation (2.50) is likely to be very close to zero, since π_k itself is constructed as a weighted average of π_i's, given by equation (2.34a).

In this section we have outlined the implications of the model involving many heterogeneous capital goods on aggregate magnitudes for which data are likely to be available. It has been found that, because the rates of technological changes are different in different industries, it is not possible to define meaningful aggregate concepts except in terms of market values. However, so long as the underlying microsystem is moving along the equilibrium path of growth, market values of output and capital stock may be used to define aggregate output and aggregate capital, deflating them by some appropriate general price index. We may utilize these data to measure the rate of interest, the average rate of technological change, and other magnitudes, and to interpret the foregoing in terms of the characteristics of the underlying microsystem. In the next section, we shall take advantage of these findings and attempt to interpret the data for the United States economy. In so doing it is necessary to remember that these theoretical propositions refer to the behavior of the system on the equilibrium path of growth, while the data are generated by the economy with all its cyclical fluctuations and the shocks from two world wars. Careful choice of periods and adjustments in data will, therefore, be necessary.

III. Introduction of Government and a Monetary System

III. A. MODIFICATIONS OF THE MODEL

My remaining task is to modify the system analyzed in Section II to allow for the roles of government and of the monetary system. I will then attempt to make the best possible guesses at the order of magnitudes of the parameters of the system, and to check the internal consistency of the model.

It is clearly necessary to make a compromise about the level of aggregation for this purpose, and I shall consider the situation in which only two commodities, one capital good and one consumption good, are distinguished. The capital good, then, takes on the meaning of aggregative capital discussed in Section II.B. In my empirical work it will be identified with the value of capital deflated by a single capital goods price index.

The system I shall use in this section is defined by modifying that given by equations (2.1)–(2.11) in Section II. Equations (2.1) through (2.5) can be carried over without any change, and will be renamed for the purpose of discussion in this section as (3.1) through (3.5). The running subscripts and superscripts should be

$$j = k; i = k, c;$$

representing the capital good (k) and the consumption good (c).

Equations (2.6) through (2.10) are modified as follows:

(3.6) $$C = \alpha_1(1 - \tau_1)wE + \alpha_2 \frac{A}{p^c}$$

(3.7) $$O^c = C + Q^c$$
(3.8) $$O^k = \dot{K} + Q^k + \delta_k$$
(3.9) $$A = p^k K + D$$

(3.10) $$r = r^k + \frac{\dot{p}^k}{p^k}$$

where Q_t^c = the rate of government purchase of the consumption good at time t

Q_t^k = the rate of government purchase of the capital good at time t

τ_1, τ_2 = the average rates of taxes on labor income and on property income, respectively

D_t = the outstanding debt of the government held by the public

All these quantities are assumed to be exogenous to the system. In particular, D is not an independent decision variable for government, and is given by

$$(3.11) \qquad \dot{D}_t = p_t^c Q_t^c + p_t^k Q_t^k + r_t D_t - \tau_1 p^c w_t E_t - \tau_2 r_t A_t$$

It is convenient to define a new concept, "disposable income" of consumers, by

$$(3.12) \qquad Y \equiv (1 - \tau_1)wE + (1 - \tau_2)rA$$

It should be noted that Y is different from the usual national income definition by the inclusion of capital gains.

Equation (2.11) will be replaced by a description of the monetary sector, which is given by

$$(3.13) \qquad M^d = M^d(A, Y, r) = p^c M^d\left(\frac{A}{p^c}, \frac{Y}{p^c}, r\right)$$

$$(3.14) \qquad M^d = M^s$$

where M^d = demand for money

M^s = supply of money, assumed to be given exogenously to the system

All together, equations (3.1) through (3.14) constitute a modified version of (2.1) through (2.11), with $i = c, k; j = k$.

The nature of the supply of money, M^s, must be spelled out. In this paper, it is assumed that the banking system issues money in exchange for individuals' indebtedness to it or for government debt. Under this assumption, the possession of money by one individual is precisely offset against someone else's debt. When all individual balance sheets are aggregated, money is completely canceled out, and the total outstanding government debt appears as an item of assets for individuals. The volume of money is then controlled, for instance, by the reserve requirement. This is the opposite of the other extreme assumption, made by Tobin among others, that all money is paper money issued by the government [4]. In reality, of course, there exist both kinds of money in the economy. I adopt the assumption stated above partly because others have used the opposite assumption and it may be interesting to compare these results with theirs, but mostly because in the United States, the volume of money that is not offset by individual indebtedness or by bank holdings of government securities is insignificantly small. It may be noted here that it is only under this assumption that the definition of D given by equation (3.11) is strictly correct.

Also, under this assumption we can derive the budget equation for consumers, corresponding to equation (2.12):

$$(3.15) \qquad\qquad \dot{A} = Y - p^c C$$

In order for this model to be complete, a demand function for government debt by the public and a market equilibrium condition for government debt must be specified. The demand for government debt by the public is ultimately a result of the portfolio selection behavior of individuals. Suppose that the demand function for government debt by the public is given by

$$(3.16) \qquad\qquad D_t^d = D^d(A_t, r_t, r_t^{k*}, \sigma)$$

where σ is a parameter representing factors (other than the rates of return) differentiating the government debt and physical capital, and the market equilibrium condition for it by

$$(3.17) \qquad\qquad D_t^d = D_t$$

Its supply is given by equation (3.11). Equation (3.14) must now be abandoned; and r^{k*}, not necessarily equal to r, is defined by

$$(3.18) \qquad\qquad r_t^{k*} \equiv r_t^k + \frac{\dot{p}_t^k}{p_t^k}$$

The possibility of the nonzero difference between r, the rate of interest on the government debt, and r^{k*}, the rate of return on capital including capital gains, arises because of the possible difference in risk associated with holdings of physical capital and of government debt. In equation (3.16) σ represents this difference in risk. Thus, equation (3.15) must be modified to make A a function of r, r^{k*}, and σ. We will then have an expanded system, consisting of equations (3.1) through (3.10), (3.12), (3.13), (3.14), (3.16), (3.17), and the new variable, D^d.

But this creates rather than solves a difficulty. I have abstracted from uncertainty throughout the analysis in this paper. In order to accommodate the problems arising from uncertainty, the real part of the system has to be modified rather substantially, introducing, among other things, market imperfections and gradual rather than instantaneous adjustment processes. Yet, in order to define the demand function for debt within the framework of this system, it is necessary to introduce the uncertainty of the return on capital. To put it another way, if there is no uncertainty associated with return on capital from the point of view of individuals choosing their portfolios, ownership of physical capital and ownership of government debt are indistinguishable from each other provided that equation (3.10) holds; the system reduces to equations (3.1) through (3.14). But in such a system, there is no explicit mechanism by which savings of individuals are divided into purchases of government debt and of physical capital. Though the problems arising from uncertainty are among the most fundamental in the analysis of economic growth and fluctuations, they cannot be dealt with in this paper. I shall, instead, adopt the following simple convention: the government, by some appropriate procedure, always succeeds in selling all the debt issues which it wishes to sell, resulting in the condition summarized by equation (3.10). As a result, the value of physical capital demanded in the economy at any time is the total net worth generated through equation (3.15), less the value of total outstanding government debt.[16]

Let us adopt the following notations,

$$q_c \equiv \frac{Q^c}{O^c}; \; q_k \equiv \frac{Q^k}{O^k}; \; d \equiv \frac{D}{p^k K}$$

and the definitions of a, π, k, and ϕ as in Section II:

$$\frac{p^c(1 - \tau_1)wE}{A} \equiv a; \; \frac{\dot{p}^k}{p^k} \equiv \pi_k; \; \frac{\dot{p}^c}{p^c} \equiv \pi_c; \; \pi \equiv \pi_k - \pi_c$$

$$\frac{\dot{K}}{K} \equiv k; \; \frac{p^k O^k}{p^c O^c} \equiv \phi$$

Suppose that q_k, q_c, τ_1 and τ_2, and d are constant over time.[17] Does there exist an equilibrium path of growth on which a, π, ϕ, r^k, and k are constant? And, if there is such a path, does it exhibit similar characteristics to those described for the model discussed in Section II?

---

[16] This situation may be relaxed slightly by assuming that the measure of uncertainty associated with holding the capital good is constant over time, and expressed by the difference between r_t and r_t^{k*}, replacing equation (3.10) by $r = r^k + (\dot{p}^k/p^k) - \rho$, where ρ is positive and constant.

[17] These are not strictly independent decision variables, as discussed below.

Examination of the analysis developed in Section II and of the modifications introduced in this section shows that the existence of the equilibrium path of growth is not disturbed by the modification introduced in this section, and that a number of the properties of the system on the equilibrium path remain unchanged. In particular, the distribution of factors among industries, given by equation (2.14), is unaffected, as are the equilibrium values of k and π, as exemplified by expressions (2.27), (2.28), and (2.29).

On the other hand, the equilibrium values of ϕ, r^k, and a are slightly altered, and the equations corresponding to (2.18) and (2.24) are given by the following:

$$(3.19) \qquad \phi = \frac{(1 - \tau_1)(k + \delta)(1 - \beta_c)}{a(1 - d)(1 - q_k) - (1 - \beta_k)(1 - \tau_1)(k + \delta)}$$

$$(3.20) \qquad r^k + \delta = \beta_k \frac{O^k}{K^k} = \frac{k + \delta}{1 - q_k} \frac{\beta_c + \beta_k \phi}{\phi}$$

$$(3.21) \quad a = \frac{\alpha_2 + k + \pi_1 - (1 - \tau_2)r}{1 - \alpha_1} = \frac{\alpha_2 + k + \tau_2\pi - (1 - \tau_2)r^k}{(1 - \alpha_1)}$$

The final equilibrium values of r^k and a are then given by

$$(3.22) \quad r^{k*} = (\alpha_2 + \tau_2\pi) \frac{\beta_c(1 - q_k)(1 - d)}{(1 - \beta_c)(1 - \tau_1)(1 - \alpha_1) + \beta_c(1 - d)(1 - \tau_2)}$$

$$+ k \frac{\beta_k(1 - \alpha_1)(1 - \tau_1) + \beta_c[\alpha_1(1 - \tau_1) - (1 - \tau_1) + (1 - q_k)(1 - d)]}{(1 - \beta_c)(1 - \tau_1)(1 - \alpha_1) + \beta_c(1 - d)(1 - \tau_2)}$$

$$- \delta \frac{(1 - \tau_1)(1 - \alpha_1)[(1 - \beta_k) - q_k(1 - \beta_c)]}{(1 - \beta_c)(1 - \tau_1)(1 - \alpha_1) + \beta_c(1 - d)(1 - \tau_2)}$$

$$(3.23)$$

$$a^* = (\alpha_2 + \tau_2\pi) \frac{(1 - \tau_1)[(1 - \alpha_1)(1 - \beta_c) + q_k\beta_c(1 - d)]}{(1 - \alpha_1)[(1 - \beta_c)(1 - \tau_1)(1 - \alpha_1) + \beta_c(1 - d)(1 - \tau_2)]}$$

$$+ k \frac{(1 - \tau_1)(1 - \alpha_1)[1 - \beta_k(1 - \tau_2)]}{(1 - \alpha_1)[(1 - \beta_c)(1 - \tau_1)(1 - \alpha_1) + \beta_c(1 - d)(1 - \tau_2)]}$$

$$+ k \frac{\beta_c[q_1(1 - d)(1 - \tau_2) - \tau_2(1 - \alpha_1)(1 - \tau_1)]}{(1 - \alpha_1)[(1 - \beta_c)(1 - \tau_1)(1 - \alpha_1) + \beta_c(1 - d)(1 - \tau_2)]}$$

$$+ \delta \frac{(1 - \tau_1)(1 - \tau_2)[1 - \beta_k - q_k(1 - \beta_c)]}{(1 - \beta_c)(1 - \tau_1)(1 - \alpha_1) + \beta_c(1 - d)(1 - \tau_2)}$$

Substitution of these values into (3.19) will then give us the equilibrium solution for ϕ.

It is clear that, when $q_k = \tau_1 = \tau_2 = d = 0$, equations (3.22) and (3.23) reduce to equations (2.31) and (2.32).

From these equations, one may conjecture about the influence of changes in fiscal policy, i.e., changes in values of q_k, q_c, τ_1, and τ_2, on the values of r, a, and ϕ in the long run, and the productivity of labor at any given point in time. However, it would be more illuminating to discuss these important questions after approximate numerical values for the parameters are given. Before proceeding to the problem of empirical estimates of parameters, however, two remaining problems must be clarified. First, the government has one more policy instrument at its disposal, namely, the supply of money; and we must investigate what consequences, if any, would result within the framework of this model when the supply of money is changed. Second, D is a consequence of past decisions on expenditures and taxes on the part of the government, and it appears that the government cannot vary the value of d arbitrarily.

In order for the system to be maintained on the equilibrium path of growth suggested above, the proportion of government debt in consumer net worth must be kept constant. This is because, on such a path, both A and $p^k K$ must grow at the rate $k + \pi$, and hence, it must be that $\dot{D} = k + \pi$, also. Substituting this in equation (3.11) and using the definition of d given above, we have

$$
(3.24) \qquad d = \frac{\dfrac{k + \delta}{1 - q_k}\left(\dfrac{q_c}{\phi} + q_k\right) - \dfrac{\tau_1}{1 - \tau_1}a - \tau_2 r}{\pi + k - r + \dfrac{\tau_1}{1 - \tau_1}a + \tau_2 r}
$$

Equation (3.24) defines the ratio of government debt to the value of total consumer net worth which must be maintained in order for the system to move along the equilibrium path of growth, given values of q_k, q_c, τ_1, and τ_2. Thus, equations (3.22) and (3.23) do not give the complete equilibrium solution for a and r, as they appear to do. In order to obtain the equilibrium solution, equations (3.19), (3.20), (3.21), and (3.24) must be taken together and solved simultaneously for a, r, ϕ, and d. This is not too difficult, but the resulting solutions for these variables are very long expressions; and it would be more useful to deal with this problem when actual numerical values of β's and α's and of k and π have been obtained.

The ratio of government debt to the value of total net worth of consumers can also be changed through monetary policies and through the resulting changes in the prices of the consumption good. Let us suppose that the demand function for money, equation (3.13), takes the special form given by

(3.25) $$M^d = m_1(r)(O^c p^c + O^k p^k) + m_2(r)A$$

where the first term on the right-hand side of this equation represents the transaction demand for money, the second term represents the asset demand for money, and m_1 and m_2 are both decreasing functions of r.[18]

It is convenient to define

(3.26) $$m(r) = \frac{M^d}{p^k K}$$

On the equilibrium path of growth, it must be the case that

$$m(r) = m_1 \frac{O^k p^k}{K p^k} \left(\frac{O^c p^c}{O^k p^k} + 1 \right) + (1 + d)m_2$$

$$= m_1 \frac{1 - q_k}{k + \delta} \left(\frac{1}{\phi} + 1 \right) + (1 + d)m_2$$

(3.27)
$$m(r) = m_1(r) \frac{1 - q_k}{k + \delta} \left[\frac{a(1 - d)(1 - q_k) - (1 - \beta_k)(1 - \tau_1)(k + \delta)}{(1 - \tau_1)(k + \delta)(1 - \beta_c)} + 1 \right]$$
$$+ (1 + d)m_2(r)$$

Note that, since $m_1(r)$ and $m_2(r)$ as well as a are all decreasing functions of r, the partial derivative of m with respect to r must be negative.

In the standard Keynesian analysis, when the money supply is changed, the level of prices is supposed to change little or at best very slowly. Consequently, the change in the supply of money is largely reflected in the credit conditions as represented by the rate of interest in the money market. In this model it is assumed that the level of prices as well as the rate of interest adjust instantaneously whenever the supply of money is changed, so as to satisfy equations (3.1) through (3.14). Because the major concern of this paper is the problem of long-run growth, the consideration that it takes time for prices and other variables to adjust to new conditions is neglected, except for the adjustment through savings as described by equation (3.15).

Now suppose that the system has been moving along the equi-

---

[18] Under the assumption of perfect certainty, it would be foolish for anyone to hold money as a part of his portfolio; consequently, m_2 really should be identically zero.

librium path defined by equations (3.19), (3.22), (3.23), (2.27), and (2.29), with the monetary authority allowing banks to increase the supply of money at the rate $k + \pi$. Suppose further that at some point in time the monetary authority permits the banks to increase the supply of money by some amount over and above the regular increase of $(k + \pi)M$. In order to increase the supply of money, banks must offer loans at a rate of interest slightly below the rate that was prevailing previously. Individuals (firms) then find it profitable to borrow money from banks, and attempt to purchase the capital good, thereby bidding up its price. This in turn induces the producers of capital goods to produce more capital goods and to demand more factors of production, raising the price of the capital good even further, along with the wage rate, and leading to an increase in the level of money income and the money value of net worth of consumers. This in turn increases the demand for the consumption good, raising its price. This process will go on until the prices of both the capital good and the consumption good are sufficiently bid up so that the equations (3.1) and (3.14) are again satisfied. However, the resulting equilibrium is not the same as the one prevailing before the increase in the supply of money took place. When the level of prices is rising, the value of a part of consumers' net worth, $p^k K$, rises, but not the remaining part, D.

How this will affect the resulting equilibrium will depend on how the increase in the money supply is brought about. In the United States, this is ordinarily done through the purchase of government securities by the central bank, enabling commercial banks to acquire additional indebtedness by the public. In this case, we have the classical "Pigou-Patinkin" effects, generating more savings.[19]

How this process ends in the long run depends upon what the government does with q's and τ's. If these parameters are maintained at the same values as those that had prevailed before the increase in the supply of money took place, then the proportion of debt in the net worth of consumers will gradually be increased, and the system will return to the original equilibrium path of growth after some passage of time. If, on the other hand, the values of these parameters are changed, and in particular, if they are changed in

---

[19] I have reported elsewhere [3] that the marginal propensity to consume net worth, α_2, is roughly 0.05. The value of total government debt outstanding plus gold stock is between, say, $300 billion and $400 billion. Therefore, 10 per cent changes in the price level will result in some $1.5 to $2 billion changes in consumption, a negligible change compared to other repercussions of such a large change in the price level.

such a way that the final equilibrium value of d is less than that which prevailed before the increase in the supply of money, the capital-output ratio in both industries will be increased, the equilibrium value of the return on capital will be less than before, and the system will move to a new equilibrium path of growth which is characterized by a higher output in both industries than would have been the case if such a change had not taken place.

III. B. SOME PRELIMINARY EMPIRICAL RESULTS

The data needed for the estimation of the parameters in the model described in Section III.A are roughly as follows:

1. Output of the consumption-good industry and of the capital-good industry, gross of depreciation.
2. Price indexes for output of the capital-good industry and of the consumption-good industry.
3. The value of capital used in both industries.
4. Depreciation of capital in both industries.
5. Man-hours employed in both industries.
6. The share of capital in both industries, or, equivalently, labor income in both industries.
7. Some method of adjusting the value of capital in both industries for underutilization of capital.
8. Data needed to estimate parameters of the consumption function; more specifically, consumption, labor income after taxes, and the value in net worth of consumers.
9. Data relating to government activities; specifically, expenditure by government, taxes on labor and nonlabor income, and the value of debt.

The sources and derivation of the data are described and discussed in moderate detail in a separate appendix, and may be obtained at cost from the author on request.

Difficulties arise mainly from four sources. The first is simply lack of information that goes back to the beginning of the twentieth century; but this is to be expected. The second is the inconsistency among the data taken from various sources. For instance, personal income in current dollars reported by Creamer [8] moves from $29.4 billion in 1909, through $69.2 billion in 1920, to $83.4 billion in 1929; while the same item, apparently having the same definition, reported by Goldsmith [21] moves from $26.9 billion in 1909, through $75.8

billion in 1920, to $85.1 billion in 1929. Since no single source can provide all the data necessary for a work of the kind attempted in this paper, the combined use of a number of different sources containing such discrepancies as that described above is at present a necessity; and this is a very serious problem indeed when working with an internally consistent model such as the one here presented. It also casts serious doubts on the meaning of the empirical results obtained.

Third, several important implications of the model presented in Section III.A. are stated in terms of current values. For instance, according to the model, the ratio of the value of labor income to the value of net worth of consumers should remain constant over time, but it has nothing to say about the ratio of "real" labor income to "real" net worth as ordinarily defined (where each component of these aggregates is deflated by its own price and then summed). However, there appears to be an increasing tendency to report "real" series alone, without showing the current-value series. The most notable example of this tendency is the work of Kendrick [28], in which very few time series are given in current prices.

Fourth, although the division between the capital-good-producing sector and the consumption-good-producing sector is a very convenient and appealing one from the theoretical point of view, in reality industries are not neatly classified in this manner; and it is necessary to make a number of rather arbitrary decisions in allocating various production activities to the two sectors. In this paper, I have largely followed the method suggested by Eckaus and Lefeber [16] in their recent paper, with some modifications. This method of allocation is described in the separate appendix referred to earlier. In retrospect, I feel that this method in its general outline is as good as any that we can devise, but a number of substantial improvements can be made, given time and patience.

Before turning to the examination of actual numerical results, it may be helpful to recall the type of questions often raised in the theoretical and empirical literature on the process of economic growth. It is often suggested that such magnitudes as the relative share of income between labor and capital, the ratio of capital to output, and the long-run saving-income ratio are extremely stable over time. Whether or not these ratios are in fact constant depends very much on the precise definitions of the variables in terms of which the ratios are computed. In my theoretical discussion, a framework has been developed that specifies which of these ratios should be expected to be stable over time. Among them, the constancies of the relative income shares are the least interesting; since I assume the Cobb-Douglas production function for all industries, the constancy of the over-all relative income share follows directly from the constancy of ϕ, the ratio of value of output of the capital-good industry to that of the consumption-good industry. That some of the other ratios should be expected to be constant on the equilibrium path of growth is somewhat more surprising. Any one of the basic equations of the model, taken by itself, does not imply such constancies; but all of them taken together apparently do. Furthermore, the model specifies the values of these ratios in terms of the values of the basic parameters of the system. It is interesting, therefore, to see, first, whether some of these ratios are in fact historically constant, and second, if they are, whether their observed values are reasonably close to those predicted by the values of the parameters of my model.

Second, there has been much discussion recently on the measurement of technological change, beginning with an important contribution of Solow [45]. This discussion, as far as I am aware, has been directed toward the measurement of technological change for the economy as a whole. We are all aware, however, of the conceptual difficulty involved in defining aggregate capital and output. In Section II.B, one possible interpretation was formulated for the link between the concepts of aggregate capital and output and disaggregated capital goods and outputs. It turns out, however, that my solution calls for the use of the value of capital and value of output, each deflated by a price index satisfying certain conditions, and not "real" output and "real" capital as usually defined. It is interesting, therefore, to compare the results which I obtain in this paper with, for instance, those of Solow, who used "real" capital and "real" output.

The parameters of the system for two periods, 1900–28 and 1951–58, are reported in Table 1. The choice of periods is, by necessity, arbitrary. The Great Depression years of the 1930's and the World War II years are certainly not relevant to a model such as the one under consideration here, and should be excluded. The period 1948–58 may be used instead of 1951–58, but I have been persuaded that the years 1948–50 should be excluded, partly because of the effects of the Korean War on the United States economy and partly because these were still years in which the effects of the depression

TABLE 1
AVERAGE VALUES OF THE BASIC PARAMETERS FOR SELECTED PERIODS, 1900–57

Periods Between		n	τ_1	τ_2	q_c	d	δ	β_c	β_k	g_c	g_k	Aggregate g
1900–01	1927–28	.014	0	0	.04	.05	.04	.43	.25[a] (.15)	.013	.013[b] (.014)	.013
1951–52	1956–57	.003	.13[e] (.09)	.20[e] (.32)	.14	.30	.04	.37	.25	.017	.012	.015

NOTE: The data needed to compute these values are available in a separate appendix, which may be obtained at cost on request to the author. The figures reported are the averages of annual values, except that the figures for 1900–28 are averages excluding 1918, 1919, and 1920. For figures on α_1 and α_2, see table in Section I and Ando and Modigliani [3].

[a] From all indications, the value of output in manufacturing in this paper is substantially underestimated relative to all other figures in the period 1900–28. As a consequence, the relative share of income of capital and, hence, β_k, appears to be substantially understated if the value of output in manufacturing is taken at face value, resulting in the figure reported in parentheses. However, if a rough adjustment is made for the underestimation of the value of manufacturing output, then β_k becomes 0.25. This is the figure used throughout this paper.

[b] The figure 0.013 is the result under the assumption that β_k is 0.25. If β_k is assumed to be 0.15, then g_k would be 0.014, reported here in parentheses.

[e] The figure is arrived at by assuming that one-half of corporate income tax is a tax on property income, while the other half is a tax on labor income, on the basis that wages would be somewhat higher if the corporate income tax did not exist. The figure in parentheses will result if all corporate income tax is considered a tax on property income.

and the Second World War were being worked out, particularly the rapid accumulation of the real assets which had been depleted.

The footnotes to Table 1 give detailed comments on the nature of the individual estimates. The following features of the estimates may be noted here.

1. Even given the roughness of the data, there appears to be very little doubt that β_c is greater than β_k. This, in turn, implies that, provided the return on capital and the wage rate is in fact the same for both industries, as required by the model, the consumption-good industry is more capital-intensive than the capital-good industry. This appears to be a surprising result at first, but when it is realized that the output of the consumption-good industry includes the service of residential structures, the result is perfectly understandable.

2. It appears that, for the earlier period, the rate of technological change in the capital-good industry was greater than that for the consumption-good industry, but this relation has been reversed for the later period.

3. The ratio of government debt to the value of physical capital, *d*, is reported to be 0.05 for the period 1900–28. This figure, as indicated in the footnote, is the average for the entire period except for the First World War years. However, it starts at 0.04 in 1900, remaining stable until the First World War years, when it rises to 0.13, and then declines to 0.08 in 1929. This gradual change in *d* might cause serious discrepancies among the observed values of *r*, *a*, and other ratios and those implied by the parameter values in Table 1.

Of the five ratios for which the model gives predictions (*a*, *r*, *k*, *π*, and *φ*), *k* and *π* really do not provide a test of the consistency of the model, since data used to measure these are directly used to obtain the estimate of g_c and g_k. Of the remaining three, *φ* is most sensitive to the short-run cyclical fluctuations of economic activity, and probably less meaningful for testing the consistency of a long-run growth model of the kind under consideration here. Because of these considerations, in Table 2, the actual values of *a* and r^k and the

TABLE 2

COMPARISON OF OBSERVED VALUES OF a^* AND r^{k*} WITH THOSE IMPLIED
BY THE MODEL AND TABLE 1, 1900–57

Periods Between		a^*		r^{k*}	
		Actual	Implied	Actual	Implied
1900–01	1927–28	.152	.151	.062[a] (.066)	.047
1951–52	1956–57	.173	.196[b] (.206)	.054	.040[b] (.039)

SOURCE: See Note, Table 1. The implied values are computed through equations 3.40 and 3.41, using values of the parameters given in Table 1. When the actual value of aggregate *k* deviates from that implied by Table 1, however, the actual value of *k* is used.

[a] The figure reported here is the average of annual values excluding 1918, 1919, and 1920. If these years are included, the figure reported in parentheses is obtained.

[b] This figure is calculated by using the values of $τ_1$ and $τ_2$ given in Table 1. If the figures of $τ_1$ and $τ_2$ given in parentheses in Table 1 are used, then the implied values of a^* and r^{k*} reported in parentheses will result.

corresponding values implied by the parameters reported in Table 1 through the use of the model of Section III.A are given.

The actual value of a^* is remarkably stable over time. For the period 1900–28, its highest value is 0.160, in 1920, and its lowest value is 0.133, in 1915, without its showing any visible trend. Furthermore, these extreme values are rather isolated phenomena, and if the highest three and the lowest three are ignored, its highest value is 0.155 and its lowest, 0.137. The figure reported in Table 1 is the average for the entire period. That the implied value of a^* for the corresponding period is so close to the actual value would appear to be very good, but this conclusion is not entirely warranted. The reason is that, while the actual value of a^* has been computed as the ratio of total labor income in the economy against the actual total net worth of consumers, which includes nonreproducible tangible assets (namely, the value of land), the model through which the implied value of a^* has been computed does not allow for the existence of land in the economy. Therefore, the actual value of a^* should be somewhat smaller than the implied value. It should be concluded, therefore, that for the period 1900–28, the implied value of a^* is somewhat too small relative to the actual value of a^*.

For 1951–57, the value of a^* is again very stable, but it exhibits a slight tendency to fall somewhat over this period, namely, from 0.179, in 1951, to 0.171, in 1957. The accumulation of net worth during the World War II years was extremely small, and the ratio a reached the peak of 0.23 in 1944. It recovered quickly, falling to roughly 0.18 in 1947, but further recovery appears to be very slow. Thus, the decline of a mentioned above may be attributed to the desire of consumers to accumulate up to the normal level those assets which were depleted during the World War II years. The value reported in Table 2 is again the average value for the period. The implied value of a^* for this period reported in Table 2 is 0.196, a figure considerably larger than the actual value of a^*. But, as suggested earlier, due to the treatment of land in the model, the implied value of a^* should be somewhat larger than the actual value. It is difficult to say how much larger, but it may be noted that the value of private land for this period is roughly 15 per cent of the total net worth of consumers, suggesting that the maximum adjustment would be to reduce the implied value of 15 per cent. This would make the implied value of a^* for this period slightly less than 0.17. In any case, the result of the comparison of the implied value of a^* with its actual value may be considered reasonably satisfactory.

The actual value of r^k for both periods fluctuates somewhat more than that of a. In particular, the value of r^k for the World War I years is extremely high. The figure reported for 1900–28 in Table 2 is the average excluding the World War I years, but the figure including the World War I years is shown in parentheses. Except for this fact, both periods can be discussed together here, since the details for both periods are very similar, i.e., the actual figures are much larger than the implied figures, though both actual and implied figures become smaller over the years.

The discrepancy between the actual and implied values of r^{k*} is quite large. Since the model from which the implied values of r^{k*} have been computed assumes perfect competition and perfect certainty, while in the real world uncertainties and various degrees of monopoly powers are important facts of life, it is to be expected that the actual rate of return on capital will be somewhat larger than the equilibrium values implied by the model. However, since we cannot measure quantitatively the effects of monopoly power and uncertainty in this context, it is impossible to determine whether the discrepancy displayed in Table 2 is too large or too small. This is one of the unsolved problems in this paper.

Before concluding this section on empirical results, I wish to report that experiments have been performed to compare the results of Solow [45] in the measurement of the rate of technological change and the conclusions reached through equation (2.50) in Section II.B. The comparison is not exact, since the data used by Solow are not identical with those used here. Solow's result is that, for the period 1910–49, the average rate of technological change was roughly 0.017 per year. According to my method, using the value of output of the consumption good and the value of capital deflated by a single price index, the rate of technological change for the similar period, after the adjustment factor shown in equation (2.50) has been allowed for, is also roughly 0.017. This finding appears to indicate that, for this period, at least, Solow's conclusion would not be altered if the method suggested by the model analyzed in this paper were substituted for his. On the other hand, for any subperiod that may reasonably be chosen for comparison, the results appear to be radically different. It is difficult to conclude anything definite from these subperiods, however, since the results for shorter periods must be affected by cyclical movements in the economy. Furthermore, the shorter the period, the more likely it is that the weakness of the data will reduce the reliability of the estimate.

Concluding Remarks

I have attempted, in this rather lengthy paper, to specify a model of United States economic growth which conforms to some of the more recent theories of economic growth, but which is, at the same time, concrete enough to act as a framework for interpreting the existing data for the long-run trend of the United States economy. It turned out that, on the one hand, the model I have developed requires some data that are not readily available, while on the other, the available data from different sources are inconsistent, presenting a number of almost insurmountable difficulties in the empirical work for this paper. Under the circumstances, within the limits of the time and resources at my disposal, I have tried to accomplish two objectives. First, to investigate the properties of the model I have specified, paying special attention to the problems of interpreting aggregative concepts and data in terms of detailed, disaggregated models; and second, to do my best to make approximations using the existing data, and to suggest the order of magnitudes of the crucial parameters in this model.

There are a number of constants that are often discussed in the literature, such as the relative share of income, the ratio of the value of capital to the value of output, and others. These ratios are useful concepts empirically, but the theoretical explanations of the constancy of these ratios have not been, in my opinion, very satisfactory. I have, therefore, specified a model which does not assume these ratios to be explicitly constant by adopting (1) the Cobb-Douglas production function, (2) different rates of technological progress in different industries, and (3) a consumption function which does not require the saving income ratio to be constant at all times; and I have inquired whether such a model is capable of implying the constancy of these ratios at least on the equilibrium path of growth. The answer to this question turned out to be affirmative. In addition, the model discussed here gives explicit solutions for these ratios as well as other ratios in terms of (1) the parameters of the production functions and the consumption function, and (2) exogenous factors such as the rate of growth of the labor force, the rates of technological change, and governmental policy variables. As a result, the model enables us to make specific numerical predictions for these ratios when its parameters are estimated and the exogenous factors are known.

Because of the difficulties in adjusting the existing body of data to information that is relevant for this model, the empirical results presented in this paper cannot be taken too seriously. However, the indications are that if it is possible to improve the approximations made here, the model presented should be moderately useful for interpreting data concerning the long-run trend of the United States economy. The improvements required of the existing body of data as well as a new set of data needed for this purpose are relatively minor, and I have little doubt that this will be possible in the very near future.

In addition to the quality of empirical approximation, a number of obvious improvements can be made in this model in order to make it more realistic and useful. The list of such future improvements surely includes: a more careful treatment of the role of government, particularly the services provided by government for private economic activities; the separation of producer durables, inventories, and structures in the concept of capital; a more detailed consideration of the monetary system; and the introduction of elements of uncertainty. Furthermore, it would be interesting to inquire how the transition of the system from one equilibrium path of growth to another would take place, following, for example, a change by the government in one of its policy variables.

In reality, the United States economy contains a number of characteristics that cause it to deviate significantly from the smooth path of equilibrium growth defined by this model. In fact, these deviations are so significant that during the period between 1930 and the late 1950s, the larger part of macroeconomic analysis was devoted almost exclusively to the study of the causes and effects of these deviations. On the other hand, as the list of references at the end of this paper indicates, fairly strong interest in the underlying economic structures has recently been shown, with less emphasis placed on the deviations discussed above. In principle, these two phenomena—the growth of the economy due to the growth of the labor force, of technological innovations, and of the accumulation of capital; and cyclical fluctuations of the economy—cannot be studied separately, since they are interrelated parts of the economic process over time.

However, given the current state of economic theory and empirical knowledge, it is extremely difficult to begin with a model which takes into account simultaneously all the complex factors affecting the growth of the economy and those affecting the cyclical fluctuations, estimates all parameters, and then analyzes the properties of the system. Under the circumstances, there seem to me to be two possible strategies in dealing with the problems of understanding the workings of the economy, involving both growth and fluctuations. The

370

first is to start with a model which lays strong emphasis on the factors causing cyclical fluctuations in the economy, and inquire whether such a model is capable of generating a steady growth path if all the exogenous factors are kept constant in some sense, and if it is, then what the properties of the growth path so generated are. The work of Duesenberry [15] is an excellent example of this approach. The second strategy is to construct a model in which the economy functions without any friction, such as the one discussed in this paper, and inquire whether such a model is capable of generating a reasonable growth path that conforms to the characteristics of the real economy when the data are adjusted for cyclical fluctuations. Then, if it does, a number of frictions can be introduced into such a model —for example, wage rigidities, nonzero time required for adjustments in markets and in relations involving stocks and flows, imperfect knowledge—and study the consequences. That such a procedure would lead to a model involving both growth and fluctuations in the case of a single-good model has been reported elsewhere [1] [2].

I think there is no inherent reason for either one of these two approaches to be superior to the other. I therefore feel that both approaches should be tried, since the problem to which both of these approaches are directed—namely, the workings of the economy, involving both fluctuations and growth—is too important to leave any promising lead unfollowed. There are some definite advantages in starting from the growth model: the growth model itself may be required to be consistent with the classical general equilibrium model; and somewhat greater insight may be gained into the contributions of each specific friction to the cyclical fluctuations, since they may be introduced separately or sequentially. This paper is meant to be a modest beginning to such an inquiry.

References

[1] ANDO, ALBERT, "A Contribution to the Theory of Economic Fluctuations and Growth," unpublished Ph.D. dissertation, Carnegie Institute of Technology, 1959.

[2] ANDO, ALBERT, and MODIGLIANI, FRANCO, "Growth, Fluctuations and Stability," *American Economic Review*, May 1959.

[3] ———, "The 'Life Cycle' Hypothesis of Saving: Aggregate Implications and Tests," *American Economic Review*, March 1963.

[4] ARROW, KENNETH, CHENERY, H. B., MINHAS, B., and SOLOW, ROBERT M., "Capital-Labor Substitution and Economic Efficiency," *Review of Economics and Statistics*, August 1961.

[5] BORENSTEIN, ISRAEL, *Capital and Output Trends in Mining Industries*, New York, NBER, 1954.

[6] CHAMPERNOWNE, D. G., "Capital Accumulation and the Maintenance of Full Employment," *Economic Journal*, June 1958.

[7] CREAMER, DANIEL, *Capital and Output Trends in Manufacturing Industries*, New York, NBER, 1954.

[8] ———, *Personal Income during Business Cycles*, Princeton for NBER, 1956.

[9] CREAMER, DANIEL, DOBROVOLSKY, SERGEI, and BORENSTEIN, ISRAEL, *Capital in Manufacturing and Mining: Its Formation and Financing*, Princeton for NBER, 1960.

[10] DHRYMES, PHOEBUS J., "A Multisectoral Model of Growth," *Quarterly Journal of Economics*, May 1962.

[11] DOMAR, EVSEY, *Essays in the Theory of Economic Growth*, New York, Oxford University Press, 1957.

[12] ———, "On the Measurement of Technological Change," *Economic Journal*, December 1961.

[13] DORFMAN, ROBERT, SAMUELSON, PAUL A., and SOLOW, ROBERT M., *Linear Programming and Economic Analysis*, New York, McGraw-Hill, 1958.

[14] DOUGLAS, PAUL, *Real Wages in the United States, 1890–1926*, Boston, Houghton Mifflin, 1930.

[15] DUESENBERRY, JAMES S., *Business Cycles and Economic Growth*, New York, McGraw-Hill, 1958.

[16] ECKAUS, R. S., and LEFEBER, L., "Capital Formation: A Theoretical and Empirical Analysis," *Review of Economics and Statistics*, April 1962.

[17] EISNER, ROBERT, "On Growth Models and the Neo-Classical Resurgence," *Economic Journal*, December 1958.

[18] FISHER, IRVING, *The Theory of Interest*, New York, Macmillan, 1930

[19] GOLDSMITH, RAYMOND W., *Financial Intermediaries in the American Economy since 1900*, Princeton for NBER, 1958.

[20] ———, *The National Wealth of the United States in the Postwar Period*, Princeton for NBER, 1962.

[21] ———, *A Study of Saving in the United States*, Princeton, N.J., Princeton University Press, 1956.

[22] GREBLER, LEO, BLANK, DAVID M., WINNICK, LOUIS, *Capital Formation in Residential Real Estate: Trends and Prospects*, Princeton for NBER, 1956.

[23] HAAVELMO, TRYGVE, *A Study in the Theory of Economic Evolution*, Amsterdam, North-Holland, 1956.

[24] HARROD, R., "Second Essay in Dynamic Theory," *Economic Journal*, June 1960.

[25] ———, *Toward a Dynamic Economics*, London, Macmillan, 1948.

[26] JOHANSSEN, L., *A Multi-Sectoral Study of Economic Growth*, Amsterdam, North-Holland, 1960.

[27] KALDOR, N., *Essays in Economic Stability and Growth*, London, Gerald Duckworth, 1960.

[28] KENDRICK, JOHN W., *Productivity Trends in the United States*, Princeton for NBER, 1961.

[29] KENDRICK, M. SLADE, *A Century and a Half of Federal Expenditure*, New York, NBER, 1955.

[30] KUZNETS, SIMON, *Capital in the American Economy: Its Formation and Financing*, Princeton for NBER, 1961.

[31] LEBERGOTT, STANLEY, "Earnings of Non-Farm Employees in the United States, 1890–1946," *Journal of the American Statistical Association*, 1948, pp. 74–93.

[32] METZLER, LLOYD A., "Wealth, Savings, and the Rate of Interest," *Journal of Political Economy*, April 1951.

[33] MODIGLIANI, FRANCO, "Comment" on "A Survey of Some Theories of Income Distribution" by T. Scitovsky, in Conference on Income and Wealth 27, 1961, forthcoming.

[34] ———, "Long-run Implications of Alternative Fiscal Policies and the Burden of the National Debt," *Economic Journal*, December 1961.

[35] NATIONAL INDUSTRIAL CONFERENCE BOARD, *The Economic Almanac*, 1940.

[36] RAMSEY, F., "A Mathematical Theory of Saving," *Economic Journal*, 1927.

[37] SAMUELSON, PAUL A., "The Evaluation of Social Income: Capital Formation and Wealth," in *The Theory of Capital*, ed. F. A. LUTZ and O. C. HAGUE, New York, St. Martin's, 1961.

[38] ———, "Parable and Realism in Capital Theory: The Surrogate Production Function," *Review of Economic Studies*, June 1962.

[39] ———, "Some Aspects of the Pure Theory of Capital," *Quarterly Journal of Economics*, 1937, pp. 469–496.

[40] SAMUELSON, PAUL A., and SOLOW, ROBERT M., "Balanced Growth Under Constant Return to Scale," *Econometrica*, July 1953.

[41] ———, "A Complete Capital Model Involving Heterogeneous Capital Goods," *Quarterly Journal of Economics*, November 1956.

[42] SOLOW, ROBERT M., "A Contribution to the Theory of Economic Growth," *Quarterly Journal of Economics*, February 1956, pp. 65–94.

[43] ———, "Investment and Technical Progress," *Mathematical Methods in Social Sciences, 1959*, ed. KENNETH J. ARROW, SAMUEL KARLIN, and PATRICK SUPPES, Stanford, Calif., Stanford University Press, 1960.

[44] ——, "Substitution and Fixed Proportions in the Theory of Capital," *Review of Economic Studies*, June 1962.

[45] ——, "Technical Change and the Aggregate Production Function," *Review of Economics and Statistics*, August 1957.

[46] TOBIN, JAMES, "A Dynamic Aggregate Model," *Journal of Political Economy*, April 1955.

[47] ——, unpublished manuscript on monetary theory.

[48] TOSTLEBE, ALVIN, *Capital in Agriculture: Its Formation and Financing since 1870*, Princeton for NBER, 1957.

[49] ULMER, MELVILLE J., *Capital in Transportation, Communication, and Public Utilities: Its Formation and Financing*, Princeton for NBER, 1960.

[50] U.S. BUREAU OF THE CENSUS, *Historical Statistics of the United States: Colonial Times to 1957*, 1960.

[51] U.S. DEPARTMENT OF COMMERCE, *U.S. Income and Output*, 1958.

[52] ——, *National Income*, 1954 edition.

[53] ——, *Survey of Current Business*, various issues.

[54] VON NEUMANN, J., "A Model of General Economic Equilibrium," *Review of Economic Studies*, 1945–46, pp. 1–9.

COMMENT

RALPH W. PFOUTS, University of North Carolina

As Ando has suggested, his models are very much in the spirit of Solow's "neoclassical" model.[1] Indeed it might be said that his models are modifications of the Solow model. As theoretical models, they seem to be eminently satisfactory. Ando spells out his assumptions rather carefully, and his models are internally consistent. If one wishes to quarrel with them, one must do so on the basis of the assumptions.

If the purpose of a model is theoretical conjecture, it is difficult even to disagree with its underlying assumptions. Surely it is legitimate and useful to postulate special conditions on the economic environment and to inquire as to the logical consequences of these conditions. So long as we feel free to use the laboratory control of special assumptions we may obtain interesting results. This is true even though the special environmental conditions assumed do not exist and have never existed; after all, it has often been observed that the real world is a special case.

[1] Robert M. Solow, "A Contribution to the Theory of Economic Growth," *Quarterly Journal of Economics*, February 1956, pp. 65–94.

However, Ando is not interested in purely theoretical conjecture. He speaks of applied capital theory, and he proposes empirical testing of the models. The objections that I wish to raise center on the models' suitability for empirical testing.

In each of the models, output or product depends on three variables: technological change, employment, and capital. The first two are determined by time series, that is, they are functions of time alone. (Strictly speaking, it is the supply of labor that is determined by time, but since employment and supply of labor are identically equal in the model, this does not matter.) In the case of technological change, the use of a time series explanation may be the most satisfactory means of handling the problem, but I do not think that it is suitable in the case of employment. Granted that we are discussing very long-run models, an assumption that employment depends only on time precludes the possibility of secular unemployment. Furthermore, it also precludes the possibility of examining causes and results of secular unemployment.

The treatment of capital is also unsatisfactory from an empirical standpoint. The difficulty lies in the passive role assigned to investment. Savings are determined by the consumption function, and the demand for investment is determined by the marginal productivity equation of perfect competition theory. Presumably each model adjusts, through the production function and the marginal productivity equation, so that savings and investment are always equal. In view of the importance often accorded investment in discussions of economic growth, the absence of a realistic explanation of the determinants of investment seems odd. Further, in view of the importance of capital as the only endogenously determined variable in the output function, it seems doubly odd that investment should assume such a passive role.

Clearly, Ando's postulates and assumptions lead to an equilibrium model of growth. Indeed, his model is of an ambulatory equilibrium type; it moves in equilibrium. Now, there is a strong precedent for this kind of equilibrium model, varying all the way from the most primitive model of the *General Theory* to, say, the Solow model alluded to above. It seems to me that such models are legitimate for theoretical purposes, but I have strong doubts that they can achieve the empirical goals toward which Ando aims.

The quest for a stable equilibrium motion leads to certain peculiar results, a few of which can be cited quickly. For example, the ratios of rate of change of output to output, of rate of change of capital to capital, of rate of change of employment to employment, and of rate of change of technological change to technological change are all constants. In the cases of labor and technology, the constants arise from the specific nature of the two time series assumed to generate these variables. It may be observed that this constancy arises fundamentally from assumption rather than from factual study. This is a questionable procedure in a model intended for empirical testing.

A further special assumption of the models is that the ratios of rate of change of output to output and of rate of change of capital to capital are equal to each other and are constant. This is a characteristic of all of the models, and it leads to peculiar results. In the simplest model we find that $k = \dot{Y}_t/Y_t = \dot{K}_t/K_t$, or $\dot{Y}_t = (Y_t/K_t)\dot{K}_t$. Thus, the rate of change of output depends on only one time derivative, that of capital. The time derivatives of labor and technological change do not matter. Fundamentally, this is a consequence of the insistence upon a stable moving equilibrium.

A feature of the models that commands immediate attention is the total absence of any lagged variables. We may note that the absence of lags is simply unrealistic. The adjustment of macroeconomic variables is not instantaneous. Econometric models are replete with lags, and they frequently prove to be important. In addition, the absence of lags forces a reliance on instantaneous time derivatives. Again, it would seem open to question that such a usage is suitable for empirical testing.

As the model stands it is undoubtedly dynamic, but it is dynamic in a peculiar way. The time path of the variables depends not only on their past values but is also conditioned by the mere passing of time. This is true because of the time series that generate technological change and employment. The passage of time feeds new values of these variables into the system instantaneously and continuously, and the system adjusts instantaneously to the new values. Thus, it is not possible for the system to remain in an equilibrium in which all variables are constant; the passage of time alone prevents this.

The model is supported by an assumption that there are no economic fluctuations. If the author were saying, "I am examining a different world in which economic fluctuations do not exist, to see what equilibrium growth conditions are like in such a world," we could not object at all. Instead, he is saying, "I am examining the real world, and I am assuming there are no economic fluctuations."

This is not sound. To compare the real world with his model, he must adjust the real world data for the effects of economic fluctuations. (I do not know how this should be done.) To rely on an analogue, we may ignore seasonal variations in theoretical discussion, but when we make use of actual data, we adjust for seasonal variations.

Of course, Ando is aware of the difficulties that arise from his models, and he believes that they can be overcome in the future by refining the models and by obtaining more satisfactory data. He may be right about this, but I am doubtful. In the empirical parts of the paper, when the observed values are not compatible with the model, he has nothing of a precise nature to suggest as a means of reconciliation. As a consequence, the empirical work presented may be suggestive, but it is far from conclusive.

The paper has welcome additions to the theory of economic growth models; in this connection the work dealing with problems of aggregation and the effects of money and of government policy may be noted. But these are theoretical advantages. In its present form the paper has little that appears to be promising for empirical research.

Reply by Albert Ando

Pfouts suggests in effect that the model I have presented has no relation whatever to the United States economy. My general answer to this criticism is contained in my paper, particularly in the concluding section.

I feel, however, that four specific points Pfouts makes should be answered in order to avoid further misunderstanding.

First, Pfouts says that investment in my model is completely *passive* because investment is determined by the marginal conditions. The meaning of the word *passive* in this context must be that I do not consider explicitly the time necessary for adjustment of capital stock by producers. I am concerned with long-run growth characteristics of the United States economy in my paper, and I consider the omission of these adjustment problems to be a justifiable approximation. Whether or not this is so is an empirical question, and must be treated as such. On the other hand, I have shown elsewhere that when frictions are explicitly introduced into this form of demand for capital, a stock-flow adjustment model of the Goodwin-Chenery type will result. In fact, for the case of a single-good model, I have already reported a study of the consequences of the introduction of such frictions, and I think this is a convenient and useful procedure to follow.[1]

Second, Pfouts seems to miss the important point that, because the *supply* of labor is given as a function of time while the *demand* for labor is given by the marginal conditions (the distinction Pfouts dismisses in parentheses), I have an option to study the causes of secular unemployment in this type of model, although I did not choose to do so. This fact is not my discovery, but was suggested by John R. Hicks in his now-famous paper, "Mr. Keynes and the 'Classics,' a Suggested Interpretation,"[2] and has been discussed by numerous authors since.

Third, Pfouts finds it "simply unrealistic" that my model does not contain any lagged variables. This statement must be based on his failure to realize that my model contains very complex lag structures implicitly, just as it contains both flow and stock variables. For instance, if Pfouts attempted to write down the consumption function utilized in my model totally in terms of flow variables, he would have found an equation involving infinite series of lagged variables.

Fourth, Pfouts seems to think that I have assumed various constants, such as the ratio of the *value* of the capital goods output to the *value* of the consumption goods output (some of the ratios he mentions are not constant, or do not play any significant role in my analysis, but this is unimportant). On the contrary, there is nothing in my model as originally set down that suggests these constants in a very obvious manner, except in the trivial sense that if these constants can be derived as implications of my model, the hypotheses specifying my model must have contained these implications in the first place.

Pfouts contends that my model is unrealistic because these constants emerge. This is a strange accusation indeed, because they have often been empirically observed and have presented themselves as puzzles awaiting *explanation* by economic theorists. I consider it a merit of my analysis that it begins with a rather flexible model containing any number of sectors, and manages to explain these aggregative constants, such as the relative shares of income and the ratio of the value of capital to the value of output.

I need not comment on his point that I must adjust data as in the

---

[1] See references [1] and [2] in my text.
[2] *Econometrica*, 1937, pp. 147–159.

case of seasonal fluctuations, since rather careful adjustments are in fact made, as explained in my text.

To sum up, I have attempted in my paper to study those periods of the United States economy in which reasonably full employment prevailed, and to inquire what kind of underlying structure may be responsible for generating certain uniformities that characterize these periods, leaving to a future study the causes which tend to make the economy deviate from such a position. If Pfouts chooses to tell me that this is not a proper procedure, then we differ in our opinions about research strategy. If, however, he does grant me the freedom to pursue such a strategy, then his criticisms appear to be based wholly on misunderstandings of my model, or on misinterpretation of the data, or both, since my model does explain a number of uniformities that have been observed in the data for the United States economy.

Notes on the Measurement of Price
and Quality Changes[1]

ZVI GRILICHES

UNIVERSITY OF CHICAGO

Introduction

AS ECONOMETRICIANS have accumulated experience in analyzing different bodies of data, their views of what are the major technical problems associated with a particular study have changed markedly. Early studies put most of the stress on "what is the relevant theory" for a particular piece of data, with "theory" providing such broad statements as "quantity purchased should be related to price and income." The next big step came when we started asking, "What is the relevant variable?" Is consumption related to measured income in the same period, to measured income in the previous period, or to some more elaborate but also rather intangible concept of expected or permanent income? Is the planned output of wheat related to current, past, or expected wheat prices? While earlier workers were not unaware of these problems, the general realization of the importance and fruitfulness of such a question owes much to the works of Friedman, Nerlove, and more recently, Muth.[2] It has now become standard operating procedure to inquire what kind of variable we "really" want when we write down price, income, or capital in one of our equations. More recently, we have started asking, "Is this a good or relevant measure of the variable?"; do the series that we actually have measure what we want or even measure well what they set out to measure?[3] As we begin to ask finer questions of the data, the quality of the available data becomes a major constraint on the work of the practicing econometrician.

The problems that I shall review in this paper arose during various

---

[1] This paper is based partly on the results of a larger research project on the econometrics of technological change supported by a grant from the National Science Foundation.

[2] See, for example, [5] [15] [13]. The numbers in brackets refer to the list of references at the end of the paper.

[3] See, for example, [14].

attempts to use available price data in two areas of special interest to me: the measurement of productivity and technological change and the study of investment behavior. On several occasions I found that what was being measured was not what I wanted, even though the two concepts had the same "name."[4] This, however, should not be interpreted as a complaint against the producers of these statistics. They have to provide all-purpose numbers and cannot guess in advance the particular combination or measure that I may want some day.

Economists use price series for two main purposes: (1) to deflate expenditures and receipts for the purpose of arriving at some conclusions about either changes in welfare (in the case of consumption expenditures and earning receipts) or changes in productivity (in the case of sales receipts, wage bills, and investment expenditures); and (2) to explain and predict changes in quantities used or purchased. In either case we are likely to have a broader concept of "price" in mind than just one of the particular numbers recorded during a transaction. Clearly, an item bought at the same "transaction" price but in one case paid a month in advance of delivery and in a second case paid three months after delivery did not "cost" the same amount. Since economists are likely to assume that it is *total* cost per unit that affects either behavior or welfare, they will usually try to convert these two different transactions into "equivalent" units, using some appropriate interest rate to achieve this transformation (and an argument always remains about the appropriate rate to use). It does not help to tell them that these are distinct transactions and cannot be compared perfectly, since this counsel leads either to despair or to the explicit introduction of an infinity of dimensions or qualities of a transaction and, hence, to despair again. To try and measure changes in welfare and productivity, or to explain the time pattern of investment or other economic series, we shall find it necessary again and again to put certain changes into the category of "price factors." Whether all these different attributes of commodities should be lumped into one index, and whether the official indexes should be broadened to include some of these, is a semantic and (perhaps) political question. The important point is that we want and need this information to evaluate and understand better the performance of our economy.

As the result of such consideration we shall usually want to define

[4] I have touched on some of these problems before in [7] [8] [9].

a commodity or transaction broadly enough to include all the characteristics and conditions of purchase and use which impose a cost or provide a benefit to the purchaser and adjust our measure whenever any *one* of these conditions changes. Thus, in a study of the demand for transportation services, not only the "price" of passage should be included but also the "time" of passage, since in almost all cases the time spent in transit is a cost rather than a "good" (except for cruise passengers). Also, since most econometric studies are implicitly "demand" studies (partly because our supply theories are much less well developed), we will be more interested in prices "paid" than in prices "charged." Unfortunately, most of the data (except wage data) is collected from sellers rather than buyers, and this brings in an additional source of bias. While much of what we want is very difficult to define, measure, collect, and compute, it is still important to keep in mind what it is that we "really" want as we go along and compromise with reality.

In the next several sections I shall describe the difficulties that arose when I tried to use some of the available price series for my purposes and shall suggest a few possible ways of arriving at more appropriate measures for the particular tasks.

Inappropriate Definitions or Measurement Procedures

Some available measures are just not very good price indexes, quality change and other problems aside. In the case of the United States Department of Agriculture's Prices Paid Index the bark is actually worse than the bite. Theoretically, it does not even desire to construct a conventional price index:

> . . . The method of pricing items for the Prices Paid Index seeks similarly to reflect changes in items bought by farmers, such as *grade, quality,* and *size of containers,* that is, to reflect accurately the *average* prices of things farmers actually buy under the economic conditions that exist at the time of purchase. For example, some items such as grease, corn meal, bread, oatmeal, and cornflakes are sold in different size containers. For these the attempt is made to estimate the average price for all such commodities bought, giving proper weight to the *changing* proportions bought in containers of different size.

> *Ideally,* to maintain conceptual similarity to the Index of Prices Received, the price paid, say for work shoes, should be the average price obtained by dividing the total sum spent by farmers for work shoes in a given period by the number of pairs bought. Thus the average price,

when multiplied by quantity bought, would equal total expenditures for shoes. However, it is impossible to obtain the data needed for such a computation, and the nearest approach appears to be to price "the kind of work shoes commonly bought by farmers." Thus, as in the case of the average price described above, any marked shift in kind or type of shoe would be reflected in the price reported.

Accordingly, in pricing most items emphasis is placed on the item "most commonly bought by farmers," or the "volume seller" . . .

Clearly, comparison of the cost of a certain make of automobile today with the cost of the same make 25 years ago is a legitimate comparison, irrespective of the fact that the two cars differ vastly as to quality and design. The car of today provides better, more dependable, and more comfortable transportation than its predecessors of 25 years ago. *But this is largely beside the point.*[5]

Two reasons are given by the USDA for desiring unit values rather than prices in its Prices Paid Index, and neither one of them is satisfactory. First, it is argued, since the Prices Received Index does not take into account quality change in the products farmers sell, the Prices Paid Index should not take into account quality change in the items farmers buy. The logical conclusion should be, however, to improve the Prices Received Index rather than ruin the Prices Paid Index. Since product quality change has probably been much less serious in agriculture than input quality change, the error introduced by ignoring it in the Prices Received Index is much smaller than the "compensating" error of ignoring quality change in the Prices Paid Index. The second reason given by the USDA for ignoring quality change is that most of it is "irrelevant" for the major purposes of the particular item. "A car is a car is a car." It provides transportation services, and it does not matter whether it is a Chevrolet or a Cadillac. And if farmers shift from Chevrolets to Cadillacs, the real price of transportation services to them has gone up. Obviously, whether certain quality changes are relevant or irrelevant is an empirical question, and it cannot be dismissed a priori.

Fortunately, the USDA does not practice all that it preaches. Where it is obviously wrong the USDA does not stick to unit values as its ideal. It does not price just "a tractor" but divides tractors into five size and type classes. Also, a substantial fraction of the recent revisions in the Prices Paid Index has been in the direction of making

---

[5] [23, pp. 32–33.] Italics supplied.

the definition of the commodity priced somewhat more specific. For example, "all soybean meal" has been changed to "41 per cent protein soybean meal," and so forth.[6] Nevertheless, many of the definitions are still quite vague, and the insistence on pricing items with all "the customarily bought" attachments leads to substantial bias in the USDA estimates of prices paid for more complicated pieces of machinery.[7]

Moreover, in some cases the adherence of the USDA to its definition leads to ridiculous and misleading results. For example, in October 1960 the USDA substituted Ramblers, Falcons, Corvairs, and Valiants for the previously priced Chevrolet, Ford, and Plymouth sixes (and the Buick Special for a standard Buick eight) without any adjustment or linking.[8] As a result of this the USDA index of prices paid for new automobiles fell from November 1959 to October 1960 by about *13 per cent*, while at the same time the Consumers Price Index (CPI) index of new automobile prices, which also introduced compacts into its list of automobiles priced in November 1960, fell only by about 2 per cent. The USDA explained: "This reduction reflects in part shifting consumer preference to the new compact autos."[9] In fact, however, this drop in the index is not the result of farmers shifting to compacts, on which we have very little evidence at the moment, but rather the consequence of the price-collecting agency's shift in its definition of the items priced without adjusting for it.

Pricing per Unit of Service Rendered

Ideally, a price index measures changes in the price of a well-defined commodity or service which is of interest to the investigator. Some indexes, however, are not even price indexes in this loose sense. For example, almost all of the construction "costs" indexes do not price a particular well-defined piece of construction (e.g., so many square feet, such and such materials, house or factory building); instead, they simply average building materials price indexes and construction wage series in the hope that the result will approximate movements

---

[6] See B. R. Stauber *et al.* [17].

[7] In a previous paper [7], I have estimated that the prices collected by the USDA for some of the more complicated farm machines, such as cornpickers and tractors, drifted upward between 1947–49 and 1958 by about 20 per cent relative to the same items in the Wholesale Price Index.

[8] [22, January 1960 and 1961].

[9] [22, October 1960, p. 3].

in the price of the product. As a result, little or no increase in productivity is allowed to appear in the construction industry, and the cumulation of such "deflated" building expenditures in various industries seriously underestimates the growth in the "true" quantity of capital invested in "structures."

Luckily, there is one area in which prices are collected for a well-defined unit of construction, and the resulting data show us how far off the results may in fact be in other areas, when the wrong kinds of measures are used because there is nothing better. The Bureau of Public Roads has collected price quotations of

. . . prices actually paid, that is, the successful bids, ordinarily the low bid, at which federally aided road construction has been undertaken in the states. As an index of prices actually paid through the mechanism of competitive bidding, it can thus reflect all those changes in the components of price that may result from changing market conditions: discounts and premiums with respect to list prices of materials; *changes in labor productivity;* and changes in contractors' margins over costs.

. . . [The resulting index constructed from these prices] employs fixed base period quantity weights, the latter referring to quantities required for the construction of one mile of road of "standard" quality in the base period, 1925–29.[10] The index consists of three components: common excavation, concrete paving and structures (bridges, underpasses, etc.), separate subindexes for which are published along with the overall index.[11] Component prices are expressed in terms of commonly employed physical units such as cubic yards of excavation and square yards of paving. Structures, an obviously heterogeneous item in contrast with the other components, are represented by the cost of three elements: reinforcing steel (per pound), structural steel (per pound) and structural concrete (per cubic yard). The price quotations refer to the unit prices charged by the low bidders to put the particular material in place or to perform the particular operation, that is, they include charges for materials, labor, overhead, and profit . . .[12]

This index and its components are available on an annual basis since 1924 and quarterly from 1931 on.

Table 1 records the postwar trend in this index and its components and compares it with some relevant alternatives. Over the whole

[10] Since this was written a revised version of this index using 1957–59 weights has been published by Stern [18]. The revision did not greatly affect the index.

[11] Bituminous paving has been added into the index in the above-mentioned revision.

[12] From Foss [4, pp. 375–376] (emphasis and footnotes supplied).

TABLE 1

BID-PRICES HIGHWAY CONSTRUCTION PRICE INDEX AND
COMPONENTS, WITH COMPARISONS, 1957–61
(1947–49 = 100)

Title and Source	1957	1958	1959	1961[a] (first quarter)
1. Total "composite mile" (BPR)	118	116	114	110
2. Composite construction costs (Commerce)	137	138	141	144
3. Construction machinery and equipment prices (WPI)	160	166	172	178
4. Average hourly gross earnings: nonbuilding contract construction (BLS)	162	167	172	185
5. Common excavation (cu. yd.) (BPR)	102	101	98	97
6. Concrete pavement (sq. yd.) (BPR)	123	123	122	116
7. Power cranes, shovels, and draglines (WPI)	160	164	169	173
8. Mixers, pavers, and spreaders (WPI)	143	150	156	162
9. Concrete ingredients (WPI)	136	139	140	142
10. Structural steel (lbs.) (BPR)	150	133	127	117
11. Total "structures" (BPR)	127	120	117	113
12. Structural steel shapes (WPI)	192	195	200	200
13. Service buildings and other structures deflator (USDA)	125	131	135	n. a.

n. a. = not available.

SOURCE: Lines 1, 5, 6, 10, and 11: *Price Trends for Federal-Aid Highway Construction*, Bureau of Public Roads, second quarter 1961; lines 2 and 4: [27] and *Survey of Current Business*, Department of Commerce; lines 3, 7, 8, 9, and 12: [28, 1959, Bull. No. 1295, and June 1961]; line 13, unpublished Department of Agriculture figures.

[a] BPR data (lines 1, 5, 6, 10, and 11) refer to first quarter. All other data are as of February 1961.

period, the BPR index rose much less than any of the other construction cost indexes, and it has trended downward since 1957 while all the other indexes have kept on rising. Table 1 also compares the price paid per "cubic yard excavated" (line 5) with the price of excavating machinery (line 7) and the wage of construction labor (line 4). Since these and similar "input" prices have risen much more than the price of "output," either the quality of construction machinery or the quality of construction labor (or other aspects of productivity) has risen very substantially over this same period.[13] This, by itself, throws some doubt on the "quality" of the construction machinery price indexes. Similar comparisons can be made for concrete pavement and concrete ingredients, for structural steel (put in place) and structural steel shapes, and for other components of this index. It is doubtful that these apparent productivity increases have been restricted to the road-building sector of the construction industry. It is my conjecture that this index is also closer to the "truth" for total construction than any of the other available alternatives. If this conjecture is true, we have seriously underestimated the growth in the structures components of our capital stock. Moreover, as Foss [4] has shown, we have also seriously underestimated both the flexibility and the variability of the prices paid for the output of the construction industry.

Among the few other series of prices per unit of closely specified service known to me are the USDA collected figures on "Average rates paid for hand harvesting 100 pounds of seed cotton," available by states since 1924. Table 2 presents a comparison of these series with the official farm wage indexes for two important cotton states, Mississippi and Texas, since 1947–49. The rates paid for picking cotton show a trend downward in the post-World War II period. The divergence between the cotton-picking rate and the average wage rates as reported by the USDA is particularly clear in the post-Korean War period. Also interesting is the substantial fall in the cotton-picking rate in Texas relative to that in Mississippi, reflecting the increasingly elastic supply of Mexican nationals to Texas agriculture. An examination of other changes that might have affected

---

[13] It can be shown, e.g., see Siegel [16], that the ratio of Laspeyres indexes of prices paid to prices received for an industry is equal to a Paasche total factor productivity index for this same industry. Kutscher and Waite [11] provide a breakdown of highway construction expenditures on various materials, on site wages, and equipment. By allocating "other" expenditures (13.5 per cent of the total) proportionally to the specified inputs, these figures can be used as weights for computing a highway construction *input* price index from Wholesale Price Index component price indexes for construction equipment and materials and BLS figures on the hourly earnings of construction workers. On a 1957 = 100 base, the resulting input price index stood at 66.2 in 1947–49 and 107.0 in 1961. At the same time and on the same 1957 base, the highway construction product price index stood at 84.7 in 1947–49 and 93.2 in 1961, implying jointly a total factor productivity index for this industry of 78.2, 100.0, 114.8, in 1947–49, 1957, and 1961, respectively, and an estimated 57 per cent rise in total factor productivity in the highway construction industry since 1947–49. Thus, without using capital stock figures an index of total factor productivity can be estimated for an industry which even the encyclopedic work of Kendrick [10] left uncovered.

these series differently in different states, such as the declining relative importance of cotton, the recent increases in mechanical harvesting, and changing yields per acre, lead me to believe that the cotton-picking-rate series probably represents rather well the marginal cost of additional low-skilled labor of constant quality to the

TABLE 2

COMPARISON OF COMPOSITE FARM WAGE RATE AND AVERAGE
RATE FOR PICKING 100 POUNDS OF SEED COTTON,
MISSISSIPPI AND TEXAS, 1954 AND 1961
(indexes, 1947–49 = 100)

	1954	1961[a]
Mississippi		
Cotton-picking rate	96	96
Average composite wage rate	107	117
Texas		
Cotton-picking rate	95	88
Average composite wage rate	119	139

SOURCE: [21, various issues] [24] [20].
[a] As of October–November 1961.

agriculture of these states. These series may reflect better than the average wage rates, which among other measurement problems are also affected by the changing skill mix of the agricultural labor force, the price of constant-quality labor. As in the case for the construction bid series, these series also exhibit a substantially larger annual variability than the alternative average farm wage series.

Collecting Data from the Other Side of the Market

Most of the price data used are employed to explain the behavior of buyers. Almost all of it, however, is collected from sellers. Both the experience of the Market Research Corporation of America and that of Michigan State University indicate that it is possible to collect price data using a "panel" of consumers. The USDA has used some of these panel data in its citrus fruit statistics; but, in general, little has been done to investigate whether in fact the prices as collected from different sides of the market differ, how they differ, and why.

Similarly, most earnings data come from employers rather than employees. In a few areas where we have some data, it appears that these two groups may see or at least report the same transaction in

389

quite different terms.[14] Chart 1 plots the official USDA index of farm wage rates (based on employers' and other "informed" persons' reports on the "prevailing" wage in their community) and an index of

CHART 1

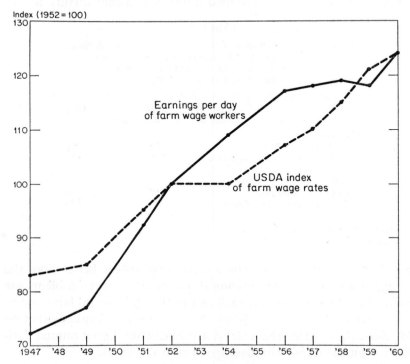

Index (1952 = 100)

Earnings per day of farm wage workers

USDA index of farm wage rates

average earnings per day of farm work collected from the household side by the Current Population and Labor Force sample for the USDA. The two series have moved rather differently over time, with the employee-reported series according perhaps somewhat better

[14] In 1945, for example, farm wage workers reported receiving on the average $44 as noncash wages (perquisites) during the year. There were 3.2 million such workers, resulting in an estimate of $141 million total noncash wages *received* by hired farm workers. In the same year, the USDA estimated on the basis of farm operator reports that noncash wages *paid* amounted to $347 million, or more than twice as much as was "received." Similarly, in the same year cash wages paid to farm workers were estimated at $1,358 million from a sample of farm workers and at $1,839 from a sample of farm operators. This type of difference has persisted. In 1959, farm wage workers reported receiving a total of $1,876 million from cash farm wages, while the USDA estimated that farm operators paid out $2,523 million in cash farm wages during this same year (see [19] [25] [26]). All of this, of course, *could* be explained away by the assumption that employers are a much better and more reliable source of data than employees, but it still leaves me wondering what actually is going on here.

390

with other information and my own impressions of what has been happening in this market.

In general, I would suggest that where possible the data be collected from the particular side of the market whose behavior is to be explained and in terms that are most directly relevant to the behavior phenomena that are to be studied. This, of course, is unlikely to lead to all-purpose numbers.

An Approach to the Measurement of Quality Change

While there is not much one can do about truly new products, and while some quality and style changes can be adequately taken care of by "linking," most of the quality changes are gradual and are not priced separately. In some areas, last year's models are not available any more on the market, and, hence, it is impossible (even if it were desirable) to use linking procedures to adjust for these changes. I have recently resurrected an old suggestion for dealing with this type of problem and have presented computations indicating that the suggested method may be both feasible and powerful.[15] In essence, it consists of viewing a commodity as a bundle of qualities, each one of which contributes (positively or negatively) to the utility or productivity derived from the commodity in question, with many or most of these dimensions or qualities quantifiable. Moreover, since at any point of time it may be possible to observe different "quality" combinations selling at different prices, one may be able to estimate (impute) the price (value) of these dimensions at the margin. One way of doing this is through cross-section price specifications regressions. Armed with these estimated "prices" of particular qualities, which may not remain constant over time, we can adjust the price of the total bundle for changes in the level of different qualities, either by adjusting the bundle at current quality prices to base period quality levels, or by valuing the change in the various dimensions by base period dimension prices. In principle, we are doing nothing more, except in a more complicated fashion, than discovering that prices of different size rugs can be compared, since apparently there is a fairly constant relationship between the size of a rug measured in square yards and its price, holding other variables constant. Armed with the computed price per square yard, price indexes can be computed, even though the previously priced 6 x 9 rugs have been replaced in the market by 8 x 9's and 6 x 8's.

[15] See Griliches [9] and Adelman and Griliches [1], and the literature cited there.

Tables 3 through 8 illustrate the possibility of and the problems associated with making such quality-change adjustments for United States passenger cars in the postwar period and the probable magnitude of the resulting adjustments. Table 3 illustrates the relationship between list prices of automobiles and several specification variables in selected years. The regressions for 1952 and 1961 had not been previously presented or computed and represent, in a sense, a successful test of the model. Because of multicollinearity of the various specifications the estimated quality prices, or weights, are not very stable from year to year. I have, therefore, preferred to use combined two-year regressions to estimate the weights to be used in the

TABLE 3

SINGLE-YEAR CROSS-SECTION REGRESSIONS, RELATING THE LOGARITHM OF NEW U.S. PASSENGER CAR PRICES TO VARIOUS SPECIFICATIONS, 1950–61

| Model Year | N | Constant | Coefficients of | | | | R^2 |
			H	W	L	V	
1950	72	1.2709	.158 (.048)	.048 (.029)	.832 (.115)	−.024 (.014)	.892
1952	51	1.7174	.097 (.042)	.105 (.030)	.578 (.127)	−.020 (.015)	.927
1957	95	2.7370	.051 (.013)	.059 (.017)	.171 (.057)	−0.11[a] (.010)	.967
1961	99	2.2530	.026 (.011)	.132 (.017)	.309 (.080)	−.011[b] (.012)	.940

NOTE: Dependent variable is the logarithm (to the base 10) of "list" (advertised delivered) price. To convert the results to natural logarithms multiply all the coefficients by 2.3. The resulting coefficient, if multiplied by 100, would measure the *percentage* impact on price of a *unit* change in a particular specification or "quality," holding the other specifications constant. Figures in parentheses are standard errors.

H = advertised brake horsepower in 100's
W = shipping weight, in hundreds of pounds
L = over-all length, in hundreds of inches
V = 1 if the car has a V-8 engine; = 0 if it has a six-cylinder or smaller engine
T = 1 if car is a hardtop; = 0 if not
A = 1 if automatic transmission is "standard" equipment (i.e., is included in the price); = 0 if not
P = 1 if power steering is standard; = 0 if not
B = 1 if power brakes are standard; = 0 if not
C = 1 if the car is designated as a "compact"; = 0 if not

[a] Plus significant coefficients for T, A, P, and B.
[b] Plus T, P, and C.

TABLE 4

U.S. PASSENGER CARS: REGRESSIONS OF LOGARITHM OF PRICE ON SELECTED
SPECIFICATIONS, TWO-YEAR CROSS-SECTIONS, 1947–48 THROUGH 1960–61

Model Years	N	Constant	H	W	L	V	D	R^2
1947–48	110	2.3854	.184 (.067)	.182 (.028)	.014 (.047)	−.047 (.016)	.0558 (.0119)	.761
1948–49	100	2.4813	.182 (.073)	.159 (.037)	.032 (.048)	−.038 (.019)	.0540 (.0138)	.736
1949–50	114	1.3494	.167 (.047)	.029 (.029)	.831 (.110)	−.014 (.014)	−.0217 (.0087)	.851
1950–51	127	1.3522	.136 (.036)	.026 (.021)	.839 (.082)	−.002 (.010)	−.0092 (.0070)	.893
1951–52	106	1.5283	.102 (.034)	.061 (.021)	.709 (.087)	−.001 (.010)	.0608 (.0075)	.920
1952–53	105	1.8785	.105 (.031)	.108 (.024)	.493 (.092)	−.027 (.012)	−.0012 (.0089)	.904
1953–54	119	2.1737	.114 (.028)	.087 (.029)	.379 (.090)	−.027 (.012)	−.0227 (.0096)	.855
1954–55	121	2.4713	.105 (.026)	.004 (.026)	.358 (.067)	−.013[a] (.010)	−.0403 (.0087)	.904
1955–56	143	2.4615	.040 (.024)	.105 (.024)	.232 (.067)	−.019[b] (.013)	.0085 (.0077)	.924
1956–57	186	2.5868	.041 (.012)	.092 (.017)	.195 (.048)	−.016[b] (.009)	.0116 (.0046)	.947
1957–58	202	2.8814	.017 (.011)	.118 (.016)	.030 (.056)	.002[b] (.011)	.0116 (.0052)	.929
1958–59	191	3.0820	.027 (.011)	.124 (.015)	−.076 (.057)	−.011[b] (.014)	.0024 (.0061)	.915
1959–60	165	3.0610	.050 (.008)	.092 (.012)	−.025 (.047)	−.026[c] (.010)	−.0010 (.0005)	.943
1960–61	177	2.7311	.033 (.008)	.107 (.014)	.120 (.058)	−.013[d] (.009)	−.0157 (.0049)	.929

NOTE: See Note to Table 3. In addition:

M = 1 if car has aluminum engine; = 0 if not
D = 1 in the second of the two years; = 0 in the first

[a] Plus coefficients for A, P, and B. [c] Plus coefficients for T, A, P, and C.
[b] Plus coefficients for T, A, P, and B. [d] Plus coefficients for T, P, C, and M.

TABLE 5

ESTIMATED QUALITY WEIGHTS, OR "PRICES": PERCENTAGE CHANGE IN PRICE
OF CARS AS RESULT OF UNIT CHANGE IN SELECTED "QUALITIES," 1937–61

	Percentage Change in Price per		
	10-Unit Change in Horsepower	100-Pound Change in Weight	One-Inch Change in Length[a]
1937–39[b]	7.1	3.0	0.15
1947	5.1	3.1	0.69
1950	3.6	1.1	1.92
1952	2.1	3.0	1.34
1957	1.2	1.4	0.39
1959	1.2	2.4	−0.16
1960	1.2	1.4	0.15
1961	0.6	3.0	0.71

[a] Wheelbase length, 1937–39; over-all length thereafter.
[b] From Court [2, p. 111].

adjustment for specification changes between these two years. Table 4 presents the combined two-year regressions for 1947–61. Again, the results for 1947–54 and 1960–61 represent a successful extension of the model into previously unexplored periods.[16] Table 5 summarizes the trend in the estimated prices of the various automobile qualities or specifications. It does make clear that substantial changes have occurred in these prices over time.

Since the CPI has priced only the "low-priced three" cars in its index (until 1961), I shall present and describe the construction of comparable quality indexes for these cars. The quality changes evaluated are changes in horsepower, weight, and length. A time series of these specifications for the low-priced three is presented in Table 6. None of these changes has apparently been adjusted for or "linked out" in the construction of the CPI.[17] Using weights derived from Tables 3 and 4, it is possible to estimate for each pair of years the change in price that is due to changes in specifications. The exact magnitude of these estimates depends on the particular set of weights used. Table 7 presents such annual estimates based on two sets of weights:

[16] The coefficient of D (the year dummy variable) in these regressions, if multiplied by 2.3×100, becomes itself an estimate of a price index. It is an estimate of the percentage change in the average *unweighted* list price of cars in the sample between the two years *holding the various specification variables constant.*
[17] See, for example, the discussion of linking in Larsgaard and Mack [12].

TABLE 6

SPECIFICATIONS AND LIST PRICES OF AN AVERAGE[a] "LOW-PRICED THREE" CAR, 1939–61

	Horsepower	Weight (Pounds)	Over-all Length	Price[b]	N[c]
SIX-CYLINDER ENGINES					
1939	80	2784	189.7	720	6
1947	92	3166	197.4	1238	6
1948	92	3134	197.6	1424	6
1948	91	3152	197.8	1363	4
1949	94	3034	195.5	1522	4
1950	95	3075	195.9	1508	4
1950	95	3081	195.6	1518	6
1951	103	3303	199.3	1779	6
1952	97	3106	194.6	1739	6
1953	103	3115	194.3	1751	6
1953	104	3138	194.5	1768	7
1954	111	3147	195.5	1781	7
1955	120	3129	198.7	1839	7
1956	135	3172	199.7	1938	7
V-8 ENGINES					
1955	163	3185	198.7	1939	7
1956	176	3246	199.7	2039	7
1957	184	3354	203.6	2240	7
1958	210	3440	206.6	2390	7
1959	202	3525	209.6	2533	7
1960	190	3615	211.5	2537	7
1961	187	3566	209.6	2542	7

[a] Average for three Chevrolet, three Ford, and two (the two lower-priced series) Plymouth models since 1953. The 1939 sample consists of two Chevrolets, two Plymouths, and two eight-cylinder Fords. The 1947–48 samples are the same as the 1939 one except that the Fords are "sixes." The eight-cylinder Fords in 1939 were included to raise the sample size to approximately the same levels as in the subsequent years. Since these eights (not V-8's) had a lower list price than comparable sixes in 1939, their inclusion will, if anything, bias the quality indexes downward. The 1948–50 samples consist of one Chevrolet, two Fords, and one Plymouth. The 1950–53 samples are back to two Chevrolets, two Fords, and two Plymouths.

[b] Arithmetic average.

[c] Number of models in average.

1. Fixed 1950 quality prices. This is comparable to the rest of the CPI, which is based on 1950 weights throughout.
2. Adjacent years weights, in which a specification change from, say, 1952 to 1953 is valued at specification prices derived from a price specification regression using data for both years jointly.

TABLE 7

QUALITY INDEXES FOR THE LOW-PRICED THREE CARS, 1947–60
(six-cylinder engines to 1956, V-8's thereafter)

	Estimated Percentage Change in Price Due to Changed Specifications	
	1950 Weights[a]	Adjacent-Year Weights[b]
1947–48	0.0	−1.6
1948–49	−4.6	−3.3
1949–50	1.6	1.2
1950–51	12.4	10.8
1951–52	−13.4	−11.7
1952–53	1.7	1.5
1953–54	4.5	3.0
1954–55	9.3	5.7
1955–56	8.1	2.9
1956–57	12.4	4.8
1957–58	16.9	3.4
1958–59	4.3	1.4
1959–60	0.6	0.3
1960–61	−5.3	−2.0
1939–47[c]	23.3	
1947–52[c]	−4.0	−5.8
1952–60[c]	57.8	25.2

[a] For all comparisons, 1950 weights used. For example, the 1937–50 figure is arrived at by multiplying the *change* in the average specifications given in Table 6, by the 1950 weights given in Table 4 and adding them together.

[b] Weights from Table 4. I.e., the 1954–55 comparison uses average 1954–55 weights, and so on.

[c] Derived for the second column by adding 100 to each of the relevant observations, multiplying, and subtracting 100. For the first column, where a fixed system of weights was used, derived by adding up the appropriate percentage changes. This is done because the underlying equation says, e.g., that a 100-pound increase in weight leads to a 2.5 per cent increase in price; and 200 pounds, to a 5 per cent increase in price rather than the 5.1 per cent that one would get by multiplying the two changes. The resulting index is lower than it would be if it were computed from annual links.

This last, and to my mind preferable, method allows the weights to shift smoothly over time, employing essentially a two-year moving average of current-specification prices to weight changes in these specifications. In Table 8 these estimated quality changes are cumulated, expressed as an index to the 1947–49 base, and used to deflate the new-automobile prices component index of the CPI.

The resulting indexes, together with the undeflated CPI, are graphed in Chart 2. While the price index deflated by the 1950 weighted quality index drops substantially more than the index based

TABLE 8

PRICE AND QUALITY INDEXES FOR THE LOW-PRICED THREE CARS, 1939–61
(1947–49 = 100)

| | | | | CPI Deflated by Quality Indexes | |
| | Quality Indexes[a] | | New-Automobile | CPI | CPI |
Model Year	G_{50}	G_A	Component of CPI[b]	G_{50}	G_A
1939	78.5		57.1	72.7	
1947	101.5	102.2	88.8	87.5	86.9
1948	101.5	100.6	95.3	93.9	94.7
1949	97.0	97.3	108.8	112.2	111.8
1950	98.6	98.4	109.9	111.5	111.7
1951	110.8	109.0	113.1	102.1	103.8
1952	97.6	96.3	124.9	128.0	129.7
1953	99.2	97.7	126.5	127.5	129.5
1954	103.7	100.6	129.7	125.1	128.9
1955	112.8	112.5	127.5	113.0	113.3
1956	120.8	115.8	126.4	104.6	109.2
1957	133.0	121.3	132.8	99.8	109.5
1958	149.7	125.5	138.4	92.5	110.3
1959	153.9	127.2	144.2	93.7	113.4
1960	154.5	127.6	144.3	93.4	113.1
1961	149.3	125.0	139.1	93.2	111.3

CPI = Consumer Price Index.

[a] Computed from Table 7. G_{50} is quality index based on fixed 1950 weights. The numbers in the first column of Table 7 were treated as index number points of an index (1950 = 100) added together (linearly) and translated to a 1947–49 = 100 base. G_A is a quality index based on adjacent-year weights, linked together (by multiplying through, assuming 1948 = 100) and translated to a 1947–49 = 100 base.

[b] From [29] and various CPI releases. For 1939 and 1947–53, as of March of the same year; for 1954, as of January 1954; for subsequent years, as of November of the preceding year.

on changing adjacent-year quality weights, even the latter index is still in the neighborhood of its 1949–50 values in 1961, indicating little or no rise in the "real" price of new automobiles. The quality-adjusted indexes are also somewhat more variable than the CPI, dropping sharply from 1950 to 1951 and rising much more abruptly from 1951 to 1952. Apparently, the 1951 pre-Korean-design models represented the manufacturers' response to the running out of the postwar demand backlog by 1949–50 and were the first substantial model changes in the postwar period. But then came Korea, price ceilings, and steel shortages, and by 1952 the manufacturers retrenched sharply, without dropping list prices, by cutting down on the power and size of their automobiles. The horsepower and size

CHART 2

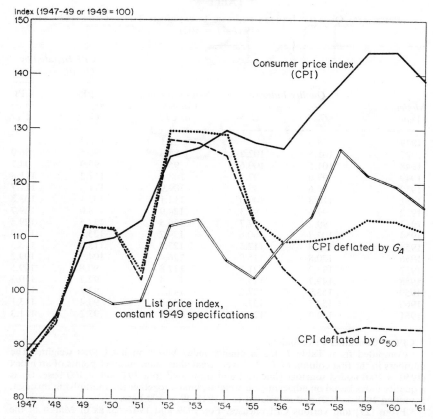

Index (1947-49 or 1949 = 100)

Consumer price index (CPI)

CPI deflated by G_A

List price index, constant 1949 specifications

CPI deflated by G_{50}

"race," which was about to begin in 1951, was interrupted by the increased demand and price ceilings generated by the Korean conflict and did not start again in earnest until after 1954. Whether the above is either an accurate or a useful interpretation of history is a question for industry specialists. I want only to suggest here that quality-adjusted price indexes may in fact be helpful and do better in explaining to us what happened than indexes that do not take such changes into account.

Before leaving this subject, I would like to mention an alternative way of computing quality-adjusted price indexes. What I have done above is to take each change in specifications and value it by estimated "prices," which either do not change or change slowly and smoothly over time. The result is a chain-link quality index with changing weights, which is eventually used to deflate a price index.

Alternatively, we could have asked the question directly: What is the price of a particular fixed bundle of qualities, say, those of 1949 models, in each of the subsequent years, allowing both the general price of the commodity and the implicit "prices" of the various specifications to change? The answer to this question can be had directly from the estimated annual regressions by inserting the appropriate fixed specification levels and reading off the predicted (interpolated) price for these base-period quantities at current prices. This type of calculation is described elsewhere and will not be reproduced here, but I have also graphed on Chart 2 an index of list prices (1949 = 100) that uses "constant" average 1949 specifications for all cars (not just the "low-priced three") and is based on the annual list-price regressions subsequently.[18] This index tells a similar story, though it rises more in the 1954–58 period. It is biased upward, however, since it does not take into account either the growth in discounting or the increased number of attachments, such as directional signals and electric windshield wipers, included in the list price. But it does represent the most desirable way of computing such an index if annual cross sections of actual transaction prices were available.

A Critique of a Criticism

. . . I believe these challenges are conceptually wrong; they rest on the assumption that intangible quality improvements can be brought into the sphere of quantitative measurement. In the end, they would make it impossible to construct measures of output and price changes that are useful to the study of economic growth.

. . . economic welfare as a measurable idea must be restricted to telling us if we are better off only by our having more goods. Any broader idea of welfare which would take account of the character of the goods available, or the satisfaction they give, may be a perfectly valid subject for speculative appraisal, but it is not measurable.

. . . our units of measurement are fixed transactions because they are the only measurable units.

. . . the advance of medical practice cannot be allowed for. If this makes it possible for a patient to be cured in half the hospital time, it would be just nonsense to say that production has remained constant while prices have fallen by 50 per cent; we must record that production has declined

[18] For details of these computations see Fisher, Griliches, and Kaysen [3].

while prices have remained constant. Of course, the patient is better off in a very real sense because he needs less hospital care. However, there is no way to measure his needs in a production index; what must be measured are the goods he buys in response to those needs.[19]

Stated in so bold a fashion these criticisms almost answer themselves. As far as I can see, Gilbert's objections to quality change measurement can be summarized as follows: (1) quality cannot be measured; (2) only "goods" and "fixed" transactions can or should be measured; (3) changes that are measured should be measured by cost and not by value to purchaser; and (4) welfare measures should be based on "goods" only. I shall try to discuss these point by point, though they are all interrelated.

The first assertion is either a tautology, achieved by adding the adjective "intangible" (unmeasurable?) to the concept of quality change, or a statement about the empirical impossibility of getting "interesting," "useful," or "good" measures of quality change. Philosophically speaking, it is hard to conceive of any phenomenon that is *in principle* unmeasurable. The simple act of "naming" or "defining" a phenomenon has the seeds of measurability in it. Moreover, history is littered with the remains of impossibility assertions. Quality changes are being measured. Perhaps they are being measured wrongly or, more likely, not well enough, and the proposed measures may thus deserve criticism on this score, but to assert that what is being done cannot be done is not particularly helpful.

The second point rests on the assumption that the relevant notions of "goods" and "fixed transactions" can be defined in the abstract, without recourse to "subjective" concepts of productivity, utility, or welfare. But the economist or statistician does not have to restrict himself to the particular form in which the data come to him. For example, a farmer may be buying "all-purpose" fertilizer in 100-pound sacks and paying a price that is quoted "per sack." Both we and the more intelligent farmer know that what he is interested in is not total poundage but the "plant nutrient content" of it. From this it is only one step, and a feasible one at that, to translate the "fixed per sack transaction" into prices paid per plant nutrient unit and perhaps to complicate it further by distinguishing different plant nutrients (nitrogen, phosphoric acid, and potash) and assigning different units to each one of these.[20] It may be necessary to make some

[19] Gilbert [6].
[20] I have an example of this in [7].

imputations, but this is no reason for shying away from such a procedure—the national accounts are full of imputations: the contribution of home ownership is imputed, the value of home consumption of farm products is imputed, and the various interpolations used in constructing series from scraps of data are also "imputations".

The choice of a transaction unit is not obvious. If I have appendicitis, my family tries to contract for a "cure." Neither the number of the doctor's visits, nor the amount of drugs used, nor the length of my stay in the hospital are under my control. They are decided by the doctor (jointly with my family) on the basis of the quantity needed to "cure" me. The cost of a *successful* appendectomy consists of the direct monetary cost of room and board, the cost of the various drugs required in conjunction with the appendectomy, physicians' and nurses' services, the indirect monetary costs of income foregone while incapacitated by the illness, and the more subjective costs of pain and of the utility or disutility of getting away from the family for a while.[21] Both the direct and indirect monetary costs are "measurable"; and if there are improvements in medical efficiency, I see no reason why they should not show up as a reduction in the "real price per unit of service" (appendicitis cure) to consumers. After all, technical advances in other areas do show up as price reductions to consumers. Why should not the same be true of medical services? Or do we want to argue that there have not been any advances in the productivity of the "health-maintaining" industry?

A similar type of "what *is* the transaction" example brings us directly to the third point: what should quality change be measured by—"cost" or "value"? The dosage of the new birth control pills (Enovid) has been recently cut in half, reducing thereby the price of this contraceptive method by half. This came about as the result of additional research which showed that half of the previously recommended dose is really enough to achieve the desired result. What is being bought here is a method of contraception. It comes in packages of twenty pink pills to be used during each menstrual cycle. The same method of contraception is now available at half the price of a year ago. True, each of the pills is somewhat smaller today, but what does that matter if the user is assured that they are equally effective for her purposes? After all, the doctor prescribed "twenty pills a month" before and is prescribing "twenty pills a month" now

---

[21] The cost of *unsuccessful* appendectomies is somewhat harder to estimate, but it could probably also be quantified. On this, see Weisbrod [31].

for exactly the same purpose. Why is this not a decline in price? True, this will lead to some trouble in our measure of this industry's output. It is producing now an equal or larger number of smaller pills than before. How we should treat this change depends on our definition of "productivity." I would choose a measure that showed no decline in output, since in this way output would be defined in units comparable to the "market" for it, and such a definition would show a substantial increase in the productivity (the satisfaction of a given set of wants with a smaller use of resources) of this industry. In fact, this is a rare actual example of the "pure-knowledge" no-increase-in-costs type of technological advance which crowds our textbooks. Since it falls so well within the usual definition of productivity, it should be measured as such.

By now it should be clear that "goods" do not mean much independently of a welfare or utility calculus. Nor does it make sense to restrict welfare and "economic growth" measures to goods-only-based output measures. An increase in aspirin consumption may indicate that we have more headaches, but this is not an obvious measure of "*well*-fare."

A large part of the disagreement, however, is purely semantic. There is no real dispute that quality changes affect both behavior and welfare. If they could be measured, they *might* help us toward better explanations of consumer and producer behavior and better measures of economic growth. The argument really narrows down to whether they are measurable, how good the proposed measures are (imprecise measures may be better than none), and finally, and most controversially, whether these aspects should be incorporated into the various official price and output measures. The last problem *is* a semantic one. As long as all aspects of economic change are adequately measured and reported, the question of which of them should be combined into one over-all, all-purpose measure is not a "scientific" one. It is probably possible to *define* aggregate price and output indexes so that they would not include these types of changes. Personally, I doubt whether the resulting indexes would be very interesting or useful. Be that as it may, the thing that I am trying to get across is that these type of changes are important, that if we have good measures of them they would prove useful, that some measures may be feasible, and, therefore, that we should try to measure them as well as we can. Whether the resulting measures should be incorporated into any one particular index is a secondary matter. The important thing is to measure these changes, since they may represent the essence of economic progress.

References

[1] ADELMAN, IRMA, and GRILICHES, ZVI, "On An Index of Quality Change," *Journal of the American Statistical Association*, September 1961.

[2] COURT, A. T., "Hedonic Price Indexes with Automotive Examples," *The Dynamics of Automobile Demand*, New York, General Motors Corp., 1939.

[3] FISHER, F. M., GRILICHES, ZVI, and KAYSEN, C., "The Costs of Automobile Model Changes Since 1949," *Journal of Political Economy*, October 1962 (abstract in *American Economic Review*, May 1962).

[4] FOSS, MURRAY F., "How Rigid Are Construction Costs During Recessions?," *Journal of Business*, July 1961.

[5] FRIEDMAN, MILTON, *A Theory of the Consumption Function*, Princeton for NBER, 1957.

[6] GILBERT, MILTON, "The Problem of Quality Changes and Index Numbers," *Monthly Labor Review*, September 1961, reprinted from *Economic Development and Cultural Change*, April 1961.

[7] GRILICHES, ZVI, "Measuring Inputs in Agriculture: A Critical Survey," *Journal of Farm Economics*, December 1960.

[8] ———, "Capital Stock in Investment Functions: Some Problems of Concept and Measurement," in Don Patinkin (ed.), *Measurement in Economics* (Studies in Mathematical Economics and Econometrics in Memory of Yehuda Grunfeld), Stanford, California, 1963.

[9] ———, "Hedonic Price Indexes for Automobiles: An Econometric Analysis of Quality Change," *The Price Statistics of the Federal Government*, New York, NBER, 1961.

[10] KENDRICK, JOHN W., *Productivity Trends in the United States*, Princeton for NBER, 1961.

[11] KUTSCHER, R. E., and WAITE, C. E., "Labor Requirements for Highway Construction," *Monthly Labor Review*, August 1961.

[12] LARSGAARD, OLGA A., and MACK, LOUISE J., "Compact Cars in the Consumer Price Index," *Monthly Labor Review*, May 1961.

[13] MUTH, JOHN F., "Rational Expectations and the Theory of Price Movements," *Econometrica*, July 1961.

[14] PRICE STATISTICS REVIEW COMMITTEE, *The Price Statistics of the Federal Government*, New York, NBER, 1961.

[15] NERLOVE, MARC, *Distributed Lags and Demand Analysis for Agricultural and Other Commodities*, Department of Agriculture, Ag. Handbook No. 141, June 1958.

[16] SIEGEL, IRVING H., "Concepts and Measurement of Production and Productivity," Bureau of Labor Statistics, March 1952 (mimeographed).

[17] STAUBER, B. R., et al., "The January 1959 Revision of the Price Indexes," *Agricultural Economics Research*, April–July 1959.

[18] STERN, E. L., "A New Base for the Highway Construction Bid Price Index Compiled by the Bureau of Public Roads," *Public Roads*, October 1961.

[19] U.S. DEPARTMENT OF AGRICULTURE, BUREAU OF AGRICULTURAL ECONOMICS, *Employment and Wages of the Hired Farm Working Force in 1945*, June 1946.

[20] ———, *Farm Wage Rates by States, Revised, 1910–1948*, January 1951.

[21] ———, *Farm Labor*, various issues.

[22] ———, *Agricultural Prices*, various issues.

[23] ———, *Major Statistical Series of the U.S. Department of Agriculture*, Ag. Handbook No. 118, Vol. 1: *Agricultural Prices and Parity*, December 1957.

[24] ———, *Statistics on Cotton and Related Data*, SB 99, June 1951.

[25] ———, *The Farm Income Situation*, July 1961.

[26] ———, *The Hired Farm Working Force of 1959*, Ag. Information Bulletin 238, April 1961.

[27] U.S. DEPARTMENT OF COMMERCE, *Business Statistics*, 1961 edition.

[28] U.S. DEPARTMENT OF LABOR, BUREAU OF LABOR STATISTICS, *Wholesale Prices and Price Indexes*, various issues.

[29] ———, *Consumer Prices in the U.S., 1953–58*, Bull. No. 1256, 1959.

[30] ———, *Consumer Price Index*, various releases.

[31] WEISBROD, BURTON A., "The Valuation of Human Capital," *Journal of Political Economy*, October 1961.

COMMENT

GEORGE JASZI, Department of Commerce

Zvi Griliches touches upon several problems of widely different character.

I agree with his discussion of the well-advertised defects of the Department of Agriculture indexes, which proclaim it a virtue to count as price change, changes in unit values that are due to shifts among qualities. I share his uneasiness about the construction cost indexes, which, as we know, tend to measure prices of inputs rather than outputs. But I do not think that his discussion contributes much to diminishing our ignorance as to the quantitative importance of the resulting bias. Griliches seems to imply that it is quite significant. I note that R. A. Gordon, in the December 1961 *American Economic Review*, has written in a manner that implies the opposite.

The problem of whether we should collect price information from buyers or from sellers is also an important one. But I am not quite sure whether I understand and agree with the way in which Griliches sorts out the issues that are involved. Does he imply that there are two valid prices in every transaction—a seller's price and a buyer's price—and that we should turn to sellers or to buyers for our information depending on whether we are interested in supply theory or in demand theory? I always thought that there was only one price to one transaction, and that the answer to the question of whether we should canvass sellers or buyers depended on who was more likely to give correct information. If this is the case, a great deal of detailed investigation is required if this question is to be dealt with fruitfully.

I share with Griliches part of his disagreement with Milton Gilbert. I think Gilbert is wrong in saying that our disabilities in measuring quality change do not lead to defects in our price and volume index numbers. I think they lead to serious defects; it would be very useful if quality change could be measured.

However, I do agree with Gilbert rather than with Griliches as to what can and what cannot be achieved in this field.

I shall spend the rest of my time in trying to explain why I am rather pessimistic about the progress that can be made. To do so I shall compare the approach to the measurement of quality change recently put forward in the United States by Griliches and by Richard Stone in England with the more conventional approach that preceded their contributions. I shall start by outlining the conventional method and explaining its limitations.

The Conventional Method

From the examination of extant price and volume indexes, it would appear at first that a bewildering variety of techniques is used to cope with the appearance of products of altered quality and of new products. On closer examination, however, this impression is strongly modified. The bulk of the procedures used reduce to one fundamental method, or at least to close variants of it, which I shall call the "conventional" method.

The essence of the conventional method is to translate quality into quantity by reference to market prices. If a new variety of a good is introduced, one physical unit of the new good is not simply equated to one physical unit of the old good. Instead, one unit of the new good is regarded as equivalent to one unit of the old good times the ratio of the price of the new good to that of the old good in an overlap period. If such an overlap period does not actually exist, an estimate is made of what the relative cost of producing the two goods would have been had both been produced in a common period.

Note that my discussion proceeds in terms of the construction of real-volume measures. It could equally well be conducted in terms of the construction of price indexes: All the problems that arise are identical.

This procedure for introducing new goods is, it may be noted, quite in harmony with that adopted for volume measurement in the absence of quality change. More expensive grades of goods are given a greater weight in such measurement than less expensive varieties —in proportion to their relative market prices.

The fundamental shortcoming of this method is, of course, that quality change will show up as volume change only if, and to the extent that, it is reflected in the relative prices of the new and old variety. If, for instance, one unit of the new good does not cost more than one unit of the old good, it will be considered to represent the same physical volume even though it renders better services. Indeed, if the new good costs less than the old good, it will be considered to represent less real volume even though it is superior. These, I should add, are general propositions which would have to be modified to apply to some of the variants of the conventional method.

It has long been felt that in the presence of quality improvement this treatment in common sense understates the increase in the volume of production. One way of expressing this is to say that the additional services rendered by the new good must be more than its additional price; otherwise, it could not be introduced. A formulation which suggests more graphically the importance of what the conventional method misses has recently been put forward by Edward F. Denison. On the basis of certain simplifying assumptions, which I need not state here, it can be said that a comparison of today's output with that of an earlier period by means of the conventional method in fact measures the physical volume of the goods known in the earlier period that could have been produced today, using the resources and the improved technology, etc., that are employed today. In other words, what our measure misses is that we do not in fact produce the outmoded products of the earlier year, but a superior collection instead. Introspection shows that this is a good deal to miss.

Although some have upheld the results obtained by the conventional method, this is not the generally accepted position. The limitations of that method have been widely admitted—even by those who see no good prospect of replacing it; and alternative techniques have been put forward with the claim that they embody more effective ways of dealing with quality change.

The Suggested Alternative

The alternative method that has received widest notice is that put forward by Stone and Griliches. It aspires to get at quality directly by deriving from a study of the past consumer response to old goods a measure of the consumer evaluation of the qualities embodied in the new good. The physical quantities represented by the new goods are then taken to be in proportion to these evaluations. More specifically, the new good is regarded as the result of the combination of two or more qualities that are associated with identifiable physical features—such as coffee bean and chicory content in the case of coffee—which have been embodied in the old products also, but not in the same proportions as in the new product. The consumers' separate evaluation of these several qualities is determined on the basis of his past behavior to the old products embodying these qualities; and the new product is valued by attaching to the quantity indicators of the several quality features which it embodies, the consumer evaluations that have been derived from this analysis. The possibility of such an analysis hinges on the existence in the past of goods embodying the characteristics in different proportions. It can then be carried through on the basis of multiple regression techniques in complex cases, and simpler ones in others.

To take a very simple case, assume that in period 1 consumers paid $2.00 for one pound of pure bean coffee and that they paid $1.50 for one pound of coffee containing half a pound of an admixture of chicory. In period 2 a new, intermediate brand containing one-quarter of a pound of chicory replaces the two old brands. According to the proposed method it will be valued at $1.75. This is an estimate, based on an analysis of consumer evaluations in period 1, of what consumers would have paid for the intermediate brand in period 1 had it been available in that period. As a result of the procedure, one

407

pound of the new coffee will be considered as equivalent to seven-eighths of a pound of the pure bean coffee, and seven-sixths pounds of the mixed coffee which it has replaced.

What are the limitations and advantages of this new method as compared with the conventional one?

It should be noted, in the first place, that it is obviously incapable —as incapable as the conventional method—of taking into account any quality change that introduces something that is really new. For it hinges on the assumption that the new differs from the old only by embodying in new proportions qualities that have existed before. This has been pointed out before.

But, secondly—and to my knowledge this point has not been made previously—the new method would in principle have to produce exactly the same results as the conventional method. This is so because the relative costs of the quality characteristics that are utilized in implementing the conventional method must be identical to the relative consumer evaluations on which the new method is based. In the coffee example just given, for instance, the conventional method of estimating the cost of the new, intermediate brand of coffee in a common period would produce a result identical to that of the new method, namely, $1.75.

The reason that this must be so is simple. The observed market price relations are compatible only with cost conditions in which the cost of one pound of pure bean coffee is $2.00 and that of one pound of chicory is $1.00. If these were not the respective costs, the prices could not be the observed market prices. But if the relative costs are as stated, the conventional method would calculate the price of the new intermediate brand at $1.75 also—three-fourths of a pound of pure bean coffee at $2.00 a pound plus one-fourth of a pound of chicory at $1.00 a pound.

This is the main point of my remarks: I think it is a mistaken idea that we can get at a better measure of quality by a study of consumer evaluations of the various features inherent in a good than by a comparison of costs. If we are confined to market data, we can measure these evaluations only to the extent that they are reflected in costs. This is all the market will reveal. Departures of relative evaluations from relative costs are prevented by adjustments in the quantities traded, and cannot show up in the observable value dimensions attached to the goods.

Future Work

If these conclusions are correct, two lines of investigation are indicated. First, we should explore the extent to which the results of the new method can be approximated by a careful, detailed application of the conventional method and the pros and cons of the two methods in statistical practice. Is it possible, on the one hand, that an application of the conventional method would be simpler and easier to evaluate step by step, as it were, than that of the multiple regression techniques usually employed in conjunction with the new method? Or, on the other hand, is it possible that the new method is a more effective way of implementing the old one in statistical practice?

Second, some consideration should be given to yet another approach, which is distinct from the two I have examined. The essence of this approach is that in the measurement of quality change it cuts loose entirely from valuations that can be derived from past cost relations or consumers' behavior. Instead, extraneous standards that seem reasonable and useful for particular purposes are introduced. For instance, calorie content may be taken as the basis of volume measurement in certain types of analysis of the volume of food consumption. The durability of automobile tires may be taken as the basic quantity dimension in some studies of transportation. It seems to me that this approach holds more promise than the two outlined before in some specific cases of applied economic analysis.

However, its limitations are severe, as further consideration of the two examples just given will show. In most studies of food consumption, it will be necessary to take account also of features other than the calorie dimension—for instance, the content of carbohydrates, fats, and proteins. Similarly, durability is not the only relevant dimension of a tire; safety and comfort in riding are also important. The difficulties involved in selecting the relevant quality characteristics, in finding good quantity indicators for them, and in assigning appropriate weights to these indicators tend to become unmanageable in most cases even of specific *ad hoc* analysis. Certainly, there is no chance at all that the method can be generalized to supersede the conventional method in the construction of over-all, all-purpose indexes of real volume.

EDWARD F. DENISON, Brookings Institution

The paper by Zvi Griliches is constructive and ingenious in criticizing available price series and suggesting alternative procedures. But Griliches does not distinguish the various issues sufficiently, and I fear this may contribute to confusion in an already confused field. Terminological differences lead him to erroneous criticism of an excellent article by Milton Gilbert.

I agree with George Jaszi's description of the conventional method of dealing with product changes and his statement that the procedures used by Griliches in his automobile calculations can only be construed as alternative statistical procedures for application of the conventional method. The method postulates that quantities of two products that sell for the same amount in a base period when both are in quantity production, or would do so if both *were* in quantity production, are the same quantity of product. (In competitive equilibrium this is equivalent to saying that quantities of two products that do, or would, use the same quantity of resources are the same amount of product, and this test is sometimes used where both products are not simultaneously produced.) The auto calculations by Griliches rely exclusively on relative prices set by sellers at points in time and consequently must conform to this standard. They give no consideration to the number of buyers who think it worthwhile to incur the additional cost of any particular new feature, let alone of any "consumer surplus" obtained by those who consider the feature more than worth its cost.

If one product partially or wholly displaces another over time it is likely that the resources devoted to its production better satisfy the wants of its buyers than would the same quantity of resources devoted to the displaced product.[1] If both products remain in production (like train and plane travel between Washington and New York) a welfare gain clearly arises because the consumer can buy the one he prefers, whereas he previously had only one choice. The fact that many travelers have shifted from train to plane indicates they prefer this alternative.[2] If the older product disappears the case is less

---

[1] This probability does not exist where there is a cycle in fashion, or other "change of tastes." In that case, consumers of each period prefer the products offered in that period, and there is no presumption that product change implies an increase in welfare.

[2] The fact that a shift takes place gradually rather than abruptly is sometimes construed as evidence of a change in tastes. On this interpretation, even displacement is not a valid indication of welfare gain. Aside from cycles in fashion, gradualness seems to me more often to reflect the time needed for information about new products to circulate and for adjustment in buying habits to occur.

definitive, since both before and after its introduction the consumer has only one choice, and some consumers would prefer the product that is not available. However, a total welfare gain is reasonably surmised on the grounds that production of the older product would have continued if many consumers preferred it to the new product, given relative prices of the two products corresponding to their relative production costs. Complete displacement thus indicates most consumers prefer the new product to the old. Displacement is perhaps the only acceptable indication of superiority, and the amount of displacement the only criterion by which to judge the number of consumers who prefer the new product. But it provides no measure of the value of the superiority and, hence, no useful criterion for price index construction. In any case, Griliches does not rely upon this test.

Griliches may say, with justice, that many price indexes do not in fact correspond well to the criteria of the conventional method. His calculations present a legitimate challenge to the CPI automobile index. Like almost everyone who has commented upon the construction cost indexes (and his comparisons here are of much interest) he stresses that they do not correspond at all to any reasonable concept of a price index. Many other price series are surely poor. If compilers of price indexes were clearly instructed to accept equivalent cost as a criterion the correspondence might improve. New techniques such as Griliches proposes could prove helpful.

However, with one exception, these techniques are not related to his criticism of Milton Gilbert. Gilbert's article stresses clearly and repeatedly, with examples, that when he says adjustment for quality change is not possible or desirable, he refers only to adjustment over and beyond that which results from the conventional method. In national income circles, at least, it is customary to use the term "quality change" in this restricted sense. If a price series fails to distinguish adequately between a more and a less costly article by simply pricing "cars" or "pills," this is considered a simple error in the price index rather than a failure to "adjust for quality." Gilbert obviously favors the correction of such errors. Once this is understood, and Jaszi's finding is accepted that the Stone-Griliches approach is irrelevant to measurement of the kind of quality change not caught by the conventional method, the most telling point that Griliches makes against Gilbert disappears. Gilbert is not asserting "that what is being done cannot be done"; what Gilbert says is not being done in fact is not being done.

411

Griliches' fertilizer example parallels Jaszi's coffee example; we need only substitute nitrogen, phosphoric acid, and potash for pure bean coffee and chicory. Gilbert certainly does not argue for counting bags of fertilizer. There is no issue here.

The appendicitis case that Griliches introduces under the category of the choice of the transaction unit is the classic example of quality change as the term is used by national income estimators. In indicating an adjustment can be made, and is called for, Griliches is truly in disagreement with Gilbert, although there is no dispute that the consumer may be better off with the new techniques.[3] This is the only part of his paper in which Griliches can claim he has a method for the kind of adjustment that Gilbert says cannot be made. But does he? Griliches cannot logically rest his case for quality improvement on the grounds that consumers get well more quickly and cheaply than before unless the whole concept of consumer choice underlying income and price measurement is changed. The evidence of superiority of new techniques seems to me rather to lie in the fact that consumption patterns have shifted. If consumers ignore the scientific evidence and shift, as they often do, to nostrums that are more costly and less effective, is there quality improvement or deterioration? If, as I suspect, Griliches' answer is improvement, his criteria for measuring its amount are not applicable; they will probably show deterioration. If the answer is deterioration, is not this a judgment based on expert rather than consumer opinion? And if his recourse is indeed to expert opinion, to how many products would he apply this standard?

Griliches says "the choice of transaction unit is not obvious," but then proceeds to specify one. I see no unique reason to agree with him that the patient really wants to buy a cure for appendicitis. Until the diagnostician told him he had appendicitis he had no such desire; when the patient entered the doctor's office he simply wanted a cure for what ailed him. But this is not satisfactory either; there is such a thing as preventive medicine, and the patient would be still better pleased if he had not become sick. We might more reasonably say the consumer's real desire is good health and long life. But then we are in worse trouble; the consumer may stubbornly

---

[3] See the quotation Griliches gives from Gilbert: "Any broader [than is provided by the conventional method] idea of welfare which would take account of the character of the goods available, or the satisfaction they give, may be a perfectly valid subject for speculative appraisal, but it is not measurable."

insist on smoking, or attending football games in the rain at the risk of incurring pneumonia, because these provide him even more satisfaction than a better chance of long life. If good health and long life are specified as the "transaction unit," is increased smoking or sports attendance in the rain, which increases his medical expenses, to be construed as a price increase for the "commodity" good health and long life? Switching the criterion for the "commodity" to be priced from what the consumer actually buys (hospital care, surgeon's time, drugs, etc.) to what he "really" wants is a dangerous and inconclusive game for the statistician to play.

I agree, on the evidence of consumption shifts to new or altered products, that output deflated by the conventional method is "biased" downward over time if viewed as an index of the satisfactions output can provide and, also, that it is unfortunate such satisfactions cannot be measured directly. But I see no reasonably objective way to measure or eliminate the bias.

The Enovid case, in which the consumer buys pills half as large as formerly because she now knows this dosage is adequate for her needs, raises still a different issue; even if we were to agree that there has been a productivity increase somewhere, has it occurred within the drug industry, or the medical care industry, or, as seems to me most reasonable, within the consumer sector, which is outside the market economy and not reflected in the national accounts or in price indexes?[4]

I am not sure why Griliches introduces his example of more headaches increasing aspirin consumption, but I trust he agrees that it has nothing to do with quality change or with price, income, or output measurement; what has changed is consumer needs or tastes.

ERNEST W GROVE, Department of Agriculture

Zvi Griliches is to be complimented on his paper. The pleasure in reading it was threefold. First, it was a pleasure to find an econometric model-builder who recognizes that the elaborate superstructure on many of his models rests on statistical data foundations of shifting sand—and not solid rock as most such builders have assumed. Sec-

---

[4] The concept of productivity increase within the consumer sector is not well developed, and I am not sure whether the Enovid case ought to be considered a productivity increase at all. If a family learns it is happier and healthier eating pieces of cake only half as large as formerly, this would not seem to be a productivity increase, but if the mother learns from a new cookbook to waste fewer ingredients in baking it would. The Enovid case might be likened to either of these situations.

413

ond, it was a pleasure to find someone with both the energy and the courage required to attempt a measure of changes in quality, and to publish his results for the critical wolves to snap at. And third, it was a pleasure to see the Department of Agriculture's index of prices paid by farmers attacked so explicitly and straightforwardly—and with such thorough justification.

That the Prices Paid Index is not a well-designed measure of price changes has long been recognized. The inappropriate procedures used, however, have not been open to any substantial criticism within the department, largely because they have had evident and authoritative backing from the top. Persons directly engaged in this work are not to blame, for such decisions have been made on a higher level.

There has been serious misguidance of the price index work in the Department of Agriculture, but there is some hope that officials now in charge will do better.

REPLY by Zvi Griliches

> That was a way of putting it—not very satisfactory . . . . Leaving one still with the intolerable wrestle with words and meanings.[1]

Jaszi calls that which is rarely applied "the conventional method." Denison says that I do not provide a solution for the quality problem, since I do not deal explicitly with the case of "new" goods. I had assumed that *quality change* is a term restricted to changes which are occurring along some dimension on which we have had at least one previous observation. Gilbert is defended for desiring to measure only goods, even when they are just a reflection of "bads." And so it goes.

"The essence of the conventional method is to translate quality into quantity by reference to market prices. . . . If . . . an overlap period does not actually exist, an *estimate is made* of what the relative cost of producing the two goods would have been . . . in a common period."[2] This is a general exhortation against sin and not an operational prescription for daily virtuous living. I can find nowhere in the "conventional" literature an actual operational *method* for estimating these changes. The method advocated in my paper—and the credit for it should really go to A. T. Court for his original

---

[1] T. S. Eliot, *East Coker.*
[2] Jaszi's comment. Italics mine.

path-breaking paper—provides an operational procedure which I believe to be applicable to a wide variety of (though not necessarily all) cases of quality change. Whether or not it would give the same answer as the so-called conventional method, I cannot tell. The "conventional" method has not been spelled out operationally. How would Jaszi *know* that it is the relative chicory and coffee bean content that determines the price of the mixture? Perhaps it is the eggshell and the label on the can that are the essence of the matter. Unless he performs an analysis similar to mine and *tests* it in some acceptable sense, he would not know the facts that he assumes. Whether we would come out with the same number at the end would depend on *how* and *when* the estimates were to be made. My impression is, however, that the "conventional" method would tend to underestimate the importance of quality change by valuing it too late and too little. The tendency is to make this estimate only when one is forced to by the disappearance of the original goods, and to make it at the prices of that time. This introduces a Paasche element into an otherwise Laspeyeres-type index and usually leads to an underestimate of the contribution of quality change. Similarly, the reliance on *cost* rather than *value* (which may have to be imputed) for making the adjustment will also tend to result in underestimation of it in disequilibrium periods. But technical change usually occurs in disequilibrium periods; in fact, it creates them.

Consider the previously discussed case of automobiles: The hedonic price indexes method would divide an automobile into five (or more) not necessarily additive components or qualities, each with its own prices: horsepower, weight, length, "V-eightness," and the "rest" (measured by the constant term). The following table sets up the data for a 1950–61 index number computation. As can be seen from it, if a quality-change adjustment were to be made in 1961, it would matter substantially whether it were made in 1950 or 1961 prices. Of course, a series of chain links would reduce the problem, but would not eliminate it entirely. The basic problems would still remain: how to measure the change, when to start measuring it, how often to do so, and how to weight the new variety of a commodity in the total.[3] Since the "conventional" *method* has no operational *procedure* for dealing with the type of changes that I described, it usually ignores them. In this sense, I am trying to

---

[3] Neither my paper nor the comments deal adequately with the problem of weighting the new commodity. But to open this up here and now would take us too far afield.

TABLE A

HEDONIC LIST PRICE INDEX COMPUTATION FOR LOW-PRICED THREE, 1950–61

Quality or Dimension	Price[a] 1950	1961	Quantity per Car[b] 1950	1961
Horsepower (in 100's of units)	0.158	0.026	0.950	1.870
Weight (1000's of pounds)	0.048	0.132	3.081	3.566
Length (100's of inches)	0.832	0.309	1.956	2.096
Cylinders (0 if six, 1 if V-8)[e]	−0.024	−0.011	0.000	1.000
"Other" (constant term)	1.271	2.253	1.000	1.000

Components for Index Computations[d]	Number	Indexes for 1961 (1950 = 100)[e]	
1. $\Sigma P_{1950}Q_{1950}$	3.1963	5. P_L	123.7
2. $\Sigma P_{1961}Q_{1961}$	3.4090	6. P_p	89.5
3. $\Sigma P_{1961}Q_{1950}$	3.2888	7. Q_L	182.6
4. $\Sigma P_{1950}Q_{1961}$	3.4574	8. Q_p	131.9
		9. $V = PQ$	163.2

[a] Coefficients of the 1950 and 1961 cross-section regressions, from Table 3, above.
[b] From Table 6, above.
[e] Since the Consumer Price Index switched to pricing only V-8's in 1956, I am following suit. One could, however, substitute the actual fraction of cars sold with V-8 engines here.
[d] The logarithm (to the base 10) of the predicted price for a given combination of quality prices and quantities per car.
[e] Antilogarithm of (3) − (1) for (5), (2) − (4) for (6), (4) − (1) for (7), (2) − (3) for (8), and (2) − (1) for (9). The result is a set of constant-quality price indexes (Laspeyeres and Paasche), a similar set of quality-level indexes per car, and a total-value index.

provide a tool which would allow conventional practice to approximate its own goals closer.

The difference between the Denison-Gilbert-Jaszi position and my own seems, however, to be more than a disagreement about the way of handling particular "index number problems." If I interpret them correctly, they believe in the possibility and desirability of constructing a value-free set of price and output indexes, independent of a welfare framework or of production or utility function considerations. I do not believe that this is feasible, but even if it were I would not be interested in it. I am interested in these indexes only to the extent that they measure changes in aggregate economic welfare or illuminate other aspects of economic behavior. Thus, while the particular regression method can perhaps be encompassed within the conventional framework, I view it as only a first step toward

416

the construction of constant utility or productivity level price indexes. To deal with really "new" commodities, I suggest in the last part of my paper that the transaction unit be redefined to be a broader concept of a service flow, corresponding more closely to the units that enter the appropriate utility or production functions, and compute (price) the cost of achieving the same level of service (often using different commodities) in different periods. This is a direct generalization of the preceding concept of a "car" as a bundle of qualities to the case of a "cure" as a bundle of services.[4] I see no more operational difficulty in specifying a base period number of appendectomies, tonsillectomies, and nervous breakdowns than the base period number of all the various pills purchased. The suggested alternative would seem to be much more informative.

An additional question raised by these comments is: To what industry should certain productivity increases be attributed? An improvement in the quality of a particular input, its nominal price remaining constant, will usually be ignored in the computation of conventional input price indexes. Thus, this improvement in quality will show up as a rise in the productivity of the input-using rather than the input-producing industry. For example, it is now possible to produce higher strength (concentration or "proof") fertilizers at a lower price per nutrient unit. This has resulted in a substantial decline in the "real" price of fertilizer to farmers and a large shift by them toward higher strength mixtures. Since the new mixtures are linked in without any direct comparison, this decline does not appear in the official fertilizer price indexes. Agriculture is thus credited with a productivity increase which is perhaps best described and understood as a technical advance in the fertilizer industry. Such a forward shifting of productivity increases, while misleading, would not matter much if we were only interested in the growth of aggregate productivity, since a consolidation of industries would eliminate this difficulty. However, in one of the largest input-using sectors, the consumption sector, we do not measure productivity at all. If we did, we might be indifferent between calling this a decline in a constant-quality price index or a rise in the productivity index. Either way, we would know what has happened. But since we are not measuring the one, we should at least try to measure the other.

---

[4] Such an approach would consider a car as only one of the inputs in the production of transportation services and would include changes in gasoline consumption per mile in its definition of quality change.

417

In addition, I believe that it is more illuminating and useful to attribute productivity to the "originating" rather than to the "using" industry. This, of course, argues for quality-corrected price indexes even in the consumption sector.

Brief remarks on some of the specific comments: (1) I find that if the highway construction price index were computed in the same way as other construction *cost* indexes, it would have risen by 47 per cent more since 1947–49. This, to me at least, implies that the bias in the other construction cost indexes is quite substantial and provides an order-of-magnitude estimate for it. (2) Besides problems of measurement and the empirical possibility that different people see the same thing differently, the evaluation of a transaction may differ if tie-ins are involved. For example: Is the price paid and received the same for all individuals when trading stamps are "given away" as part of the purchase? Additional examples of this sort occur when some of the perquisites or fringe benefits given by the employer are really inputs in the production process and have no direct utility of their own to the employee—such as nurses' uniforms. (3) "We can measure [quality changes] . . . only to the extent they are reflected in costs." Counter example: consumer evaluation of various past quality changes could be measured in the used car market—where there is no direct relationship of prices to costs. (4) The aspirin example was introduced to show that "goods only" indexes are of limited use or interest.

Index

427